W9-BGN-865

"[*Perfect*] is as deep as any man can go into a baseball game that lasted only two hours and six minutes. [Paper's] insights on the likes of Jackie Robinson, Duke Snider, and Billy Martin are complete, objective, and—perhaps most important—baseball-centric. What Paper loves is the game itself."   —Chuck Klosterman, *Esquire*

"Fascinating . . . the game story contains countless moments of discovery and awe. . . . Paper stays true to the book's title, producing a fitting testament both to a singular performance and its cast of characters . . . a heck of a story."   —*The Washington Post*

"Baseball purists and nonfans alike will find a lot to enjoy in *Perfect*. . . . Relying on interviews with every living player who appeared in the game, family members, fans, and commentators, Paper provides nineteen minibiographies and does it in an inventive way."
                                              —The Associated Press

"There have been more World Series since 1912 that deserve the 'classic' label, but only one game can be called perfect. . . . Lew Paper recounts the game through the eyes of the nineteen players who saw action that afternoon at Yankee Stadium, basing his story on interviews with surviving players, sportswriters, and family members. . . . The author has succeeded in getting under the skin of the players, juxtaposing their stories with key moments. . . . Mr. Paper is especially good at capturing poignant story lines."   —*The Wall Street Journal*

"Paper writes each profile with a fan's passion. It's to his credit that chapters on oft-covered icons such as Robinson, Mantle, and Berra are all compelling as well. A must read for baseball fans, this book is a terrific tribute to when baseball really was the national pastime."
                                              —*Publishers Weekly*

continued . . .

"This gem of a story brilliantly re-creates one of the greatest moments in baseball history by interweaving the intense drama of the game with superb portraits of the key players who shared in the historic moment. *Perfect* captures our hearts as it carries us back to the golden age of baseball and the more innocent world of the 1950s. Though it was a sad day for me as a Dodger fan, I am now mature enough to read and savor this wonderful account."

—Doris Kearns Goodwin, Pulitzer Prize–winning author of *Team of Rivals* and *Wait Till Next Year*

"If you think you know all there is to know about Don Larsen's perfect game, think again. In *Perfect*, the true story of that historic game and the men who played it is revealed. . . . With this charming, meticulously researched book, Lew Paper has connected for a resounding hit."

—Jonathan Eig, author of *Luckiest Man: The Life and Death of Lou Gehrig* and *Opening Day: The Story of Jackie Robinson's First Season*

"An extraordinary book, a startling approach...a fascinating pitch-by-pitch detail of the most famous game in World Series history with individual bios of the nineteen players in the game that give a penetrating picture of . . . the game's Golden Age."

—Robert W. Creamer, author of *Babe: The Legend Comes to Life* and *Stengel: His Life & Times*

"So you think you know everything about Don Larsen's perfect game in the 1956 World Series . . . not until you have read Lew Paper's classic."

—Tim McCarver, FOX sports broadcaster

"All baseball fans know about Don Larsen's perfect game, but Lew Paper does something more. . . . By the end of the book, you will know each player as a friend. Special game . . . special players . . . special book. . . . I couldn't put it down, and neither will you."

—Joe Garagiola, former Major League Baseball player, Hall of Fame broadcaster, and author of *Baseball Is a Funny Game*

"Lew masterfully captures the thoughts of 'Gooney Bird,' the supporting cast of players, and Don's World Series masterpiece. I"s authentic. *Perfect* jumps out from that fall afternoon in Yankee Stadium. . . . It's real life. Whatta writer!"

—Tony Kubek, former New York Yankee shortstop (1957–65), NBC broadcaster, and coauthor of *Sixty-One*

"A terrific book. Don Larsen's perfect game was one of those once-in-a-lifetime events for those of us lucky enough to witness it. Lew Paper takes us behind the scenes and allows us to get to know all the participants."

—Peter Golenbock, author of *Dynasty: The New York Yankees 1949–1964* and *Bums: An Oral History of the Brooklyn Dodgers*

OTHER BOOKS BY LEW PAPER

John F. Kennedy: The Promise and the Performance

Brandeis: An Intimate Biography

Empire: William S. Paley and the Making of CBS

Deadly Risks (a novel)

PERFECT

Don Larsen's Miraculous
World Series Game
and the Men
Who Made It Happen

LEW PAPER

NEW AMERICAN LIBRARY

New American Library
Published by New American Library, a division of
Penguin Group (USA) Inc., 375 Hudson Street,
New York, New York 10014, USA
Penguin Group (Canada), 90 Eglinton Avenue East, Suite 700, Toronto,
Ontario M4P 2Y3, Canada (a division of Pearson Penguin Canada Inc.)
Penguin Books Ltd., 80 Strand, London WC2R 0RL, England
Penguin Ireland, 25 St. Stephen's Green, Dublin 2,
Ireland (a division of Penguin Books Ltd.)
Penguin Group (Australia), 250 Camberwell Road, Camberwell, Victoria 3124,
Australia (a division of Pearson Australia Group Pty. Ltd.)
Penguin Books India Pvt. Ltd., 11 Community Centre, Panchsheel Park,
New Delhi - 110 017, India
Penguin Group (NZ), 67 Apollo Drive, Rosedale, North Shore 0632,
New Zealand (a division of Pearson New Zealand Ltd.)
Penguin Books (South Africa) (Pty.) Ltd., 24 Sturdee Avenue,
Rosebank, Johannesburg 2196, South Africa

Penguin Books Ltd., Registered Offices:
80 Strand, London WC2R 0RL, England

Published by New American Library, a division of Penguin Group (USA) Inc. Previously published in a New
American Library hardcover edition.

First New American Library Trade Paperback Printing, October 2010
10 9 8 7 6 5 4 3 2 1

New American Library Trade Paperback ISBN: 978-0-451-23123-9

THE LIBRARY OF CONGRESS HAS CATALOGED THE HARDCOVER EDITION OF THIS TITLE AS FOLLOWS:

Paper, Lew.
    Perfect: Don Larsen's miraculous world series game and the men who made it happen/Lew Paper.
        p. cm.
    Includes bibliographical references.
    ISBN 978-0-451-22819-2
    1. Larsen, Don. 2. Pitchers (Baseball)—United States—Biography. 3. Perfect games (Baseball)
    4. World Series (Baseball) (1956) 5. New York Yankees (Baseball team) 6. Baseball players—
    United States—Biography. I. Title.
    GV865.L32P36 2009
    796.357092—dc22   2009017670
    [B]

Set in Sabon
Designed by Ginger Legato

Printed in the United States of America

In memory of my father:

a wonderful man who introduced me to the magic of baseball.

CONTENTS

Prologue: The Moment of Truth   1

1   Top of the First: Don Larsen   11

2   Bottom of the First: Sal Maglie   20

3   Top of the Second: Jackie Robinson and Gil McDougald   37

4   Bottom of the Second: Sandy Amoros   66

5   Top of the Third: Carl Furillo   75

6   Bottom of the Third: Roy Campanella   88

7   Top of the Fourth: Billy Martin   108

8   Bottom of the Fourth: Duke Snider   122

9   Top of the Fifth: Mickey Mantle   142

10 Bottom of the Fifth: Pee Wee Reese   164

11 Top of the Sixth: Yogi Berra   182

12 Bottom of the Sixth: Andy Carey   203

13 Top of the Seventh: Jim Gilliam   216

14 Bottom of the Seventh: Enos Slaughter   227

15 Top of the Eighth: Gil Hodges   251

16 Bottom of the Eighth: Joe Collins   268

17 Top of the Ninth: Hank Bauer   281

18 The Last Pitch: Dale Mitchell   298

19 Aftermath   311

    Epilogue   357

    Acknowledgments   361

    Endnotes   365

    Selected Bibliography   401

    Index   407

PROLOGUE

The Moment of Truth

The tall right-hander peers down at the catcher from his perch on the pitcher's mound under the fading afternoon sun in the cavernous environs of Yankee Stadium. It is the fifth game of the 1956 World Series, and the soaring facades of the stadium cast a giant shadow over much of the field while a slight breeze blows against the flags in the outfield. It is a relatively warm day with only a hint of autumn in the air, and a thunderous noise is sweeping through the 64,519 fans in attendance, almost all of whom are now standing in anticipation of witnessing a miracle in baseball history.

Yogi Berra, the Yankees' perennial All-Star catcher, looks up at Don Larsen from his crouch. Larsen's ears protrude from his cap and explain the nickname that has followed him everywhere: "Gooney Bird." It seems to fit Larsen perfectly: an almost pear-shaped body draped on a six-foot-four-inch frame with long, dangling arms.

None of that is on Berra's mind now. His heart is pounding and his eardrums are throbbing with the roar of the crowd as he focuses on the next pitch. He cannot lose his concentration. He has called each pitch that Larsen has already thrown against the Brooklyn Dodgers that day. All ninety-six of them. And no one can have any reason to second-guess the burly catcher. Twenty-six Dodger batters have come to the plate, and twenty-six Dodgers have made an out.

Over the course of thousands of major-league baseball games that have been played in the twentieth century up to this point, there have been only four perfect games in which no batter reached base. The last one was pitched by Charlie Robertson for the Chicago White Sox thirty-four years ago in 1922. To be sure, there have been more than one hundred no-hitters marred by a walk, a fielding error, or some other circumstance that allowed a batter to reach base. But there has never been a no-hitter in a World Series. And never before has a pitcher come so close to pitching a perfect game in a World Series. Only one more out separates Larsen—an otherwise mediocre pitcher—from an immortality that has eluded baseball's most illustrious pitchers.

This is a new experience for Larsen. But not for Berra. In October 1947, Bill Bevens, another second-rate Yankee pitcher, stood on the same threshold of baseball immortality in the fourth game of the World Series against the Dodgers in Ebbets Field. Like Larsen, he took a no-hit game into the ninth inning and then got the first two men out. But that was not a perfect game. Far from it. Bevens had given up ten walks—a World Series record. One run had scored, and the Yankees had a 2–1 lead. Two men were on base—the result of walks. Still, the Yankee pitcher had only to get one more out to do what no other pitcher had done in World Series play—pitch a no-hitter. But Cookie Lavagetto, the Dodgers' aging third baseman, slammed a Bevens pitch against the right-field wall for a double and two runs, turning a near-miraculous pitching performance into a 3–2 Yankee defeat.

The memory of that loss looms large in Berra's mind because the Yankees are winning by a score of only 2–0. "Anything can happen," he remembers thinking. Yankee manager Casey Stengel understands the risk as well, and he has Yankee ace Whitey Ford warming up in the bullpen if Larsen should falter. Still, Berra has hopes that Larsen can do what Bevens could not. Not only for Larsen's sake but for the team's as well. "I wanted to win the game," Berra later said. "That's what I wanted to do."

For all his contribution in calling the specific pitches, Berra knows that much of the credit has to go to Larsen. The twenty-seven-year-old pitcher from Michigan City, Indiana, has demonstrated pinpoint control with a no-windup delivery that has baffled the Dodger batters. They are used to the big deliveries that virtually all pitchers of the day use and that give the batter time to adjust for the tiny ball that comes hurtling toward them at speeds up to ninety-eight miles an hour. As Berra would later say of Larsen's contrasting approach, "The ball just kinda came out of nowhere."

Larsen had first experimented with the no-windup delivery toward the end of the 1956 season. It was not an idle experiment. In a game against the Boston Red Sox, Larsen became convinced that Del Baker, the Red Sox third-base coach, was able to identify the kind of pitch Larsen was about to throw by watching his delivery. Larsen assumed that other team coaches were also stealing his signs and thwarting his success, and he was determined to do something about it. He asked Yankee pitching coach Jim Turner if he could use a no-windup delivery in his next outing. Turner chuckled at the proposal but said he didn't mind.

The impact was immediate—and favorable. Larsen pitched the Yankees to four victories in the final pennant drive in September, boosting his won-lost record from a pedestrian 7–5 to an impressive 11–5. The Red Sox's Ted Williams, perhaps the greatest hitter of Larsen's generation, was among those who noticed the difference in Larsen's performance. "The guy that kills me," Williams would later admit, "is Larsen. I can't hit that son of a bitch. He's standing there like a statue. Hardly any motion. And then the ball's on you."

Although teammate Bob Turley also began using it at about the same time to gain more control and reduce walks, Larsen said he could never remember where he got the idea for the no-windup delivery. When a sportswriter asked him for the source of his new delivery, Larsen—an avid reader of comic books—responded that "the comic book ghoulies sent me the message to try it."

Larsen's late-season success with the no-windup delivery earned him the opportunity to start the second game of the 1956 World Series at Ebbets Field. However, the experience fell far short of his expectations. Although he thought he had "excellent stuff" that day, Larsen's control was anything but pinpoint. Before the second inning was over, he had walked four men and given up a hit. The Yankees appeared to be in danger of losing a 6–1 lead, and Casey Stengel, the sixty-six-year-old Yankee manager with a bowlegged walk, had waddled out to the mound to replace the Indiana native.

Larsen was angry at Stengel for taking him out of the game. After all, he had given up only one hit and the Yankees still had a comfortable lead. He stormed off the mound and made no secret of his feelings when he reached the dugout. "I don't give a damn if I ever pitch a game for the Yankees or Stengel again," he told his teammates. Later he was more philosophical about it. "Casey Stengel," he observed, "always said that when a pitcher doesn't have control, he's pitching to the hitter's strengths." But after that second game, Larsen knew—or at least thought he knew—that his pitching chores in the 1956 World Series were over. Stengel, Larsen assumed, was not about to take another chance on a pitcher who had shown the wildness that Larsen had displayed in those two innings. The World Series was too important.

Making assumptions about Stengel's strategy, however, was always risky business. The man was unpredictable. And, in time, nowhere would that unpredictability be more evident than in Stengel's selection of a pitcher for the pivotal fifth game of the series at Yankee Stadium on Monday, October 8. Each team had won two games, and Stengel's choice for the Yankee starting pitcher had to be someone who could inspire confidence among his teammates. Don Larsen hardly seemed to be the right candidate.

Larsen certainly continued to think so, and he spent his evenings enjoying himself, assuming that he would not be called upon to pitch again. Rumors would later circulate that Larsen spent the evening before the fifth game engaged in heavy drinking until the early-morning hours and that he arrived at the stadium the next day with a bad hangover. The truth is otherwise. He had nursed a few beers with his friend, Arthur Richman, a sportswriter for the *New York Daily Mirror*, at Bill Taylor's Restaurant on West Fifty-seventh Street in Manhattan, a favorite hangout for baseball players. Teammates Mickey Mantle and Rip Coleman stopped by for part of the time, and Larsen left the restaurant sometime before midnight. In the cab ride back to his apartment at the Concourse Plaza Hotel in the Bronx—only a couple of blocks from

Yankee Stadium—Larsen predicted good things for himself at the game the next day. "I'm gonna beat those guys tomorrow," he told Richman, "and I'm just liable to pitch a no-hitter doing so, too."

It was nothing but playful bluster. Larsen did not expect to do anything more than sit on the bench. Still, other omens seemed to be at work. Across town in Times Square, the father of Yankee third baseman Andy Carey passed by a novelty shop that created fake newspaper headlines. Carey's father had become friends with Larsen over the years through a mutual acquaintance, and he had two newspaper headlines printed. The first read, "Larsen Pitches No-Hitter." The second said, "Gooney Birds Pick Larsen to Win Fifth Game." When he returned to the Concourse Plaza Hotel, where he too was staying, the elder Carey pasted one of the headlines—the one that mentioned the no-hitter—on Larsen's door so that he could see it when he returned. But then he had second thoughts—the headline might prove to be a jinx. So he returned to Larsen's door, where the paper remained untouched, took it back, and flushed it down the toilet after shredding it. The second headline he kept for himself (which his son later had framed as a permanent memento).

Although he did not frequent novelty shops in making pitching assignments, Stengel's rationale in crafting strategy often appeared to be inscrutable, and many observers sometimes wondered whether he consulted some kind of crystal ball. In many, if not most, situations, the Yankee starting pitcher would not learn of his assignment until he walked into the clubhouse the day of the game. Frank Crosetti, the wiry third-base coach, would arrive early in the morning and place a baseball in the selected pitcher's shoe. It was a Yankee tradition known to all the players.

The first players to spot the ball in Larsen's shoe that day were right fielder Hank Bauer and first baseman Moose Skowron. Even before they saw it, however, Bauer had asked Crosetti who was pitching, and when Crosetti told him, Bauer had a short response: "Oh, shit." Bob Turley came into the clubhouse shortly afterward and walked over to his locker, which adjoined Larsen's. He looked down and saw the ball in Larsen's shoe. He too was "flabbergasted," and, like Bauer, said, "Oh, shit. Somebody's joking. He ain't going to pitch." But the ball was still there when Larsen sauntered into the clubhouse, still assuming that he would be sitting on the bench. Larsen stared at the ball in disbelief without saying a word and gulped.

The right-hander slowly undressed in silence, put on his game underwear, walked into the training room, and lay down for a short nap. He then arose, put on his uniform, discussed the strengths and weaknesses of the Dodger hitters with Berra, and walked out onto the field shortly before the starting time of one o'clock to warm up with Charlie Silvera, the Yankees' bullpen catcher. He had been given a second chance, and he would make the most of it.

And now, with two outs in the bottom of the ninth, Larsen needs to get only one more out to walk off the mound in glory.

As Berra considers Larsen's next pitch, Dale Mitchell—a left-handed batter who is pinch-hitting for Dodger pitcher Sal Maglie—settles into his batting stance. Larsen and Berra had not discussed Mitchell because they did not expect him to play. The omission is not a critical one. Mitchell is well-known to both Berra and Larsen. Before joining the Dodgers in the middle of the 1956 season, Mitchell had spent more than ten seasons with the Cleveland Indians. In that span, the thirty-five-year-old outfielder had amassed a .312 lifetime batting average. Larsen had pitched against him as a Yankee and in his earlier struggles as a pitcher with the St. Louis Browns and then the newly franchised Baltimore Orioles. Both Larsen and Berra know from that experience that Mitchell will not be an easy out. "I knew he was a pretty good hitter," Berra later said. "He punches the ball. The kind of guy you've got to watch." For his part, Mitchell is confident that he can do what no other Dodger has been able to do that afternoon. "I had hit off Larsen a lot," he would recall, "and I really felt I could've gotten on base."

There are at least two fans in Yankee Stadium who share Dale Mitchell's optimism. When he walked to the plate in the late-afternoon sun, Mitchell's name was announced over the public-address system, the words echoing throughout the stadium. In a box seat behind the Yankee dugout, Dale's wife, Margaret, placed her arm around their seven-year-old son, whose nickname was Bo, leaned over, and whispered a stern warning. "Son," she said, "keep your mouth shut if your dad gets a base hit right now. Otherwise, these Yankee fans might kill us." Bo understood at once that his mother was not joking. "This was serious," he later remembered.

Although he cannot guarantee a hit to break the game open, Mitchell is confident that he will at least make contact with the ball. Because Dale Mitchell rarely strikes out. In 3,984 official plate appearances over more than eleven years of regular-season play, the Oklahoma native has struck out only 119 times. In one season with the Indians he had had 640 at bats with only eleven strikeouts, and in another year he had had 511 at bats with only nine strikeouts. And in thirty previous plate appearances in three World Series, he has never struck out. So Larsen and Berra know that there is little hope of getting Mitchell to strike out. They will have to count on the fielding.

The other seven Yankees in the field no doubt know that as well, and they share the tension—and fear—of the moment. Like Berra, however, they are thinking of more than Larsen's possible place in baseball history. "We were thinking about winning the damn game," remembered Andy Carey. From his vantage point in center field, Mickey Mantle alternates between dread and hope as to whether Mitchell might hit the ball to him. "The crowd was on its feet and I was so nervous I could feel my knees shaking," Mantle later recalled. "I played in more than 2,400 games in the major leagues, but I never was as nervous as I was in the ninth inning of that game, afraid I would do something to mess up Larsen's perfect game."

Over in right field, Hank Bauer is hoping that Mitchell does not hit one of his trademark line drives that will require him to dive for the ball and risk getting his cleats caught in the drainpipe—not only because of the chance of losing the ball but also because he knows that the drainpipe in right field had been the cause of Mickey Mantle's first major knee injury in the 1951 World Series. But no player is more nervous than Larsen. "I was so weak in the knees out there in the ninth inning," he later said, "I thought I was going to faint," and when Mitchell came to bat, "I was so nervous I almost fell down. My legs were rubbery and my fingers didn't feel like they were on my hand."

The other nervous participant is perhaps the most important—Babe Pinelli, the umpire who is calling balls and strikes behind the plate. Just one week shy of his sixty-first birthday, he is calling his last game behind home plate. In a span of almost a thousand games over the course of twenty-two years—beginning when Babe Ruth was playing for the Boston Braves in 1935—Pinelli has never officiated a perfect game behind the plate. This will be his last chance. His retirement has already been planned, and there will be no more World Series for the much-respected National League umpire. And so Pinelli too is a captive of the drama. He later remembered it as the "most agonizing" game he ever umpired. Now, in the ninth inning, with Mitchell at the plate, Pinelli is crouched over Berra with sweat soaking through his uniform and feeling so short of breath that he almost feels faint. The eyes of the baseball world are upon him, and he cannot afford to make an obvious mistake.

The tension is palpable in the stands as well, where cheers and shouts have filled the stadium with every pitch in the ninth inning. It is hard not to take notice, and radio announcer Bob Wolff proclaims with confidence, "I'll guarantee that nobody, but nobody, has left this ballpark."

The excitement of the moment has even permeated the Dodger camp. When Mitchell stepped into the batter's box, Clem Labine was warming up in the Dodger bullpen beyond left field so that he could replace Dodger pitcher Sal Maglie if the Dodgers should somehow manage to tie the game or even pull ahead. But he realized that he could be about to witness a unique moment in baseball history. So he stopped throwing and moved up to the railing, where fellow Dodger pitcher Roger Craig was also watching.

Labine looks over to Craig. "Roger, what do you think? If he does it, this is probably something we'll never, ever see again in our lives."

Craig thinks for a second. "I hope he does it."

"I have to tell the truth," Labine says. "I hope he does too."

In other circumstances, Berra would talk to batters about something other than the game. Where they were going to dinner that night. How their golf game was faring. And sometimes a personal matter that would create confusion or even anger. Anything, Berra explained, "to distract them from the ball on the way." (When longtime Detroit Tiger All-Star outfielder Al Kaline came to the plate on one occasion, Berra casually remarked, "I hear you're being traded to Chicago. Think you'll like Chicago?") Many players caught on to Berra's ploy and would let him know that his overtures were not welcome. One time he asked Ted Williams, an avid angler, where he was going fishing after the game, and Williams—one of the most focused hitters of all time—had a quick response: "Shut up!" Berra was not deterred and would persist in his friendly dialogue with Williams and other players.

But there is no dialogue with Dale Mitchell. The Yankee catcher does not want to be diverted from the task at hand.

It did not take long for Larsen to reach a commanding count of one ball and two strikes on the Dodger pinch hitter. Mitchell took a strike, swung mightily at yet another pitch, took a ball, and then fouled off a pitch that appeared destined for the strike zone.

Mitchell is surely nervous as Larsen gets ready for the next pitch, but the Yankee pitcher hardly appears to be a portrait of equanimity. Larsen steps off the mound to the right, takes off his cap for the ump-teenth time and wipes his sweaty brow with his forearm. He trudges back to the mound, picks up the dirt-stained resin bag, and dusts the white contents onto his pitching hand. As thousands of fans in the stadium observe and millions more watch or listen on television and radio, Larsen glances around to Mickey Mantle in center field, turns back, steps on the pitcher's rubber, and glares down at Berra. The catcher's fingers are shaking, but Larsen can read the sign.

With the pitcher ahead on the count, Berra would normally call for a slider or even a curve. Something with a little movement and perhaps a hope that the batter will flail away at a bad pitch. But not now. Not today. Larsen has the magic touch, and so Berra calls for a fastball. Larsen's fastball has worked so well all afternoon. There is no reason to lose faith in it now. ("His sliders were good, so were his curves," Berra later explained, "but his fastballs were faster than I'd ever seen.") Larsen has no reason to quarrel with Yogi's decision. "Every ball that was hit hard" by the Dodgers that afternoon, the Yankee pitcher ac-knowledged immediately after the game, "came off" his slider. And so the fastball seems like the right choice to him as well.

Larsen gives a slight nod, grips the ball with his two forefingers, and with one quick movement hurls the leather sphere toward the batter.

———

When Dale Mitchell first advanced to the plate, Dodger broadcaster Vin Scully told his television audience that "no man in baseball history has come up in a more dramatic moment," and *The New York Times* later called it the "greatest moment" in World Series history. But it is not enough to know that Don Larsen stood on the brink of a success that no other pitcher had enjoyed. An appreciation of Larsen's performance—and how he came to that enviable position—requires an understanding of the other players who were on the field that day: their backgrounds, their skills, their hopes and fears, and, most especially, how and why they found themselves at Yankee Stadium for that fifth game of the 1956 World Series. Because this is not just a story about Don Larsen. This is also a story about eighteen other players who were an integral part of the drama that unfolded on that warm fall day.

1

Top of the First: Don Larsen

Don Larsen's mother could have watched on television when her son strode to the mound in Yankee Stadium shortly before one o'clock on that October afternoon for the fifth game of the 1956 World Series. But Charlotte Larsen, a sixty-one-year-old housekeeper for a retirement home in La Jolla, California, stayed away from the television and radio, afraid that her "presence" would somehow compromise her son's performance. "I make it a rule never to watch Don when he pitches," she later explained to a reporter. "Seems like every time I watch him, he loses. So I just don't do it." His father, James, a salesman in a Berkeley, California, department store, had separated from his wife many years earlier and had no such reservations. He watched the game on a television set at the local YMCA.

Seeing Don on television no doubt brought back fond memories of the days when the elder Larsen played catch with his young son in the basement of their home in Michigan City, Indiana, a small industrial town near the Michigan border. Even then, Don knew he wanted to be a major-league baseball player. "I didn't pay much attention to it," his mother later said, "because he didn't seem to have any special talent for the game."

His mother's doubts did not deter Don from pursuing his dream of becoming a major-league baseball player. The irony was that the ambitious youngster—who had grown to more than six feet tall by the time he reached his teens—was more proficient at basketball than baseball, and when his family moved to San Diego, California, in 1944, he had no trouble making the basketball team at Point Loma High School and being selected for the Metro Conference team with an average of nineteen points per game. He also pitched for the school's baseball team, where the coach concluded that the young athlete was "a better prospect as a hitter than as a pitcher." But Don wanted to be a pitcher, and he was not discouraged by the coach's sentiments. He pitched for a local American Legion baseball team and performed well enough to catch the eye of Art Schwartz, a scout for the American League's St. Louis Browns.

When Don graduated from high school in 1947, Schwartz took the eighteen-year-old prospect and his father out to dinner and offered Don a contract to play with one of the Browns' minor-league teams. Don had already been offered some college basketball scholarships, but they held no appeal for him. "I was never much with the studies," he later explained, "and I didn't really have an interest in going to college and studying my life away." So he signed the contract proffered by Schwartz, which included an $850 bonus.

His introduction to professional baseball a few weeks later was less than auspicious. He was assigned to the Browns' farm team in Aberdeen, South Dakota, and he took a train in late June to join the team. No one met him at the train station, and, not knowing what to do, he went to one of the town's few hotels. They had no rooms available, and so he spent the night sleeping in the lobby. The next day he traveled to the ballpark, only to learn that no one knew of him. Unable to get into the ballpark, he had to buy a ticket to the doubleheader that was being played that day. And not wanting to bother anyone, he took his seat along the first-base line, luggage in tow, trying to figure out what to do. After the first game, Larsen was able to catch the attention of one of the team's players, who retrieved Don Heffner, the manager. Heffner explained that he had expected Larsen a few days earlier and for that reason had not made any arrangements for his later arrival.

It was smooth sailing from there. Larsen was able to move up the minor-league ladder and, along the way, develop new friendships. Bob Turley, who would later be Larsen's teammate on the St. Louis Browns, the Baltimore Orioles, and then the New York Yankees, remembered their first meeting in Pine Bluff, Arkansas, where the Browns' minor-league teams would meet for spring training. Turley first spotted Larsen in the mess hall "beating the hell out of a pinball machine." He was, said Turley, "a fun-loving guy" who "liked to go out and have a beer or two and talk to people in bars."

The Korean War ignited shortly after the 1950 season began, and in due course Larsen received his draft notice. He spent two years in noncombat roles and, upon his discharge in 1953, he was promoted to the St. Louis Browns. The promotion was a mixed blessing in one respect: the Browns were a perennial losing team that had finished last or next-to-last twenty-two times. Still, it was not something to be turned aside. "I'll never forget," Larsen later said, "how excited I was when I found out I made the club."

He made his first appearance on April 18 in Detroit and soon established himself as one of the Browns' brighter prospects, with a 7–12 won-lost record on a team that lost a hundred games and again finished last. The Browns also appreciated Larsen's prowess as a hitter (having established a major-league record for pitchers by getting seven consecutive hits at one point in the season), and he was occasionally used as a pinch hitter. But all of that potential was compromised by Larsen's inability to honor the midnight curfew established by manager Marty Marion. His mantra was "let the good times roll," and years later he would say, "You give the best you can on the field. Who cares what you do afterwards as long as you show up and do well?"

It may have been an appropriate approach in Larsen's mind, but Marion found it difficult to accept. The Browns' manager finally took his frustrations to team owner Bill Veeck. "Look, Bill," he said, "we have to teach this guy Larsen a lesson. I think if we send him down to [the Browns' farm team in] San Antonio right now, it might throw a scare into him and get him straightened out." Veeck—more concerned with victories than team discipline—disagreed. "There's no sense in trying to reform him," said the Browns' owner. "I still think he'll be a big winner someday, even though he winks at all the rules."

Larsen's social habits continued unchecked when the team relocated to Baltimore (as the Orioles) in 1954 (leading Jimmy Dykes, the new manager, to say that "the only thing Don fears is sleep"). But hopes for Larsen as a "big winner" in 1954 proved unduly optimistic. He won only three games and lost twenty-one. But that losing record had to be placed in context. The team scored only 483 runs that season—or about three runs per game—which made it difficult for any capable pitcher to succeed. And beyond that, two of Larsen's victories came in well-pitched games against the New York Yankees.

Larsen's success against the Yankees was not lost on manager Casey Stengel, and on November 18, 1954—after the season ended—it was announced that Larsen was part of a sixteen-player deal that would bring the young right-hander to New York (along with Orioles teammate Bob Turley). The Yankees—eager to strengthen a pitching staff that had lagged behind the pennant-winning Cleveland Indians—had high hopes for their new acquisitions. "With Turley and Larsen," said Yankee general manager George Weiss, "we plug our major weakness. They are two of the finest and fastest right-handers in the game. Both are young and both figure to get better."

Weiss' hopes for Larsen proved to be premature. He arrived at spring training with a sore arm, and Stengel as well as some of the other Yankee players wondered whether he had the same drive to succeed that motivated them. "He had probably a hell of a lot more ability than ninety-nine percent of all the pitchers in baseball," said one teammate. "He was a good hitter. He could run. He could field the ball. But he was a lazy type." That concern grew when the 1955 season started. His pitching performances were not impressive, and Stengel decided that Don needed further conditioning with the Yankees' farm team in Denver, which was managed by former Yankee catcher (and future Yankee manager) Ralph Houk. Larsen did not take the news of his demotion well. "I'm going to take my sweet time reporting," he told his teammates, "and I don't give a damn if I ever come back here."

It proved to be nothing more than false bravado. Larsen did report to Houk at Denver and, to everyone's delight, did remarkably well, compiling a 9–1 won-lost record in a couple of months. On July 28, Houk gave him the good news: the Yankees wanted him back.

Larsen started his first game on Sunday, July 31, and pitched the Yankees to a complete game victory over the Kansas City Athletics. It was a good omen. Larsen proved to be instrumental in the Yankees' final pennant drive, winning key games (including a thirteen-inning outing against the Red Sox) and finishing the season with a 9–2 won-lost record and a respectable 3.06 earned run average. He also impressed Stengel with his hitting ability, and there were many times when the Yankee manager would bat Larsen seventh or eighth in the lineup instead of last, as was usually the case with pitchers. (There was the time, for example, when Stengel posted the lineup showing that Larsen would be batting seventh, second baseman Jerry Coleman eighth, and Billy Martin, assigned to third base, batting ninth. Martin stormed into Stengel's office demanding to know why he was batting ninth. "Larsen should be hitting ahead of me," Martin conceded, "but there's no way you can have Jerry Coleman hitting in front of me!")

Larsen was given the starting assignment in the fourth game of the 1955 World Series against the Dodgers, but it was not an experience to remember. He gave up five runs in four innings as the Yankees lost 5–3. While the Yankees went on to lose the series to the Dodgers, Larsen was proud of his accomplishment over the course of the 1955 season. "I had stretched beyond my childhood dreams by pitching for the Yankees and in the World Series," he later said. "Even though we lost the championship to the Dodgers, I was thankful to have even been there in the first place."

He had good reason to be hopeful for the future. He had proven—despite the World Series loss—that he was a tough competitor who could come through in high-pressure situations. That was no small matter. The Yankees were, to a man, a fiercely competitive group, and they did not tolerate a teammate who seemed to be giving less than everything he had. (The unyielding drive to win was perhaps captured best when Eddie Lopat, one of the Yankees' premier pitchers of the early 1950s, confronted Mickey Mantle in the dugout during Mantle's rookie year in 1951 when the nineteen-year-old player failed to get a jump on a ball hit to the outfield because he was still moping about a strikeout his last time at bat. Lopat had been pitching, and he did not hesitate to convey his displeasure. "You want to play?" Lopat demanded of Mantle. "If not, get your ass the hell out of here. We don't need guys like you. We want to win.")

In addition to his talent, Larsen had an affable manner that made him easy to like. Indeed, said Turley, "everybody liked him." They also recognized his interest in entertainment after the game. Although there were many occasions when Don would drift out of the clubhouse after a game to socialize with someone other than his teammates, they had enough contact to realize that Don had a startling capacity for liquor. "Larsen was easily the greatest drinker I've known," Mantle later observed, "and I've known some pretty good ones in my time." Larsen also had a penchant for diversity when it came to drinking. "He'd never drink the same thing twice," said first baseman Joe Collins. "If he had five drinks, he'd have five different drinks." His teammates would tease him good-naturedly about his drinking habits, but, as Collins remembered, they were also prepared "to accept him for what he was."

Stengel was also prepared to accept Larsen for who he was, and that became evident when Larsen wrapped his brand-new Oldsmobile around a telephone pole at five o'clock in the morning in St. Petersburg, Florida, shortly after spring training had commenced for the 1956 season. Larsen admitted to Stengel that he had been frequenting some "waterholes" earlier in the evening and that he had fallen asleep at the wheel (and fortunately escaped any major injury). Although he made much in team meetings about honoring his curfew, Stengel—an avid drinker himself—was prepared to tolerate a player's deviations from his policy as long as it did not affect the player's performance. And so, when reporters later confronted him about Larsen's accident and whether he had violated the team curfew, Stengel was nonchalant. I'm not sure what to do, he told the reporters, because "Larsen was either out too late or up too early."

Stengel used Larsen interchangeably during the 1956 season as a starter and a reliever, and by season's end, he had pitched in thirty-eight games and compiled a respectable 3.26 earned run average in 180 innings. Larsen had also adjusted to life as a Yankee in New York City, living a seemingly carefree existence that did not leave any room for savings on his $12,000 annual salary. On the morning of the fifth game of the World Series—after he had learned that he would be the starting pitcher—Larsen approached Bill McCorry, the Yankees' traveling secretary, and asked for a $200 advance on his series earnings. "I've gotta get home to California when this thing is over," he explained to McCorry, "and I don't have a nickel." "Win today," McCorry replied, "and I'll see that you get your money."

As Larsen was told later that day—and as he should have already known—he was not the only one in need of an advance on his World Series earnings. As far as his teammates knew, Larsen was a bachelor (with one reporter referring to Larsen shortly before the 1956 World Series as "a devil-may-care playboy"). But those perceptions changed quickly when word got out on the morning of October 8, 1956, that Larsen was in fact married and that his wife had filed a complaint with a New York court because of his failure to make support payments for her and their fourteen-month-old daughter. "While this baseball hero is enjoying the luxuries of life and the plaudits of the public," Mrs. Larsen's attorney told the press, "he is subjecting his fourteen-month-old baby girl and his wife to the pleasures of a starvation existence." Vivian Larsen, it turned out, had met the Yankee pitcher in 1954 when she was a twenty-seven-year-old operator for a Baltimore telephone company and Don was a pitcher for the Baltimore Orioles. Larsen thought they had parted company after the season was over, but Vivian called him in California to let him know that she was pregnant. Abortions were illegal, and at first he suggested that Vivian put the baby up for adoption. That was out of the question, Vivian told him. So Larsen decided that the only honorable course of action was to get married (which was accomplished in April 1955). But Larsen made it clear to Vivian that the marriage had to be kept secret, that the union was only "for the sake of the child," and that "he was not ready to settle down and preferred to live a life of free and easy existence." They never lived together, but Vivian migrated to the Bronx near Yankee Stadium, and there she stayed with their daughter, expecting $60 a week in support money from her husband.

Whatever his thoughts about Vivian and their young daughter, Larsen does not appear to be distracted when Dodger second baseman Jim Gilliam steps into the batter's box to start the fifth game of the 1956

World Series. A five-foot-ten-inch switch-hitter who is batting left-handed against the right-handed Larsen, Gilliam—who goes by the nickname of "Junior"—has been the Dodgers' only .300 hitter in the 1956 season (batting exactly .300). "He's very selective," Berra told Larsen before the game, "and he'll make you pitch to him"—a point that no doubt registered with Larsen, because he had walked Gilliam when he pitched to him in the second game of the series. Larsen starts off with a fastball that is low and outside for a ball. On the next pitch Gilliam hits a ground-ball foul that caroms off the right-field wall and is retrieved by Hank Bauer in right field. Larsen follows with a fastball that is called a strike. Gilliam steps out of the batter's box and looks at plate umpire Babe Pinelli, not believing that the pitch was really a strike but, as radio announcer Bob Neal observes, "The evidence is up on the scoreboard" with a count of two and two. Larsen follows with a "sneaky slider" that results in a called third strike, and Gilliam walks slowly back the dugout. Larsen has his first out.

Dodger shortstop Pee Wee Reese, batting right-handed, steps up to the plate. Reese fouls off the first pitch and then takes a ball. Reese takes the next pitch for a called strike but holds his bat while Larsen throws two more pitches, each of them balls. With a full count of three and two, Reese—mindful of Larsen's lack of control in the second game—no doubt hopes that he will be the beneficiary of a walk. But it is not to be. Larsen throws a slider for a called third strike, and there are now two outs.

Larsen watches as Dodger center fielder Duke Snider steps into the batter's box. He is a left-handed power hitter who has hit forty or more home runs in the last four seasons and led the National League in that department in 1956 with forty-three. Recognizing Snider's tendency to pull the ball, all of the Yankee outfielders—Enos Slaughter in left, Mantle in center, and Bauer in right—shift toward the right-field foul line, which is only 296 feet from home plate. Shortstop Gil McDougald shades over toward second base, Billy Martin is playing deep at the edge of the outfield grass at second, and first baseman Joe Collins is situated well behind the bag near the right-field foul line. Knowing that Snider is a good fastball hitter, television announcer Mel Allen surmises that "Larsen will show Snider a change of pace," and, after missing the plate with his first pitch, Larsen throws a slow fastball that Snider anxiously swings at and misses. As Bob Neal tells his radio audience, Larsen had taken something off the pitch, and Snider was "way out ahead on his swing." After throwing another pitch that is wide of the plate, Larsen hurls a fastball down the middle, and Snider hits a line drive into right field that Bauer catches with ease.

Having gotten through the first inning without a problem, Larsen slowly walks off the mound toward the Yankee dugout for some rest and a quick cigarette in the tunnel that connects the dugout to the clubhouse.

Bottom of the First: Sal Maglie

With the top of the first inning over, eight Dodger players move up the steps of the visiting players' dugout on the third-base side of the field. Seven of them run to their various positions while Roy Campanella, the Dodgers' rotund catcher, moves behind the plate. The ninth player, with the number 35 emblazoned on the back of his jersey, emerges more slowly and walks toward the pitcher's mound with a purposeful gait. He is thirty-nine years old—a senior citizen among baseball players of his generation—but there is nothing to indicate that he has a retiring personality. Quite the contrary. There is something ominous about him. He stands about six feet, two inches and weighs around 185 pounds and has the blue baseball cap with the white B pulled low over his forehead. You can see the whites of his deep-set eyes, which have a penetrating glare, and his mouth is turned downward in seeming disgust. He has not shaved, and the dark beard contributes to the aura that he is tough, perhaps mean. Indeed, in a *Sports Illustrated* article the year before, Robert Creamer had referred to him as "the angel of darkness."

Players familiar with Sal Maglie understand Creamer's reference. Maglie, they know, will use his considerable talent to intimidate batters. He might not succeed as well as he would like on every occasion, but the other team's players know that he will be in control when he steps on the mound. "When I'm pitching," he once explained, "I own the plate." And there is nothing he will not do to protect his turf. "When I was on the mound," he later said, "I was in business. I didn't give a damn if my grandmother was in there."

It is a perspective that inspires respect from other pitchers. Dodger hurler Carl Erskine is among them. He later told me that Maglie was one of the two pitchers he admired most (the other being the Yankees' Allie Reynolds) because, "when he pitched, there was no question who was in charge of the game." The Yankees certainly know that. Maglie has already pitched the Dodgers to a 6–3 victory in the first game of the series at Ebbets Field, striking out ten men in the process.

There is a certain irony in Maglie's presence in a Brooklyn uniform. He had disliked the Dodgers from the first days when he broke into the major leagues as a New York Giant in 1945, and that emotion did not leave him until the day he joined the team in May 1956. "When I pitched against the Dodgers," he later told Jim Bouton when they were both on the Seattle Pilots, "I didn't care if it was the last game I ever pitched. I really hated that club."

There is another irony that makes Maglie's appearance in a World Series game even more remarkable, and he no doubt appreciates that irony more than anyone. Because, the truth be known, he was not a very good ballplayer when he was growing up in Niagara Falls, New York.

It was a neighborhood of mixed religious, ethnic and national groups—Jews, Irish, Poles, and, of course, Italians. In the early years, his father, an immigrant from Foggia, Italy, ran a small grocery store to support his wife and three children. Sal was the middle child with a younger and an older sister. As he got older, his father proposed that his son learn a trade and arranged for him to work in a barbershop. The experiment was short-lived. "I went there once," Maglie later recalled, "went out the back and through the alley and never came back." In retrospect, the escape from the barbershop was no surprise. Even as a young boy, Sal was not interested in a trade. He was interested only in basketball and baseball.

His success as a basketball player was easy to understand. "I've always loved basketball," he once said. He played for his high school team and set a municipal record by scoring sixty-one points in a game. But his accomplishments in basketball were not solely attributable to his enthusiasm or his skills in dribbling and shooting. His attitude made the difference. "I've always played sports rough," he later explained. "I scored because I used every inch of my body under the backboards. I pushed a little and elbowed a little and, finally, I scored. If the other team played rough, I played rougher."

By the time he graduated from high school in 1937 at the age of twenty (apparently because of a course he had failed and had to repeat), Sal had an offer for a basketball scholarship at Niagara University. In another time and place, it might have been worth pursuing. But the young athlete could not accept it. The Depression had enveloped the nation, money was tight, and his family needed help. So Sal took a job in the shipping department at Union Carbide in Niagara Falls. The pay was good, but he lived for the weekends when he could play semipro baseball—because as much as he enjoyed basketball, baseball was his first love. The problem was that he could not achieve the same level of success on the diamond as he could on the court. There was the time, for example, when he was pitching for a semipro team while he was still in high school and was approached by a Dodger scout after the game. "Kid, are you going to school?" the scout inquired. "Yes," said Maglie. "Keep going," the scout replied.

Sal was not discouraged. He continued to explore opportunities for playing professional baseball after he left high school. But it was not easy. Almost everyone who watched him pitch in the semipro leagues told him that he had an awkward motion that would ruin his arm. Few were willing to give him any encouragement about a career in professional baseball. The obstacles were hard to ignore. When he went to the tryout for the Rochester Red Wings in 1937, he threw only three pitches before he heard the coach yell, "Next."

His break finally came in the summer of 1938. Steve O'Neill, manager of the Buffalo Bisons minor-league team, decided to take a chance on Sal—not so much because of his pitching skills but because of his notoriety as a local basketball star. Anything to draw crowds. The contract did not promise any substantial financial benefits—a $275 signing bonus and a monthly salary of $250 during the season. Still, it was a chance to be a professional baseball player, and Sal was not going to let it slip away.

His first outing on August 13, 1938, was less than auspicious. The twenty-one-year-old rookie knew little about etiquette in professional baseball, and, when O'Neill called on him to relieve with the bases loaded in the eighth inning of a game against the Newark Bears, Maglie headed straight for the mound without warming up. "That's how little I knew," Sal later recalled. Although he ultimately did take his warm-up pitches, the result was not inspiring. His first pitch in the game sailed over the batter's head, and several others had the catcher "doing handsprings." After he had walked three batters and hit one in the rear, O'Neill mercifully took him out.

He saw action in only four more games that season and no doubt hoped that the following year would prove to be more productive. It was a false hope. Sal attributed much of his poor performance in that second season to the infrequency of his playing time. There would often be many days, sometimes weeks, between pitching assignments. You cannot pitch well, he told his manager, if you work only sporadically. However much he understood, O'Neill was not about to give a failing pitcher more work. So Maglie asked to be sent down to the inferior PONY League, where he could play more often. O'Neill warned the young pitcher that he was moving in the wrong direction and that he might never come back. But Maglie stood his ground.

The strategy proved successful. Sal did well enough in the PONY League to earn a promotion in 1941 to the Elmira Pioneers in the Class A league (where he won twenty games). To those who later marveled at the dramatic turnaround in his fortunes, the young pitcher had a simple answer: "In Elmira, they let me play, that was all."

There was, however, more to the story. Maglie was an intense competitor who focused on all aspects of the game in an effort to capitalize on every possible advantage. There was no relaxing during the game—not even when he sat in the dugout while his team batted. He studied the other pitcher's motion, the opposing batters' stances, and the dynamics of the field. As he later explained, "In the dugout I always had my head in the game. There is always something to learn." Even when he was playing in the major leagues, his teammates knew not to trouble Maglie in the dugout during the game. "You don't want to bother Sal when the other team's batting," said Dale Mitchell, who roomed with Maglie on the road when they were with the Dodgers, "because he's studying all the time."

The hard work paid dividends for Sal in 1942. His stellar pitching performance at Elmira caught the eye of New York Giant scout Eddie Ainsmith, who reported that the Niagara Falls native "hasn't much of a curve, but he could develop." The Giants drafted Maglie on the basis of that recommendation, and in the spring of 1942—with the nation at war—Maglie was assigned to the Giants' farm team in Jersey City in the International League, the top rung in the minor-league ladder. He could have been wearing combat fatigues instead, but he had a sinus condition that made him unfit for service. So Maglie spent the 1942 season honing his skills and posting a 9–6 won-lost record.

The opportunities for advancement expanded exponentially at the end of the 1942 season because the major-league teams' rosters had been depleted by the war effort. Maglie was in a position to exploit that situation but decided that he could not in good conscience play a game while his peers risked their lives in defense of the country. He placed himself on the voluntary retirement list and took a job as a pipe fitter in a Niagara Falls defense plant. But he did not live alone in Niagara Falls. In early 1941 he had married Kay Pileggi, a slim brunette with a bright smile who was two years his junior and his former high school sweetheart. It was an enduring and valuable relationship for Maglie. (She was, he would later say, "a wonderful woman" and "my best friend in baseball.")

As the war wound down, Maglie—who had preserved his pitching proficiency by playing for a Canadian team on weekends—rejoined the Jersey City Giants in June 1945, hoping, no doubt, that he could continue the progression toward the big leagues. His performance, however, was unremarkable. Still, big-league teams were hurting for players because so many remained in the service, and Mel Ott, the Giants' manager, put out a call to bring Maglie up to the parent club.

On August 9, 1945, Sal was summoned to the mound at the Polo Grounds to pitch against the St. Louis Cardinals, who had loaded the bases with one out. Maglie may have thought back to his first experience as a professional baseball player in Buffalo in 1938 when he was also asked to relieve with the bases loaded. But unlike that fiasco, Maglie performed well, walking one batter and then retiring the other two and leaving the game unscathed. The short but successful performance earned him a starting opportunity on August 14—the very day on which the Japanese surrendered. Maglie did not disappoint. He pitched the Giants to a 5–2 complete game victory over the Cincinnati Redlegs.

It was only a start. Sal pitched six more complete games, including three shutouts, and finished the season with a 5–4 record and a 2.35 earned run average. For Maglie, however, the more enduring memory of that season was the first game of a Sunday doubleheader with the Dodgers in September before 54,740 fans in the Polo Grounds. He was called in to relieve in the tenth inning with the score tied. He breezed through that inning but fell apart in the next inning when he walked two batters and saw Dixie Walker, the Dodger left fielder, get a hit that won the game. "For some reason that made me resent the Dodgers," Maglie later recalled. It was a bitterness that would stay with him all the years he pitched with the Giants.

But that was all in the future. The 1945 season left Maglie feeling proud of his accomplishment. He had finally made it to the big leagues. But he was no fool. He knew that staying there would require hard work. So he was receptive to the proposal of Dolf Luque, a Giant coach, that he play winter ball in Cuba for a team that Luque was going to manage in Cienfuegos.

Luque, a fifty-five-year-old Cuban native, was a colorful figure who had pitched in the National League for twenty years between 1914 and 1935, with considerable success. Luque told Maglie that the key to success was a willingness to pitch high and inside so that the batter was always kept off balance. Never, said Luque, should you allow the batter to feel comfortable at the plate. "Luque believed in protecting the plate," Maglie later explained, "and I became a believer too."

Sal was able to turn Luque's advice into sterling pitching performances, and so the Niagara Falls native was in good shape and full of expectations when he arrived at the Giants' spring training camp in

Miami Beach, Florida, in February 1946. Those hopes were buoyed when Ott greeted him by saying, "We're depending on you, boy." And soon thereafter he signed a contract for $7,500. It was all enough to make Maglie believe that he had finally come into his own.

For reasons he could never fathom, Sal's aspirations for a meaningful spot in the Giants' pitching rotation soon evaporated. He pitched in a few exhibition games, including one on March 30 in which he pitched five strong innings and struck out seven batters. "And then," said Maglie, "I never got a chance to pitch again—not even batting practice." Maglie did not have the courage to confront Ott about the manager's refusal to use him. He sat in silent frustration, wondering whether he had a future with the Giants.

There was, however, another option. Jorge Pasquel, a thirty-eight-year-old Mexican, was using his considerable wealth to lure American players to join the Mexican baseball league—where he had substantial interests—in the hope that he could make that league a more profitable venture. In January 1946—while he was still in Cuba—Maglie had been approached by Bernardo Pasquel, Jorge's younger brother, who had offered him a $7,500 salary with a $3,500 signing bonus. Maglie, believing that his future with the Giants was secure, turned it down immediately. Bernardo understood, but gave the young pitcher his card and told Maglie to contact him if he had a change of heart.

While he was fuming about Ott's refusal to use him in spring training, George Hausmann and Roy Zimmerman, two other Giant players, contacted Maglie because they had heard that he had received an offer from the Mexican League, and they wanted to know if Maglie had a telephone number for the Pasquels. When Sal said that he had Bernardo's card in his hotel room, Zimmerman and Hausmann arranged to meet Maglie there so that they could make the call and secure offers to join the Mexican League (which they ultimately did).

Rumors about the Pasquels' efforts were swirling around all the major-league spring training camps, and it did not take long for Ott to learn that Hausmann and Zimmerman had used the telephone in Maglie's hotel room to make contact with the Mexicans. Unfortunately, Ott assumed—wrongly—that Maglie had been the recruiting agent for the Mexicans.

Maglie knew that something was up when he walked into the club-house the next morning. It was, he remembered, "deathly quiet." Ott summoned Maglie to his office, shut the door, and berated him for try-ing to steal American players for the Mexican League. Ott refused to let the pitcher tell his side of the story. Instead, the manager marched out of the office with Maglie in tow and demanded that all the players line up. He then proceeded to ask each man whether he intended to "jump" to the Mexican League. When he finally came to Maglie, Ott received an affirmative response. Sal Maglie was going to play baseball in Mexico. He contacted Bernardo Pasquel and secured a $10,000 sign-ing bonus and a salary commensurate with his Giant salary.

It was not a precipitous decision for Maglie. "I was sore about the brush-off I had been getting all spring," he later explained, "and I knew I was marked lousy for sure now. I could get almost as much money in Mexico as the Giants were paying me. I was twenty-nine, and I had only a few years left to build up a little nest egg for me and my wife." So he and Kay discussed the matter before the confrontation at the clubhouse and decided that, if Ott's attitude remained unchanged and the Pasquels met his conditions, he should seize the opportunity—even though major-league baseball commissioner Happy Chandler had issued an edict that any player who joined the Mexican League would be banned from American baseball for five years.

In retrospect, Maglie's decision to go to Mexico proved to be a profitable one—his manager in the Mexican League was none other than Dolf Luque, and the Cuban veteran continued to pour wisdom into his American protégé. Maglie was assigned to the team in Puebla, a small village located seven thousand feet above sea level near the Si-erra Madre mountains, and he was forced to survive in conditions that were nothing short of primitive. "A train track ran through the out-field," Maglie later remembered, "and when a train had to go by, the game stopped, a gate opened in right field, the train chugged across center field and then went out through the gate in left."

The poor playing conditions were compounded by the means of transportation. The players had to travel from town to town in old buses that were constantly breaking down and that were filled with local villagers who had had brought along chickens, goats, and other livestock (a situation that finally convinced Maglie to charter a private plane to make the trips to distant towns). And then there was the weather. Located high in the mountains, Puebla could be comfortable, but the humidity and heat were overwhelming in Veracruz, Tampico, and other towns on or near the coast. "You could take a dozen showers down there and still not cool off," said Maglie.

There was another aspect to the weather that had a more lasting effect on Maglie's career. In Puebla, he saw that his curveball barely broke and that his fastball had more velocity. In contrast, his curveball broke more sharply in the lower elevations while his fastball had less movement. Maglie therefore learned to make his curveball break in high altitudes. Having mastered the curve in higher altitudes, Maglie saw that the ball would break that much more sharply when he pitched at lower elevations. "I was just a thrower before I jumped," Maglie later said. "Dolf Luque and the altitude taught me how to pitch."

With that instruction and experience, Maglie proved to be the most accomplished pitcher in the Mexican League—winning twenty games in 1946 and twenty-one in 1947—and earned the adulation of Mexican fans. But the adulation of the fans could not hide the stark reality of the Pasquels' business venture. Despite their early willingness to invest whatever money it took to entice American players to cross the border, the Pasquels could not generate enough revenue from the games to pay the high salaries that had been promised. By the end of the 1947 season, the venture was over and the American players had no alternative but to return to the States.

Chandler's five-year ban was still in place, and so Maglie retreated to his home in Niagara Falls with an uncertain future. He bought a gas station and kept his eyes open for other opportunities to play baseball. As luck would have it, something materialized in Canada. Sal was recruited to pitch for the Drummondville Cubs in the Quebec Provincial League for the 1949 season. The signing of the former New York Giant generated headlines in Canada's local media, and the area fans were not disappointed. Maglie won eighteen games during the regular season and then another five in the play-offs to lead the Cubs to a championship in October. The fans rejoiced by carrying him off the field.

Two months before that joyous conclusion, Maglie learned that he could leave the Cubs and return immediately to the Giants. The opportunity arose because lawsuits by the excluded players had persuaded Chandler to drop the ban on the Mexican "outlaws," as they were called, and allow them to rejoin their teams. Maglie resisted, largely because he wanted to make sure that he was well positioned—physically and emotionally—to make it a success. "I was in such bad shape," he later explained, "that I was afraid of queering my chances of sticking." So he decided to wait until the 1950 season.

When Maglie arrived at the Giants' training facility in Phoenix the following spring, he was a far different player from the one the Giants had last seen four years earlier. He now had three different curveballs, one of which would break down sharply when it was almost on top of the plate. ("That man can do things with a curve I never saw before," said Steve O'Neill, his former manager at Buffalo and now a major-league coach.) He also had far more self-confidence than he had possessed as a rookie in 1945. And, perhaps most important, he now had a strategy for keeping the hitters off balance.

He would often throw a fastball at the batter's head—sometimes even behind his head—so that the batter could never feel comfortable at the plate. Maglie never intended to actually hit the batter (in part because he did not want to put a man on base). And he picked his targets carefully (Brooklyn catcher Roy Campanella being one—before Dodger games, Maglie would often proclaim to his teammates, "Campanella's going down on the first pitch"). Still, there were some players—like Don Zimmer of the Dodgers in later years—who would never see a Maglie knockdown pitch because the pitcher knew they might get hurt. ("I didn't dare throw at him," Maglie later said of Zimmer, "because I knew he'd freeze.") But other batters—those he left sprawled on the dirt—believed that Maglie was indeed trying to hit them. Fearing another inside pitch close to the body, the batter would often step back from the plate and be set up for a sharp-breaking curveball on the outside corner. The approach worked wonders for Maglie, and, not surprisingly, he later confessed that the knockdown pitch was "the best pitch in baseball."

There was another major change when Maglie arrived for spring training in 1950: Mel Ott was gone and Leo Durocher was now the manager. A man with a fiery temper and an unbridled sense of competition, Durocher was interested in only one thing on the field: winning. And he was prepared to do whatever it might take to achieve that goal. So Maglie took heart when Durocher greeted him in Phoenix by saying, "I'm very happy to see you. I see you want to pitch."

Despite that encouragement, Maglie, now thirty-three, did not feel secure when the Giants broke camp and began the season. At first, Durocher used him sparingly in relief, and Maglie began to wonder whether he was, literally and figuratively, on his last legs. But then, on July 14, he was called in to relieve in a game against the Boston Braves in the third inning. Maglie shut the Braves down for the rest of the game, secured the victory, and gave Durocher the incentive to give him a chance. On July 21, the manager called on Maglie to start a game against the St. Louis Cardinals in Sportsman's Park. The Mexican outlaw pitched the Giants to a 5–4 victory with a performance that impressed his teammates and startled the Cardinals. ("Where have you been keeping that guy?" Stan Musial, the Cardinals' premier player, asked Giants' broadcaster Russ Hodges. "He's got the best curve I've ever seen.")

Durocher immediately placed Maglie in the Giants' pitching rotation, and the Niagara Falls native responded with a record that was nothing short of remarkable. He proceeded to win ten more games in a row in less than two months, including four straight shutouts— matching a record held by four other National League hurlers. He also brought himself to the brink of tying the major-league record of five shutouts and simultaneously came within four outs of breaking the National League record for consecutive scoreless innings (forty-six and a third) held by former Giant pitcher Carl Hubbell.

Maglie finished the season with a record of eighteen wins and four losses, leading the league in winning percentage. He also finished the season with a new nickname—"The Barber." There remains some uncertainty as to the origin of the nickname. Some claimed it was pinned on Maglie by Durocher, who said that Maglie looked "like the barber at the fourth chair." But the more probable genesis of the nickname was a comment by Jim McCulley, a reporter with the *New York Daily News*, who said he coined the nickname because Maglie "shaved the plate and came so close to the batters."

In either case, the nickname demonstrated that Maglie had arrived, and in 1951 he proved that his performance in 1950 was no accident. He won twenty-three games while losing only six over the course of 298 innings, helping the Giants overcome a thirteen-and-a-half-game lead by the Dodgers in August to finish in a tie for first place and forcing a play-off series of three games. Each team won one play-off game before the third and deciding game was held at the Polo Grounds on October 3, 1951. Durocher understandably asked Sal to start the pivotal game.

Maglie held the Dodgers for seven innings, and the score was tied at 1–1 as he began the top of the eighth. But after a few hard ground balls, a walk, and a wild pitch, Maglie walked off the mound at the end of the inning with the Giants trailing 4–1. He was lifted for a pinch hitter in the bottom of the eighth inning and, racked by despair, walked back to the clubhouse to watch the rest of the game with Giant owner Horace Stoneham. Although the situation looked bleak, Stoneham was not ready to surrender. "Sal," he told his star pitcher, "the game's not over yet. Have a beer." And then—after the Giants had whittled the Dodger lead down by one run—Maglie and Stoneham watched as Bobby Thomson hit a three-run home run in the bottom of the ninth to give the Giants a 5–4 victory and the National League pennant. The excitement spilled out of the field and throughout the sports world as radio and television announcers screamed, "The Giants win the pennant! The Giants win the pennant!" "I picked up Stoneham," Maglie recalled, "and we danced around." No small feat, considering that Stoneham weighed about two hundred pounds.

The World Series proved to be a disappointment for both Maglie and the Giants. The team held a 2–1 advantage when Maglie started the fourth game at the Polo Grounds on October 8, 1951. The first problem was the schedule. The game had to be postponed for one day because of rain, and the delay interfered with Maglie's rhythm. "I was the sort of pitcher," he later said, "who had to go every fourth day like it was clockwork." Maglie compounded the lack of rhythm with another mistake—a large meal at an Italian restaurant the night before the game, which left him feeling "plain heavy" the following day. He lacked the sparkle of earlier outings, and the Yankees got to him early, with Joe DiMaggio hitting a home run and leading the Yankees to a 6–2 victory. Maglie never saw action in that series again. The Yankees won the next two games and the World Championship. And so, in retrospect, Maglie would later say of the experience, "I believe I ate us out of that series."

Maglie continued to perform well for the Giants in 1952, finishing with an 18–8 record, but he began to experience a pain in his back that limited his mobility and often required him to sleep on a board to alleviate the discomfort. The cause of the problem was ultimately diagnosed as a strained ligament (which produced a lemon-size lump at the base of his spine). He spent a few days in traction at New York's Columbia Presbyterian Hospital, returned to the Giants by the end of the season, and by the beginning of the 1953 season was telling people that "my back feels better than ever."

That may have been so, but the relief was only temporary. Sal began to experience pain in his shoulder after the season began, and then he heard something snap in his back while pitching in a game against the St. Louis Cardinals. X-rays at the hospital revealed that he had a slight curvature of the spine, a tilted pelvis, and a right leg that was about three-quarters of an inch shorter than his left leg—perhaps the result of pushing off the pitching rubber so hard for so many years. He was placed in traction for five days and then given a lift for his right shoe. The lift produced only minimal relief, and Maglie finished the 1953 season with lingering pain and a disappointing 8–9 won-lost record.

Sal returned to the Giants with less pain and renewed hope in 1954. His performance matched his expectations, and he produced a 14–6 record, which included a complete game victory over the Dodgers at Ebbets Field on September 20 to win the pennant. Durocher took some credit for Maglie's revival. "Now that dago pitcher," the Giant manager once said to a reporter with reference to the Barber, "is a different kettle of fish. If I let him get happy, he don't pitch good. So I get him mad. I say, 'Whatsa matter, you stupid wop, you choking?' He gets so mad he wants to kill me."

The World Series was anticlimactic for Maglie. He had the honor of starting the first game at the Polo Grounds against the Cleveland Indians—who had established an American League record with 111 wins during the regular season—but was lifted in the eighth inning when Indians first baseman Vic Wertz stepped up to the plate with two men on base and the score tied at 2–2. Don Liddle strode to the mound, and on the first pitch Wertz drove the ball over Willie Mays' head in center field for what seemed to be a certain hit. But Mays—knowing that the fence was 475 feet from home plate—turned his back, ran at full speed, and caught the ball on the run over his shoulder about thirty feet from the fence. It was a spectacular play that saved the game for the Giants, who ultimately won 5–2 and then swept the next three games for the World Championship.

Maglie returned to the Giants in 1955, but, by the middle of the season, the honeymoon with the New York club came to an end. His pitching performance was still of a high caliber—he won nine of his fourteen decisions—but the Giants were concerned that the thirty-eight-year-old hurler had only limited time left as a productive player. After a game on July 30, Durocher signaled to Maglie that they needed to have a conversation in the dugout. "Sal," the Giant manager explained, "the time has come to say good-bye. We need young blood on this club." And that was how Maglie learned that he had been traded to the Cleveland Indians.

Sal hoped to demonstrate that his pitching skills were still intact. "I'll show 'em," he told a reporter. "I'm not as old as everyone thinks." But the high expectations were sidetracked by the competition for pitching assignments. The Indians already had four accomplished pitchers in their starting rotation—Early Wynn, Mike Garcia, Bob Lemon, and Herb Score—as well as an aging Bob Feller, and there was simply no room for another starter. As a result, Maglie started only two games during the remainder of the season and saw only limited relief appearances in eight other games.

He reported for spring training in 1956 in good shape, but he knew from the start that his prospects of playing a meaningful role on the

Indians were bleak. Life then took an unexpected turn after Maglie pitched against the Brooklyn Dodgers in an exhibition game in Jersey City on April 30. He was sharp, and he held the World Series champions to one hit in the final four innings. Shortly afterward, Indian general manager Hank Greenberg called Buzzie Bavasi, his counterpart on the Dodgers, and asked whether Brooklyn might be interested in acquiring the former Giant pitcher. After checking with manager Walter Alston and team captain Pee Wee Reese, Bavasi called Greenberg back and asked how much the Indians wanted for Maglie. A hundred thousand dollars, said Greenberg. "You've gotta be crazy," Bavasi responded. Greenberg persisted, Bavasi resisted, and finally the Indians—desperate to get rid of Maglie and his salary—agreed to accept $100 (although Bavasi said that, to avoid embarrassment, the Indians could issue a press release with any figure they liked, and later reports indicated that Maglie was sold for $14,000).

The trade may have been a propitious one in the view of Alston and Reese, but Dodger outfielder Carl Furillo was, as Bavasi later remembered, "furious." Furillo had been a favorite target of Maglie's when he was with the Giants, and there was many a time when Furillo found himself sprawled in the dirt at home plate to avoid a Maglie knockdown pitch. With those confrontations fresh in his mind, Furillo was not happy to see Maglie become a Dodger. "You dumb dago bastard," he yelled at Bavasi. "What'd you get that dago for?"

Eager to mollify one of the team's star performers, Bavasi turned to diplomacy. He gave Furillo $200 and told him to take Maglie out to dinner at Toots Shor's, a favorite restaurant for ballplayers on West Fifty-first Street in Manhattan. He then called Shor and told him to pick up the tab for the meal, thus allowing Furillo to keep the $200.

As Bavasi had hoped, the dinner helped to ease Furillo's anger at Maglie and contributed to the good relationship the two men enjoyed afterward. "Carl Furillo," Sal would later say, "became one of my best friends on the club." Nor was Furillo an exception. All of the Dodgers were surprised to see Maglie join the club but eager to embrace him as a teammate. It was, said Carl Erskine, "the strangest sight to see him in our clubhouse," but, he added, the transition was a smooth one because "Maglie was a gentleman in every sense of the word." The good feelings were mutual, and Maglie would later say of his Dodger teammates that "I got more of a kick out of them than I ever did in all my years with the Giants."

The acquisition of Maglie proved to be a pivotal one for the Dodgers. They were locked in a battle for the pennant with the Milwaukee Braves, and the former Giant pitcher gave them a critical advantage—and a pennant. His first start on May 30 was a bumpy one, as he allowed four runs in five innings. But by July he fell into a groove, winning ten of his next twelve decisions, including a no-hitter against the Philadelphia Phillies on September 25 at Ebbets Field. He then added another complete victory against the Pittsburgh Pirates on September 29, and the Dodgers won the pennant the next day.

No one doubted the value of the contribution Maglie had made. He finished the season with a 13–5 won-lost record, which was all the more remarkable because he had missed almost the first two months of the season. His teammates certainly understood his value. "We wouldn't be up here now if it were not for Maglie," said Campanella. The sportswriters agreed, and Maglie finished second in the voting for the Most Valuable Player award.

However much he enjoyed praise from his teammates and sportswriters, Maglie knows they are no guarantee of success in the fifth game of the 1956 World Series. And so he is a study of concentration as Yankee right fielder Hank Bauer, a right-handed batter, steps into the batter's box to start the bottom of the first inning.

Bauer had two hits against Maglie in the first game, and the Dodgers are playing the Yankee outfielder deep and to the left in recognition of his substantial power. Bauer tries a surprise bunt on the first pitch, but the ball goes foul. Maglie does not like surprises, and the second pitch sails behind Bauer's head. Radio announcer Bob Neal tells his listening audience that "Maglie looks to his hand to indicate that the ball slipped." But those familiar with Maglie's interest in keeping the batter off stride are surely skeptical. Bauer is obviously among them. He stares long and hard at Maglie, his anger almost palpable. It has no impact on Maglie. After another ball, a missed swing, and a foul, Bauer lifts a pop fly to the edge of the outfield grass that is caught by short-stop Pee Wee Reese.

Yankee first baseman Joe Collins, a thirty-four-year-old left-handed batter, follows Bauer to the plate. After a called ball and a strike, Collins bunts the ball down the third-base line. Dodger third baseman Jackie Robinson fields the ball cleanly and throws Collins out at first.

The Dodger infielders move to the right as Mickey Mantle, the Yankees' switch-hitting center fielder, steps up to the plate to bat left-handed against the right-handed Maglie. Having played against him in three previous World Series, the Dodgers are all too familiar with Mantle's prodigious power, and they hope to limit his success with an unusual infield shift—Dodger first baseman Gil Hodges moves deep behind the bag, second baseman Junior Gilliam moves back to the edge of the outfield grass between first and second base, and shortstop Pee Wee Reese relocates to the right side of second base (with third baseman Jackie Robinson in the shortstop position). The infield shift proves to be of no utility on this occasion. After missing the ball on a gigantic swing on the first pitch and then taking two balls, Mantle sends an easy fly ball to Sandy Amoros in left field, and the inning is over.

Top of the Second:
Jackie Robinson and Gil McDougald

After he finishes his warm-up pitches, Larsen prepares himself for another round with the Dodgers, no doubt hoping that he can survive longer than he had in the second game. The first Dodger to step into the batter's box to start the second inning is the right-handed Jackie Robinson. The ebony color of his skin stands in stark contrast to the light gray uniform he wears.

Although thirty-seven and carrying more weight than he did nearly a decade earlier when he became the major league's first black player, Robinson remains a dangerous hitter. Having faced him in the 1955 World Series, Larsen is well aware of Robinson's skill with a bat, and that perception was reinforced when he and Berra reviewed the Dodger lineup before the game. "We can't throw anything soft to Jackie," the Yankee catcher explained. "Anything tight and up is his wheelhouse, so we gotta be careful to keep the ball away from him." Still, the Yankee outfield shifts to the left in case Robinson does get an inside pitch that he can pull.

Robinson's advanced years do not reflect lethargy. Quite the contrary. There is something electric about him. Something that suggests that anything is possible. Because, however much he may have aged,

Robinson has not lost his burning desire to win. Nor has he forgotten his roots and the symbol that he now represents in baseball history.

It is, to be sure, a remarkable story. His grandparents were slaves in the Deep South before the Civil War, and racial segregation was still a part of daily life when he was born near Cairo, Georgia, on January 31, 1919. Robinson's father, Jerry, worked as a sharecropper on a plantation while his mother, Mallie, took care of young Jackie and his four older siblings. But the family was not destined to stay in Georgia for long. Six months after Jackie's birth, Jerry went to the train station with another man's wife and never returned. A strong-willed woman determined to improve her lot, Mallie packed the family up shortly afterward and took them by train to Pasadena, California, to join some family members there. Once in Pasadena, Mallie was able to find a small house for her family on Pepper Street in a largely white neighborhood, and it was there that Jackie Robinson spent his formative years.

For young Jackie, the departure from Georgia was a fortunate change of venues. California would give him opportunities that probably would never have been available in the Deep South—though racism was still rampant out west, and there were many activities that Jackie and his young friends could not enjoy. (Unable to use the community pool when they chose, Jackie and his friends would often swim in the nearby reservoir, and one hot summer day they were discovered by a sheriff, who packed them off to jail. "Looka here," said the sheriff when he first saw the young boys. "Niggers in my drinking water.")

The racism that Robinson encountered outside the home was made bearable by the support and guidance that he and his siblings received inside the home from Mallie. As Jackie later recalled, she "indoctrinated us with the importance of family unity, religion, and kindness toward others." And so, throughout his adult life, Jackie Robinson would remain religious (often saying prayers on his knees before going to bed), devoted to his family, and committed to doing what he could to improve the lives of others.

Long before adulthood, however, he had demonstrated the skills and temperament that would be his trademarks as a major-league baseball player. He was a talented youngster with extraordinary eye-hand coordination. One of his classmates in Pasadena remembered that young Jackie "could do things in games and sports that the other kids could not do." But those superior skills also reflected a sense of competition that many of his peers found offensive. "Jackie wasn't a very likable person," said another classmate, "because his whole thing was just win, win, win, and beat everybody."

His athletic skills allowed him to star in football, basketball, track, and baseball in high school, earning him recognition from the local paper as the high school's "outstanding athlete" in his junior and senior years. In 1937, the five-foot-eleven-inch, 135-pound Robinson enrolled in Pasadena Junior College, where his mastery of all those sports continued. "It is doubtful," said the *Pasadena Post* at one point, "if Pasadena ever has had a greater all-around athlete, and that is saying a lot in a city where champions are produced as regularly as the years roll by."

Robinson's athletic accomplishments enabled him to enroll at UCLA in 1939 with an athletic scholarship. Now weighing about 175 pounds, Jackie excelled in football, basketball, baseball, and track, becoming UCLA's first four-letter man. He was hailed by one local newspaper as "the greatest ball-carrier in the nation," won the Pacific Coast Conference basketball scoring title in 1941, and set a conference track record for the long jump (twenty-five feet). Ironically, baseball proved to be his worst sport (where he played shortstop and finished his first season with a batting average of only .097). But his shortcomings in that one sport were of little moment. Jackie Robinson had made his mark. He had not only the adulation of other students but also the attention of college coeds, both black and white.

However much he must have enjoyed that attention, only one woman captured his emotions—a freshman he had met in the UCLA student lounge. He was, he later said, attracted by her "looks and charm." For her part, seventeen-year-old Rachel Isum, a slim African-American woman with keen intelligence, was immediately drawn to UCLA's premier athlete. He was, she remembered, "very impressive—a handsome, proud and serious man with a warm smile and a pigeon-toed walk." But the quality that most impressed Rachel was Jackie's humility. "He was a big man on campus when he met me," she later remembered, "and I was a lowly freshman. But he related to me as a person and not as being a big star on campus."

They began to date, and, as Rachel later confessed, she was "the aggressor," waiting for Jackie after games or work and otherwise doing whatever she could to increase the frequency of their contact. In November, Jackie invited Rachel to the school's homecoming dance, and from that point on Robinson was committed to a relationship with this young woman from Los Angeles.

By the early winter of 1941, Jackie had exhausted his eligibility to play football for UCLA, and at that point—being a C student with no interest in academics—he decided to leave school without waiting for graduation. In March 1941 he accepted a position with the National Youth Administration, part of President Franklin D. Roosevelt's New Deal program, to help troubled youths in San Luis Obispo. The outbreak of war in Europe made that assignment a short-lived one, because the army decided to utilize NYA's facilities.

Left to fend for himself, Jackie accepted an offer to play semipro football with the Honolulu Bears for the 1941 season. Although he enjoyed some memorable moments, the team was not very good, and he sustained a serious injury to his right ankle, which had already been damaged in earlier football exploits. He was glad to return home in December and was on a ship coming back to California when he learned of the Japanese attack at Pearl Harbor.

Robinson received his draft notice in March 1942 and filed an application with the army for Officer Candidate School. His application was summarily dismissed at first, but Jackie knew all about racial discrimination and the importance of perseverance. And so, before long, his OCS application was accepted, and in time it was Second Lieutenant Jack Roosevelt Robinson who occupied the army barracks at Fort Riley in Kansas.

Despite his success in overcoming the obstacles to become an officer, Robinson soon learned that army life was rife with racism. The most enduring experience occurred in July 1944. One evening Jackie took a bus to nearby Camp Hood, spent a few hours at the colored officers' club and then caught an army bus to return to the hospital. As he was walking toward the rear, he spotted the wife of a fellow black officer seated in the middle of the bus, and he sat down next to her for the ride back. As more passengers boarded the bus, the driver left his seat to tell Robinson that he had to move to the rear. Jackie knew his rights and refused to move. The bus driver called the military police and, when they arrived, the driver pointed to Robinson, saying, "There's the nigger that's causing me trouble."

The MPs took Robinson off the bus, held him in a room on a suspicion that he was drunk and trying to cause a riot (even though Robinson had never had a drink in his life), and ultimately had him arrested for "behaving with disrespect" toward the MP commanding officer (who had shown up at the scene) and for failing to obey the commanding officer's order that he remain seated on a chair in the room to which he had been taken.

Always the fighter, Robinson wrote to the NAACP about the trumped-up charges, and the matter received considerable publicity in the press. By the time the court-martial proceedings convened in August 1944, the army was no doubt aware of the adverse publicity that would ensue if Robinson were convicted, and so, after four hours of testimony, Robinson was acquitted.

Although he may have won the legal battle, Robinson was not a welcome presence in the armed services. They took note of his ankle injuries and had him honorably discharged. Robinson immediately returned to his home in Los Angeles with one principal goal in mind: to marry Rachel Isum.

That was no small challenge. He had remained in touch with Rachel in the years after he had left UCLA, and, despite several separations, the relationship remained strong. But Rachel had another agenda that did not entirely coincide with Jackie's. "I could see marriage suffocating me," she later said, "and I really was not eager to rush into it." And so she made it clear that there would be no wedding until she completed her studies at UCLA in the spring of 1945 and he got a job to support them.

Ironically, before he had left the service, another GI had talked to Robinson about opportunities that might be available with the Kansas City Monarchs, one of the Negro leagues' top teams. Jackie tried out in the spring of 1945 and received an offer to play for $400 a month. Anxious to succeed in his new job, Robinson made his mark in the Negro leagues that summer. He played shortstop, posted an impressive .345 batting average, and won wide recognition for his superlative talents. But he was not happy. Playing with the Monarchs meant constant travel in old buses and cars, dingy rooms in dilapidated hotels, and greasy food from segregated restaurants. It was, Robinson later said, "a pretty miserable way to make a buck."

Fate then intervened in the guise of Branch Rickey, the sixty-three-year-old general manager and part owner of the Brooklyn Dodgers. Rickey was a lawyer who had devoted his life to baseball, and he had a dream: to integrate the major leagues. It was a dream that had evolved from his days as a coach for the Ohio Wesleyan University baseball team in the early 1900s. Rickey had taken the team to South Bend, Indiana, for a game against Notre Dame, but the hotel resisted when he tried to register the black player on the team. In a compromise, Rickey agreed to share his room with the young player and sent him up the stairs while Rickey completed the arrangements. When he entered the room, Rickey saw the black student sitting on the bed in a state of despair and pulling at the skin on his hand. "Damned skin," the student cried. "If I could only rub it off." Then and there Rickey decided that he would do something about segregation in baseball.

It would not be easy. Segregation was an accepted part of baseball life at that juncture, and Rickey had to bide his time. In the meantime, he enjoyed considerable success as a field manager and general manager for the St. Louis Browns in the American League and then the St. Louis Cardinals in the National League, introducing many innovations (like a minor-league farm system where young players could be nurtured) and fielding Cardinal teams that won nine pennants and six World Championships in twenty-five years. But Cardinal owner Sam Breadon decided not to renew Rickey's contract after the 1942 season, and the rotund sextagenerian found a new home with the Brooklyn Dodgers, who had won the pennant in 1941 and were beginning to look like perennial contenders.

As he aged, Rickey no doubt sensed that time was running out on his dream of integrating baseball, but there remained one unyielding obstacle: Judge Kenesaw Mountain Landis. He had been appointed as baseball commissioner in 1920 in the wake of the Black Sox Scandal (when eight players on the Chicago White Sox were accused of fixing the 1919 World Series). Landis ruled the game with the proverbial iron fist, and he had an unwavering view about blacks in baseball—it would never happen under his watch. But Landis died in November 1944, and former United States senator Albert B. Chandler was chosen to replace him.

Rickey could not have been more pleased. When asked about the growing pressures to allow blacks to play in the major leagues, Chandler responded, "If a black boy can make it in Okinawa and Guadalcanal, hell, he can make it in baseball." Upon reading that quotation, Rickey began to move forward with his plans to integrate baseball.

There was no shortage of talented black players from whom to choose, but the first player had to be special. However much Chandler supported equality in baseball, there remained a stronghold of opposition to having black players in the major leagues. There would be resistance, there would be pressure, and there would be no assurance of success. The first black player would therefore need not only the skills to excel on the field but also the fortitude to handle the inevitable abuse that would follow him wherever he went. Rickey intended to find that special player and dispatched Brooklyn scouts throughout the country to investigate Negro players who might be available.

Clyde Sukeforth was the scout designated to check out the Monarchs' star shortstop at a game in Chicago and to bring him back if Robinson had the skills to play in the major leagues. Rickey did not want to advertise his true intentions, and he had circulated the notion among his scouts that the Dodgers were going to form a new Negro team—the Brooklyn Brown Dodgers—to play in a new Negro league. But that subterfuge did not sit well with Robinson, and he kept pressing Sukeforth, "Why does Mr. Rickey want to see me?" Sukeforth tried to explain the situation as he understood it, and the young athlete finally agreed to take the train back to Brooklyn with the Dodger scout.

The meeting occurred on August 28, 1945, in Rickey's office at 215 Montague Street in Brooklyn. Robinson was led into the office and saw a large man with bushy eyebrows and a cigar sitting behind a oversized desk. Rickey was given to long sermons (a quality that led sportswriters to refer to his office as the "Cave of Winds"), and Robinson soon learned that there was no topic more deserving of a sermon than integration in baseball.

Rickey no doubt startled Robinson with the opening question: "You got a girl?" It was not an idle question. A devout Methodist, Rickey was, according to one sportswriter, offended "by alcoholism, extramarital sex, and the word shit." Robinson explained that he was indeed engaged. Rickey was pleased. "When we get through today," he replied, "you may want to call her up, because there are times when a man needs a woman by his side." Rickey then proceeded to reveal his true intentions. There was not going to be any Brown Dodgers team. Rickey wanted to bring Robinson into the Dodger organization so that he could eventually play in the major leagues. "I know you're a good player," Rickey continued. "What I don't know is whether you have the guts." The Brooklyn GM explained that there would be many people in and out of baseball who would oppose Robinson's presence on the field and who would do whatever they could to prevent the experiment or, failing that, try to make it an embarrassing disaster. "We can't fight our way through this, Robinson," Rickey intoned. "We've got no army. There's virtually nobody on our side." Robinson, always ready, if not eager, to fight discrimination wherever it appeared, did not understand. "Mr. Rickey," he asked, "are you looking for a Negro who is afraid to fight back?" Rickey's response made a deep impression on the young player sitting before him. "Robinson," he said, "I'm looking for a ballplayer with guts enough not to fight back." And so Rickey made Robinson promise that, no matter how vile the taunts or actions of other players, he would simply turn the other cheek and focus on his performance on the field.

Robinson left the meeting "thrilled, scared and excited." He had an offer to play for the Montreal Royals, a Dodger farm team, which included a $3,500 bonus and a salary of $600 a month. He not only had a new future. He now had the means to marry Rachel.

The wedding was held at Independent Church in Los Angeles on February 10, 1946. Two weeks later, the young couple traveled to Daytona Beach, Florida, for spring training (where they learned that they could not stay with the rest of the team at the hotel—which did not allow blacks—but had to share a nearby private home owned by blacks).

As Rickey had predicted, spring training was filled with tension. Some of it was hard to ignore—threats from anonymous sources of what would happen if Robinson showed up on the field, games that had to be canceled because the particular town did not allow blacks to play on the same field as whites, and epithets thrown at Robinson from the stands.

Rickey realized that the best way to overcome opposition was to show the Dodgers how valuable Robinson could be to the team, and he urged the former Monarch star to be as daring as he could be on the field. "Give it all you've got when you run," said Rickey. "Gamble. Take a bigger lead." Robinson was conscious of the need to succeed and did what he could—but the pressures were taking their toll. "I couldn't sleep," Robinson later recalled, "and often I couldn't eat." He and Rachel consulted a doctor, who thought that the young player might be on the verge of a nervous breakdown.

Rickey understood the unrelenting pressures that his protégé was enduring, but also knew that there was no easy escape. "Always, for as long as you are in baseball," he told Robinson, "you must conduct yourself as you are doing now. Always you will be on trial. That is the cross that you must bear." Bearing that cross was made possible in no small part because of Rachel's steadfast support. She knew that she could not change the racism they encountered, but she could, as she later said, "be a constant presence to witness and validate the realities, love him without reservation, share his thoughts and miseries, discover with him the humor in the ridiculous behavior against us, and, most of all, help maintain our fighting spirit."

Vindication came on April 18, 1946, in Robinson's first game with Montreal in Jersey City before a capacity crowd of more than 25,000 against the New York Giants' farm team. He got four hits—including a home run—in five trips to the plate and was instrumental in the Royals' 14–1 victory (and was, as one sportswriter recounted, "mobbed trying to leave the field by fans of assorted ages and colors"). It was a harbinger of things to come. He led the International League in hitting with .349, scored a league-leading 113 runs, and stole forty bases.

Jackie's elevation to the Dodger club for the 1947 season was widely anticipated, but Rickey was taking no chances. Toward the end of the 1946 season, he told Buzzie Bavasi, the general manager of the team's farm club in Nashua, New Hampshire, to determine whether there were any skeletons in Robinson's closet. The general manager was instructed to go to California, but Bavasi went instead to Montreal to watch Robinson in action and to gauge the reactions of others. Upon his arrival, Bavasi was given a seat near home plate, right behind the seats occupied by the players' wives. There he watched as the other players' wives (all white) turned to Rachel with a variety of questions as the game progressed. Bavasi was impressed with her demeanor and her commentary. When he returned to Brooklyn, Rickey asked what he had learned. Bavasi had no hesitation: "If Jackie Roosevelt Robinson is good enough for Rachel, he's good enough for us."

Still, Robinson could not relax when he joined the Dodgers for spring training in Havana (where he was once again forced to live in different quarters from his teammates). Rickey told him that he had to prove himself on the field one more time in a series of seven games that pitted the Montreal Royals against the Dodgers' parent club. "I want you to concentrate," Rickey instructed, "to hit that ball, to get on base *by any means necessary*. I want you to run wild, to steal the pants off them, to be the most conspicuous player on the field—but conspicuous only because of the kind of baseball you're playing." Robinson obliged, hitting .625 and stealing seven bases in the series.

His success on the field did not assure his acceptance in the clubhouse. When the team traveled to Panama for some exhibition games, Robinson learned that a petition was being circulated by some of the Dodger players to persuade Rickey not to bring Robinson up to the parent club. The petition was initiated by Dodger outfielder Dixie Walker, an Alabama store-owner, and it basically said that those who had signed did not want to play with a black. The petition was apparently signed by several other Southern players on the team, but most of the other players refused to sign. Outfielder Pete Reiser, for one, told Walker that he "was a goddamned fool" for circulating the petition.

One of those who agreed with Reiser was manager Leo Durocher. He was enraged when he learned about the petition. He had been urging Rickey to bring Robinson up in 1946, and he did not want his plans to use Robinson in 1947 to be compromised by dissension among the players. Durocher wasted no time in conveying his view to the team. He called a meeting at midnight in the barracks where they were staying and marched out of his room in a yellow bathrobe, looking, as one player remembered, "like a fighter about to enter the ring." "I don't care if the guy is yellow or black, or if he has stripes like a fuckin' zebra," he told the assembled players. "I'm the manager of this team, and I say he plays. What's more, I say he can make us all rich." He then paused and said, "An' if any of you can't use the money, I'll see that you're traded." He looked around the room. "I don't want to see your petition. I don't want to hear anything about it," he screamed. "Fuck your petition. The meeting is over. Go back to bed." And that was the end of the petition.

Despite his vigorous defense of Robinson's right to play in the major leagues, Durocher was not there when Robinson made his debut at Ebbets Field on April 15, 1947, with the number 42 on the back of his Dodger uniform. Chandler had suspended the Dodger manager from baseball on April 9 because of his reputed association with gamblers and other underworld figures. Burt Shotton, the new Dodger manager (who wore a shirt and tie instead of a uniform in the dugout), was the antithesis of Durocher—a quiet, soft-spoken man who tried to promote harmony on the team. And that was no longer an issue for Robinson, because even the Southern players on the team were now prepared to accept his presence—a perspective that was perhaps captured best by the comment of second baseman Eddie Stanky, who had grown up in the South. "I don't like you," he told Jackie, "but we'll play together and get along because you're my teammate."

Stanky's presence on the Dodgers did, however, create one challenge for Robinson: he could not play second base, and—because Reese still had a hold on the shortstop position—the Pasadena native was asked to play first base, a position with which he had little familiarity. The tension of mastering a new position was compounded by the hostile reaction of the other teams' players. The Philadelphia Phillies, and especially their manager, Ben Chapman (a former teammate of Babe Ruth's), were particularly abusive. ("Hey, nigger, why don't you go back to the cotton field, where you belong?") And shortly before the Dodgers traveled to Philadelphia for a series in early May, Phillies general manager Herb Pennock (another former teammate of Babe Ruth's) telephoned Rickey to tell his Brooklyn counterpart, "You just can't bring that nigger here with the rest of your team. We're not ready for that sort of thing yet in Philadelphia." Rickey disagreed and bluntly told Pennock that the Dodgers would take a forfeit if Philadelphia failed to field a team.

Pennock eventually backed down. But the hostility followed Robinson and the Dodgers as they moved around the National League circuit. In each case, the Dodgers rallied behind their teammate— Rickey saying at one point that, through his abuse, Ben Chapman "did more than anybody to unite the Dodgers."

Opinion nonetheless remained divided among baseball players whether integration was serving the best interests of baseball. But there was unanimity on one point: Jackie Robinson drew enormous crowds wherever he played. Some of it no doubt was curiosity; some of it certainly reflected support from the black community; but much of it was a tribute to the excitement that Robinson generated on the field. It was not merely his ability to steal bases (which he did with regularity, leading the league with twenty-nine). It was primarily the fire he ignited both before and after he got on base.

The opposing team's players knew that they could not relax if Jackie Robinson was at the plate. Would he try a surprise bunt down the third-base line? Or would he swing for the seats, as he could easily do (hitting forty-eight extra-base hits in 1947, including twelve home runs—tying him for the team lead in that department)? And what would happen when he got on base? If he reached first base, he would dart back and forth, yelling at the pitcher and daring him to throw the ball to first base. ("You can't pick me off," Jackie would shout. "I'll steal second on you!") He would use the same tactics even when he was on third base, and there were many times during his career (nineteen, to be exact) when he actually did steal home. And even if Robinson did not attempt a steal, his daring tactics could still succeed as the pitcher, flustered by the constant distraction, would balk or throw a wild pitch or otherwise fail to concentrate on the batter at the plate.

It was, all in all, high entertainment—at least for everyone other than the opposing team. "Jackie Robinson," said Hall of Fame radio announcer Bob Wolff, "was the most exciting ballplayer that I've ever covered. From the moment he got on base, the whole ballpark came alive. There was a drama going on no matter what else was happening. The pitcher started to fidget. The shortstop started to move in a little bit. The second baseman got closer to second. Everything—the whole panorama of the game changed." Opposing players agreed that Robinson could indeed change the dynamics of the game. "Robinson was," said Pittsburgh Pirates slugger Ralph Kiner, "the only player I ever saw who could completely turn a game around by himself." And so the Dodgers were glad to have the former UCLA star in the lineup. "As long as he was in the game," said Dodger pitcher Rex Barney, "you had a chance to win. He played baseball with such abandon."

By the time the season ended, Robinson had amply justified Rickey's faith in him. He played in all but three of the Dodgers' games, batted .297, and won the first major-league Rookie of the Year award (which would later be divided between rookies in the American and National Leagues). And, as Leo Durocher had predicted in spring training, Robinson had led his team into the World Series for the first time since 1941. But more important—from Robinson's perspective, at least—he had won the respect of his teammates, including those who had opposed his inclusion on the team in spring training. As the Dodgers moved toward the pennant in late September, Dixie Walker—author of the failed petition against Robinson—told *The Sporting News* that, with the possible exception of catcher Bruce Edwards, no other player had "done more to put the Dodgers up in the race as Robinson has."

When he reported for spring training in 1948, Robinson was twenty-five pounds over his initial playing weight of 195. For those who knew him, the excess weight was no surprise. Robinson loved food. ("His attack on a wedge of apple pie, topped with two scoops of vanilla ice cream," said one sportswriter, "was an exercise in passion.") Durocher, having returned as manager, made Robinson endure stringent workouts and eating restrictions.

While he struggled to control his weight, Robinson also had to wrestle with the racism that he still encountered as the Dodgers moved through their exhibition schedule in the South. At one point, Shotton held a meeting in the clubhouse to explain that someone had threatened to shoot Robinson if he showed up on the field in Atlanta for an exhibition game. The room was quiet for a few minutes as everyone pondered the threat, and then outfielder Gene Hermanski broke the silence. "I've got an idea," he said excitedly. "Why don't we all wear uniforms with the number 42, and that way the guy won't know who to shoot!" Everyone broke out in laughter and then scurried onto the field, knowing that the team would hang together in the face of such threats—although shortstop Pee Wee Reese did ask Robinson, now playing second base because of Stanky's trade to the Boston Braves, to move a little farther away from him. ("The guy may be a bad shot," said Reese.)

Although he started the regular season off slowly, Robinson soon regained his earlier batting form and wound up leading the Dodgers in virtually every offensive category, including batting average (.296), runs batted in (eighty-five), and extra-base hits (fifty-eight, which included twelve home runs). But the Dodgers faltered as a team, and by July, Durocher (who had returned as manager in April) had been fired as skipper in an arrangement that allowed him to become the manager of the hated Giants (where he and Robinson developed a bitter antagonism that reflected their equally competitive spirits). Burt Shotton resumed the reins of the Brooklyn club, but the Braves ran away with the National League pennant.

Throughout his first two years, Robinson had been careful to abide by Rickey's admonition that he turn the other cheek and not create any waves. But by the spring of 1949 Robinson had begun to sense that the time for passivity had passed and that he should now be free to speak his mind if confronted with racial bigotry on or off the field. His teammates had accepted him as one of their own, he had received recognition as one of the game's better players, and the firestorm of protest that had accompanied his first days as a Dodger had subsided. He discussed the matter with Rickey, and they agreed that Jackie would now be free to speak his mind. And so, at a clubhouse meeting in spring training, Robinson told his teammates that he was no longer going to suffer in silence. "From this point on," he said, "I take nothing from no one, on this team or on any other team, not from umpires or anyone else."

The new attitude—and batting instruction from George Sisler, the Hall of Fame player of an earlier era—provided spectacular results. Robinson led the league in hitting with a .342 average, stole thirty-seven bases (leading the league in that department as well), and drove in 124 runs. His achievements were acknowledged by the sportswriters, who selected him as the league's Most Valuable Player. His performance on the field boosted his team's morale, and the Dodgers won the pennant again (only to fall to the Yankees once more in the World Series).

One of the year's most notable events for Robinson, however, took place outside the ball field. On July 18, 1949, Robinson flew to Washington, DC, to appear before the House Un-American Activities Committee. The committee wanted Robinson "to give the lie to statements by Paul Robeson." A well-known actor and black activist, Robeson had been quoted as saying that it was "unthinkable" that blacks would fight to save America—where they had suffered intolerable racial discrimination—in any conflict with the Soviet Union. Robinson, HUAC hoped, would show the country that Robeson's comments did not reflect the view of all blacks in America.

Robinson's testimony provided that desired assurance—but with a cautionary note. "White people must realize," he told the congressional committee, "that the more a Negro hates Communism because it opposes democracy, the more he is going to hate the other influences that kill off democracy in this country—and that goes for racial discrimination in the army, and segregation on trains and buses, and job discrimination because of religious beliefs or color or place of birth." As for Robeson's reported comments, Robinson dismissed them, saying that they sounded "very silly."

Robinson's testimony before Congress illustrated the new perspective he had adopted. No longer would he stand quietly in the background while witnessing acts of discrimination on and off the field. No longer would he hold his fire when asked about issues and events involving racial issues. Sportswriters, accustomed to subdued responses when he first arrived at Ebbets Field, now found Robinson to be out-spoken when discussing matters that touched on racial discrimination. Some of the reporters accepted the change in attitude as inevitable. Others, like Dick Young of the *New York Daily News*, found it disruptive and therefore enjoyed talking with other black players, like catcher Roy Campanella, who did not have any cause to advance. "The trouble between you and me, Jackie," Young said at one point, "is that I can go to Campy and all we discuss is baseball. I talk to you and sooner or later we get around to social issues. It just happens I'm not interested in social issues." But Robinson was, and he would trumpet his views on social issues whenever he could (including the occasion in 1953 when he bluntly said on a television program that the New York Yankees—who had never had a black player on their roster and would not until 1955—"have been giving Negroes the runaround").

Robinson's willingness to be assertive on social issues was not always well received. The country was only beginning to correct the racial discrimination that pervaded virtually all aspects of life, and Robinson's pointed remarks often made people feel uncomfortable or, in some situations, generated open hostility. By 1954, *Sport* magazine said that Robinson was "the most savagely booed, intensively criticized, ruthlessly libeled player in the game." And Robinson himself felt obliged to counter the attacks with an article in *Look* magazine entitled, "Now I Know Why They Boo Me."

In the meantime, he continued to provide the Dodgers with sterling performances in the field. In 1950, he had a .328 batting average (second-best in the league) and almost led the Dodgers to another pennant (which they lost on the last day of the season to the Philadelphia Phillies). And in 1951, he had another good year, batting .338 (third-best in the league) and hitting a career-high nineteen home runs. He was also instrumental in preserving the Dodgers' tie with the Giants, who had that remarkable comeback after being down thirteen and a half games in the middle of August. In the last game of the season, with the Giants now settled in first place, the Dodgers were pitted against the Phillies at Shibe Park in Philadelphia with the score tied in the twelfth inning and the bases loaded. Phillies first baseman Eddie Waitkus (the player whose strange encounter with an obsessed female fan was the inspiration for Bernard Malamud's novel *The Natural*) hit a scorching line drive toward right field that appeared destined for a hit and a Phillies victory. But Robinson, playing second base, timed his jump perfectly and snared the ball in what was described by a *New York Times* sportswriter as "one of the greatest, if not the greatest, clutch plays I have seen." Robinson then sealed the victory (and a tie with the Giants) with a home run in the fourteenth inning. Still, even Jackie Robinson had his limits. He could not secure the Dodgers' success in the three-game play-off series that followed with the Giants, and the Dodgers once again went home empty-handed.

By this time, Robinson was making close to $40,000 in salary—tops among the Dodgers. But the increase in pay was not the only change that had taken place. Walter O'Malley, the principal Dodger owner, had engineered an arrangement in 1950 to buy Rickey's stock in the team and force him out as general manager (replacing him with Bavasi). Although he had supported Rickey's efforts to integrate baseball, O'Malley was having second thoughts about the selection of Robinson as the test case. A fastidious lawyer, O'Malley was one of those who bridled at Robinson's new outspoken approach. It was creating adverse publicity and was not what O'Malley wanted for his club. By 1956, O'Malley reached the breaking point and bluntly told Bavasi, "I'm sick of him popping off and his outbursts. Get rid of him!" And so Bavasi began making plans to trade Robinson to the Giants after the 1956 season was over.

Long before then, O'Malley had made another change that was to Robinson's liking: he replaced Burt Shotton with Charlie Dressen as manager in 1951. A short (five-foot-five-inch) man with a stocky build, Dressen was enamored with the word "I" and had an apparent belief in his own infallibility when it came to making decisions. But he did heap praise on Robinson, constantly reminding his second baseman in 1952 of his importance to the club—and then, with the prospect of a rookie (Junior Gilliam, another African-American) who could play second base with flair, Dressen moved Robinson to third in 1953 and benched third baseman Billy Cox, who was widely recognized as a superb fielder. ("That ain't a third baseman," Casey Stengel once remarked after watching Cox in a World Series. "That's a fucking acrobat.") But Cox's hitting was not what it used to be, and Dressen believed the change at third would better serve the club's interests. The only problem was that Dressen forgot to tell Cox about the move, and the veteran third baseman was bitter when he read about his demotion in the newspapers. ("How would you like a nigger to take your job?" he rhetorically asked sportswriter Roger Kahn at the time.) Robinson ultimately defused the situation, praising Cox as "the best third baseman" and "the most underrated player in baseball."

Despite the controversy, the new third baseman responded well to his manager's oft-stated compliments—as did the team as a whole—and the Dodgers of 1952 and 1953 dominated the National League, easily winning the pennant both years (and losing the World Series in each of those years to the Yankees). Robinson handled third base with aplomb and contributed to the team's success with his bat as well (hitting .308 and .329, respectively, in those years). But then Dressen killed the goose that laid the golden egg by demanding that O'Malley reward his accomplishments with a two-year contract instead of the standard one-year deal. O'Malley did not like to lose control, and Dressen found himself without a job for the 1954 season.

Walter Alston, who had managed the Nashua farm club when Bavasi was the general manager, became the new manager for the club. For Robinson, the change proved to be an unwelcome one. Unlike Dressen, Alston was not effusive in his praise of the Dodgers' new third baseman. And, beyond that, Alston had a completely different approach to management that Robinson found unsatisfactory. In contrast to Dressen's ebullient personality, the new Dodger manager was a quiet man who did not believe in ruffling feathers. (On one occasion, Robinson was shocked to see that he, but not Alston, had run onto the field to challenge an umpire's call that a Duke Snider hit that bounced back into the field from the bleachers was a double instead of a home run. "If that guy hadn't stood standing out there at third base like a wooden Indian," Robinson told one teammate with reference to Alston, "this club might go somewhere.") The tension grew in the clubhouse, and at one point Alston challenged Robinson to a fistfight that was forestalled only when Roy Campanella stepped in between them, saying, "When are you two guys gonna grow up?"

The tension did not bode well for Robinson or the Dodgers during the 1954 season. Robinson was beginning to slow down (in part because of the increased weight he could not shed), and Alston sometimes played him in left field and at other times simply kept him on the bench (although Robinson did manage to hit fifteen home runs and bat .311 in 124 games, the fewest he had played since joining the Dodgers in 1947).

Alston's quiet manner and revised strategy did not bode well for the Dodgers, and the Giants ran away with the pennant. For his part, Robinson began to think about retirement. "I was getting fed up," he later said, "and I began to make preparations to leave baseball." But he really had nowhere to go—at least not yet—that could pay him the same salary the Dodgers were providing. So he reported for spring training in 1955, slightly overweight and slower afoot but ready to do what he could to bring the pennant back to Brooklyn.

The other Dodgers were equally motivated, and it showed. The team set a major-league record by winning the first ten games of the season and ultimately breezed to a pennant, finishing thirteen and a half games in front of the Milwaukee Braves. Sadly, Robinson was not a major factor in the Dodgers' success. Alston played him in only 105 games and, for the first time in six years, he batted below .300 (a very mediocre .256) with only eight home runs (thus marking the first time in his career that he hit less than twelve in a season). Still, he was a bundle of energy and daring, and, if there was any doubt, he removed it in the first game of the World Series in Yankee Stadium. The Dodgers were losing 6–4 in the top of the eighth inning, and, after getting on base through an error, Robinson eventually found himself on third and determined "to shake things up." Dancing and darting off third base, Robinson made a dash for home plate as Yankee southpaw Whitey Ford went into his pitching motion. Yogi Berra caught Ford's pitch and, in his view, tagged Robinson out. The umpire disagreed, and Robinson had his nineteenth steal of home. Later, after the Dodgers beat the Yankees to win their first World Championship, one commentator gave special recognition to the former UCLA athlete for "breathing life into a Dodger team which from the start of this series seemed destined for the embalmer."

However much observers and teammates appreciated his contribution to the Dodgers' World Series victory, Robinson was, literally and figuratively, on his last legs when the 1956 season began. He was able to raise his batting average to .275, but he played only seventy-two games at third, and players as well as sportswriters openly speculated about Robinson's imminent retirement.

Jackie ignored the speculation and often showed the spark that had made him so valuable to the Dodgers for so many years. There was the time early in the 1956 season when New York newspapers quoted Giant scout Tom Sheehan as saying that "the Dodgers are over the hill. Jackie's too old, Campy's too old, and Erskine, he can't win with the garbage he's been throwing up there." The next day Erskine pitched a no-hitter against the Giants at Ebbets Field, and, as soon as the last out was recorded, Robinson ran up to Sheehan, who was sitting behind the Giant dugout, pulled the article from his back pocket, and waved it at Sheehan, saying, "How do you like that garbage?" As Erskine later said, "That was Jackie. A fierce competitor." But those moments of glory were few and far between, and Robinson knew the end of his baseball career was near.

Robinson shows no signs of retirement as he faces Don Larsen in the top of the second inning in the fifth game of the 1956 World Series. Standing deep in the batter's box, the Dodger third baseman is a study of concentration as Larsen prepares to throw his first pitch of the inning. It is a waist-high fastball. Robinson snaps the bat at the ball and fouls it off. Larsen checks Berra's sign for the next pitch, and, as he does so, twenty-eight-year-old Yankee shortstop Gil McDougald, a slim six-foot-one-inch player with a freckled face and a determined look, steadies his gaze at the batter, knowing that a ground ball is always possible when Larsen is pitching well.

McDougald's approach to playing the infield distinguished him from many of his peers. He was not content to leave fielding strategy to happenstance. He was, said Bob Wolff, "a thinking man's ballplayer" who always "positioned himself knowing where the pitch should be." And he knew all about the expected location of the pitches from talking to Yankee pitchers before and during the game. He would quiz them on how they intended to pitch to different batters, move wherever he thought the action would be, and rebuff requests from the pitcher to move elsewhere. There was the time, for example, in July 1951 when McDougald, then a rookie, was playing third base while Yankee ace Allie Reynolds was trying to preserve a no-hit game against the Cleveland Indians. Stengel, wearing number 37 on his uniform, motioned for McDougald to move closer to home plate against Indians batter Bobby Avila to protect against a bunt while Reynolds kept yelling at McDougald to move behind the bag to prevent any ground ball from escaping into the outfield. After hearing (and ignoring) Reynolds' repeated demands, McDougald finally trotted over to the mound and said to Reynolds, a Native American, "Hey, Indian, what's your number?" Reynolds was perplexed by the question. "What the hell are you talking about?" McDougald was quick to explain: "If your number don't read 37, don't tell me where to play."

McDougald's assertive attitude reflected the self-confidence of an intensely competitive player. He wanted to win at almost any cost and was prepared to place faith in his own knowledge and skills to achieve that goal. Former teammate Tony Kubek remembered that McDougald "could just explode because he was so competitive." And Bobby Brown, a veteran third baseman on the Yankees from the late 1940s and early 1950s, agreed, saying that McDougald was "very, very tough" and "very good in big games."

McDougald's competitive fire had evolved while growing up in the 1930s in San Francisco's Mission District, where he played basketball and baseball on city courts and fields. The family (which included Gil's older brother) lived in a two-story flat. Although his father had a job at the post office, they often needed welfare stamps to buy food in those Depression years. But Gil never regarded himself as being poor. The community parks always had ample sports equipment, the facilities were maintained well and so, when he looked back on those times, McDougald would say that "you had everything you needed."

The young athlete nurtured his talents and was able to make the varsity basketball and baseball teams at Commerce High School. He excelled in both sports but enjoyed basketball more and was able to make the All-City team. He weighed only about 140 pounds and did not stand much taller than five feet, eight inches as a senior in high school, but that was good enough for the University of San Francisco, which offered him a basketball scholarship. Gil was excited about the prospect of playing college basketball—until he started going to practices. The coach had a conservative game-plan that the freshman player found very frustrating. "'Pass the ball around and don't shoot until you can get a layup,'" McDougald later remembered. "I said to myself, 'Jesus Christ.' I wanted to move." So he transferred to the City College of San Francisco where he could play the kind of basketball that he liked. But then something happened: "I got more interested in baseball."

There was no shortage of opportunities to play baseball in San Francisco—or to catch the eye of a major-league scout. The city had proven to be a fertile source of major-league players (including Joe DiMaggio), and scouts were a constant presence at the semipro games around the city. McDougald began to play the infield for the Bayside Braves, a semipro team that had been a traditional recruiting base for the Boston Braves in the National League. In due course the Braves offered McDougald a contract in 1948 but it had no bonus. Joe Devine, a Yankee scout who had been keeping tabs on McDougald since his days at Commerce High, offered the young player something better: a contract with a $1,000 bonus. It was an easy decision, and McDougald was told to report to the Yankees' farm team in Twin Falls, Idaho.

Gil now had enough faith in his future to marry his former high school sweetheart, an energetic brunette named Lucille Tochilin. Still, success did not come easily to McDougald in those first days at Twin Falls. He did well enough at the plate if it was a fastball, but he had trouble hitting curves. He began to tinker with his batting stance, and he soon found that he could hit curveballs more easily with an open stance that had his left foot placed to the left of his right foot and the bat hanging down rather than being held up. It might have looked strange, but no one could argue with the results. The San Francisco native batted .340 in that first year with Twin Falls and continued the solid hitting with a .344 average the following year with the Yankee farm team in Daytona Beach, Florida.

McDougald was moved up to the Yankees' farm team in Beaumont, Texas, where his new manager was Rogers Hornsby, the renowned Hall of Fame second baseman who had the highest lifetime batting average (.358) in the National League. Hornsby made no effort to change his second baseman's unorthodox batting stance. Like McDougald, Hornsby had been criticized for his own stance when he was a player, and he knew that there were times to leave well enough alone. "If you feel comfortable batting the way you do," he told his young protégé, "go ahead."

Hornsby had to be satisfied with his positive approach. McDougald batted .336 for Beaumont in 1950 and won the league's Most Valuable Player award. Not surprisingly, the Yankees invited McDougald to join them at spring training in Phoenix for the 1951 season. The invitation came none too soon—McDougald had told Devine that he would play in the minor leagues for only three seasons. "Joe," the prospective rookie said, "if I'm not staying with the Yankees, I'll be seeing you back here in San Francisco. Because that's it."

In the beginning, it appeared that Gil might be required to make good on his threat to return to San Francisco. Stengel did not give him any opportunities to play in spring training games, and the young player sat in frustration on the bench. And then someone wanted to take a photo with McDougald, Stengel, and Hornsby, who was with the team. While the photographs were being taken, the Beaumont manager asked his former star how he was doing. "Enjoying the bench," McDougald sarcastically replied. Hornsby turned to Stengel. "Case," he said, "he's the best ballplayer you've got on your whole damn ball club and you're sitting him down?" The next day McDougald was in the lineup.

Still, there was a problem of where to play Gil. He had spent most of his minor-league career at second base, but the Yankees had an established second baseman in Jerry Coleman. Shortstop was not an option because that position was taken by Phil Rizzuto (who had won the league's Most Valuable Player award in 1950), and Bobby Brown and Billy Johnson had been alternating at third base. Brown was only twenty-six, but Johnson was now thirty-three (an advanced age in those days) and had not been a stellar performer in 1950 (batting only .260). So there was hope that McDougald might make it at third—if he could replace Johnson.

Gil started the season off well. In his first game against the St. Louis Browns, the twenty-two-year-old rookie had a home run and a double. McDougald continued to hit well when given the chance, but Stengel played him only sporadically. McDougald remained convinced that he was destined for a return to the minor leagues if Johnson remained on the team, and, as the May 15 cut-off deadline approached, there was no indication that Stengel was planning to get rid of Johnson. "Well," Gil told Lucille on the evening of May 14, "it looks like we're heading back to San Francisco, because I'm quitting if he thinks I'm going to Kansas City."

Convinced that his intuition was correct, McDougald showed up at the Yankee clubhouse early on the morning of May 15 and began to pack up his things. He did not want to discuss his decision with any of his teammates and hoped to be gone before any of them showed up. But Pete Sheehy, the Yankees' longtime clubhouse manager, was there, and he was surprised to see Gil packing everything up. "What're you doing?" he asked the Yankee rookie. "I'm cleaning out my locker, Pete. I'm on the way home." "Oh, no," Sheehy responded. "What for? Billy Johnson's been traded to the St. Louis Cardinals. You're staying."

From that point forward, McDougald was the Yankees' regular third baseman, and he fulfilled Hornsby's predictions, hitting .306 (tops among Yankee players) and slamming fourteen home runs (one more than fellow rookie Mickey Mantle). The Yankees won their third straight pennant, and McDougald found himself starting at third base in every game of the World Series against the New York Giants.

It was a World Series that McDougald would long remember. In the third inning of the fifth game at the Polo Grounds, Yogi Berra was on third base and Joe DiMaggio was on second. The next batter was former Cardinal and Giant slugger Johnny Mize, who was now playing first base for the Yankees. Giant manager Leo Durocher was familiar with Mize's power from his days in the National League (where Mize once hit fifty-one home runs in a season) and decided that it would be better to pitch to McDougald, who was scheduled to follow Mize. So Durocher ordered the Giants' pitcher to give Mize an intentional pass to first base (meaning that the bases were now loaded with three players who would later be inducted into the Hall of Fame).

McDougald was prepared to avenge the slight. But as he approached the batter's box, Stengel called him back to the dugout. McDougald assumed that Stengel was going to lift him for a pinch hitter, and the rookie third baseman was not happy. "I'm ready to bop him over the head if takes me out," he later recalled. But McDougald's assumption proved to be incorrect. Stengel only had a request. "Hit one out, Mac," was all he said. McDougald returned to the batter's box and proceeded to hit a home run over the left-field wall—thus becoming only the third player in almost fifty years of World Series play to hit a grand slam. (There was one other time when Stengel made a similar request of McDougald. The Yankees were behind 1–0 in a spring training game in St. Petersburg, Florida, against the St. Louis Cardinals. "Don't you have anybody who can hit?" Cardinal owner Gussie Busch playfully teased the Yankee manager. Stengel called over McDougald, who was the next hitter, and said, "Go on and hit one out." McDougald then blasted a home run over the left-field wall. "See, Mr. Busch," Stengel remarked as McDougald returned to the dugout. "It's no problem if we want to hit.")

The Yankee victory in the 1951 World Series was capped by McDougald's selection by the sportswriters as the American League Rookie of the Year. And so, when talk turned to Joe DiMaggio's retirement at the end of the 1951 season and who would replace him as the Yankees' "money player," Connie Mack—the longtime owner and manager of the Philadelphia Athletics—had a quick response: "Why, Gil McDougald, of course."

With endorsements like that, McDougald was able to bask in the glory of a superb year and talk on the banquet circuit about his plans for the 1952 season. Those plans appeared to get an unexpected lift when Jerry Coleman was called to duty by the Marines. The Korean War had dragged on and the country needed the services of the Yankee second baseman.

McDougald was hopeful that Coleman's loss was his gain. And so he openly talked with the press about his desire to play second base instead of third. "Around second base," he explained, "you get more action. You have more fun. You figure in more double plays. At third, you don't see the signs so often, and the first thing you know, a batted ball comes at you without warning."

However much he may have understood McDougald's perspective, Stengel had another second baseman in the wings whom he liked (Billy Martin), and McDougald wound up playing most of the games at third base for the next two seasons (until Martin was drafted into the army). Other decisions by Stengel, however, sometimes seemed incomprehensible. On one occasion in a game against the Washington Senators, the manager lifted McDougald for a pinch hitter with the bases loaded even though McDougald was on a hitting streak. While McDougald simmered in the dugout, the pinch hitter—Johnny Mize—hit a home run. "Right then and there," McDougald later said, "I figured I'd never second-guess the manager."

McDougald's faith in Stengel's choices did not always ensure a harmonious relationship. In fact, there were points of frustration and anger as McDougald tried to persevere under Stengel's regime. One matter of contention was McDougald's batting stance. Although the results had been rewarding in 1951, McDougald could never pull his average above .300 in the years that immediately followed. Stengel kept pressing Gil to make a change, not only to increase his average but also to enhance his ability to move a runner from first to third. McDougald had a tendency to pull the ball, and a hit to left field, Stengel explained, was likely to leave the runner at second. The runner could more often move to third base, he said, if McDougald could "spray the ball" to center field or right field.

At first, McDougald was "mad as heck" at Stengel, but then he too saw that there were benefits in hitting the ball up the middle and to right field. In 1956, he finally yielded to the pressure, changed his batting stance, and batted .311—the second-highest batting average on the team that year and the first time he had batted over .300 since his rookie season. It was enough to make him feel good about his manager—

especially because they had already cleared the air on their running feud before the 1956 season began.

It had happened when the Yankees took a goodwill tour in Japan after the 1955 season. Stengel—a man who savored his liquor and liked to keep his players at bay—told them that they were not to congregate in the hotel bars during the trip. That venue was reserved for him (where he would often stay until the early-morning hours, talking with sportswriters or whoever else might be there). But on one evening during the tour, McDougald, feeling warm and thirsty, decided to go down to the bar for a beer. It was about one o'clock, and there was no one there. And then suddenly, out of nowhere, Stengel appeared. McDougald thought the old man might be angry, but the Yankee manager sat down next to him at the bar and began an amiable conversation. It gave the young player the courage to confront Stengel about something that had been troubling him for years. "You must hate my guts," he told his manager. "Five years now, and there isn't one thing I've ever done that's made you happy. Why don't you just get rid of me, and you'll save a lot of aggravation, and I certainly won't get an ulcer, which will have to come along." "Well, I'm not trading you ever," Stengel responded. Then why, McDougald shot back, "are you getting on my back?" "Very simple," said Stengel. "You're a better player when you're mad." And he added, "I plan on keeping you mad." After that disclosure, McDougald understood—and appreciated—the intuition that Stengel brought to his managing role.

The Japanese tour proved to be a turning point for McDougald in other ways as well. Phil Rizzuto did not make the trip, and Stengel asked Gil if he would be willing to try playing shortstop. Rizzuto was thirty-eight years old and showing signs of age. The need for a new shortstop was fast approaching. McDougald was an ideal candidate. He had already established himself as an All-Star third baseman and then, beginning in 1954, as an All-Star second baseman. There was thus ample reason to believe that McDougald could play shortstop as well.

Gil accepted Stengel's invitation, and by the end of the tour sportswriters were reporting that McDougald "looms as the 1956 shortstop of the Bombers." For his part, the twenty-seven-year-old player was excited about the prospective change. It was better than either second or third, he later explained, because "you're at the center of the stage. You see every pitch. It's easier to position yourself when you see every pitch that's being called by the catcher. So you're ready to move in whatever direction you feel according to the pitch and the batter."

McDougald's interest in the new position was reflected in his performance. By June, sportswriters were calling him "one of the finest shortstops of the major leagues" and saying that his "spectacular work has counted heavily in making the New York infield the finest producer of double plays in the majors."

McDougald's considerable fielding skills are of paramount importance as Don Larsen sends his second pitch to Jackie Robinson in the top of the second inning of the fifth game of the 1956 World Series—a fastball that drifts into the Dodger third baseman's power zone. Robinson swings hard, and the ball zooms off the bat down the left side of the infield between third and short. Yankee third baseman Andy Carey leaps at the ball but can only tip it with the edge of his glove. The ball sails toward McDougald, who is, as he later recalled, "going into the hole" between third and short because he is not sure that Carey will reach the ball. As the ball flies off Carey's glove, McDougald tries to catch it for the out. But the ball drops in front of him instead. With lightning speed, he picks the ball up on the short hop and fires it over to Joe Collins at first base. First-base umpire Hank Soar quickly gives the signal that McDougald's throw has indeed beaten Robinson to the bag. To the veteran umpire, there is no question that Robinson reached first base after the ball did: "His foot was about six inches above the bag when Joe Collins caught the ball."

In retrospect, both Carey and McDougald realized that fate had played a role in catching Robinson. "I was in the right place at the right time," Carey later acknowledged. But another key factor was Robinson's age. "We would have never gotten Robinson out," Carey added, "if the game would have been played two or three years earlier when he still had his speed."

Dodger first baseman Gil Hodges steps into the batter's box as Larsen retrieves the ball from his infielders and prepares for his next pitch. Now thirty-two, Hodges is still regarded as the strongest man on the Brooklyn team, and he has also wielded a powerful bat up to that point in the series, hitting .500 (seven hits in fourteen at bats) and driving in eight runs (only one behind the World Series record set by former Yankee first baseman Lou Gehrig). Larsen's first pitch is a fastball that misses the plate, but the second pitch is a fastball that catches the outside corner. Hodges swings hard but misses. With the count even at one ball and one strike, Berra proceeds to call for two sliders on the next two pitches. Hodges sees the first one called as a strike by Pinelli and then swings and misses on the second, giving Larsen his third strikeout.

Sandy Amoros, the Brooklyn left fielder who hits from the left side, follows Hodges to the plate. A twenty-six-year-old Cuban native with dark skin, Amoros is only five feet, seven inches tall but weighs 170 pounds and is powerfully built. He also wiggles the bat in the air before a pitch is thrown, a habit that seems to underscore his ability to hit the long ball despite his small size.

Larsen works the count to two balls and two strikes against the Dodger batter. He then throws a slider, and Amoros hits a high pop fly that drifts toward shallow right field. Bauer races in at full speed as the ball proceeds to drop, but it is clear that he will never get there in time. In the meantime, second baseman Billy Martin begins backpedaling, keeping his eye on the ball, and at the last second puts his glove up, catches the ball, and falls over backward—but holds his glove high to show the second-base umpire that he has not dropped the ball. Amoros is out, and Larsen begins his slow walk back to the Yankee dugout.

Bottom of the Second: Sandy Amoros

Yankee catcher Yogi Berra steps into the batter's box to start the bottom of the second inning as Sal Maglie glares at Roy Campanella for the sign. Although he stands only five feet, eight inches tall, Berra weighs about 195 pounds and is a power hitter who holds the American League single-season record for home runs by a catcher (thirty), having turned the trick twice—once in 1954 and again in 1956.

Maglie knows he has to keep the ball on the outside corner of the plate to prevent Berra from pulling the ball to right field. But even if he succeeds in keeping the pitch away from Berra's preferred power zone, Maglie recognizes that the Yankee catcher is capable of driving the ball down the left side of the field as well. Stationed in left field, Sandy Amoros knows about Berra's propensity to pull the ball and moves toward left center field. But he too knows all about Berra's ability to hit a pitch down the left-field line. He has only to recall that memorable moment from last year's World Series.

It was October 4, 1955, a sunny and warm fall day and, for the 62,465 fans at Yankee Stadium, one filled with tension. After facing the Yankees in five previous series beginning in 1941—and losing every one of them—the Brooklyn Dodgers were on the verge of winning their first World Series Championship. The cry in Brooklyn had always been "Wait until next year," and it finally appeared that "next year" would soon arrive.

The Dodgers were ahead 2–0 as the Yankees came to bat in the bottom of the sixth inning. Brooklyn manager Walter Alston, eager to increase the lead, had sent the left-handed George Shuba to the plate to pinch-hit for second baseman Don Zimmer, a right-handed batter, in the top of the sixth inning. No one could doubt Alston's judgment. Bob Grim, a right-handed pitcher, had come in to relieve Yankee starter Tommy Byrne, a southpaw, and conventional wisdom dictated that a left-handed batter would have more success against a right-handed pitcher than a right-handed batter. But Shuba failed to get a hit, and, when the Dodgers returned to the field, Alston needed to find a replacement for Zimmer at second base. He therefore moved Junior Gilliam, one of the Dodgers' more versatile players, from left field to second and told Amoros to play left field.

It proved to be a critical maneuver. Johnny Podres, the Dodgers' twenty-three-year-old starting pitcher, had done well up to that point, but it soon appeared that he was tiring. After getting the first batter out, Billy Martin walked and Gil McDougald bunted safely for a hit. The tying runs were on base as Yogi Berra stepped to the plate. Fearing that Berra would pull the ball if he connected, Alston moved all the outfielders to the right. Amoros was almost in straightaway center field, with center fielder Duke Snider in right center field and right fielder Carl Furillo hugging the line. But Berra caught a pitch on the outside of the plate and lifted a high fly toward left field. "When he first hit it," Podres later recalled, "I picked up the rosin bag by the pitcher's mound, and I said, 'Well, there's an out.'" But then he looked up and saw the ball slicing toward the left field line—with the outcome uncertain.

Amoros already knew what Podres now realized—that the ball could drop in for a hit and at least two Yankee runs to tie the game. Amoros was a speedy runner. ("Little Flying Ebony," *The Sporting News* had called him.) And so, when he saw Berra's fly ball drifting toward the left-field foul line, Amoros did what he did best. "I run like a hawk," he later said in his broken English.

As he raced toward the left-field foul line, Brooklyn fans and players alike worried that Amoros would shy away from the nearby fence and miss the ball. But Amoros displayed no fear. Just before he reached the stands at full speed, he stuck out his right hand (because he was left-handed) and watched the ball drop into his glove. Over in the nearby Dodger bullpen, pitcher Billy Loes watched in alarm, thinking that Amoros might juggle the ball and drop it. "Hold on to that damn thing!" he screamed to his teammate.

But Loes had no reason to be concerned. Amoros held on to the ball, pivoted, and fired a bullet to shortstop Pee Wee Reese, who was waiting by the third-base line and yelling for the left fielder to throw him the ball. Reese then turned and fired a perfect peg to Gil Hodges at first base to double up McDougald, who had already raced from first base beyond second on the assumption that Berra's fly ball would drop in for a hit.

The inning over, the Dodgers were energized and the Yankees deflated. Podres completed the next two innings without difficulty, and, amidst the celebrations that ensued, the team as well as the press agreed that Amoros' remarkable catch made the difference. It was, said *The Sporting News*, a "$100,000 catch" that "will not be forgotten as long as the World Series is played." Reese, who played in every one of the World Series in which the Dodgers faced the Yankees between 1941 and 1956, said that being the middle man in the play "was the biggest kick I got out of seven World Series." And in a 2003 review of a hundred years of World Series play, *The New York Times* called Amoros' catch one of the "ten greatest moments" in World Series history. For his part, Amoros, the epitome of modesty, simply said, "Lucky, lucky, I'm so lucky."

It was not, however, luck. It was a reflection of skills and dedication that Amoros had been honing since his early days in Cuba. Home was Matanzas, a city located about sixty miles east of Havana near the north shore of Cuba. His father, an itinerant laborer, died when Edmundo (not yet known as Sandy) was three and left little money to his wife and six children. The mother was dedicated to doing what she could for her children and took a job in a local textile mill. But Edmundo had no interest in working in a factory or in pursuing education when he got older. His only interest was baseball. And he was good at it.

The young boy played for his local school at first and then moved on to amateur baseball leagues in Cuba. He played second base for his province and distinguished himself as one of the best players in the league, leading his team to a national championship that was played in Havana. His talents (including a spree of six home runs in seven games) led to his selection for the Cuban All-Star team, and, at the age of eighteen, Edmundo was on his way to Guatemala to play in the Caribbean World Series (where he compiled the top batting average of .450).

It was all a wondrous journey for a teenager who had never traveled outside of Cuba, but Edmundo had a dream—to play baseball in the United States. And he knew it was a dream that could come true. Jackie Robinson had already broken the color barrier, and Minnie Minoso, another black Cuban who had been Edmundo's hero as a young boy, would soon nearly win (and in the eyes of some, should have won) the American League's Rookie of the Year award in 1951.

By then, Edmundo had already completed his first two years of professional baseball, playing left field for the Negro league's New York Cubans in the United States. But his break came in Cuba while playing in the winter leagues in 1951. Al Campanis, a would-be Dodger player and a scout for Walter O'Malley, saw Amoros play while Campanis was managing another team in the Cuban league. Amoros was one of the league's leading hitters, but the first quality Campanis noticed was the young outfielder's speed. "I saw him hit a ball on one bounce to the second baseman," Campanis later remembered, "and nearly beat it out. That opened my eyes." In due course, Amoros was signed to a Brooklyn contract and shipped off to the club's farm team in St. Paul, Minnesota, for the 1952 season.

Despite his small size, Amoros made people take notice of his power. In an early season game at the team's home field of Lexington Park, the St. Paul Saints' manager, Clay Bryant, asked Amoros to pinch-hit in the tenth inning with the winning run on first base. Amoros sent a 450-foot drive to left center field that would have gone for an inside-the-park home run if Bryant had not stopped him at third after the winning run had crossed the plate. The drive—identified by the press as "one of the longest triples in Lexington Park history"—was surprising to Bryant and other observers not only because of Amoros' size. It was that much more amazing because the ball seemed to fly off Amoros' bat with "what appeared to be a flick of the wrists."

The hard-hit triple was not an aberration. Amoros tore up the American Association League with a .337 batting average and nineteen home runs. The local press began to refer to him as "the batter with the miracle wrists" and "a second Willie Mays." The Dodgers also took notice and, at the end of August 1952, Bryant was told to send the young player up to the parent club to help the team win a pennant (which they did).

By this point it was no longer Edmundo. Bryant and his players saw a resemblance between Amoros and featherweight boxing champion Sandy Saddler. The name Sandy was affixed and the name Edmundo was soon forgotten. One personal characteristic, however, remained unchanged: Amoros spoke little English and relied on teammates with fluency in Spanish to communicate with other people. The language barrier prevented Amoros from developing any close relationships on the Dodgers and often created difficulties when he tried to manage the daily rituals of life. (Duke Snider recalled that Amoros ordered pie à la mode in restaurants with great frequency because it was one of the few things he could say in English.)

However difficult it made the daily tasks of life, the language barrier could not conceal Amoros' buoyant personality. Almost always there was a smile, a laugh, and a playful attitude (which would be displayed in any number of ways, perhaps by his coming to the park on a hot summer day in a straw hat and a heavy overcoat or smoking one of the large Cuban cigars he favored). "Sandy is always smiling when he hits or when he doesn't," said one of his teammates from the minor leagues. His fellow Dodgers agreed. "He was always smiling," Johnny Podres recalled, "and never complained about anything." Even the landlady from whom he later rented an apartment in Brooklyn was impressed by his cheerful demeanor. "He's always very happy," she told an inquiring reporter. "He just drives up in his car and jumps out, says hello and greets everybody. You can never tell what happened to Sandy at the ballpark by looking at him when he comes home."

Unfortunately, home did not mean Brooklyn after the 1952 season. He had been used only sparingly in that final pennant drive, and management decided that Sandy needed some additional experience before he could stay with the parent club. So the young Cuban was sent to Montreal for the 1953 season. Amoros performed well, leading the league with a .353 average and, with twenty-three home runs, again demonstrating the ability to hit with power. Fielding was another matter. In his first season at St. Paul, the sportswriters had called him "one of the best left-field flyhawks in Lexington Park in a dozen years," and no one could doubt Amoros' speed in chasing down fly balls. Making judgments on how to play a hitter and what to do with the ball after he retrieved it was a different issue, and some wondered whether Amoros could do better.

Still, Amoros' prospects for joining the Dodgers in 1954 seemed bright—especially because the team's new manager was none other than Walter Alston, who had managed Amoros at Montreal. Sportswriters speculated that those prospects were that much brighter because Amoros had achieved a .421 batting average during spring training.

Alston did not share reporters' upbeat assessment of the young Cuban's talents, saying that "Amoros needed more minor league experience." "He has been a streak hitter as long as I've known him," the new manager opined. "When he's hitting, he'll hit anybody, right or left and hard throwers or soft throwers. And when he's not hitting—why, anybody can get him out." While many had earlier touted Amoros' fielding, Alston found fault with his performance, saying that he sometimes failed to get a good jump on a fly ball and that he often threw to the wrong cutoff man in the infield.

Not everyone was prepared to take Alston at his word. Even before the Dodgers opened the season at Ebbets Field, there was, as one sportswriter explained, "an undercurrent of suspicion" that Amoros was being held back for reasons having nothing to do with his performance on the field. The team already had five black players, and some sportswriters speculated that "the Dodgers are reluctant to add another

Negro to the squad." Another reporter similarly surmised that the Dodgers may have reached "the saturation point" with black players.

The Dodgers, of course, denied that there was any such "saturation point" for black players. Still, when the season began, there was much discussion among the Dodger ranks and in the press about whether Amoros should be played or sent back to the minors. ("For some reason," said one reporter, "the Dodgers treat Amoros as if he were a constitutional amendment. He can't go in or out of the lineup without a referendum.")

After struggling with the issue, Alston made the decision to send the young Cuban back to Montreal, where he once again did well, hitting .352, with fourteen home runs in only sixty-eight games. It was a record that could not be ignored and, with the Dodgers faltering in the pennant race, Amoros was called back to Ebbets Field after the All-Star break. Even Alston had to be satisfied. In only half a season, Amoros hit .274 with thirty-three extra-base hits, including nine home runs. And there could be no valid complaints about his fielding—as *The Sporting News* reported after the season, Amoros had "raced to the foul line or deep into left-center field and made catches on sheer speed of foot."

It was a performance that seemed to make a difference when Amoros reported for spring training in 1955. There was no talk about sending him back to the minor leagues, and Alston played him frequently when the season began. Amoros responded to the show of confidence, hitting .341 through the end of July. But then he was overcome with a sore back that landed him in the hospital. He was placed on the disabled list for a few weeks, and, by the time he returned, his batting eye had lost its sparkle and Alston had regained his misgivings about Amoros' value to the team. It was not, to say the least, a favorable combination. Amoros played only sporadically for the rest of the season and saw his batting average dip to .247.

Despite the accolades, the pivotal catch in the seventh game of the 1955 World Series did not give Amoros any security for his future. When he reached the Dodgers' spring training camp in 1956, he learned that he would have to vie with several other players for the left-field position. The competition proved considerable, and, while the Dodgers kept him on the team, he again played only sporadically (although he was able to hit sixteen home runs in only 292 at bats).

It was the kind of roller-coaster year that had already marked Amoros' short tenure in the majors. In one of the last games of the 1956 season—when the Dodgers were desperately trying to overtake the Milwaukee Braves in the pennant race—Amoros misplayed a fly ball in the sun in a game against the Philadelphia Phillies and then failed to charge a hard-hit single to left field, thus allowing the runner on first base to go to third. The Phillies won the game 7–3, and Dodger pitcher Don Newcombe slammed his glove against the wall on returning to the dugout after the first misplay, muttering to anyone who would listen, "Get him out of there if he can't catch a ball." Alston acknowledged that the young outfielder had "a bad day," but added, "I'm keeping him in the lineup, and he may help us to win the games we must win from now on."

Alston would not regret his decision. In the final season series with the Pittsburgh Pirates a few days later, Amoros hit two home runs in the first game of a doubleheader to assure pitcher Sal Maglie of a victory and the Dodgers of a chance at winning the pennant. And when the Dodgers did finally clinch the pennant the following day, Alston was quick to tell reporters that Amoros would be in the starting lineup for the World Series against the Yankees. "He's a streak hitter," the Dodger manager explained, "and he's hot right now."

Amoros is watching closely from the outfield as Maglie begins pitching to Yogi Berra in the bottom of the second inning of the fifth game of the 1956 World Series. After taking a called strike from Maglie, Berra swings at a curveball on the outside corner and lifts a high fly ball that starts to drift toward the left-field foul line. This ball is not hit as deep as the one in 1955, and, although he is running at full speed, Amoros can see that he will not get to the ball before it drops. Shortstop Pee Wee Reese knows that as well and is running toward the left-field foul line with his back to the plate. As the ball starts to fall, Reese makes what radio announcer Bob Neal calls "a fine catch" in which Reese "went almost out to the line and, with his back to the infield, reached up in the air and grabbed the ball."

The next batter is Enos Slaughter, a forty-year-old North Carolina native and a left-handed batter. He can pull the ball, but Amoros is playing him in straightaway left field (while Snider and Furillo have shifted toward the right-field foul line, leaving a large gap in left center field). Alston's placement of the outfielders proves to be a good read. Slaughter hits an outside pitch to Amoros, who moves slightly to his right to catch it.

Yankee second baseman Billy Martin, a right-handed hitter, moves up to the plate. Although not a power hitter, Martin has already hit two home runs in the series, including one against Maglie in the first game. But Martin cannot duplicate the feat now. He strikes out swinging (although Campanella drops the ball and has to tag Martin out).

The Dodgers retreat to the dugout, and already Bob Neal is saying that the game is shaping up to be "a real pitchers' battle between Sal Maglie and Don Larsen."

Top of the Third: Carl Furillo

Fern Furillo, a petite brunette, sits in the stands with the other Dodgers' wives as her husband, Carl, moves to the plate to face Don Larsen in the top of the third inning. She is proud of Carl. He is the team's perennial right fielder and, standing six feet tall and weighing almost two hundred pounds, he conveys the impression of being the strong, silent type. Indeed, in his first days with the Dodgers in 1946, people took notice of that strength and began calling him the "Rock."

Carl and Fern had grown up in Stony Creek Mills, a small town in the Pennsylvania Dutch Country near Reading, and she can no doubt remember the time when her brother Charlie had tried to protect her against the advances of this man who now stands waiting for Larsen's first pitch. Fern Reichart had met Carl in the early 1940s, but then he was shipped overseas with the army to fight in the Pacific. He carried her picture with him and contacted Fern upon his return. They started to see each other regularly, and he would usually pick her up in the large Studebaker that the Dodgers had given him in that spring of 1946. When he brought her home, Carl would often park the car in front of her house, and the time spent in the automobile did not go unnoticed in the Reichart household.

Fern was the youngest of thirteen children, and her brothers were very protective of her. "Who the hell's that guy out there you're with all the time?" her brother Charlie demanded at one point. Shy and not wanting to disclose her relationship with the young man who had achieved fame as one of the area's first major-league ballplayers, Fern deflected the question. "Charlie," she replied, "you don't want to know who it is." Her brother could not be turned aside. "Come on," he persisted. "Who is it?" And if she didn't tell him, said Charlie, "I'm going to grab him and rip him out of the car." "Trust me," Fern replied. "You don't want to do that." But Charlie would not accept that cryptic response, and Fern finally told him that her companion was Carl Furillo. Her brother was incredulous. "What the hell's he doing dating you," he rhetorically asked, "when he's probably up in New York with all those high-society women?" And so, still not believing his sister, Charlie went out to the car one evening and pulled the car door open to see who was dating his sister. Out popped Carl Furillo—towering over Charlie and leaving no doubt that Charlie would be the loser in any physical confrontation.

It was an experience that Fern and Carl (as well as Charlie) would laugh about in later years. But it was not the only fond memory they would take from Stony Creek Mills. Their roots were there and, no matter where Carl's career took him, he and Fern would always return to the small community that they called home.

In the early years, Carl could not have anticipated that he would someday find himself playing baseball for the Brooklyn Dodgers. (When a school counselor asked him what he wanted to be when he grew up, the young boy responded, "I would like to be an undertaker.") He was the sixth child born to Michael and Philomena Furillo, who had migrated to the United States from a town near Naples, Italy. They eventually settled in Stony Creek Mills, where they were one of only a few Italian families. Life was not easy in the beginning, and it became that much more difficult after the Depression enveloped the country. But they were a tight-knit family who drew comfort from each other, and there was always food on the table, in part because they had some land to grow their own crops.

Carl went to school in those early years, but education was considered a luxury in the Furillo home. He dropped out after the eighth grade. "At that time," he later explained, "things were a little hard." The family needed money, and young Carl was asked to spend his time picking fruit for $5 a day or working in the local cotton mill instead of sitting in a classroom. In later years, the lack of education often created a handicap as well as some comical moments. There was the time, for example, when Carl was asked to complete a questionnaire for the Dodgers which inquired about the "state of his health"—to which Furillo responded, "Pennsylvania." But Carl was smart enough to know what he had missed. "He always thought," said his older son, "that an education was the best thing in the world."

Carl Furillo may not have had the education he wanted, but he did have one remarkable talent—the ability to throw a baseball harder and farther than most of his peers. When he played the outfield, he could fire the ball back to the infield and prevent the batter from taking an extra base or, better yet, catch him trying to take that extra base. Josh Haring, a scout for the St. Louis Cardinals, took note of that talent as he watched Carl play softball games in the Stony Creek Mills sandlots and on baseball teams for local organizations. "How much you getting in the dye house?" Haring asked an eighteen-year-old Furillo in 1940. When the teenager with the short dark hair and the angular face said $18 a week, Haring had a quick response. "I can get you a job, a good one—baseball," the scout explained. "With Pocomoke City in the Eastern Shore League. Pays $80 a month, and I think you'll wind up a big-league ballplayer."

For Furillo, there was no question whether he would accept the offer—not so much because he loved baseball but because his family needed the money and he knew there was no future in the mills. So Carl Furillo became a professional baseball player. But always—even long after he had become the All-Star right fielder for the Brooklyn Dodgers—he would regard baseball as a place to work. And so, when Carl Jr. asked his father whether he was scared when he first came up to the Dodgers in 1946, Furillo had an easy answer: "No. It was my job."

He did well when he joined the Pocomoke club that summer. Eager to take advantage of his strong throwing arm, the manager initially tried to have Carl pitch every five days and play the other four days in the outfield. But Furillo had little control as a pitcher and, beyond that, he found it to be a "rough grind" to be constantly switching positions. So he was ultimately confined to the outfield, and the continuity proved to be to his liking. He wound up hitting .319 and stroking nine home runs in only seventy-one games.

He was promoted to the Cardinals' farm team in Reading, where he caught the Dodgers' attention. When their efforts to buy his contract failed, the Dodgers pursued the only alternative they had left—they bought the whole Reading club for $5,000. As Buzzie Bavasi, the Dodgers' point man on the deal, later recalled, the purchase netted the Dodgers "thirty uniforms, a bus, and Carl Furillo."

The Dodgers assigned Furillo to their top farm team in Montreal for the 1942 season, but his climb to the major leagues was disrupted when he received his draft notice. Carl joined the 77th Infantry Division of the army and spent the first eighteen months of his service in the States and Hawaii. But then the division was sent overseas to become part of the force that invaded Guam, the Philippines, and ultimately Okinawa. Carl was eventually transferred to the quartermaster unit, which required him to provide supplies and brought him that much closer to the combat front. At one point Furillo was hit by a Japanese mortar—an experience he would not soon forget. "I thought my whole face was ripped," he later remembered, with "blood pouring." But the wound was not life-threatening and Furillo—mindful of the deaths and serious injuries incurred by his comrades—refused the medic's offer to submit his name for a Purple Heart, which was awarded to almost every soldier wounded in action.

By July 1945, Carl had been brought back with his unit to the Philippines to plan for the invasion of Japan. It was to involve thousands upon thousands of servicemen, who would depend on untold quantities of various supplies. The chances of success were high, but the expected cost in lives was staggering. Furillo and the rest of his unit had been told that "the first three waves would be wiped out going into Japan." It was not something that could give the young soldiers in his division hope—because they were to be part of the third wave. And then President Harry S Truman decided to drop the atomic bomb on Hiroshima on August 6. The surrender of Japan shortly afterward could not have come too quickly for Furillo and the other members of his division.

Carl soon returned to the States, but his wartime experience was not a subject for family discussion. He would not talk with Fern very much about those years in the army, and when his two sons later pestered him with questions about his service, Furillo at first turned a deaf ear. When his sons would not let the subject drop, he allowed each of them to ask one—but only one—question. Carl Jr. asked the question that had troubled him the most: did his father kill any Japanese soldiers? His father nodded. Yes, he had killed some Japanese soldiers. Furillo's other son, Jon, was overwhelmed by the response and decided not to use the one question allotted to him. He was not interested in hearing any more. But Carl Jr. was, and he asked his father the second question: Did that bother him? To which Furillo had another simple response: "Yes. Very much." And that was the end of the discussion.

Within weeks of returning home from the service in January 1946, Furillo was in Sanford, Florida, for a special instructional school that the Dodgers had decided to hold for returning veterans. Now twenty-four years old, Furillo was hoping that he could rejoin the Montreal Royals, and he worked hard to get himself in shape. The dedication paid dividends, and in April, manager Leo Durocher told Furillo that he was not being sent to Montreal—he was going to be brought up to the parent club. Carl could not have been more excited. As he later told a reporter after he had arrived in Brooklyn, "I can't believe it yet. It's all a dream. I went to Sanford this spring figuring I'd be the luckiest guy in the world if I stuck with the Royals—and here I've wound up on the Dodgers themselves. It's out of Ripley."

There was, however, one disappointment in joining the Dodgers: the salary. Durocher had explained to Carl when they arrived in Brooklyn that he would be given a contract for $3,750. "I can't even survive on that," the young player told his manager. Take it or leave it, Durocher replied. It was not a response designed to endear the rookie to his manager. "I hated his guts from that day on," Furillo said.

Whatever his feelings toward Durocher, Furillo did not let it interfere with his performance. He played left field and then, when center fielder Pete Reiser slammed into a wall chasing a fly ball at Ebbets Field, the Stony Creek Mills rookie was moved to center. His batting was certainly respectable (.284 in 117 games), although he did not display the power that would later be a trademark (hitting only three home runs).

Hitting was only part of the story. Seasoned observers took note of Furillo's throwing capabilities, and as early as April, sportswriters were referring to his "rifle arm." The more they watched, the more the reporters were impressed—at one point asking the Dodger manager whether he had ever seen "another guy with an arm like that?" Before long the sportswriters were calling Furillo the "Reading Rifle," and opposing players were proceeding more cautiously on the base paths, knowing that a throw from Furillo could reach the infield more quickly than a player might otherwise suspect. (There was the time in later years when Pittsburgh Pirates pitcher Mel Queen had been heckled by the Dodgers because of his failure to get a hit, and then, when he came to bat in a game in which Ralph Branca was pitching a no-hitter, Queen surprised everyone by lining what appeared to be a single to right field where Furillo was then playing. As he ran to first, Queen turned his head toward the Dodger dugout with a smirk of satisfaction, only to turn back and see that Furillo had picked the ball up on one hop and thrown him out at first. Branca ultimately finished the game with giving up only one hit, and Dick Young of the *New York Daily News* reported the next day that "the strong Sicilian arms of Ralph Branca and Carl Furillo threw a one-hitter against the Pittsburgh Pirates at Ebbets Field yesterday.")

Although he could draw much satisfaction from his first year, Furillo could not know for sure what the future would hold for him when he reported for spring training in 1947. But his fortunes did not command as much attention as those of another player: Jackie Robinson. All the players (except Robinson) were housed in a converted army barracks in Cuba, and Furillo could hear some of the players from the South talking among themselves at night about the prospects of having a black man on the team. "They were talking about Jackie coming up," Furillo later remembered, "and the Southern boys didn't want this in the worst way." For his part, Furillo was more concerned about his own status. And so, when Bobby Bragan, one of the Southern players, asked him how he would feel if Robinson "came after your job," Furillo had a quick response: "I'd cut his legs off." It was, he later acknowledged, "a stupid remark," but Furillo later said that he had no interest in signing the petition that Dixie Walker circulated among the team to say that they did want to play with Robinson. Having grown up in a small community where Italians were a distinct minority, Furillo knew that ethnic and racial discrimination was not confined to blacks.

Still, Furillo's response to Bragan circulated among the players, and Robinson himself was led to believe that Furillo had been part of Walker's cabal. And so, when a movie about Robinson's life was produced a few years later, it included a scene in which Branch Rickey asks a young Italian player on the team who supported the petition how he would feel if he had been the object of ethnic or racial discrimination. When he heard about the scene, Furillo assumed that the Italian player was intended to be him, and he was angry at being falsely accused of supporting the petition. "They pushed the blame on me," he told Fern, "and the sons of bitches were those Southern kids." But Furillo was not one to confront Robinson or anyone else with the truth as he knew it. He kept his silence, and years later Robinson would say in his autobiography that Furillo was one of the "ringleaders" of the Walker petition.

There is evidence to support Furillo's later explanation that he was not one of the petition's "ringleaders." Bavasi told me that Furillo had come to him shortly after the petition had been circulated and said, "I can't sign this." Robinson's comment was nonetheless accepted by his subsequent biographers, and they too would point to Furillo as one of the players who had "circulated" the petition or who had "backed the revolt."

None of the controversy, however, had any impact on Furillo's value to the team. He continued to play left field until Reiser again collided with the center-field wall in Ebbets Field, and Furillo was once again shifted to center field. His batting during the season showed some improvement (.295 in 124 games with eight home runs), and he produced the highest batting average (.353) of all the regulars in the World Series against the Yankees.

Carl was a man of few words, and he was certainly no match for the long-winded Branch Rickey when the Dodger outfielder was summoned to Brooklyn in the early spring of 1948 to sign a contract for the forthcoming season. Furillo was well aware of Rickey's parsimony when it came to paying his players. (As former Dodger and sometime movie actor Chuck Connors later observed, Rickey "had players and money, and he didn't like to see the two of them mix.") So Furillo was prepared to wait out the Brooklyn general manager until he got something close to the salary he wanted. Rickey talked to Furillo for almost four hours, explaining his theory of baseball management and why the Dodgers' contract offer was reasonable. "I couldn't even say beans," Furillo later recalled. But he left without accepting Rickey's terms— prompting Rickey to call a friend afterward and say, "Why, you can't even talk to Furillo. He's so stubborn." But the two men ultimately did reach agreement, and for Furillo, the 1948 season proved to be a pivotal one.

On July 15, 1948, Durocher left to become the manager of the Giants, and Burt Shotton, the new manager, decided to move Furillo from center field to right field. Given Furillo's throwing capabilities, the decision made eminent sense. Having Furillo in right—where the distance to second and third base from the outfield was the greatest—would minimize the opportunities for opposing batters to take the extra base on a hit. The challenge confronting Furillo, however, was the structure of the right-field wall at Ebbets Field.

The wall sloped upward at an angle away from the field for about fifteen feet, then straightened out at an angle perpendicular to the field for about another fifteen feet. A twenty-eight-foot wire-mesh fence sat on top of the wall, and in the middle of the wall was the scoreboard with a large Bulova clock sitting on top. Trying to anticipate how the ball would respond after hitting the wall was no easy task. "A fly ball or a ball bouncing once or twice before it hit the wall," remembered one loyal fan, "would ricochet off that wall in the weirdest direction you ever saw. It never seemed to go the same way twice."

Furillo knew all about the trickery of the right-field wall, and he meant to master it. "He was a workman," teammate Carl Erskine later said of Furillo. "I studied every angle of that fucking wall," Furillo later explained. He would have teammates hit him flies so that he could see how the ball responded to different situations. In time, he knew every quirk. When a sportswriter later asked him how he learned to play the wall so well, he had a simple response: "I worked. That's fucking how."

Furillo's dedication not only helped the Dodgers win ball games. That effort also benefited Abe Stark. A sign on the right-field wall in Ebbets Field promoted Stark's clothing business: HIT SIGN, WIN SUIT. In all the years Furillo played right field, Stark never had to give away a single suit. (When Buzzie Bavasi's son later established a minor-league team in Everett, Washington, he checked with his father about Abe Stark's promotional sign, and Bavasi explained that Stark never had to give away a suit. So Bavasi's son sold a similar sign to a local clothier, and when Bavasi went to Everett for the opening game of the season, the first batter hit the sign and won a suit. Bavasi's angry son came up to him after the game, yelling, "I thought you said you never gave a suit away!" "We never did," the father replied. "But we had Furillo.")

In addition to mastering the right-field wall, Furillo also worked on his hitting, and the results of that effort were there to see as well. Between 1948 and 1951, he never hit lower than .295 (reaching .322 in 1949), and he learned to take advantage of the short left-field wall in Ebbets Field, hitting eighteen home runs in 1949 and 1950 and driving in 106 runs in each of those two years (which was all the more remarkable because Furillo was often the leadoff hitter in the lineup). But then his practice of sliding headfirst into bases took its toll. Grit became embedded in his eyes, and it started to bother him, especially when he was batting. He would sometimes see spots and was often unable to focus on the ball that was coming toward him at speeds approaching a hundred miles per hour. The results were reflected in his batting performance in 1952—an average of .247 with only eight home runs (half of what he had produced the year before). The team's trainer was unable to correct the situation and, believing that he had no other option, Furillo had an operation on both eyes in a New York City hospital in January 1953.

The operation proved to be a wise move. The earlier difficulties with his eyes disappeared, and now, as he later explained, the baseballs coming toward him in the batter's box "looked like balloons." His hitting improved dramatically, and by September, he had reached new heights. His batting average was close to .340 and he had already belted a career-high twenty-one home runs. But none of those achievements could guarantee what would happen when the Dodgers opened a series at the Polo Grounds against the Giants on September 5. The pressure was always considerable when the two New York teams played each other, and the tension was particularly evident whenever Furillo came to bat.

The first game did nothing to ease the friction between the two teams. Furillo had four hits in leading the Dodgers to a 16–7 rout of their New York rivals (increasing his batting average to a league-leading .345). So there was no love lost between Furillo and his former manager, Leo Durocher, when the Dodger right fielder came to bat in the next day's game. In his second time at the plate against Ruben Gomez, the Giants' rookie pitcher from Puerto Rico, Furillo saw Durocher yelling at him from the Giant dugout. Furillo thought he heard the Giant manager say, "Stick it in his ear," just before Gomez hit Furillo on the left wrist. As he trotted down to first base, Durocher was, as Furillo remembered, "yapping at me" and motioning to come get him if he wanted to fight. Furillo could take it no longer and, as he recalled, "I went after him." He raced into the Giants' dugout, jumped on Durocher, and put an armlock around his neck. With his baseball cap having been knocked off, people could see the top of Durocher's bald head start to turn purple. The two men fell to the ground, and players from both teams tried to pull them apart. In the course of the struggle, the pinkie on Furillo's left hand was broken.

The broken pinkie signaled the end of the season for Carl Furillo. Still, he was able to win the National League batting champion with a .344 average and return in time for the World Series with the Yankees (where he batted .333 with a home run and two doubles in the losing effort).

The Dodgers could take much satisfaction from Furillo's performance in 1953 and his stature after eight seasons with the club. He was a superb fielder, a keen hitter, and a fierce competitor. But he was not really one of the boys when the game was over. He was, said Duke Snider, "one guy on the club we didn't pal around with much." Furillo himself would agree. "I don't ever recall them saying," he later said of his teammates, "'Carl, we're having a get-together. Why don't you come over?'" And when later asked about the Dodger wives with whom she socialized, Fern Furillo simply said, "I didn't."

To some extent, the social gap was a matter of happenstance. Many of the players with whom Furillo was closest on the field—Snider, Reese, and Erskine, among others—lived in the Bay Ridge section of Brooklyn, and Furillo lived much farther away in Flushing. Players from Bay Ridge would carpool to Ebbets Field and then ride home together afterward, all of which made it that much easier for them to make social plans together. But part of Furillo's social isolation from the other players was a matter of personality. Even Erskine—one of Furillo's closest friends on the club—would later say that his teammate "was rough around the edges." (There was the time, for example, when Furillo was rooming on the road with Tommy Brown, a six foot-one-inch utility fielder, and he asked Brown to turn the light off so he could go to sleep. Brown resisted, words were exchanged, and the next morning Harold Parrott, the Dodgers' traveling secretary, was forced to tell the press that Brown had been taken to the hospital because of an altercation with some unidentified men who had encountered him in a parked car with one of the men's girlfriends—when in fact Furillo had simply become infuriated by Brown's nasty responses.)

But Carl had his soft side too. ("To get a friend," he would always tell his sons, "you've got to be a friend first.") It was a sensitivity that few saw, and sometimes he had to struggle with the disappointments he had with some of his teammates (such as the unfair implication in Robinson's movie that he had signed Dixie Walker's petition). When he was confronted with those disappointments, his first reaction was not to complain but to walk away and say to himself, "I don't want to have nothing to do with none of them." That perspective eluded Furillo's teammates at the time, and later—when they learned of his hurt feelings—they would express surprise and sorrow. "We never suspected," said Erskine, "that he felt like an outsider."

That was not to say that Furillo was without friends. Quite the contrary. In his neighborhood, he was a beloved celebrity. "When he was in New York," said his son Carl Jr., "he was like a god." Erskine agreed, remembering that Furillo had "an entourage like Muhammad Ali whenever he went somewhere." One of his favorite places to go with friends was Tex's, a local Italian restaurant. Furillo took almost everyone to Tex's, and in due course they learned that one of their host's favorite dishes was the scungilli (cooked snails). So Dick Young of the *New York Daily News* started referring to Furillo as "Skoonj," and before long, everyone—teammates as well as fans—was referring to the Dodger right fielder by that nickname.

In the meantime, Furillo continued to command respect among his teammates and Brooklyn's fans with solid performances. In 1954, playing in all but four of the team's 154 games, he batted .294, hit nineteen home runs, and drove in ninety-six runs in the season that saw Durocher's Giants take the pennant. He improved that record in 1955—a .314 average with twenty-one home runs and ninety-five runs batted in while playing in only 140 games. Furillo's performance that year was all the more remarkable because Dodger manager Walter Alston often batted him eighth in the lineup—a change that would have disturbed other players, but not Furillo. "What's the difference where you bat?" he told a reporter at one point during the season. "Just so you hit."

That 1955 season was particularly memorable because of the Dodgers' victory over the Yankees in the World Series. It was, Furillo later said, "a thrill of thrills." It was not just the World Series ring he received—the achievement was that much more special because of the fans' reaction. "No matter where the hell you went," Carl remembered, "everybody couldn't do enough for you. Never in my life have I ever seen a town go so wild."

The 1956 season brought gratification as well. The Dodgers were an aging team, and it was not easy to overcome the challenge of the largely younger team fielded by the Milwaukee Braves (which included future Hall of Fame inductees Hank Aaron and Eddie Mathews). Although his average slipped to .289 (with twenty-one home runs), the Stony Creek Mills native remained critical to his team's success. "If the Dodgers push through to win this pennant," said one sportswriter in late September, "a lot of the credit will have to go to Furillo, because Carl was hitting and winning games for the Brooks when victories were vital."

As the Dodgers' thirty-four-year-old right fielder steps up to the plate in the third inning of the fifth game of the 1956 World Series, Larsen knows that Furillo will be a "tough out" and that he should "never come inside to his power." Larsen sends a fastball to the outside of the plate which appears to be a ball to the Yankee hurler, but, to his surprise, home plate umpire Babe Pinelli calls it a strike. Larsen's next pitch is a fastball to the same spot, and Furillo lifts a fly ball to right field that Hank Bauer fields with ease.

Roy Campanella follows Furillo to the batter's box. Although 1956 was a difficult, injury-prone season for the longtime Dodger catcher, he is batting .333 in the series and is still a dangerous hitter. Larsen knows all about Campanella's capabilities, and so he keeps the ball on the outside of the plate away from Campanella's power zone. Within minutes, the Dodger catcher becomes the victim of a called third strike.

Sal Maglie comes to the plate and receives a warm ovation from the crowd. A right-handed batter, Maglie is a relatively good hitter, and that becomes apparent immediately. The Dodger pitcher swings at Larsen's first pitch and sends a line drive over second base that has all the markings of a ball that will drop into center field for a hit, but, as radio announcer Bob Neal tells his listening audience, "with Mantle's great speed, he was able to outrace it and grab it."

Larsen marches off the mound toward the dugout with the satisfaction of having retired the first nine batters to face him.

Bottom of the Third:
Roy Campanella

It was an event he would never forget, and, more than that, one he would relive in his mind over and over again for more than thirty years. The patches of ice on the winding road leading to his home on the North Shore of Long Island. The large Chevy sedan sliding out of control toward the telephone pole, and the realization that there is nothing he can do to avoid the collision. The thud of the impact and the sudden disorientation as the car flips over and, without a seat belt, he is thrown to the floor and wedged in between the front seat and the dashboard. And that sickening feeling when he tries to turn off the ignition but cannot move his arms—or, indeed, feel anything. He has no medical training, but he knows that he is paralyzed. He lies there, immobile and unable to do anything but cry out for help—but it is about two o'clock in the morning, and there is no one around to hear him. And so, fearing that the running car will explode in a ball of fire at any moment, he repeatedly recites the 23rd Psalm—a remnant of early childhood when he would attend services at a Baptist church every Sunday and his mother would tell him to say that prayer if "things went wrong." He is finally discovered by a policeman two hours later, and, although they are able to extricate him from the car, they will not be able to disabuse him of his self-diagnosis. It is January 28, 1958, and Roy Campanella, the Dodgers' thirty-six-year-old catcher, is the victim of a spinal cord injury that will leave him paralyzed from the neck down for the rest of his life.

Neither Sal Maglie nor his catcher can foresee the event that will later transform Campanella's life. As he walks onto the field in the bottom of the third inning in the fifth game of the 1956 World Series, however, Maglie can see that the shadows from the right side of the stadium have moved closer to the pitcher's mound. But he is focused only on getting the Yankee batters to strike out or hit balls that can be fielded by his teammates. And, like the other Dodger pitchers, he knows that Campanella has the experience to call the pitches to help him achieve that goal. ("No one dared shake him off," Carl Erskine later said of Campanella.) And more than that, Maglie is confident that Campanella can—despite a compact frame of five feet, nine inches and more than two hundred pounds of weight—move swiftly to field a bunt or catch a foul ball or throw out a runner who is trying to steal a base or even thinking about it (his most remarkable feat on that score being the time he picked off the Giants' Willie Mays at first base while in a catcher's squat). "Campy is a picture catcher," one sportswriter later observed. "He makes it look so easy."

For his part, Campanella never dreamed when he was growing up in Nicetown, a northern section of Philadelphia, that he would be catching in a World Series game. He played the game as a boy only because he loved it. And then he learned about racial discrimination in the big leagues and knew that his skills alone would not be enough to give him the opportunity to play there. Not that Campanella was entirely unhappy about the situation. Quite the contrary. Long before the Dodgers discovered him, he had fashioned a comfortable life in baseball.

In large part, Campanella's perspective was a product of his upbringing. John Campanella, his father, was a first-generation Italian whose parents emigrated from Sicily to Homestead, Pennsylvania. Roy's mother, Ida Mercer, was a black woman who grew up in Chesapeake City on Maryland's Eastern Shore. After marriage, John and Ida were drawn to Nicetown, a neighborhood populated principally by

Italian, Polish, and Irish families (and very few blacks). They had four children, with Roy being the youngest.

It was a close-knit family where hard work was valued highly. At the age of twelve, Roy had to get up at two o'clock in the morning to deliver milk for a local dairy. When he returned from that task around five a.m., he would load the truck from which his father sold vegetables, and, after completing that chore, eat breakfast and go to school. It was a grueling schedule that Roy would recall with pride as an adult, long after he had made a name for himself in baseball. "My dad's work ethic, which was tremendous, and his sense of discipline in terms of his craft," Roy's older son later observed, "was something I'm sure he got from my grandfather."

Ida's influence on her youngest child was no less important. She was a religious woman who had no tolerance for ethical indiscretions. If Roy found an abandoned glove on a local ball field, she would make him return it—even though the family did not have enough money to provide Roy with his own glove. And when Roy discovered four dollars on a street one day, Ida became apoplectic when she saw it in his pants pocket, believing that he had stolen the money. "I took quite a pummeling before I could finally convince her I had actually found all that money," Roy later remembered.

Like other neighborhood kids, Roy was enthralled with baseball. They would play pickup games on sandlots where equipment was at a premium. Even if equipment was available, it did not always fit properly. (There was the time eleven-year-old Roy was catching in a game with older kids, and he dispensed with the mask because it was too large and impeded his ability to see the ball clearly. As soon as he took the mask off, the batter tipped a foul ball that smacked him in the face and broke his nose. "He was catching again," one of his sisters later explained to their father. "And without a mask. Can you imagine anyone so stupid?") His interest in the game extended to professional baseball as well. For twenty-five cents he could sit on the top of a row house across the street from Shibe Park, home of the Philadelphia Athletics, and watch the game for a fraction of the cost of a bleacher seat (a venue that gave him the opportunity on June 3, 1932, to watch the Yankees'

Lou Gehrig become the first major-league player in the modern era to hit four home runs in a single game).

Roy was never aware of any racial discrimination in those early years. And then, as he was walking home from school one day when he was a teenager, another student referred to him as a "half-breed." "I didn't know what it meant," Roy later confessed. But he knew enough to know that it was a slur of some kind. So he hit the offender and ran home to his mother for an explanation. Yes, she said, Roy's father was a white man, but, she added, it was nothing that should cause him any shame. "He gives us what many folks, white or colored, can't buy with all the money in the world," she said. "He gives us love, Roy."

It may have been clear in his mother's mind, but Roy would encounter rough language and vicious taunts from schoolmates as the years progressed, and he was not one to simply turn the other cheek. "I learned fast," he later said, "to be pretty good with my fists." Still, he was able to continue sports in school, and one of the sports that continued to interest him was baseball. But he also excelled at track (running the hundred-yard dash and doing the broad jump), and he pursued that activity in junior high school rather than baseball. And then one spring afternoon, George Patchell, the junior high school baseball coach, saw the 150-pound eighth grader hit a softball over the fence in the field across the street from the school. Patchell summoned Roy to his office the next day. "You're fourteen," the coach told Roy, "and I'm a grown man. But I can't hit a ball that far." To Patchell, the next step was obvious. "So," he told the precocious player, "I wish you would come down to the gym after school today and enroll for the baseball team." Roy obliged and, when everyone was asked to step into a circle for their desired position, he saw that no one had chosen to be catcher. Roy decided to fill the void.

It proved to be a wise choice. With his build and natural instincts, Roy was able to develop skills as a catcher that far exceeded what might otherwise be expected from someone so young. By the time he was fifteen, he was playing American Legion ball with players much older than him. But he held his own, both on the field and at the plate.

In time, Roy's reputation as a talented catcher reached the ears of

Tom Dixon, one of the owners of the Bacharach Giants, a local black semipro team. As Roy was leaving the field after a Legion game in the summer of 1937, Dixon approached the young catcher and asked if he wanted to play for the Giants, who traveled to different cities on the weekends for games. "I'd sure like to play with your team," the startled teenager replied, "but I'm afraid my mother wouldn't let me."

Roy knew what he was talking about. When Dixon and Jack McGowan, the team's owner, visited the Campanella home, Ida made it clear that she had no interest in letting her youngest child travel to parts unknown with strangers just to play baseball. And in no event, she explained, could her son play on Sunday. That was a day reserved for church and prayer. McGowan pushed back, saying that he too was a churchgoing person and that he would ensure that her son attended services. And more than that, he said he would pay her son $35 for playing two games on the weekend. In those Depression days, that was a considerable sum—in some weeks, more than her husband made with his vegetable truck. Religion was certainly important, but there was no getting around the value of having enough money to pay the bills. And so Ida yielded to the pressure—but before he left on his first trip, she gave Roy a Bible, which he would take with him on his journey through baseball and which he would still have decades later when he was struggling with the challenges of his paralyzed condition. ("The Bible and Campy have always been good friends," his wife, Ruthe, would later say.)

It did not take long for Dixon to recognize that he had made a smart decision in bringing Campanella on the team—and, to the young player's good fortune, Dixon did not want to stand in the way of his protégé's advancement. Dixon therefore had a quick response when he and Campanella encountered Biz Mackey, the legendary catcher for the Negro National League's Baltimore Elite Giants, at the Woodside Hotel in Harlem. "Tom," Mackey asked, "I need a catcher—a good young kid I can break in to give me a rest. I'm beginnin' to get beat. You know anyone?" "You're standin' right next to him," said Dixon.

Mackey subsequently met with Roy in Philadelphia and offered the fifteen-year-old catcher the opportunity to play with one of the premier teams in the Negro National League for $60 a month. Campanella protested that he was making more than that with the Bacharach Giants. "But that isn't the big leagues, son," Mackey responded. "This is only a start. There's no telling how much you can be making in just a few years." Mackey then gave Campanella an Elite uniform to try on, and the teenager was sold.

It was a summer job that Campanella loved from the beginning. School was a legal requirement until he reached sixteen, but Roy had no interest in scholastic studies. ("I just couldn't work up any steam for the books," he would later explain.) And so, when the Elite Giants offered him $90 a month to play on a regular basis, Roy pressed his parents to allow him to quit school. They could not resist the inevitable, and on November 20, 1937—one day after his sixteenth birthday—Roy Campanella left academia for good.

Life in the Negro National League was rewarding for a player devoted to baseball, but, like Jackie Robinson, Campanella learned that it was hardly luxurious. The team traveled from city to city in dilapidated buses, ate meals in restaurants that did not get high marks for cleanliness or quality, and stayed in hotels that provided little comfort. And never could a player afford to sit out a game because of injury or fatigue. (Years later, in describing life in the Negro National League to Carl Furillo, Campanella explained that there were only thirteen players on a team—eight fielders, four pitchers, and "a utility man who took care of bats and stuff." Furillo was incredulous. "What happened if more than one guy got sick or hurt?" he asked. "Nobody ever got sick or hurt," Campanella replied. "If a guy didn't play, he didn't get paid.") Campanella displayed the endurance to play as much as needed—sometimes catching two doubleheaders in a single day. And he demonstrated skills behind the plate and at bat that earned him a selection to the league's All-Star teams.

On September 3, 1939, he married Bernice Ray, a girl from his neighborhood. Two daughters were born in the first two years of the marriage, but it was not a union that would stand the test of time. Roy decided to play winter ball in Puerto Rico and then accepted an offer from Jorge Pasquel to play in the Mexican League during the winter, pushing his annual income above the $5,000 mark. But it was not a schedule conducive to married life (and, in fact, the couple never had their own home, living instead with their parents). It soon became clear to both of them that the relationship could not endure, and, as Roy later said, "We just agreed to call it quits."

Still, the marriage did provide one incidental benefit: the local draft board gave the married father a deferment after Pearl Harbor to allow him to work at a defense plant making armor plating for tanks instead of requiring him to don a uniform. But Roy had little interest in that job when he saw a coworker get his arm "smashed to a pulp" by a hammer press. "I got a family to worry about," he told the foreman, "and a baseball career." He was switched to another department, and then—for reasons he never understood—his draft board told him he could return to baseball.

By the summer of 1942, Campanella was recognized as one of the most accomplished players in the Negro leagues, and it gave him the confidence one day to approach Hans Lobert, the Philadelphia Phillies' manager, during a game at Shibe Park. "You can use a catcher," Campanella said. "And I'm a good catcher. I can help this club." Lobert suggested that Campanella call the team's president, who told the black star that he was powerless to accept the offer. "The social times are not ready yet for Negroes in organized baseball," the Phillies' president explained.

However much he disliked that answer, Roy was content to return to the Negro leagues. He only wanted to play baseball—whatever the venue. He had seen film clips of Boston Red Sox outfielder Ted Williams skipping happily around the bases "like a kid" after he had hit a three-run home run in the bottom of the ninth inning to enable the American League to win the 1941 All-Star game. The image captured Campanella's perspective on baseball. "I don't care how old you are," he would later tell a sportswriter. "You have to have that spirit." And so, in later years, long after he had become the most respected catcher in the National League, he never tired of saying that "you have to be a man to be a big-league ballplayer, but you have to have a lot of little boy in you too."

His positive attitude was evident to those who watched him play on a daily basis. "Campy is the most relaxed ballplayer I've ever seen," said Dodger vice president Fresco Thompson after the Nicetown native had been with the Dodgers for more than six years. "There seldom is a crisis for him because he loves playing so much." Dodger general manager Buzzie Bavasi understood that perspective. Long after Campanella had achieved fame as a Brooklyn Dodger, Bavasi sent him a contract and asked him to fill in the salary number that he wanted, Bavasi assuming that the modest player would insert a figure lower than the one Bavasi was prepared to give him. But Campanella turned the tables on Bavasi by signing the contract and returning it without filling in the blank. "You know I'll play no matter what you give me," he told Bavasi. "I'll play for nothin' if I have to. You can write in the number yourself." And so Bavasi was forced to give his catcher the raise he deserved.

Campanella's enthusiasm for the game was infectious and helped to make him a popular figure wherever he went. His Dodger teammates, for one, loved it in later years when he would walk into the clubhouse after a victory the day before, wearing a big Panama hat while chewing on an unlit cigar, and proclaim in his squeaky voice to anyone in earshot, "Same team that won yesterday is gonna win today."

That optimism extended to almost any situation. And so Roy had no anxieties when Charlie Dressen, a Dodger coach, approached him during an All-Star game between Negro league and major-league players in Newark's Ruppert Stadium in October 1945. Dressen cryptically said that Branch Rickey wanted to meet with the black catcher the next morning at the Dodgers' offices in Brooklyn. Campanella had heard that the Dodgers might be forming a new black team—the Brown Dodgers. He was not sure that a newly formed Negro team would be of any interest to him, but he agreed to meet with the Dodgers' general manager.

The first thing Campanella noticed about Rickey were the man's eyebrows. "They were thick and wild-growing," the veteran catcher later recalled. He also saw that Rickey had a large notebook on his desk that, he soon learned, possessed all kinds of information on Campanella's private life and baseball career.

At first, the two men said nothing to each other while Rickey surveyed the man who sat in front of his desk. After a few minutes, the older man broke the silence. "How much do you weigh?" he asked

Campanella. "About two-fifteen," said the five-foot-nine-inch catcher. "Judas Priest!" Rickey roared. "You can't weigh that much and play ball." "All I know," Campanella replied, "is that I've been doin' it every day for years."

Rickey proceeded to explain, as only Rickey could, how important it was to find ballplayers with the right qualities. "I've rejected a number of possibilities," he said, "who I'm sure have the ability. They're lacking other requisites. It's either character, habits, or what have you. You're different," he told Campanella. "Your record is good—no arrests, no trouble, good family, a hard worker who loves baseball, a man who gets along well with people." And on and on it went. But never once did Rickey make Campanella an offer—or say anything specific about a new Negro league team. And so Campanella—assuming that Rickey was talking about the soon-to-be-formed Brooklyn Browns—told the Brooklyn general manager that he was making good money and was otherwise satisfied playing summer ball in the Negro leagues and winter ball in the Mexican or Caribbean leagues. Rickey did not clarify the situation for Campanella as the meeting ended. He asked only that the young player not sign any contracts without talking to him first. "I don't sign no contracts," Campanella replied. "I just play ball."

Campanella took the train back to his home in Baltimore and recounted the details of the meeting to his wife, Ruthe, a vibrant black woman whom he had first met on one of his trips to New York City and whom he had married earlier that year. "Honey," he told Ruthe, "that man sure can talk. He talked so much that he gave me a headache."

Whatever Rickey had in mind, it was not enough to deter Campanella from returning to Venezuela to play winter ball. The first segment of the schedule would be a series of games with All-Stars from the Negro leagues, and they all agreed to meet in New York City for a short vacation before embarking on the trip to South America. Shortly after arriving at the Woodside Hotel in Harlem, Campanella encountered a black player from the Kansas City Monarchs who would be joining them on the Venezuela trip—Jackie Robinson. After a casual conversation, Robinson suggested a game of cards to pass the time. Campanella agreed, and before long the two men were sitting in Campanella's hotel room, playing cards and talking about any number of things. And then Robinson mentioned that he had heard that Campanella had met with Rickey. The Elite Giant catcher was startled that Robinson knew of the meeting. "How did you know?" he asked. "I was over there myself," said Robinson. "What happened with you?" Campanella then confessed that he had no interest in playing for a newly formed black team. "I'm an established star in our league," said Campanella, "and I'm not going to give it up to take a chance on something that's just getting started and might not last."

Robinson then told Campanella in confidence that he had just signed a contract to play for the Montreal Royals with the expectation that he could soon join the Brooklyn Dodgers. "It's the end of Jim Crow in baseball," Robinson boasted. "I'm all excited. I'm proud, and I'm scared too."

Campanella, realizing his mistaken assumption, just stared at Robinson. He now knew that Rickey had been interviewing him about the possibility of joining the Dodgers—not the Brooklyn Browns. But it was too late, or at least so Campanella thought, to turn back now. He went to Venezuela as planned and played the scheduled games, all the time wondering if he would ever hear from Rickey again. Then, on March 1, 1946, he received a telegram from Rickey: PLEASE REPORT BROOKLYN OFFICE BY MARCH 10. VERY IMPORTANT.

Campanella was too excited to wait. He got on the first plane to New York and was in Rickey's office the following day. Bob Finch, Rickey's assistant, explained that Rickey was at the team's spring training camp in Florida but did indeed want to sign the young catcher to a contract. The initial thought was to have him play with Montreal, but when Finch called Rickey in Florida, the Brooklyn general manager explained that there had been some unpleasant repercussions from Robinson's presence and that it would be better to find another home for Campanella. Finch then called the team's farm club in Danville, Illinois, but they too made it clear that a black player would not be welcome. The third call went out to Buzzie Bavasi, at that time the general manager of the team's farm club in Nashua, New Hampshire, a blue-collar town dominated by a local textile mill and French-Canadian immigrants—but with almost no blacks. Finch explained to

Bavasi that Rickey wanted to assign two players to the Nashua team—
Campanella and a nineteen-year-old pitcher named Don Newcombe.
"Can they play?" Bavasi asked. "We think they can," said Finch. "Then
what's the problem?" Bavasi responded. Finch did not mince words:
"They're colored." Bavasi's reacton was all that Finch could have
wanted. "If they can play," said the Nashua general manager, "that's
no problem."

Nashua proved to be a hospitable environment for Campanella and
Newcombe. Although Rickey had cautioned him to turn the other
cheek in the face of verbal abuse, Campanella encountered very little
hostility from the fans. In fact, the only inflammatory incident he could
recall occurred when Sal Yvars, a twenty-two-year-old catcher on the
New York Giants' farm team, threw dirt in his face as he stepped into
the batter's box. Despite Rickey's admonition, Campanella could not
help but see red. "Try that again," he snapped at Yvars, "and I'll beat
you to a pulp." Yvars heeded the warning, and the incident was never
repeated.

In the meantime, the Nicetown native quickly established himself as
the team's leader on the field and at the plate. Campanella's skill with
a bat and glove were complemented by his ever-endearing personality.
He was cheerful, optimistic, and uncommonly polite. (There was the
time in the beginning when Claude Corbitt, an opposing team's leadoff
hitter, came the plate with nothing more than an interest in getting a
hit. "Good evening, Mr. Corbitt," said the Nashua catcher. "How are
you tonight?" Corbitt later said that he was "so stunned I could barely
tap the ball back to the pitcher.") Others also took note of Campanella's effusive personality, and it was later reported that he "was perhaps the most popular player in Nashua."

By the end of the season, Campanella had compiled a .290 average
with forty-one extra-base hits in only 113 games and was chosen as the
New England League's Most Valuable Player. "He was the best player
in the league," Bavasi later crowed. "Nobody could touch him." Campanella returned to Baltimore a happy man with high expectations for
the future.

The Dodgers did not disappoint him. While Jackie Robinson was
elevated to the parent club for the 1947 season, Campanella was as-

signed to the Dodgers' top farm team in Montreal. The rotund catcher's performance made it clear that the Canadian club was merely a stepping-stone to the big leagues. His batting average remained well above .300 until the end of the season, and, while his hitting cooled off as the year ended, he was still given the league's Most Valuable Player award.

Hitting was only part of the story. The MVP award also reflected Campanella's skills behind the plate. Frank Shaughnessy, the International League's president, said that the Dodger prospect was "the outstanding catcher in the minors." Paul Richards, a former big-league catcher who managed the Buffalo team in the International League and would later achieve fame as a major-league manager, agreed, saying that "Campanella is the best receiver in baseball." And beyond it all was that ebullient personality. It was hard not to like the man. "The Royal farmhands accepted him more readily than Robinson the year before," said one sportswriter. "Perhaps this was due to the fact," he added, "that Jackie was more serious."

However much satisfaction he could take from his record with Montreal, Campanella was feeling anything but confident about his chances of moving up to the Brooklyn club in 1948. The 1947 Dodgers included Bruce Edwards, who had handled the catching responsibilities superbly in 1947 by batting .295, being selected for the National League All-Star team, and earning manager Leo Durocher's respect as "the best catcher for the National League." Campanella was well aware of Edwards' accomplishments and could not help but feel that "it just didn't look like there was any room for me."

Still, he was invited to the Dodgers' spring training camp in the Dominican Republic in February 1948, and, after only a few weeks, Durocher realized that Campanella was far superior to the Dodgers' other backup catcher—Gil Hodges—and perhaps as good as Edwards. Rickey confirmed Durocher's conclusion in a private meeting with the young hopeful. "Roy," said Rickey, "you're the best catcher we have, and I'm going to bring you up to the Dodgers." Campanella's elation was immediately eclipsed by Rickey's next comment: "You will be brought up as an outfielder."

Campanella was understandably confused. Rickey explained that, while he knew the former Negro league star had the skills to be a major-league catcher, the Dodger general manager had a higher priority—the further integration of the minor leagues. Campanella would be sent to the club's farm team in St. Paul, Minnesota, to become the first black player in the American Association league. Playing Campanella in the outfield in spring training would provide the ostensible excuse to send him back to the minor leagues for further training. "Mr. Rickey," Roy responded, "I'm a ballplayer, not a pioneer." But he was a good soldier and agreed to the plan.

The experiment in St. Paul was a success and, fortunately for Roy, short-lived. "Roy Campanella has found a new friend in St. Paul," explained one sportswriter, "the 315-foot fence at Lexington Park, home of the Saints." The St. Paul catcher set a league record by hitting eight home runs in his first seven games, and after twenty-five games he had blasted eleven home runs and driven in thirty-three runs—a record that Rickey could not ignore, especially because the Dodgers were languishing in sixth place with Edwards on the injured list and Durocher screaming for the return of the Nicetown native. After a doubleheader in Minnesota on June 30 (only days after Ruthe had given birth to their first child, a boy named Roy Jr.), Alston gave Campanella the good news. He was going back to Brooklyn.

When he walked into the Dodger clubhouse at Ebbets Field the next day, the manager greeted Campanella as only Durocher could: "Ha. Fat as ever." But the most important message had come from Rickey at an earlier meeting in his office. "All our pitchers are white," the general manager explained, "and you're going to have to get them to believe in your signal calls."

That proved to be an easy prescription for Campanella to fill. He was only twenty-six years old, but he already had more than ten years of professional experience and a refined sense of how to guide a pitcher. He would study the statistics of opposing batters before each game and review their strengths and weaknesses with the pitcher. But that was only a starting point. "A catcher must know the pitcher's emotional stability, his physical characteristics, and his mental capacity," Campanella would later explain. "He must know just what the other team can do and what it may want to do. He must know the other manager's philosophy of baseball and his tactics as well as he does his own."

Campanella's success with the Dodger pitchers reflected more than detailed information about the opposing team. Campanella also had the personality to make it work. Part of it was the constant chatter emanating from that cherubic face (made smooth by Nair instead of shaving cream). The other part was the never-ending stream of advice. Before the games he would invariably remind the pitcher to "just throw what ol' Roy calls and I'll make you a winner." It was the kind of attitude that inspired confidence (although Carl Erskine would often tease Campanella after a defeat by showing his teammate the box score from the next day's newspaper which said that Erskine was the losing pitcher and asking "if it shouldn't say, 'Campanella, losing catcher'"). If a pitcher encountered trouble during the game, Campanella would saunter out to the mound with some advice to help the pitcher relax. It was a conference that Pee Wee Reese—the Dodgers' regular shortstop during all of Campanella's years with the team—would invariably attend. "I don't want to miss a word he says," Reese once explained to a sportswriter. "He's funnier than Bob Hope."

Campanella's value to the team extended well beyond his skills on the field. His bat was an explosive force. In his first game on July 1, 1948, he rapped out a double and two singles. Two days later he hit two home runs to propel the Dodgers to a 13–12 victory over the Giants. While he batted only .258 in his first season, he hit nine home runs, drove in forty-five runs, and received credit from Durocher as a principal factor in the team's resurgence from sixth place to third place in the standings. Not surprisingly, Edwards never made it back as the club's regular catcher. Campanella caught 130 games and was instrumental in the Dodgers' drive to the 1949 pennant, hitting twenty-two home runs and driving in eighty-two runs while raising his batting average to .287.

His teammates not only appreciated their catcher's contribution to the team's success. They also recognized that his perspective on race relations was far different from Jackie Robinson's. The former UCLA star was ever sensitive to racial slurs and eager to eradicate the remnants of racial discrimination in baseball. Campanella viewed the issue with a different lens. "I tried not to notice the things that bothered Jackie," he later explained. "Not that I didn't mind them. It's just that

some men can have the same problems and yet face them differently."
For Campanella, it was enough that he and Jackie had made it to the
big leagues. As Erskine commented, "Campy was completely satisfied.
Jackie was never satisfied."

The difference in attitude would manifest itself in numerous ways
and on many occasions, especially in those early years of integration.
There was the time when Robinson and Campanella could not join the
other Dodgers for a steak dinner after a spring training game in some
Southern town. Harold Parrott, the club's traveling secretary, brought
dinners to the two black players, who were still sitting on the team bus.
Campanella could see his teammate seething and urged restraint with
words that could not be found in the dictionary. "Let's have no trouble,
Jackie," the Dodger catcher cautioned. "This is the onliest thing we can
do right now, 'lessen we want to go back to them crummy Negro
leagues." Another time the Chase Hotel in St. Louis agreed to allow the
black Dodgers to stay with the rest of the team (although they would
not be permitted to eat in the dining room). Robinson jumped at the
chance to remove one more barrier to racial segregation, but Campanella, believing it had to be all or nothing, declined, telling his black
teammate, "I'm no crusader."

There were, of course, incidents that pushed Campanella's carefree
approach to the brink (the most notorious being in 1953 when Milwaukee Braves' hurler Lew Burdette called Campanella a "nigger"
after brushing him back with two knockdown pitches, causing Campanella to march toward the mound with bat in hand, only to be inter-
cepted by other players). But those incidents were few and far between,
in part because Campanella recognized that opposing players would
"always try to get under your skin any way they can." None of that
was acceptable to Robinson, whatever the reason, and he sometimes
took exception to Campanella's passive perspective. "Jackie would get
impatient with Campy because he wanted him to speak up more,"
Rachel Robinson later acknowledged, "and Campy would get frustrated with Jackie because he thought he spoke up too much." It was
an ongoing difference of opinion, she added, that "often led to periods
of tension between them, usually provoked by sportswriters."

For his part, Campanella never let the tensions escalate to open hostility—no matter what the sportswriters said about his relationship with Robinson. "Listen," he would tell his young son whenever those stories appeared in the press. "Don't let that stuff worry you. I only read it in the crapper, and that's it." And so, while sportswriters and teammates might take notice of their different perspectives on race relations, the two men retained harmonious relations with each other, sometimes carpooling to Ebbets Field together, often eating together, and always being there to support each other. Never would differences of opinion affect their play on the field. Their commitment to the Dodgers' success was too deep-seated. Indeed, Campanella always believed that it would be that much better "if I could let my bat do my talking for me."

Campanella's hopes on that score were soon fulfilled. In 1950, he was on the verge of breaking the team's home run record (Babe Herman's thirty-five round-trippers in 1930) when he broke his thumb trying to catch a foul tip in early September and had to settle for thirty-one. In 1951, he smashed thirty-three home runs before being beaned by Turk Lown of the Chicago Cubs about two weeks before the season ended. Bleeding profusely from the ear, the Dodger catcher was rushed to the hospital with general manager Buzzie Bavasi in tow. "You don't have to stay with me, Buzzie," said Campanella. "You know I'm all right." "If I don't stay," Bavasi replied, "you'll walk out of here."

Bavasi's caution was justified. Campanella was dizzy for almost two weeks and had to remain in the hospital until the last days of the season. When he returned, he pulled a muscle trying to stretch a double into a triple. By the time the Dodgers reached the play-offs with the Giants, the pain in his right thigh was considerable. "I couldn't swing, I couldn't run, and it even hurt when I threw," he later recalled. Still, he wanted to play. His team needed him, and he was not one to disappoint his teammates. But the laws of physics could not be ignored. His play in the first play-off game was weak and, after the Dodgers lost, he asked manager Charlie Dressen to bench him and use backup catcher Rube Walker. When Bobby Thomson hit his historic home run in the ninth inning of the third game, Campanella was on the bench, crying out, "Sink, you devil. Sink!" But the ball did not sink until it reached the left-field stands.

Although there was no World Series for Campanella that fall, his performance during the year (which included 108 runs batted in and a .325 batting average) was rewarded by his selection as the National League's Most Valuable Player.

The following season was a different story. Roy suffered multiple injuries to his thumbs, his elbows, and his hands from foul tips, collisions at the plate, and wild pitches from opposing hurlers. He played in only 128 games and saw his home run production drop to twenty-two and his batting average fall to .269 (although he did drive in ninety-seven runs). The Dodgers did win the National League pennant, but their catcher was of little help in the World Series against the Yankees. He had only six singles in the seven-game series and did not drive in a single run.

There was no reason to think that Campanella was nearing the end of his career, but Walter O'Malley later met with the Dodger catcher to ask if he might be interested in becoming a coach after retirement. "Nobody knows more than you about catching," O'Malley explained, "and you know more about pitching than most pitchers. Besides," he added, "you have a way with you. You're popular with the players. There's no question in my mind but that you'll make a fine teacher." O'Malley said there was only one condition to his offer: Campanella had to take off weight so that he could set an example for the other players.

Whether the coaching offer was real or feigned, it had an immediate impact on the Dodger catcher. When he reported to spring training in February 1953, Campanella weighed only 205 pounds—about eighteen pounds less than he weighed the previous season. The results were reflected not only on the scales but also in his performance. He established new major-league records for both home runs by a catcher (forty-one) and runs driven in by a catcher (142). Not surprisingly, when the baseball writers later met to select the league's Most Valuable Player, Campanella easily outdistanced the competition. "That's exactly as it should have been," Arthur Daley observed in *The New York Times*, "because Round Roy, the Jolly Dodger, was easily the most valuable operative in the league."

Campanella's good fortune in 1953 appeared to evaporate in 1954.

Beset by severe injuries to his hands, he could not regain the batting form he had enjoyed the year before, and his batting average sank to a lowly .207 while playing in only 111 games (although he did steal home for the first time in a game against St. Louis in June). Once again, however, the former Negro league star seemed to rise from the ashes the following year.

The 1955 season did not have a promising start. Mindful of his injuries and poor performance in 1954, Alston had Campanella batting eighth in the lineup and, unlike Carl Furillo, the Dodger catcher did not take kindly to the gesture. "That's fine encouragement he is giving me," Campanella sarcastically told a sportswriter, "sending me to hit with the batboy."

However angry he may have been with his manager's decision, Campanella did not let it affect his performance. Although an injury to his knee from a foul tip had him out of the lineup for two weeks, he soon began hitting the ball with authority and moving up the lineup. As the Dodgers moved to a thirteen-game lead in the standings by the middle of the summer, Campanella's picture graced the cover of *Time* magazine, which paid tribute to his considerable contribution as the team's catcher. "No active player in American baseball fills that formidable job better than the burly, bulging, cocoa-colored catcher named Roy Campanella, currently enjoying one of the best seasons of his long career on the best team in baseball." The magazine then presciently observed that, "to Dodger rooters, 1955 is the year of destiny, and destiny is the bulky shape of Roy Campanella."

As predicted, the Dodgers captured the National League pennant with ease and then went on to defeat the Yankees in the World Series. Campanella proved to be a critical component of that success. He hit thirty-two home runs and drove in 107 runs in only 123 games during the season and posted the third-highest batting average (.318) in the league. His role in the team's World Series victory was no less important—two home runs and then a double in the seventh game that led to the Dodgers' first run. It was indeed a remarkable year, which was capped by his third MVP award and a new annual contract for $50,000—the most money ever paid to a Dodger player.

To anyone who asked, Campanella would provide assurances that he had many years left to his playing career, but his body showed otherwise in 1956. His hands continued to give him problems—the nadir being the time in June when he tried to pick a runner off at first base but inadvertently broke his right hand when it struck the batter's bat. The result was predictable. He could not grip the bat or throw the ball with the same authority, and the frustration of the experience was sometimes difficult to handle. "It meant such pain," remembered his son Roy Jr., "that I think even his disposition occasionally off the field wasn't as sanguine or as playful as it usually would be." Campanella's injury was, unfortunately, a poorly kept secret, and by the end of the summer, sportswriters were reporting that Campanella "simply cannot throw with his beaten right hand, and opposing clubs now know that." The statistics reflected the downslide. Although he caught 121 games, he hit twelve fewer home runs in 1956 and saw his batting average drop ninety-nine points to .219.

There are no thoughts of retirement as Campanella gives Sal Maglie the sign for the first batter in the bottom of the third inning at Yankee Stadium on October 8, 1956. The Dodgers need to win the fifth game, and the Brooklyn catcher is all business as Gil McDougald steps into the batter's box.

The Yankee shortstop swings at Maglie's first pitch and sends a ground-ball foul to the left side of third base, which is picked up by Frank Crosetti, the Yankees' third-base coach. Maglie follows that pitch with a sharp curve, prompting radio announcer Bob Neal to say that "the Barber, not to be outdone by the great pitching so far of Don Larsen, is matching him, pitch-for-pitch." Maglie then tosses another curve, which McDougald hits sharply down the third-base line, but Robinson is there and easily beats the Yankee shortstop with a throw to first base.

Andy Carey, the Yankees' third baseman, follows McDougald to the batter's box. A right-handed hitter, Carey pops Maglie's second pitch up into foul territory to the right side of the plate. Campanella flips off his mask and quickly moves under the ball for the second out.

Don Larsen—who had a single in the second game that drove in a run—moves up to the plate. "Larsen is big enough and strong enough and brave enough to swing that bat," Neal tells his listening audience. But the right-handed Larsen has no success now against his adversary. After getting to a count of one ball and one strike, Larsen hits a pop-up to the left side of the plate. Campanella jerks his mask off again and easily pulls in the ball for the last out.

Having retired the first nine Yankees he faced, Maglie walks off the mound to the security of the Dodger dugout.

Top of the Fourth: Billy Martin

Bob Wolff watches from the press box as the Yankees take the field in the top of the fourth inning. "In those days," he remembers, "the dream of every broadcaster was to be a World Series announcer." And now he has been given the chance. He had toiled for many years as the voice of the Washington Senators on both television and radio before being selected to provide the play-by-play commentary on the 1956 All-Star game that was played in the nation's capital in July. People liked what they heard, and soon enough Gillette—the sponsor of the 1956 World Series broadcasts—called upon Wolff to make his first appearance in the fall classic by doing the radio broadcast with Bob Neal. It was not only a welcome acknowledgment of Wolff's considerable skills in the broadcast booth. Gillette's decision also gave the Senators' broadcaster the opportunity to watch the Yankee players he knew so well. And few Yankees commanded as much attention from Wolff as Billy Martin, the slim, five-foot-eleven-inch California native who had patrolled second base for the club during the season and is now performing the same role in the series.

"Billy Martin," Wolff would later say, "was a one-of-a-kind ballplayer who played with such intensity that, in a way, you didn't forgive, but you understood why, at times, the intensity was too much for his own good." Wolff had no difficulty remembering an incident—long after Martin had been traded from the Yankees and was playing for the Minnesota Twins—that epitomized the second baseman's inability to control his emotions. The manager had taken him out of the game after he had struck out, and Martin, enraged by the slight, had stormed away in the dugout after throwing his bat and glove down in front of the manager. Wolff—only about seven years older than Martin—wanted to impart the kind of guidance that an older brother would give to a sibling. He had already predicted that Martin would someday be a manager. He went down to the clubhouse after the game and encouraged the frustrated player to view his own behavior from that perspective. "If you do that stuff," Wolff cautioned him, "you're not going to be a manager. You wouldn't like it if you were a manager and the player did that to you."

Years later—after he had compiled an exceptional record as a manager for five different teams in the American League—Martin approached Wolff at a luncheon being held at Yankee Stadium as part of an Old-Timers' Day celebration. "I just want you to know," said the now-experienced manager, "I've never forgotten those words of advice you gave me. It meant a lot to me." Wolff was touched by the gesture. "So my feelings about Billy Martin," he later admitted, "have always been tinged with a feeling that this guy may have made many mistakes, but he had goodness in his heart."

The show of gratitude was not something that came easily to Billy Martin. Growing up in West Berkeley in the 1940s, his social life revolved around the gangs who hung out in Kenney Park, and his predominant concern in those early days was to avoid getting beaten up by other kids—many of whom would poke fun at his abnormally large nose. "Pinocchio" or "Banana Nose," they would often call him. They no doubt assumed that Martin would slink away because of his small size. (He was four feet eleven inches tall and weighed only ninety-five pounds when he entered high school.) But appearances—at least in the case of young Billy—were deceiving. "They figured they could take advantage of me," he later explained. "This is where they made their mistake. I was stronger than I looked." He had spent hour after hour hitting a punching bag. ("It got to the point," he remembered, "where I could make that bag talk.") And so, he would later say with considerable pride, "I never got whipped."

There is little doubt that Billy got his small size and his fighting spirit from his mother. Jenny Salvini—who stood only four feet eleven inches herself—was one of ten children whose volatility and irreverence were belied by her petite figure. ("I have the best-looking ass in town," she once told her son, "and don't you forget it.") Her parents—immigrants from Italy—had little money but great faith in established traditions, one of which was to arrange for their daughters' marriages. One day in 1917, Jenny's parents told their sixteen-year-old daughter that she would be married later that month to one of the men who rented a room in her parents' house in West Berkeley.

It was not, to say the least, a marriage made in heaven, and three years later Jenny, now with a young son, was divorced and dating Alfred Manuel Martin, a tall man with a small mustache and a wandering eye. Their relationship lasted longer than Jenny's marriage to the boarder, but life took a turn for the worse in 1927 after they got married and Jenny became pregnant with Billy. Al began spending many evenings away from home, and his wife soon learned that a high school girl was wearing her husband's watch. "I went to the school," Jenny later explained, "took the watch off the girl, and beat the hell out of her."

It reflected a perspective that the mother passed on to her younger son—after she had thrown Alfred Manuel Martin out of the house— "Take shit from no one." Those words became Billy Martin's mantra. Never—not even when he was a sixty-year-old manager for the New York Yankees—would he walk away from a fight. (Mickey Mantle once said of his good friend that "he was the only man alive who could hear someone give him the finger.")

Although the second marriage had soured, Jenny named her infant son after his father: Alfred Manuel Martin Jr. It may have been evident on the birth certificate, but it was hardly clear to the young boy as he grew up. He spent much of his time in those early years with his grandmother, who repeatedly called him Bellissimo—meaning "beautiful" in Italian. Others (who did not speak Italian) interpreted the words to mean Billy, and soon enough that was the name by which he was known.

Billy never knew otherwise until that day in seventh grade when the teacher kept asking for Alfred Manuel Martin. When no one answered, the teacher proceeded to call out the names of the other students until Billy was the only one left standing. In response to the teacher's inquiry, the young student said that his name was Billy Martin. The teacher then explained that he was not Billy Martin but Alfred Manuel Martin Jr. The surprised teenager ran home after school and confronted his mother with the obvious question—why had she not told him? "Because," she explained, "I didn't want you to know you had the same name as that jackass."

Jenny had the good fortune to meet another man—Jack Downey—who had a more suitable perspective, and he soon became Jenny's third husband and the father young Billy had never known. Downey was a hard worker who treated the family well, and his effort did not go unappreciated. ("Because of Jack," Martin later said, "we always had a roof over our head and plenty of food, even in the middle of the Depression.") Not that life was always tranquil in the house. Jenny demanded respect from her children (which later included another son and two daughters), and she was not shy about making her feelings known if one of them showed any sign of disobedience. There was the time when Billy's younger brother, Jackie, interrupted Jenny at the dinner table after she had told her children not to "butt in" when she was talking. Jenny's reaction was swift. As Billy remembered, she "punched him on the mouth so hard she made his teeth bleed."

Billy exuded that same combative attitude when he played high school sports. He had talent in basketball and baseball, but he was ultimately kicked off the varsity team in both sports because of fights—in basketball, with a fan who kept calling him "Pinocchio" (and who was subjected after the game, as one Martin friend recalled, to "the quickest barrage of punches I've ever seen"), and in baseball, with an opposing team player who had threatened to "get" Billy after the game (but who was knocked out cold by Martin in the confrontation that ensued in the locker room after the game).

None of those experiences soured Billy on a career in baseball.

To anyone who asked what he would do after high school, he would say that he was going to play baseball with the New York Yankees. It was a bombastic prediction—Billy Martin did not have the kind of talent that might attract the many scouts who scoured the Bay Area for major-league prospects. Still, he did have an abundance of determination, and that quality was duly noted by Red Adams, the trainer for the Oakland Oaks in the Pacific Coast League. He had seen Billy play in high school and had watched him when he worked out at the Oaks' field. Adams relentlessly pestered the team manager—Casey Stengel—to take a look at this young high school graduate.

Stengel finally agreed. On a June day in 1946, Adams brought Martin to the Oaks' field where Stengel could test the young player's skill in fielding grounders at shortstop. At first, the grounders were not very challenging. Martin handled them with ease, and Stengel began hitting the ball harder and harder. Martin fielded them all and finally yelled to the manager, "Is that the best you got?" Stengel pushed as hard as he could, but nothing got through. "That little son of gun," Stengel later told Adams. "I've hit him so many grounders, I think he's trying to wear me out. He doesn't catch them all, but he doesn't back off from any either."

The result was an offer for Billy to play in the Oaks' minor-league team in Idaho Falls. It was a modest start, with Billy hitting only .254 and making sixteen errors in thirty-two games. But there were no fights—only a belief among the Oaks' management that the young player could improve with further seasoning. So, in the spring of 1947, Stengel sent him down to the club's farm team in Phoenix, where young Billy Martin became, as one sportswriter said, "the sensation of the Class C Arizona-Texas League." He led the league with a .392 batting average, hit forty-eight doubles, and drove in a remarkable 174 runs in only 130 games. It was a record that could not be ignored, and Stengel promoted the young player to the Oaks in 1948.

It was the beginning of a close relationship between the two men that would—except for one period of seven years immediately after Martin was traded from the Yankees—survive until Stengel's death in 1975. "That fresh punk," Stengel told reporters when Martin first joined the New York club in 1950, "how I love him." The feeling was reciprocated by Martin, who would always be prepared to do whatever his manager wanted. When Stengel called a clubhouse meeting of the Yankee players in the early 1950s to say that he would give one hundred dollars to any player who would let himself get hit by Harry Byrd, the sidearm-throwing pitcher for the Philadelphia Athletics, Martin earned himself three hundred dollars. And never would the Berkeley native tolerate another teammate ignoring a directive from the crusty manager. Yogi Berra learned about Martin's devotion to Stengel when he called for a pitch in one game that was different from the one Stengel had demanded and the batter hit a home run. Martin ran into the dugout after the inning was over to confront the All-Star catcher and ask why he had "crossed up the old man."

Not surprisingly, Martin emulated much of Stengel's style when he became a manager. Stengel had been a disciple of the legendary John McGraw, who had managed the New York Giants at the turn of the twentieth century during the "dead ball era" when the emphasis was on running, fielding, and strategy. Lessons learned from those days became the guidepost for Stengel in his career as a manager. Like McGraw, he did not always use the same players day-in and day-out. Instead, he platooned them according to a complex set of factors that were never entirely understood by the players but often resulted in left-handed hitters being played more often against right-handed pitchers and right-handed hitters being played more often against left-handed pitchers. There would also be a mix of bunts and steals and other plays to keep the opposing team off balance—all of which was absorbed by Martin. He too would use a mix of platooning, base running and bunts to keep the other team off balance when he assumed managerial reins after his playing days were over. "I never saw opposition managers pitch out more when a guy got on base and do crazy things because they were managing against Billy," said former teammate and longtime broadcaster Tony Kubek. "Billy was Casey's boy, and I think Billy picked up much of that from Stengel."

However much they liked each other, Stengel could not ignore reality when Martin first started playing for him in Oakland in 1948. Martin played second, short, and third, and, while he batted a respectable .277, it was hardly the kind of performance that would justify a promotion to the major leagues. When he received word that the Yankees had hired him to take the helm for the 1949 season, Stengel had to tell the Berkeley native that he would have to remain with the Oakland club. "It wasn't too bad," Martin remembered, "because he told me it wouldn't be long before he called for me."

True to his word, Stengel—impressed with Martin's improved performance at Oakland that year (a .284 average with thirteen home runs and ninety-one runs-batted-in)—had the Yankees buy his contract shortly after the 1949 season was completed. As he had predicted, Billy Martin, the brash kid from West Berkeley, was going to play for the New York Yankees.

The promotion was accompanied by considerable fanfare in the press (one sportswriter noting that "Martin is a scamper kid with a generous nose and rather large feet"). The young rookie lived up to his billing. From the first days of spring training in 1950, he displayed the kind of spirit that would be the hallmark of his playing and managerial career. When the Yankees played an exhibition game against the Dodgers, Martin began screaming at Jackie Robinson (who had won the National League's Most Valuable Player award in 1949), "You big busher. It's a good thing you're not in my league. I'd have your job in a week." And when longtime Yankee coach Frank Crosetti held a drill to show infielders how to execute a doubleplay, Martin was quick to say, "No, no, that's not the way you do it, Cro." But nowhere was that spirit more evident than in Martin's approach to Joe DiMaggio, the team's All-Star center fielder.

Other players—even those who had known DiMaggio for years— found him to be cold and aloof, a man who could sit for hours in the locker room with a cigarette while he sipped a cup of coffee or nursed a beer and said very little to those around him. (Tommy Henrich, who played next to DiMaggio in right field for eleven seasons, said that the San Francisco native "was a loner to us on the team as much as he was a loner to the general public.") The other players were friendly but respectful when DiMaggio walked into the clubhouse, invariably dressed in an expensive suit with a white dress shirt and silk tie, and rarely would anyone have the confidence to initiate a conversation with the Yankee star. Martin disregarded that established etiquette, using informality when addressing DiMaggio ("Hi, Dago"), playfully emulating the veteran player's peculiar dressing habits in the locker room (taking off his pants first while still wearing his shirt and tie), and even pulling pranks on the solemn center fielder (including the time he had DiMaggio sign a ball with a pen that squirted blue ink all over DiMaggio's white dress shirt—which drew an angry look from Joe until Billy explained that it was invisible ink that would soon disappear).

Martin's confidence in the locker room was matched by his exuberance on the field, especially after the first game of his big-league career. The Yankees were losing 9–0 to the Red Sox at Fenway Park in Boston. The game appeared to be a lost cause when Stengel sent Martin into the field in the sixth inning. In his first major-league at bat in the eighth inning, Martin hit a double off the left-field wall to drive in a run. DiMaggio followed with a home run, and other Yankees continued to bombard the Red Sox pitchers until Martin came up for a second time in the inning with the bases loaded. He proceeded to hit a single to drive in two more runs and, by the time it was over, the Yankees had won the game by a score of 15–10. The sportswriters crowded around DiMaggio's locker after the game, but he pointed to Billy at the locker next to his and said, "What about that kid? He's the one you should be talking to."

Although he had set a new record by getting two hits in his first two major-league at bats in the same inning, Martin did not see much action afterward. Stengel continued to use Jerry Coleman at second base, and Martin was forced to sit next to the manager on the bench most days. Stengel enjoyed the company of the young player, but it was not enough—in part because the Yankees had Snuffy Stirnweiss, a veteran second baseman who had enjoyed some stellar years with the team. Stengel informed Martin one day in May that he was being sent to the Yankee farm team in Kansas City to bring the club down to the required roster of twenty-five players. "You'll be back in about thirty days," Stengel promised, "and when you come back, you'll stay here." Martin was not happy, and Stengel encouraged him to express his frustration to George Weiss, the Yankee general manager.

A rotund man of medium height and strong convictions, Weiss was a humorless guardian of the club's prerogatives. He was not receptive to the young player's complaint. "You're going to go down there, son," Weiss responded angrily after Martin expressed his opposition to being sent to Kansas City. "You've got to learn." Martin started to cry and, as he left the office, began shouting at the somber man behind the desk. "You'll be sorry," Martin said. "I'll show you."

The Yankees eventually sold Stirnweiss' contract to the St. Louis Browns, and Martin returned to the club in June. But the twenty-six-year-old Coleman was having a good year at the plate and was widely recognized as one of the smoothest-fielding second basemen in the American League. So Martin was forced again to spend most of his time on the bench with Stengel. Still, Billy was excited just to be there and continued to be one of the team's principal voices during the games, always shouting encouragement for his teammates or throwing barbs at the opposing team's players.

Although he played in only thirty-four games that first season, the Yankees gave Billy a full cut on his World Series share, which he used to have an operation to reduce the size of his nose and to marry Lois Berndt, a girl he had known at Berkeley High School. It was, so Martin hoped, the beginning of a new life as a major-league ballplayer. And then he got his draft notice. The Korean War was raging and the army needed soldiers. Martin had other goals. He wanted to be with the Yankees when they broke for spring training in February. He began complaining to the army shortly after he got to Fort Ord in California that he was trying to support his stepfather (who had suffered a heart attack) and mother as well as two brothers, a sister, and his wife's family—all on a private's salary. In due course the army released him on hardship grounds, and by March he was with the Yankees in Florida.

However much he enjoyed being with the team, 1951 proved to be a frustrating year for Martin. Jerry Coleman was still available, and the Yankees had a new rookie—Gil McDougald—who had a talent for playing second as well as third. The result was not a good one for Billy. He eventually played in only fifty-one games, had no home runs, and drove in only two runs—six fewer than he had driven in the year before. In retrospect, the only noteworthy event for Martin in 1951 was meeting Mickey Mantle.

Martin had already read about the power exploits of the nineteen-year-old rookie from Commerce, Oklahoma. When he saw him at the spring training camp, Martin approached Mickey and simply said, "Hi, Pardner." A shy teenager who had difficulty conversing with strangers, the Oklahoma native held out his hand and mumbled, "Mantle." Thus began a friendship that would last the rest of their lives. The two of them began to spend time together before the games (often having water-pistol fights), after the games (often quizzing long-time clubhouse manager Pete Sheehy about his days with Babe Ruth and Lou Gehrig), going out to dinner after the games, and, after Mantle got married in December 1951, spending summer evenings at each other's rooms in the Concourse Plaza Hotel in their bathing suits (because the hotel had no air-conditioning). It was a friendship that Mantle cherished, especially in those first days with the Yankees, and later he would say that "my best pal on the Yankees during my earlier years with the club was Billy Martin."

The friendship was no less important to Martin in those early days, especially when Lois sent him divorce papers in the fall of 1952 shortly after their daughter Kelly was born. Martin was not one to easily absorb emotional setbacks, and Lois' decision to leave him was no exception. He moved to Kansas City for the winter, but he spent much of his time on the phone with his wife, begging her to return. Nothing had changed by the spring of 1953 when he was rooming with Mantle on the road, and the breaking point came when Martin finally realized that Lois was not going to change her mind. As Mantle remembered, Billy "literally tore" their hotel room apart. Mantle did what he could to console his roommate, and, as Martin later confessed, "Only my friendship with Mickey saved me from going over the edge."

There was, however, a cost to both of them for that close friendship: alcohol. As a teenager, Martin had vowed never to drink until he was twenty-one, and he was forced to break that promise only because of a spiking wound he suffered while playing for the Oaks in 1948. Anxious to stitch up the wound, the club physician asked someone to fetch some bourbon. Martin drank the alcohol and watched while four players held him down and the doctor completed the procedure.

Ironically, Mantle too had never had anything to drink while growing up in Oklahoma. But Billy and New York's nightlife changed all that, and by 1953 Mantle and his good friend began to frequent bars and restaurants, where they could indulge their new habit. At first, it was simply fun. "If you could drink all night, get a girl, get up the next day, and hit a home run," Mantle remembered, "you passed the test." The drinking expanded when Billy came to Commerce to spend the winter with Mantle and his wife after the 1953 season. Both players were now making more money than they had ever anticipated, and, unlike most other players, neither felt the need to secure an off-season job. They would get up in the morning, tell Mickey's wife, Merlyn, that they were going hunting or fishing, and wind up in a bar by noon. It was a lifestyle that would prove to be their undoing in later years, but, at the time, it seemed like harmless pleasure to both of them.

In the meantime, Martin's star began to rise on the playing field. By 1952, Jerry Coleman had been called back to duty by the marines, McDougald was playing most of the games at third, and Martin had settled into playing second base. Neither his play nor his bat reflected any exceptional talent, but his competitive spirit was extraordinary. ("Billy wasn't pretty to watch," said Mantle, "but he would always find a way to beat you.") And, as before, he was always ready to accept any challenge from opposing players. So Martin did not hesitate when Jimmy Piersall, the emotionally troubled shortstop for the Red Sox, persisted in baiting Martin throughout the spring and then ridiculed the Yankee second baseman's still enormous nose during a warm-up before a game at Fenway Park. ("Hey, Pinocchio," Piersall yelled, "what's with the schnoz?") Martin responded by saying, "Let's go." The two men threw down their gloves and raced to the tunnel underneath the stands that joined the clubhouses for the Red Sox and the opposing team. They were followed by a retinue of players and coaches from both teams who were anxious to stop the fight, but the two protagonists arrived first. Piersall threw a punch to the side of Martin's head, but the Berkeley native quickly brought Piersall to his knees with two rapid punches to the stomach. Piersall was later placed in a mental institution because of continuing emotional struggles, all of which made Martin feel "terrible" about the altercation.

Still, Stengel delighted in Martin's aggressive attitude. "It should wake my other tigers up," he told a sportswriter. But some of his teammates sometimes bridled at Martin's take-no-prisoners approach to any mistakes on the field. Moose Skowron, who joined the Yankees as a first baseman in 1954, remembered his first experience with Martin. He let a throw to first base sail over his head for an error. Martin watched the play in disbelief and then threw his glove up in the air as an expression of his frustration. "I went after him in the dugout," said Skowron, and a fight would have ensued if Mantle had not intervened to say, "Enough is enough." But Skowron yelled a final warning to the Yankee second baseman: "Don't show me up on the field."

Whatever their individual experiences, Martin's teammates nonetheless understood his value to the team. He was a spark plug who was ever vigilant to do what he could to help the team succeed. The more critical the situation, the more focused he became. "He was always there for the big play," remembered Yankee third baseman Andy Carey.

Nowhere was that perspective more evident than in the seventh game of the 1952 World Series at Ebbets Field. The Yankees were leading that pivotal contest 4–2 when the Dodgers loaded the bases in the seventh inning. Stengel, following instincts that remained inscrutable to outside observers, allowed the left-handed Bob Kuzava to remain on the mound to pitch to the right-handed Jackie Robinson with two out. Kuzava threw a sharp curve that resulted in a high pop-up between the pitcher's mound and first base. Kuzava kept calling for first baseman Joe Collins to catch the ball, but it soon became clear that Collins had lost the ball in the sun. As the ball started its descent, Kuzava watched in horror as Dodger players were running around the bases—meaning that the score would be 5–4 if the ball were allowed to drop. And then, out of nowhere, Martin raced in from second base and caught the ball right before it reached the ground. The play ended the inning and proved to be the turning point in the Yankees' ultimate victory.

Martin rose to the occasion again in the 1953 World Series, getting a record twelve hits in the six-game contest, which included a hit that drove in the winning run in the ninth inning of the sixth game. "The Yankees," said one sportswriter in describing the scene after that hit, "bounded screaming from the dugout and mobbed the big-beaked kid who, more than anyone else, brought them the title and some $8,200 apiece in the lushest classic of all time." The achievement brought Martin the coveted Babe Ruth award as the series' Most Valuable Player and a baby-blue Cadillac from his friends in Berkeley.

None of those accomplishments could prevent the army from recalling Martin to active service, and he was forced to spend the entire 1954 season in uniform. For Stengel, Martin's absence left a void that was difficult to fill. "Martin made himself the best second baseman in our league," he told one sportswriter. "I know that some people will fight me on that statement. They don't like Billy because he is so cocky. Well," Stengel continued, "what's wrong with being full of scrap, eager to take advantage of every opportunity?" Not surprisingly, the Yankee manager was delighted when Martin was discharged by the army and finally able to join the team for the pennant drive in September 1955. "Martin should help us, whether at short, or at second, or even just sitting on the bench," he told *The Sporting News*. "He will help the spirit of this club."

For his part, Martin was eager to fulfill Stengel's expectations—not only for the sake of the club but for his as well. He had lost virtually all his money and most of his material possessions, including that baby-blue Cadillac. "I don't know how hungry you guys are," he told his teammates shortly after rejoining the club, "but I'm hungry. I need the money. I want to win this pennant real bad." Inspired by their returning teammate—who hit .300 for the month (the only time in his career that he would reach that magic number)—the Yankees won the pennant and, as a reflection of their gratitude, voted Martin a full series share despite his absence for most of the season.

Martin should have had much to look forward to in 1956. But clouds were already beginning to form around his future as a Yankee. The club had a minor-league player—Bobby Richardson—who not only had considerable promise as a second baseman but, as a devout and nondrinking Christian, had more appeal to George Weiss than the volatile Martin. Although he had a respectable year in the field and at the plate in 1956 (with nine home runs and a .264 batting average), Martin understood that much of his vulnerability reflected Richardson's availability, and the California veteran would periodically tease the newcomer's wife about her husband's future, saying, "I've written to the draft board, and I'm sure he's going to be drafted pretty soon."

Billy Martin, wearing the number 1 on the back of his uniform and with his mind obviously focused only on the game, is leaning over, his hands on his knees, waiting for Don Larsen's first pitch in the top of the fourth inning of the fifth game of the 1956 World Series. Larsen hurls a slider to Junior Gilliam, and the Dodger second baseman sends a grounder to Martin's left. It is nothing compared to the grounders Stengel hit to him on that tryout many years ago in the Oaks' park, and Martin fields the ball easily for the first out.

Pee Wee Reese steps into the batter's box, and Larsen throws him a low slider. The Dodger shortstop tries to check his swing, but the bat makes contact with the ball and sends another slow grounder toward Martin. The Yankee second baseman fields this one with ease as well, and there are now two outs.

After falling behind Duke Snider with two balls, Larsen—eager to get a strike—throws a "mediocre" fastball that, as Larsen later recalled, must have looked to Snider like "a beautiful present on Christmas day." Snider swings and, from the crack of the bat, Yankee fans know it can be trouble. The ball flies in a high arc toward the upper deck in right field. Radio announcer Bob Neal's voice rises with excitement as he describes the ball being hit "deep into right field. It is going in the upper deck . . . foul." It was, however, extremely close. As first-base umpire Ed Runge later said, the ball was foul only "by six inches."

Larsen is now feeling vulnerable and wondering whether he can survive the inning. "I had dodged a bullet," he later said, "but I knew Duke would now be even more determined to beat me." But it was not to be. After a called strike and two foul balls, Larsen slips a slider past Snider for a called third strike.

As Larsen walks off the mound to the security of the Yankee dugout, Neal is telling his listening audience that "the first twelve Dodgers to face Don Larsen have been retired in order."

Bottom of the Fourth:
Duke Snider

As he trots out to the vast expanse of center field in the bottom of the fourth inning, Duke Snider can no doubt remember his first visit to Yankee Stadium as a player. It was the first game of the 1949 World Series, and he was twenty-three years old. He had just completed his first full season with the Dodgers, but that experience had not prepared him for the emotions of that first encounter. Perhaps it was the aura of the stadium's history—which was well-known to him from listening to baseball games on the radio as a boy. Or perhaps it was seeing the preserved lockers of Babe Ruth and Lou Gehrig in the clubhouse—especially because he had always regarded Gehrig as his favorite player.

Whatever the reason, Snider's knees "felt like rubber" when he was introduced over the public address system in that first World Series game and had to run out to the third-base line to stand with his teammates. But all of that anxiety disappeared when the late-afternoon sun threw its rays directly into center field in the middle of the game, and, not having any sunglasses, he was forced to ask Joe DiMaggio if he could borrow his. And then, as he watched the play from center field with the famous Yankee center fielder's lenses, he could not help but say to himself, "I've come a long way."

Indeed he had. Not that his father would have been surprised. Ward Snider, a semipro baseball player himself, had high hopes for his only child. That perspective was epitomized by the nickname Ward gave his son. When he came home from kindergarten one day, five-year-old Edwin Donald Snider heard his father say, "Here comes His Majesty, the Duke." It may have been a playful gesture, but it was the name his father would always use and by which the young boy became known as he progressed through school—his mother, Florence, being the only exception, continuing to call him Edwin.

Home in those early days was a small apartment behind a grocery store in Boyle Heights, a working-class section of Los Angeles. Ward had a job with Goodyear Tire & Rubber Company, and he would come home from work with hands covered by blisters from the hot molding equipment. But none of that would prevent him from taking his young son outside in the early evening and on the weekends to teach him the fundamentals of baseball. Although Duke was right-handed, Ward made his son learn to swing a bat left-handed. First base was a few steps closer, the father explained, if you batted left-handed. And, he added, most parks were better suited for left-handed hitters, with shorter distances to the fences in right field.

Duke could not have had any regrets about his father's instruction— by the time he matured as a player, few could hit a baseball as well as Duke Snider. "He could swing harder than anybody," recalled Gene Mauch, one of his high school friends (and later a big-league player and manager himself). "And he had such a graceful swing. He looked better striking out than any of us did hitting a triple."

To be sure, the young athlete had a natural affinity for the game. But his skill at the plate was also a product of incessant practice. His parents insisted that he fulfill certain obligations—drying the dishes after dinner, mowing the lawn, and taking care of other household chores— but decided that he need not get a job. Instead, Duke could spend his spare time practicing athletics. That was no small sacrifice for the Sniders, because money was always tight (and would lead his mother to do whatever she could to preserve what they had—such as stuffing card-board in her son's sneakers to make them last longer).

For his part, young Duke made the most of his parents' generosity. "While lots of other kids in the neighborhood spent their spare time at the beach," he remembered, "I was getting my suntan playing softball." The focus on softball was not accidental. There was no Little League in his community and thus no opportunity to play baseball until the local playground organized a baseball league when he was ten years old. Most of those early summers (even after the creation of the playground's baseball league) were spent on the softball field, and Duke was able to lead his team to three championships.

Duke had no difficulty in making the transition to baseball when he entered high school in 1942. Reflecting on his high school career in sports many years later, he would say, "I never knew what failure was." He could not only hit and play center field but could pitch as well (hurling a no-hitter with fifteen strikeouts against Beverly Hills High School in his first game). Duke had a similar proficiency in playing football and basketball. Pete Rozelle, Snider's high school classmate and later the commissioner of the National Football League, said that "the most amazing football game" he had ever seen—which included more than thirty years of watching professional teams—was the high school game in which a young tailback named Duke Snider threw a sixty-three-yard pass in the closing seconds to beat a rival team.

Summers were now spent with much older players on the Monte-bello Merchants, a local semipro baseball team. "I wasn't excelling," Snider remembered, "but I was holding my own." Recognition of that talent no doubt led the manager to give Duke a chance to play third base, but the change in positions did not suit the young player. "I wasn't so hot," Snider later recalled. "The balls came down the line too fast." He soon returned to the security of the outfield, and even there he was slow to field ground balls that made it through the infield. (When Dodger teammate Pee Wee Reese complained to him many years later about that shortcoming, Duke traced the problem back to those days in high school. "I had been an infielder," he explained, "and I hated those ground balls. And I still hate them.")

That deficiency in fielding ground balls was of no moment to Bill

Schliebaum, the Compton High School baseball coach. After discussing the matter with Duke, he responded to a letter he had received in June 1943 from Branch Rickey, the new general manager for the Brooklyn Dodgers. The letter was identical to ones that Rickey had sent to high school coaches throughout the country in search of talent. For his part, Schliebaum was delighted to tell Mr. Rickey about "Edwin Duke Snider." Schliebaum explained that the young athlete "is definitely not interested in going to college and wishes only to make a success of baseball." Although Duke was only a sixteen-year-old junior at the time, Schliebaum expressed confidence that his young protégé would succeed as a professional player. Duke Snider, he told Rickey, "is one of the finest baseball prospects I have ever seen."

Rickey was impressed, and in September, Snider received an invitation from Brooklyn scout Tom Downey to attend a tryout in Long Beach, California. Downey liked what he saw, and shortly after Duke graduated from high school in February 1944, Downey showed up at the Snider apartment with a typewriter. When the high school graduate asked about the typewriter, Downey had a simple response: "You're going to sign today." Downey offered the teenager a $1,000 bonus and a $200 monthly salary or a $750 bonus and a $250 salary. Ward was with the navy in the Pacific Theater somewhere, and Florence was forced to make the decision with her seventeen-year-old son. "It didn't take long to figure out that one," Snider later remembered. And so he signed a contract for the higher salary and made plans to travel to the Dodgers' spring training camp in Bear Mountain, New York, near the West Point Military Academy (because wartime travel restrictions foreclosed the use of Florida).

Although scouts from the Cincinnati Reds and St. Louis Cardinals had also pursued Snider, they were not as quick to offer a contract, all of which was to the young athlete's liking. Duke had been a Dodger fan for several years and wanted nothing more than to play with the Brooklyn team. Ironically, his love for the Dodgers had emerged from the team's failure to win the 1941 World Series against the Yankees. Duke had already been attracted to the Dodgers because of Pete Reiser, the team's twenty-two-year-old center fielder, and Pee Wee Reese, the team's twenty-three-year-old shortstop. It was not only their accomplishments that appealed to the high school hopeful. "The way they played baseball was very exciting to me," he later explained.

In the fourth game of that 1941 series, the Dodgers were one out away from winning the game by a score of 4–3 when catcher Mickey Owen let a third strike against Yankee outfielder Tommy Henrich get by him. Henrich made it to first base, and the next Yankee batters exploded for hits that resulted in more Yankee runs and another Dodger loss. "It broke my heart," Duke later said, "when they got beat the way they did."

There was no heartache, however, when Duke made it to the Dodgers' spring training camp in the spring of 1944—only excitement. The young athlete arrived in time to see snow for the first time in his life and to experience the joy of playing with major-league players (getting his first hit off of a Yankee pitcher in an exhibition game). But he was not yet ready for the big leagues, and, when the season began, Rickey dispatched him to the team's Class B farm club in Newport News, Virginia.

Living in the South was a new cultural experience for the California native. He quickly learned about the different social mores of the region when he got on a city bus for the first time. "I put my money in the little slot," he remembered. "I walk to the back of the bus, and I sit down." It was not something that endeared him to the other people on the bus. "I got dirty looks from some of the black people," Duke remembered. "I got dirty looks from some of the white people." Perplexed at first, he looked up and saw the sign that said "colored section." And that was the last time he sat in the back of the bus in the South.

Whatever discomfort he felt on the bus, it had no impact on Duke's performance on the field. The seventeen-year-old prospect dominated the league, hitting .293 with a league-leading nine home runs (which was unusually low because the league relied on re-covered balls that had little bounce). He returned to California that September with heightened expectations about his professional baseball career but soon learned that any advancement would have to be deferred as long as the war continued. He received the draft notice shortly after his eighteenth birthday. Instead of making plans for the next baseball season, he found himself on a navy tender that serviced submarines in the Pacific.

To his good fortune, he never saw combat, spending most of his time making repairs to submarines, stocking them up for the next tour of duty, and washing dishes in the mess hall. But he was not complaining. As he later said, "My number one priority during the war was to survive it."

His discharge from the navy finally came in June 1946, and the Dodgers invited him to another tryout camp in Long Beach that was being supervised by the general manager's son, Branch Rickey Jr. Duke had been able to play some baseball when stationed in Guam and other distant points, and his skills had not diminished during his nineteen-month tour of duty. The younger Rickey therefore recommended that Duke play with the Dodgers' Fort Worth team in the Texas league, an assignment that would be a promotion and bring him that much closer to playing in the big leagues.

Although now six feet tall and weighing almost two hundred pounds (with short dark hair that would soon turn prematurely gray), Duke found the early days difficult, and the manager was forced to keep him on the bench for many games. As Duke later said of that time with the Fort Worth team, "Success did not come quickly for me." But the manager finally agreed to give the young player a chance to play in a series in Houston, and Duke responded with two home runs and a new hitting streak. By the end of July, Branch Rickey decided to travel to Fort Worth to check out Duke's progress, and Snider responded by hitting a 430-foot home run into the wind and over a twenty-foot fence. ("Judas Priest!" Rickey exclaimed when he saw the blast.) Duke's hitting remained steady through the play-offs (with seven home runs), and, by the winter of 1947, he received an invitation to join the Dodgers' spring training camp in Havana.

Even before the season began, the twenty-year-old rookie was being touted as a possible replacement for Reiser—who had an incurable (and injury-causing) propensity to run into fences while chasing fly balls. Rickey himself had earlier reported that Snider had "steel springs in his legs and dynamite in his bat." That comment was echoed in the press, with one sportswriter saying that Snider is "a straightaway left-handed hitter who would be a valuable asset if he could learn to pull a ball and hit the right-field fence at Ebbets Field." Another sportswriter suggested that the California prospect could "be the player who will win the pennant for the Dodgers." It was all pretty heady stuff for someone who had never played a single major-league game.

Duke Snider was not the only rookie attracting the attention of sportswriters in that spring training camp. Snider, for one, was not surprised by the Dodgers' decision to bring Jackie Robinson up to the parent club. He had seen Robinson in action at Pasadena Junior College and UCLA, and, as Snider later recalled, "I marveled at the way he could play baseball." And so he had no difficulty rebuffing Dodger right fielder Dixie Walker's request to sign a petition protesting the inclusion of Robinson on the club. "This guy is an idol of mine," Duke told his new teammate. "I'm not gonna sign that thing."

The discord over Robinson's presence was a momentary distraction for the twenty-year-old rookie from Boyle Heights. Duke found that first postwar spring training to be exhilarating—attending Branch Rickey's lectures on the "Dodger way" to play the game, taking drills on sliding, bunting and other fundamentals, and, realizing, when he put on that white uniform with the blue lettering, that it had a special meaning for him—especially after he became the club's regular center fielder in 1949. "I think the happiest moment in my baseball career," he later told one interviewer, "was when I put the Brooklyn Dodger uniform on and knew that I belonged in that uniform." When clubhouse manager John Griffin asked him at the beginning of the 1947 season which number he wanted, Duke did not have to think about a response. He wanted number 4—the same number that Lou Gehrig had worn. Griffin was reluctant at first, saying that no one had worn that number since the departure of Dolph Camilli, a popular first baseman who had been traded to the Giants in 1943. But Duke was not to be turned aside, and Griffin finally yielded, saying only, "Don't embarrass that number."

Griffin did not have to worry. The player who wore that number 4 over the next fifteen years would establish a record that warranted induction into baseball's National Hall of Fame and that helped to bring many pennants and fans to Ebbets Field. Not that Griffin could have known that in 1947. Snider's first days on the club were hardly the stuff of legend. He did get a pinch-hit single in the first game of the season.

But that success was short-lived, and he spent the next few weeks in a struggle to master big-league pitching. "I was a free swinger," he later said about those first days on the club. "If the ball looked halfway decent, I took a cut at it." Not surprisingly, he found himself spending more time sitting on the bench than playing in the field.

Snider did not take his lack of success well. "Duke was temperamental when he first came up," said Spider Jorgensen, the Dodgers' rookie third baseman in 1947. "He sulked a lot, both when he wasn't hitting and when he wasn't playing." Duke himself was very conscious of his dark moods and attributed much of it to the high praise he had received for so long. "I was always reading and hearing about how great I was destined to be," he later explained, "how I had the potential to become one of the greatest baseball players of all time. That puts a lot of extra pressure on an athlete, and what pressure wasn't already on me I managed to add myself."

Whatever the explanation, Duke was not yet ready for the big leagues. Midway through the season, he and Gil Hodges—another rookie initially selected to be the team's third-string catcher—were summoned to a meeting with Branch Rickey. "You two young men," the general manager explained, "are the Dodgers' power combination of the future. In about three years from now, you two guys are going to be leading the team in home runs." But, he added, they each needed more work to reach that plateau. Rickey said that they should not be disappointed with the decision to send both of them back to the minor leagues, where they could play with greater regularity and hopefully refine their skills. "I want you two gentlemen to be patient," Rickey advised them, "and to work hard to improve yourselves, because you both have a bright future ahead of you."

Duke was sent to the club's farm team in St. Paul, Minnesota, where he hit a very respectable .316. The Dodgers called him back to the parent club in September, but he saw little action and wound up hitting a meager .241 with only eighty-three plate appearances for the entire season. His prolonged absence made him ineligible to play in the World Series against the Yankees, and so he had to watch the series from the stands. Still, he was happy to be a member of the team—and excited for what awaited him when he returned home.

Her name was Beverly Null, a vivacious brunette whom Duke remembered as "a cute little girl" who "sat near the front of the class" in high school. He was too shy to ask her out for a date himself and decided instead to dispatch a friend to make the initial inquiry. When his friend communicated an affirmative response, Duke and Bev began spending considerable time together until Duke graduated. The fire still burned bright, however, and they stayed in touch after he began his baseball career. They renewed the relationship when Duke was stationed in San Diego shortly before his discharge from the navy. They were married in California a few weeks after the World Series ended in 1947.

Thus began a union that would survive the frequent separations required by Duke's life in baseball. Many years later—long after he had retired—their devotion to each other was still evident to those who saw them together. "Bev is definitely an influence in his life," said Nancy Gollnick, the director of the Dodger fantasy camp in Vero Beach, Florida, and someone who had occasion to see the two of them frequently beginning in 1995. "It's a great love. You can see that in everything." Duke himself would later tell me that, after fifty-nine years of marriage, Bev is a "super wife. A super mother. A great companion. And just an ideal person for being the wife of a major-league ballplayer."

That psychological support was no doubt important to Duke during the 1948 spring training camp in the Dominican Republic. The young player was still swinging at bad pitches. Eager to channel Snider's raw talent into a productive performance, Rickey traveled with Snider back to the Dodger camp at Vero Beach and initiated a program of instruction that would hopefully help the young outfielder identify the strike zone. "Mr. Rickey made me his personal project," said Snider. Each day Duke would stand at the plate with a bat in his hand and a mechanical device by his side and be asked to say whether a pitched ball was inside or outside the strike zone (without taking a swing). It was a tedious but critical exercise, and years later Snider would say that Branch Rickey "taught me an awful lot about how to hit."

The instruction produced immediate benefits at the beginning of the season—including two home runs in a game against the Philadelphia

Phillies. But Duke soon fell into a hitting slump, flailing away at bad pitches, and the decision was made to send him to the Montreal Royals farm team. "All you need, kid," said manager Leo Durocher, "is a little more experience." Rickey was more specific. "Show me some big numbers up there, son," the general manager told the departing player. "Make me bring you back."

Snider took Rickey's message to heart, and by the middle of the season he had blasted seventeen home runs and driven in seventy-seven runs. And so, when Rickey made a personal visit to Montreal in July, Snider could not help but ask the obvious question. "Mr. Rickey," he said, "don't you think seventy-seven RBIs in seventy-seven games is enough to bring me back?" The general manager did not have any trouble answering that question—especially because Pete Reiser's injuries precluded him from playing with any regularity. "Pack your bags and catch the next plane to New York," Rickey told a relieved Duke Snider. "Tomorrow you're going to play center field for the Brooklyn Dodgers."

Snider displayed a new confidence at the plate in the Brooklyn uniform. He had fewer strikeouts and—given the limited time he was with the club—a relatively high number of extra-base hits (including six triples and five home runs). That performance was enough to keep Duke in the lineup for 1949, and he responded by batting .292, hitting twenty-three home runs, and driving in ninety-two runs—which included the winning run in the final game of the season against the Phillies to enable the Dodgers to clinch the pennant. His contribution to the Dodgers' success did not go unnoticed in the press, with one sportswriter saying that Snider "can run like an antelope, throw with the best of them, and hit with real power."

Snider's satisfaction with his performance that last day of the season evaporated after the World Series began. Instead of plaudits for more winning hits, he felt only the frustration of dramatic failure. As Rickey had predicted, he and Hodges (who was now playing first base) had led the team in home runs, but the boy from Boyle Heights could not hit a single one during the five-game series. And more than that, he tied a series record (initially established by the great Rogers Hornsby) with eight strikeouts. "I was very disappointed with myself because I was trying too hard and wasn't myself," he later explained. "I hadn't learned to relax in a real pressure situation like that."

The folks back home in Compton saw it differently, and they gave the returning player a parade and a dinner replete with testimonials. The young athlete was embarrassed by the attention—especially in light of his poor showing—and, when given the chance to say a few words, he apologized. "I tried to be somebody that I wasn't," he told the crowd. "If I ever get in the World Series again, I'm going to make it up to you."

And try he did to get the Dodgers into the World Series in 1950. He batted .321, led the league in hits with 199 (which included thirty-one home runs), and drove in 107 runs. The high point of the season was the second game of a Memorial Day doubleheader against the Philadelphia Phillies at Ebbets Field. Duke connected for three home runs in his first three at bats and then missed getting a fourth home run—and thus tying the modern-day record set by Lou Gehrig—when he hit the top of the wall on his next at bat. (It was, he later recalled, "the hardest ball I hit all day.")

The joy of that accomplishment was almost—but not quite—eclipsed by another hit that Snider got on the last day of the season in another game against the Phillies at Ebbets Field. With both teams tied for first, a victory meant the pennant. Utility outfielder Cal Abrams was on second base when Snider stepped into the batter's box to face Robin Roberts—the Phillies' premier pitcher—with the score tied 1–1. Stan Lopata, the Phillies catcher, gave the sign for Roberts to try to pick Abrams off second, but Roberts missed the sign and threw the pitch to home plate. Snider then hit a single past second base that, under other circumstances, should have been enough to bring Abrams home with the winning run—and a Dodger pennant. But Phillies' center fielder Richie Ashburn had seen the pickoff sign and had moved in closer to second in the event the pickoff throw went in the outfield. It was a fortuitous move for the Phillies—Ashburn fielded Snider's hit cleanly and, because of his proximity to home plate, was able to get the ball to Lopata in plenty of time to nail Abrams, who had made the mistake of rounding third and racing toward home.

The next season proved to be another exasperating experience when the Dodgers lost the third play-off game to the Giants on Bobby Thomson's ninth-inning home run. Snider was in center field when he saw the ball soaring toward the Polo Grounds' short left-field stands and began running toward those stands in the event the ball bounced off the wall and got by Dodger left fielder Andy Pafko. Over in the Giant bullpen near left field, pitcher Jim Hearn heard the roar of the crowd as Thomson's ball landed in the stands and turned around, only to see "Duke Snider on his knees in center, pounding his glove on the grass." Snider was indeed gripped by despair. "When I saw that ball go into the stands," he later said, "I saw dollar signs flying away."

The money was the least of it. He had enjoyed a respectable year at the plate, with twenty-nine home runs and 101 runs driven in. But in Snider's view, it was not enough. "I felt I had let the club down," he later told a sportswriter, because of his failure to get a hit that could have turned the play-off game around. He went to owner Walter O'Malley after the game, saying that "my spirit is down to my ankles" and that he would not blame O'Malley if he decided to trade him. The offer was not one O'Malley wanted to accept. "We plan to have you around for a long time," he told the frustrated center fielder. (In the meantime, Snider kept a dinner date with his parents after the game but, depressed with the afternoon's outcome, had difficulty in maintaining a conversation—prompting his mother to finally ask, "What's the matter?")

However disappointed he may have been by the 1951 play-off series, Snider was satisfied with the life that he and Bev had created for themselves. The family—which now included a two-year-old boy named Kevin and would soon expand to three more children—lived in a house in the Bay Ridge section of Brooklyn during the baseball season. The experience was made that much more enjoyable by the presence of several other Dodger families. They would play bridge together, have barbecues together, and even commute together to games at Ebbets Field or the Polo Grounds.

The camaraderie that Snider shared with many of his teammates did not extend to Carl Furillo. The two men played side by side for almost fourteen years, with Snider in center and Furillo in right, and they spent considerable time practicing with each other in the outfield to make sure that they did not collide in pursuit of a fly ball. "We never had any problems with a ball hit between us," Snider later said. "Never ran into each other." For his part, Furillo similarly recalled that "Snider and I got along good" and that "we played the outfield beautiful together." But Snider would rarely see Furillo in social situations outside the park. For his part, Furillo regarded Snider as "a prince" and "a funny duck" who was "always crying" if he had to face a left-handed pitcher (who was usually more difficult to hit than a right-handed pitcher) or if "he wasn't hitting the ball and was in a slump."

Furillo was not the only one to notice Snider's aversion to left-handed pitchers or his propensity to feel sorry for himself in the face of frustration at the plate. Dodger pitcher Rex Barney, for one, agreed that Duke "was a magnificent ballplayer" but that he was also "a pain in the ass and a crybaby" who would come into the clubhouse "pouting" if he did not do well. "If he had a bad day," said Reese, who was one of Duke's closest friends on the team, "he didn't like it. And he couldn't take it. And we would say, 'Okay, Duke. Who took your candy today?'" Snider himself acknowledged that he had difficulty dealing with his frustrations. "My problem was that I had excelled in athletics all my life," he later explained, "and that I really didn't know what adversity was until I came to the Dodgers. I had to learn that every day wasn't a bed of roses, and that took some time. I would sulk. I'd have a pity party for myself. I admit it."

Snider's willingness to feel sorry for himself sometimes affected his play. On one occasion he stopped running to first base after hitting a ground ball to the infield because he assumed it would result in his being thrown out. When he returned to the dugout, Jackie Robinson pulled him aside and said, "Duke. Home to first base. That's ninety feet. Not seventy-five." Another person who tried to change Snider's attitude was perhaps the most important—Charlie Dressen.

The relationship between the two men was not a pleasant one when Dressen first became the Brooklyn manager in 1951. Snider resented Dressen's large ego, and the new manager believed that his star center fielder was too temperamental. Relations did not improve when Dressen called a club meeting before one game to complain about the players' spending more than their allotment for food on the road and, as one example, cited one player's additional charge of seventy-five cents for a dish of creamed cauliflower at a Philadelphia hotel the previous night. As Dressen droned on, Snider—anxious to get on the field to warm up for the game—interrupted the manager's lecture, saying, "Cripes, Charlie, what the hell is the big deal? If it's so important, take it out of my allowance for last night."

The breaking point came in a game against the Giants in July 1952. Snider was on second base when the Dodger batter drove a single into right field—a situation that should have enabled Snider to score easily. Instead, as one sportswriter explained, "he certainly wasn't getting away to a good start, and after he got started, he circled third base in a wide arc and wound up being thrown out" by the Giant right fielder "by perhaps ten feet."

Disgusted with Snider's mental lapse, Dressen benched him in the team's next game in Cincinnati. News reports speculated that Duke's salary would be cut by as much as 25 percent—all of which, as one sportswriter later explained, "brought a crisis in the lives of the whole Snider family." Bev immediately got on the telephone with her husband, and, in a flurry of subsequent calls, Walter O'Malley himself telephoned Mrs. Snider to assure her that there would be no cut in Duke's salary. The spate of telephone calls also resulted in discussions between Snider and Dressen, and the next day Snider was seen by one sportswriter "grinning and talking animatedly with his manager—something that had not been observed before then."

The change in attitude had an impact on Snider's performance, and he was able to finish the 1952 season with a .303 batting average along with twenty-one home runs and ninety-two runs driven in. But, more important, the Dodgers won the pennant, and he was given an opportunity to avenge his poor performance in the 1949 World Series. And avenge it he did. Facing Yankee stalwart Allie Reynolds—who had struck him out three times in the first game of that 1949 series—Snider nailed a home run that helped the team win the first game of the 1952 series. Although he would hit three more home runs in the series (and thus tie a series record held by Ruth and Gehrig), the first one was magical. Delighted to have overcome his initial anxieties of World Series play, Snider was too excited to even "remember going around the bases." Still, the Dodgers ultimately lost the series to the Yankees, and, once again, the team and its fans had to wait until next year.

The Dodger team of 1953 included outstanding performances by many of the team's regulars, but few could compare with Snider's achievements. He batted .336 (fourth in the league), established a new Dodger single-season record of forty-two home runs (second in the league), tied for third in doubles (with thirty-eight), and drove in 126 runs (third in the league). One sportswriter observed that the Dodger center fielder had had "a magnificent season" and that, with his best years yet to come, "it must be wonderful to be only twenty-seven years old and Duke Snider." But the performances of Snider and other Dodgers during the season were not enough to overcome the Yankees' dominance in the World Series, and, as Snider remembered, people began to wonder whether the New York rival had a "jinx" on the Brooklyn club.

The disappointment with the Dodgers' loss of the World Series did not have any impact on Snider's performance in 1954. He continued to pound the ball with consistency and power, and that productivity inevitably led to comparisons with the other two center fielders who played for New York teams—Mickey Mantle and Willie Mays. The comparison with Mays was a particularly frequent topic among sportswriters because, like Snider, he played in the National League. The debate was featured in midseason articles in *The Sporting News*, with one sportswriter saying that Mays—who had a dramatic running style and could make "basket" catches in the outfield—had a "showmanship" that Snider lacked, but another sportswriter countered that Snider displayed an "excellence" in making catches that compared favorably with his crosstown rival. From a statistical perspective, the two players had season records that were remarkably similar (Snider hitting forty home runs and driving in 130 runs, while Mays hit forty-one home runs and drove in 110 runs). Indeed, on the last day of the season, Snider, Mays, and Giant right fielder Don Mueller were all tied for the league lead in batting with a .342 average—but Snider went hitless on that last day while Mays had three hits, thus enabling the Giant outfielder to ultimately prevail with a .345 average.

Snider regarded the comparison with Mantle and Mays as only so much "media hype." In his mind, his individual performance was secondary to whether the Dodgers were winning—but he did acknowledge that he "was happy just to be compared with" Mantle and Mays, telling one interviewer, "Heck, if I am compared with those two, I'm a pretty good ballplayer."

Any doubts on Snider's comparison with Mantle and Mays were removed by the California native's performance in 1955. "There," Phillies' manager Mayo Smith told one sportswriter while pointing to Snider during a game in May, "is a helluva player. You can have Willie Mays. I'll take Snider." Dodger manager Walter Alston, who was rarely effusive in discussing his players' accomplishments, echoed that perspective, saying, "I don't think I've ever seen an outfielder who can go so high to catch a ball while running at full speed." The comments of Smith and Alston were echoed in *Sports Illustrated*, which concluded that Snider was the preferred player among Mays and Mantle not only because of his fielding skills but also because he was "the most dangerous hitter in the National League."

Ironically, both Snider and Mays were keeping pace through much of the 1955 season with Babe Ruth's record of hitting sixty home runs—although Ruth hit a remarkable seventeen home runs in September, which often made such comparisons deceiving. Duke's home run productivity collapsed in August after he was hit in the knee by a pitch, leaving him with forty-two home runs (while Mays finished with a league-leading fifty-one). Still, Snider led the league with 136 runs driven in, was chosen by *The Sporting News* as the Major League Player of the Year, and finished only two votes behind teammate Roy Campanella in the voting by the sportswriters (who were not terribly fond of Snider) for the league's Most Valuable Player award.

Despite his considerable contribution to the Dodgers' success in winning the pennant (and, with four home runs, winning the World Series), Snider jeopardized his standing with the fans with a temperamental outburst in August. The outburst reflected habits that could not be so easily changed. He continued to worry if he did not succeed at the plate. ("No player agonized more," said Carl Erskine, "when he didn't perform well.") And he was quick to anger if sportswriters made critical comments—although Reese told him to shrug them off, saying that "there's nothing older than yesterday's newspaper."

Snider certainly understood that the sportswriters' criticism came with the territory and that he should not fall apart emotionally if his performance did not always satisfy everyone's standards. Still, he became enraged when the fans began booing him unmercifully during one late-season doubleheader at Ebbets Field in which he went hitless in nine times at bat. When reporters gathered around his locker after the second game, the California native did not restrain himself. "You guys want something to write about?" he rhetorically asked. "The Brooklyn fans are the worst in the league. They don't deserve a pennant." Reese overheard the ill-chosen comments and gave his teammate the opportunity to reconsider, saying, "Wait, guys. Duke doesn't really mean that. Do you, Duke?" But Snider insisted that he did mean it and that the reporters should print it.

Duke had second thoughts about his comments when he saw the newspaper headlines the next morning. When Bev said that she would attend the game that evening, Duke tried to dissuade her. "No, you're not," he told his wife. "Those fans are going to tar and feather me." Bev pushed aside his caution and was sitting in the stands when Snider encountered a round of loud boos in his first plate appearance. But he got a hit, and the booing became less pronounced on his second time at bat. When he got another hit, there was some scattered applause. And when he got a hit on his third plate appearance, the jeers gave way to a standing ovation. The Duke was back in the fans' good graces.

It proved to be a temporary reprieve. Roger Kahn, who had covered the Dodgers in 1952 and 1953 for *The New York Herald Tribune* (and later wrote the best-selling memoir *The Boys of Summer*), asked Snider if he would be interested in cooperating on an article that would appear in *Collier's* magazine. The article, Kahn explained, would provide Duke with a platform to convey the frustrations that Snider had expressed to the New York writer during one of their many conversations in 1953. Snider agreed, and the article appeared in the issue of May 25, 1956.

The article ran under the headline, "I Play Baseball for Money—

Not Fun." Although Kahn wrote the article, it was portrayed as Snider's firsthand complaint that professional baseball did not provide the joys it appeared to have and that, during one World Series game, he was dreaming about the day when he could "settle down to raising avocados in the California sunshine."

To Snider, the disillusionment with baseball reflected a variety of factors. Youngsters who "throw skate keys and marbles" at his head while he is standing in center field. Older fans who "bounce beer cans" off his legs "during dull moments in the games." Sportswriters who write critical stories even though they know "just as much baseball as my four-year-old daughter." And a travel schedule that forced him to "spend half my life in strange towns, a thousand miles away from Beverly and the kids." He acknowledged that he was making about $50,000 a year through his salary, World Series checks, and endorsements. It was not, however, enough to justify the "headaches." Baseball "is no fun," he concluded, "but it's better than suffering the heartaches of a sour press and hooting fans."

In writing his autobiography many years later, Snider complained that he did not remember reading the article "until it appeared in Collier's." However, The Sporting News carried a story at the time in which the Dodger outfielder was quoted as saying, "I wasn't misquoted at all." In either event, the Collier's article generated predictable criticism in the press. Red Smith of The New York Herald Tribune took Snider to task for being unhappy with a $50,000 income for seven months' work. "Chances are," wrote Smith, "he hasn't more than the foggiest notion of how the other 99.99 percent lives."

Ironically, at the time the article appeared, Snider was on his way toward establishing a new Dodger record for home runs in a season (a league-leading forty-three) and once again leading the team to another World Series with the Yankees (although Duke later expressed disappointment with his performance that season because his .292 batting average represented the first time in five years that he fell below the .300 mark). He was also making plans to develop the avocado ranch in southern California that he had mentioned in the Collier's article—a sixty-acre parcel near the Camp Pendleton marine base that he had purchased with a friend.

Duke Snider appears to be a study of concentration—with no thoughts of avocados—as Hank Bauer steps into the batter's box to start the bottom of the fourth inning of the fifth game of the 1956 World Series. The afternoon shadows are now covering a third of right field as Sal Maglie takes the sign from Campanella and throws a curveball to the Yankee right fielder. Bauer fouls that pitch off and then works the count to one ball and two strikes before hitting a routine ground ball to third base. Jackie Robinson grabs the ball and fires it to first base for the out.

Yankee first baseman Joe Collins follows Bauer to the plate. He fouls off one pitch but soon becomes Maglie's second strikeout victim with a sharply breaking curveball that home-plate umpire Babe Pinelli calls for a third strike.

Maglie has now retired the first eleven Yankees to face him, and, as Mickey Mantle steps into the batter's box, the Dodger pitcher is no doubt hoping to make it twelve in a row. While Mantle gets ready for the first pitch, the Dodger infield shifts again to the right side of the field. Mantle gives no indication that he is even aware of the shift, let alone that it bothers him. But that can provide no satisfaction to the Dodgers. Mantle is a threat regardless of where the fielders position themselves. And they instinctively know what Mantle later discloses, long after he retires from baseball—that he is almost always swinging for the fences. (When interviewers would later ask him if he ever went up to the plate "just trying for a home run," Mantle would invariably smile and say, "Every time.")

Mantle fouls off a pitch, takes a ball, and then gets a called second strike on another sharply breaking curveball. ("It is almost unbelievable," says radio announcer Bob Neal, "to see this ball, the way it is jumping around.") The count moves to two balls and two strikes, as the Yankee center fielder continues to foul pitches off to the left side of the plate. And then Maglie comes in with a fastball. Mantle swings hard, and the ball leaps off the bat in a low trajectory. "There's a drive into right field," screams Neal. A pause. And then, as the ball barely flies over the short fence and into the stands near the 344-foot mark, the radio announcer loudly describes what is obvious to the fans in the stadium: "And there's a home run for Mickey Mantle."

As the Yankee center fielder trots around the bases with his head down, Maglie stares ahead, angry with himself, but equally frustrated by the circumstance of Mantle's round-tripper. To those who would ask him about the game in later years, Maglie would complain that Mantle's hit was "the shortest home run in baseball" and that, "in any other field, it would have been an out." Certainly that would have been true if the game had been played in Ebbets Field, where the right-field fence stood more than thirty feet tall (meaning that Mantle's home run probably would have been at best only a double or, with Carl Furillo handling the carom, perhaps only a single). But they are not playing at Ebbets Field, and Maglie turns his attention to Yogi Berra, who has stepped up to the plate with the Yankees now leading by a score of 1–0.

Maglie quickly gets a one ball–one strike count on the Yankee catcher. Berra then swings at a curveball and sends a line drive into left center field. Snider is off to his right with the crack of the bat and with the outcome uncertain. "Snider is digging for it," Neal yells, "and still coming on." And then, as Neal tells his listening audience, the Dodger center fielder makes a "diving, grabbing catch of the ball." Yankee broadcaster Mel Allen is equally impressed, telling a national television audience that Snider's effort is "one of the most sensational catches you'll ever see."

Maglie now walks back to the Dodger dugout, no doubt wishing that he could take back that one bad pitch to Mickey Mantle.

Top of the Fifth: Mickey Mantle

For those who tuned in to watch ABC Television Network's *Good Morning America* on August 1, 1995, the sight was unexpected and the message grim. The man in the videotape had the familiar smile and the country drawl they knew so well. But he did not look like the robust athlete who had captured the nation's imagination forty years earlier. His face was gaunt, and the white baseball hat he wore looked like it was too big for his head.

He did not waste time with formal introductions. "Hi," he said as the video opened. "This is Mick." He did not dwell on where he had been or why he was now speaking to this national television audience. He assumed that most had seen the never-ending headlines over the preceding weeks and were familiar with the medical problems that had previously driven him to Baylor University Medical Center in his hometown of Dallas. He proceeded to relate the results of a recent checkup. The news was not good. "The doctors found a couple of spots of cancer in my lungs," he explained without emotion. "Now I'm taking chemotherapy to get rid of the new cancer. I hope to be back to feeling as good as when I left here."

It proved to be a false hope. He was dead within two weeks. "This was," one of his attending physicians later said, "the most aggressive cancer that anyone on the medical team has ever seen." And so thousands made the pilgrimage to the memorial service in the Lovers Lane United Methodist Church in Dallas to listen to eulogies from NBC broadcaster Bob Costas, former teammate Bobby Richardson, and other speakers who extolled the virtues of a man who had meant so much to so many.

As he stands in center field waiting for Don Larsen's first pitch of the fifth inning of the fifth game of the 1956 World Series, Mickey Mantle cannot know the fate that lies before him. But if he could have foreseen all of those adoring crowds and all of those laudatory speeches at the funeral, he would have been embarrassed. Few things trouble the Yankee switch-hitter more than the attention people shower on him.

Not that he was ignored while growing up in the 1930s in Commerce, a small town in the Dust Bowl of eastern Oklahoma. Quite the contrary. Few boys received as much attention as young Mickey did from his father. Mutt Mantle, as his son remembered, "lived and died for baseball." And he had a plan. His firstborn son was going to be an outstanding major-league baseball player.

From all appearances, it was a preposterous notion. Mutt Mantle was a coal miner who could barely afford the necessities of life. Mickey was born in a two-room, unpainted house at the end of a dirt road in Spavinaw, Oklahoma, and the Mantles never had a telephone or indoor plumbing until their nineteen-year-old son used his first World Series check to buy his parents a new house.

Mutt not only lacked money. He had no connections to organized baseball. All of that left Mutt with only one choice—he would mold his son into a player whose talents would capture the attention of a major-league club. "The feeling between Mutt Mantle and his son," Mickey's wife, Merlyn, later observed, "was more than love. Mick was his work, just as much as if his father had created him out of clay." And for his part, Mutt's son was a willing subject. "I just wanted to please him more than anything else," Mickey commented many years later. (The pressure to please his father, however, had its costs—Mickey would wet his bed until he was sixteen years old.)

The starting point of the father's dream was the boy's name. Mutt wanted to name his son after a player whose achievements would be the guidepost for future development. For reasons that were never entirely clear, Mutt decided to name his son after Mickey Cochrane, the Philadelphia Athletics' All-Star catcher. (Cochrane's first name was actually Gordon, and Mantle would later express gratitude that his father remained ignorant of that fact. "I hope there are no Gordons here today," he told the audience as he was inducted into the National Hall of Fame in Cooperstown, New York, in 1974, "but I'm glad that he didn't name me Gordon.")

Mutt, a muscular man of medium build, would come home from the mines in the late afternoons, the ever-present Lucky Strike cigarette dangling from his mouth, and his young son would greet him with an old glove and a worn-out tennis ball. They would then spend the rest of the day practicing the basics of baseball.

Mutt knew enough to know that future major-league managers—much like the Giants' legendary John McGraw—would "platoon" players (so that some right-handed batters would face limited playing time against right-handed pitchers and some left-handed batters would face limited playing time against left-handed pitchers). Guided by that expectation, Mutt decided that his son—a natural right-handed batter—should learn to hit left-handed. Mutt, a right-handed player, would pitch to young Mickey while he batted left-handed, and Mutt's left-handed father would toss the ball to his grandson when he was practicing his swing from the other side of the plate. It was a disciplined approach, and never could young Mickey deviate from his father's plan. (Some years later, Mutt watched from the stands as his teenage son batted right-handed against a right-handed pitcher in a sandlot game. The father did not waste any time in leaving his seat and sending Mickey home with a stern admonition: "Don't you ever put on that baseball uniform again unless you switch-hit like I taught you.")

Mickey's mother remained largely a passive observer through all of this. A small woman with dark, curly hair, Lovell Mantle was not given to expressing her emotions, and Mickey would later say that he could never remember getting a hug from his mother or any statement of love. Still, there was no doubt about Lovell's devotion to her family, and Merlyn would later acknowledge that she "was a tireless and protective mother." (She was also a strict disciplinarian, and Mickey would vividly remember the time she smacked his young son David with the back of her hand—something he too had experienced as a child—and that, said Mickey, was the last time he left her alone with any of his children.)

As Mickey got older, Mutt decided to explore the benefits of farming, becoming a sharecropper on a 160-acre tract of land five miles outside of Commerce where he could grow corn and raise dairy cows. It was an idyllic time for young Mickey, who could ride his horse, Tony, to school. But it did not last more than a couple of years. Torrential rains caused the nearby creek to flood, and, when all the crops were lost, Mutt was forced to abandon the farm and return to the mines.

None of those setbacks interfered with Mickey's athletic progress— which was nothing short of phenomenal. To be sure, he was blessed with a natural ability in anything that required eye-hand coordination, but there was so much more to explain his success in whatever sport he chose—whether baseball, basketball, or football. He had a remarkable strength in his arms (which Mickey said he got from milking cows twice a day and later from a summer job digging ditches for the local graveyard). And he could run with a speed that made heads turn. When he attended his first spring training camp with the Yankees in 1951, Mantle was clocked in running the ninety feet from home plate to first base in the astounding time of 3.1 seconds. After watching him run the bases during an exhibition game, Cardinal second baseman Red Schoendienst screamed, "Look at that guy go. He must be part jackrabbit!"

Mickey did not confine his athletic activities to baseball when he was growing up. In retrospect, that was a grave mistake. At football practice one afternoon in 1946, the fifteen-year-old halfback got kicked by a teammate who tackled him. By the next morning the ankle was swollen to twice its normal size and discolored with a purple hue. Unfortunately, the Commerce physician was not able to diagnose the injury because the town did not have an X-ray machine. When infection set in, Mutt decided to take his teenage son to the hospital in nearby Picher, Oklahoma. The diagnosis could not have been worse for the budding athlete: osteomyelitis, a chronic inflammation of the bone that can sometimes be controlled but never cured. Seeing no permanent alternative, the attending physician told Lovell that they would probably have to amputate the leg. "The hell you are!" responded the doting mother. Unwilling to accept the Picher physician's verdict, she and Mutt took Mickey to the Crippled Children's Hospital in Oklahoma City, where doctors applied the new wonder drug—penicillin—to reduce the swelling, eliminate the fever, and enable their son to return home.

By the spring, Mickey was able to play baseball without any handicap—and began to attract attention with his power at the plate and his speed on the bases. One of those he impressed most was Barney Barnett, owner of the Baxter Springs Whiz Kids in the Southeastern Kansas Ban Johnson League, a team one step above sandlot ball that often attracted scouts looking for players with major-league potential. That was no small benefit, because there could be little doubt about the potential of this 150-pound shortstop who could blast home runs well beyond the four-hundred-foot marker in center field—regardless of whether he was batting left-handed or right-handed.

Yankee scout Tom Greenwade recognized Mickey's potential when he watched a Whiz Kids game in Baxter Springs one day. After four innings, Greenwade rose to leave, and Barnett asked what he thought of the team's shortstop. "I think I've seen enough," said Greenwade. "I want to talk to Mutt." A sudden rain shower forced people to run for cover, and Mickey soon found himself in the front seat of his father's LaSalle with the Yankee scout. "How would you like to play for the Yankees?" Greenwade asked. Greenwade explained that he could not sign Mickey to a professional contract until he had graduated from high school but told him not to sign with another team in the interim. "I'll be back," the Yankee scout promised.

Greenwade would later say—after his prospect became the talk of the Yankees' 1951 spring training camp—that "Mick is the kind of player you dream about finding." But the Yankee scout had a different assessment when he met with Mickey and Mutt in his big Chrysler after a Baxter Springs' game in May 1949. "Right now," Greenwade told his captive audience, "I'd have to rate him a lousy shortstop. Sloppy. Erratic arm. And he's small." And then a pause. "However," he added,

"I'm willing to take a risk." He offered Mickey $400 to play for the Class D Yankee farm team in Independence, Kansas, for the remainder of the summer.

Mutt was not happy. "He can make that much playing Sunday ball and working in the mines during the week," the disappointed father told the Yankee scout. Greenwade agreed to include a bonus of $1,100, and Mickey Mantle became the property of the New York Yankees.

That first season in professional baseball produced mixed results for the seventeen-year-old Commerce native. He was able to bat .313 but his play at shortstop—with forty-seven errors in eighty-nine games—was less than spectacular. Mickey himself remembered that his throwing was so erratic that the team "had to put a chicken-wire screen behind first base as a backstop to prevent somebody in the stands from getting killed." His manager—Harry Craft, who later became a big-league manager—touted Mantle's hitting accomplishments to Yankee management but told the front office that he "would like to see him shifted to third or the outfield."

Somehow the fielding recommendation got lost in the shuffle, because Mickey was promoted to the Joplin farm team in the Western Association league for the 1950 season but still found himself playing shortstop. The errors continued, but the hitting only improved. Mickey finished the season with a .383 batting average while blasting twenty-six home runs and driving in 136 runs in only 137 games.

The reward for that performance was an invitation to join the parent club in St. Louis on September 17 for the final two weeks of the season. Mickey did not play in any games, but he did have an opportunity to get a taste of the big leagues—and the club got a glimpse of this minor-league player's bountiful potential. He and Moose Skowron—a nineteen-year-old prospect who had played football at Purdue University—would take batting practice with the team and astound everyone with their ability to drive balls into the seats. "They put on a great show of power hitting," remembered pitcher Whitey Ford, then completing his rookie year with the team.

It was enough to give Mickey hope that he could soon join the Yankees as a player, and he was elated when he received a letter in January 1951 from Yankee farm director Lee MacPhail directing him to join the team's special instructional camp in Phoenix in February. Expectations were soaring even before Mantle arrived in Phoenix. The sportswriters had already had identified him "as the No. 1 minor league prospect in the nation," and manager Casey Stengel, for one, was anxious to see whether this country boy could make the grade—but not as a short-stop. (Mantle played shortstop in the first days of spring training, but it soon became clear that his fielding had not improved. "He was a real scatter-arm," Gil McDougald remembered. "I can picture him throw-ing to first base. Everybody in the grandstand would scatter.") The decision was made to move him to the outfield, where throws to first base would present less of a problem. For his part, the nineteen-year-old rookie was delighted with the change. "I like the idea of shifting to the outfield," he explained to a sportswriter. "It is not as tough as the infield, and out there I get a chance to use my legs."

Stengel asked longtime Yankee outfielder Tommy Henrich to tutor Mantle on the fundamentals of the new position. Mantle's other in-struction came from watching DiMaggio. "I study Joe all the while," Mantle remarked to one sportswriter. "I marvel at his grace and non-chalance." DiMaggio also gave the prospective outfielder periodic di-rection on where to play—and Mantle was only too happy to oblige. Not that the two men shared any kind of friendship—indeed, the two players hardly spoke to each other.

Part of the problem was Mickey's personality. He was still a shy teenager who did not understand the publicity that surrounded his ar-rival at spring training. Stengel had asked the press to be gentle with the bashful rookie, saying, "The kid has never seen concrete." But sportswriters had a job to do, and they forged ahead. The results were not always satisfying. (There was the time when a reporter sat down next to Mantle in the clubhouse, his pen at the ready. "I hope you're not going to ask me a whole lot of questions," the rookie began. "I'm no good at answering questions.")

Mickey's difficulty in conversing with unknown sportswriters was that much greater when it came to Joe DiMaggio. Unlike Billy Martin—who relished the challenge of confronting idols—the Oklahoma native was dumbstruck. "I couldn't even mumble hello," Mantle later remem-bered. "He had this aura. It was as if you needed an appointment just to approach him." For his part, DiMaggio was not the kind of person to ease the tension that Mickey felt. There was no slap on the back, no invitation to join him for a beer after the game, and no inquiry on how the young rookie was dealing with the pressures of being a top prospect in the Yankees' spring training camp.

It was an unpleasant experience that Mantle would never forget—and that would guide his relationship with teammates after he had achieved the stardom that the press had envisioned for him in 1951. In later years Yankee rookies and other newcomers to the team would find—to their great surprise—that, unlike the great DiMaggio, the Yankees' famous switch-hitting center fielder was a man who would take the initiative to make them feel comfortable. It could be an invitation to dinner or a practical joke. (Tony Kubek, a shy twenty-year-old rookie in 1957, was astounded when Mickey approached him after a game in Chicago and asked him to dinner with Whitey Ford and Billy Martin. After dinner, the four Yankees went to a jazz bar, and Kubek excused himself to go to the restroom. When he returned, the other players were gone and the waiter was waiting with the check—which Kubek could not afford to pay. After watching the rookie grope for explanations, the waiter finally disclosed with a smile that the bill had already been paid by Mantle.) Or there could be a small gesture. (When pitcher Bob Turley was traded to the Yankees after the 1954 season, he walked into the clubhouse in spring training in 1955 and found in his locker a bottle of "greenie"—a lime-lemonade drink popular among the players at the time—with a note from Mantle. "Thank God you're here," the note read. "I don't have to face you anymore.")

Mantle made concerted efforts to endear himself to his teammates in other ways as well. He would invariably be the one cheering his teammates on from the dugout when they came to bat—something DiMaggio would rarely do. And unlike DiMaggio—who would usually leave the stadium by a side door after a game to avoid crowds—Mantle would leave through a route that would take him into the anteroom where the players' families were waiting, and he would then spend time talking with the wives and children who were there. Then there was Elston Howard, who joined the Yankees in 1955 as the team's first black player—when the team stopped during spring training at restaurants in the South that did not accept blacks, Mickey would have dinner with Elston on the bus.

Mantle's effort to gain favor with his teammates bore abundant fruit. "He was the perfect teammate," Kubek would later say of Mantle. "That's what he always wanted to be considered. And a good part of that was because he did not want to be like Joe DiMaggio." Yogi Berra—who played with DiMaggio for five years—agreed, saying that Mantle "was more one of the guys than DiMag" and that "all of us loved Mickey Mantle because he was the best teammate you could have."

However much he wanted to distance himself from DiMaggio's image in later years, Mantle found himself being compared to the Yankee Clipper at the 1951 spring training camp by players and sportswriters alike. And for good reason. This nineteen-year-old rookie from Oklahoma, it seemed, could do everything—and do it better than anyone else. His home runs were a constant source of discussion—especially the ones he hit in a series of exhibition games in Los Angeles. One of the home runs (at USC's Bovard Field) sailed over the 439-foot sign in the outfield, passed the width of the football field next to the stadium, and was estimated to have traveled about 650 feet from home plate by the time it landed. Mantle ended spring training with a home run at Ebbets Field—his ninth of the camp (tops for all Yankee players) and a .402 batting average.

Spring training only fueled hopes that the Yankees had now found a replacement for the ailing DiMaggio (who would retire after the 1951 season). "I don't know that I ever saw a young player who had as much talent as he had," said Yankee third baseman Bobby Brown. "He had power from both sides of the plate. He could run faster than anybody I ever saw. He could outthrow anybody that you would want to see. He could do everything." When later asked by a sportswriter if Mantle had any weakness, St. Louis Browns' manager Marty Marion responded, "He can't throw left-handed." And so the press began to trumpet Mantle's coming with stories that he might even surpass the achievements of Babe Ruth and Lou Gehrig.

However understandable, the publicity only heightened the pressures that the Yankees' new outfielder was already feeling. "Casey kept bragging on me and the newspapers kept writing it," Mickey later observed. "I don't mind admitting," he added, "that there was incredible pressure on me because of what Casey was saying."

Mantle began the 1951 season playing right field next to DiMaggio in center, and batting third in the lineup—just ahead of DiMaggio. Mickey initially gave the fans what they wanted—hitting long home runs, stealing bases, and occasionally dragging a bunt down the first-base line for a hit. But the honeymoon faded quickly when opposing pitchers learned his weaknesses at the plate.

Frustrated by his inability to deliver what Stengel and the fans expected, Mantle would get especially angry if he struck out (which became more and more frequent as the weeks passed), and he did not restrain himself when he reached the dugout after a whiff. Hitting his foot or a bat against the watercooler became a common reaction. Stengel, the master at reverse psychology, would try to calm the rookie down by giving him a bat and telling him, "if he wanted to end his career, he should hit himself over the head and get it over with." The psychology did not work, and fans began to express their disappointment with boos from the stands.

The pressures on the young player were compounded by his draft status. Even before he arrived in spring training camp, his local draft board had classified him as 4F—unfit for military service—because of his osteomyelitis. Many fans and sportswriters found the board's decision incomprehensible when they saw this muscular teenager scampering around the field while the Korean War was raging. "So Mantle has osteomyelitis," one sportswriter commented. "What's the big deal? He doesn't have to *kick* anybody in Korea."

In the meantime, Mantle continued to live life as well as he could. After his first year of professional baseball, he returned to Commerce to resume the social life, such as it was, that he had in high school. One night he and a friend had a double date with two girls from Picher— but Mickey was more interested in his friend's date: Merlyn Johnson, a pretty brunette who was one year younger than Mickey. The two soon began dating, going to movies and other social events (but never drinking alcohol), and years later Merlyn would say that October 6, 1949—the day she first saw Mickey Mantle at a local football game—

was the day her life "changed forever." Merlyn soon became consumed with her love for this blond-haired boy with the quick smile. "I loved Mickey Mantle so much," she would later say, "that I wanted to crawl inside him and live underneath his skin."

By January 1951, Merlyn's parents had announced the engagement of their daughter to the Yankee rookie. But all was not what it appeared to be. Mickey Mantle was now finding that there were many temptations—and pitfalls—to life in New York City. As Mantle later explained, "I guess I developed my first taste for the high life then."

Her name was Holly Brooke, an attractive brunette and a budding showgirl. She met the Yankees' new right fielder at a party and soon became his constant companion at social events or in quiet evenings at his room in the Concourse Plaza Hotel. Merlyn knew nothing of Holly's existence. Nor was Merlyn there to counsel her fiancé when Alan Savitt, a short, heavyset man with a razor-thin mustache, talked the young player into signing a contract that would entitle Savitt to be his agent and retain 50 percent of Mickey's earnings for ten years. Mantle's suspicions should have been raised when Holly later told him that Savitt had sold her half of his interest in the agency relationship, but Mickey was no doubt blinded by the emotions of his new social life.

However much he treasured the trappings of life in the big city in that 1951 season, nothing, it seemed, could help Mantle's deteriorating performance at the plate. The inevitable occurred when the Yankees arrived in Detroit for a series with the Tigers in July. One of the clubhouse managers told the rookie that Casey wanted to see him, and Mickey understood the consequences as soon as he saw the Yankee manager. There were tears in his eyes, and Stengel began by saying, "This is gonna hurt me more than you." The team had decided to send the struggling player to its farm team in Kansas City in the hope that he could regain the form that had astonished so many during spring training.

It may have seemed logical to the Yankee management, but Mickey was devastated. Holly remembered that Mantle called her immediately afterward "and bawled like a baby." His mood did not improve after he started playing for the minor-league team. After getting a drag bunt hit in his first game, Mickey had twenty-one additional plate appearances without getting a hit. Mickey Mantle, the extraordinary prospect from Commerce, had hit rock bottom.

After waiting a few days, he made the call to his father. "I'm not hitting, Dad," he explained. "I just can't play anymore." Mickey was hoping, maybe expecting, that his father would provide some comfort that would enable his son to weather the storm. But Mickey miscalculated. Mutt did contact Merlyn, and the two of them immediately made the five-hour drive to the Aladdin Hotel in Kansas City, where Mickey was staying. But the elder Mantle had no sympathy for his son's plight. As soon as Mutt and Merlyn entered the hotel room, Mickey tried to review his frustration at the plate. Mutt was not prepared to listen. "I don't want to hear that whining!" he said with clenched jaws. "I thought I raised a man, not a coward!" And with that, Mutt grabbed his son's suitcase and began throwing his son's clothes into it, telling Mickey that he was going to take him back to Commerce, where he could work with him in the mines.

It took some time before Mickey could convince his father to let him stay in Kansas City and give it another shot. Mutt finally relented (or appeared to relent), and when he returned to the ball field the next day, Mantle was a different player. He began getting hits (ultimately driving up his average to .361), blasting home runs (eleven), and driving in runs at a pace (fifty in forty games) that no doubt pleased the Yankee management. By the end of the August, Mickey Mantle was wearing Yankee pinstripes once again.

The new uniform was not the only change. Instead of returning to the Concourse Plaza Hotel, Mickey accepted an invitation to join Hank Bauer and Johnny Hopp, two veteran players, in an apartment over the Stage Delicatessen in Midtown Manhattan. Thus began a steady diet of matzo-ball soup and corned-beef sandwiches, all of which helped push his weight up to about 190 pounds.

Other benefits ensued from the new apartment. Bauer tried to tutor Mantle on the ways of city life and, as part of that instruction, helped the rookie secure a lawyer to terminate the oppressive agency contract that Savitt had foisted on the young player. But the Yankee veteran did not extricate Mantle from the relationship with Holly. And, so, when Mutt came to New York in October for the World Series against the

New York Giants, Mickey was able to introduce his new girlfriend to his father. Mutt was not pleased. "Mickey," he later admonished his son, "you do the right thing and marry your own kind." And that was the end of Holly.

However disappointed he might have been with the termination of that relationship, it was eclipsed by the excitement that enveloped Mickey as the World Series approached. He had played with confidence in that last month of the season (finishing with thirteen home runs and sixty-five runs driven in), and Stengel had him start the first series game (which the Yankees won) in right field next to DiMaggio. Shortly before the second game, the Yankee manager pulled the rookie aside to ask him to help out DiMaggio, who would be playing center field despite the discomfort of an injured heel that had plagued him all season. "Take everything you can get over in center," Stengel told Mantle. "The Dago's heel is hurting pretty bad."

Anxious to please, Mantle had not forgotten that directive when Willie Mays, the Giants' rookie center fielder, lofted a ball into right center field in the sixth inning. Mantle, expecting that he would have to field it, turned on the speed and raced toward the descending ball and then, just as he was about to catch it, heard DiMaggio call out to him, saying, "I got it." Mantle stopped abruptly and, as he did, his cleats got caught in a hidden drainpipe. His knee twisted on impact, and he immediately dropped to the ground with a bone sticking out of the side of his leg. DiMaggio leaned over the stricken player and said, "Don't move. They're bringing a stretcher." Mantle, overcome with excruciating pain, said nothing in response, but in later years he would say "that was about as close as Joe and I had come to a conversation."

The injury Mantle sustained on that October afternoon would haunt him for the rest of his career. ("I wouldn't play another game the rest of my career," he later remarked, "without hurting.") But it was nothing compared to the heartbreak he felt when he learned of his father's condition shortly afterward. Mutt—who had lost considerable weight since the visit to Kansas City in July—had gone with Mickey to the Lenox Hill Hospital in Manhattan, but when the younger Mantle leaned on his thirty-nine-year-old father in getting out of the cab, Mutt collapsed on the pavement no less quickly than Mickey had fallen on the field earlier that afternoon. Tests were conducted, and Mickey soon heard the doctor's diagnosis of his father: Hodgkin's disease, a form of cancer for which there was no cure.

Mickey was all too familiar with the disease and its destructive impact—his grandfather as well as other male relatives had succumbed to Hodgkin's disease either before or shortly after they turned forty. The attending physician explained to the Yankee right fielder that there was no hope and that the best course of action was to take Mutt home "and let him enjoy the time he has left."

Mickey did take Mutt home and in December fulfilled his father's request by marrying Merlyn. ("Next to me," Merlyn later said, "the groom's father was the happiest person in the room.") But Mutt Mantle never got to see the grandchildren he had envisioned when he advised his oldest son to marry the girl from Picher. Eager to spare his family the trauma of watching him waste away, Mutt checked himself into a hospital in Denver and died there—alone—on May 6, 1952.

Stengel was the one to break the news to Mickey over the phone while the team was in New York for a series with the Cleveland Indians. At that point, the Yankee manager was playing Mantle only sporadically because his hitting was anemic (with only two home runs). That all changed when Mickey returned from his father's funeral. On May 20, Stengel started him in center field, and Mantle responded with four straight hits—two batting right-handed and two batting left-handed. From that point on, Mantle became the team's regular center fielder—and began to show the power that he had first displayed in the 1951 spring training camp. (There was the time in July when first baseman Joe Collins, who batted second in the lineup ahead of Mantle, slammed a gigantic home run into the upper deck of Cleveland's Municipal Stadium. As he crossed home plate, Collins said to Mantle, who was about to step into the batter's box, "Go chase that." On the next pitch, Mantle blasted a home run into the upper deck that landed in a spot higher and farther away from the plate than Collins' shot. When Mantle came back into the dugout, he casually walked past Collins on the way to the watercooler and said with a grin, "What'd you say?" To which Collins good-naturedly responded, "Go shit in your hat.")

Although he hit only twenty-three home runs (well behind Cleveland's Larry Doby, the league leader with thirty-two), Mantle's overall batting performance in his first full season placed him among the league's most productive batters—with a .311 batting average (third in the league), thirty-seven doubles (second in the league), and 291 total bases from all his hits (second in the league). Those achievements were complemented by Mickey's critical contribution to the team's defeat of the Dodgers in the seven-game World Series, batting .345 with ten hits (including two home runs). It was, said *The Sporting News*, "a spectacular World Series in which Mantle played a spectacular role."

That performance in the fall classic—coupled with his season record—catapulted Mantle into a national sports figure. Stories of Mickey's background and exploits filled the sports pages, and the public was understandably anxious to learn more about this twenty-one-year-old prodigy. But it was not easy. When a sportswriter for the *Chicago Tribune* traveled to Oklahoma to interview Mickey in conjunction with a book on "The Mickey Mantle Story," the Yankee center fielder was incredulous. "You mean," he said to the reporter, "the *Tribune* actually paid your expenses down here to Commerce, Oklahoma, just to see me?"

Mickey's performance in the exhibition season the following spring did nothing to quell the enthusiasm for this emerging star. He batted .421, causing *The Sporting News* to identify him as the "Yankee candidate for the American League batting championship." And then there was his home run in an exhibition game against the Pittsburgh Pirates in Forbes Field that sailed over the right-field roof—which was more than ninety feet high—thus matching a feat that had been previously accomplished only by Babe Ruth. Shortly after the season began, Mantle hit another four-bagger that inspired awe among sportswriters and led *The Sporting News* to talk about "the saga of the truly titanic home run."

With Washington Senators' southpaw Chuck Stobbs pitching to him on April 17 in the capital's Griffith Stadium, Mickey, batting right-handed, slammed a ball that, according to the Senators' broadcaster Bob Wolff, "just zoomed" off Mantle's bat and made Wolff ask himself, "Did that really happen?" The ball cleared the left-field fence on the rise at the 391-foot mark, hit the football scoreboard that stood sixty feet above the last row of bleachers, flew past Fifth Street behind the stadium, and landed on a side street well beyond the stadium's walls. "Everybody was screaming in the press box," remembered Yankee publicity director Red Patterson. So he decided something had to be done to memorialize the event. He was, after all, in charge of Yankee publicity.

Patterson left the press box, bought a hot dog and a beer, and some minutes later returned to the press box to tell his colleagues that he had determined that the ball had traveled 565 feet. No one challenged Patterson's measuring techniques. They had all seen the blast, and it was indeed incredible. The next day's headlines repeated the figure and said that Mantle's "565-foot drive" compared well with the feats of Babe Ruth and earlier power hitters. The measurement may have rested on faulty methodology, but no matter. The era of the tape-measure home run was born.

There was thus hope that Mantle could surpass the achievements of the 1952 season. But that hope was soon compromised by repeated injuries to his legs that forced Mickey to miss almost thirty games and limited his home run production to twenty-one (although he did drive in ninety-two runs, five more than he had in 1952). Whatever disappointment he may have felt about his season's record was soon erased by another memorable home run in the World Series against the Dodgers.

In the top of the third inning of the fifth game at Ebbets Field, Brooklyn manager Charlie Dressen called in Russ Meyer, a six-foot-one-inch right-hander, to pitch to Mantle with the bases loaded. Dressen warned his new pitcher not to give Mantle any fastballs, and Meyer obliged by throwing the Yankee center fielder a curve. Batting left-handed, Mantle swung at the pitch and drove the ball high into the left-field bleachers for a grand-slam home run (making him only the fourth player to hit one in a World Series). Sportswriter Roger Kahn, who was covering the game for *The New York Herald Tribune*, remembered the ball "landing with such force that some said they heard the sound of furniture breaking." For his part, Meyer, who pitched in the major leagues for thirteen seasons, later said that Mantle's home run "was the longest and hardest ball ever hit off me."

It should have been a good omen for the 1954 season. But obstacles remained. Another operation on Mantle's knee was required during the winter and, not one to worry about postoperative rehabilitation, he showed up at spring training unable to run, let alone play. ("When you're young," Mantle later said, "you think you're indestructible. I didn't even do the exercises they gave me to do.") Still, the press continued to inflate his reputation, with one sportswriter repeating Stengel's preseason prediction that Mantle was "capable of taking the batting title held by Mickey Vernon and the runs driven in and the home run leadership held by Al Rosen."

None of those predictions materialized, but there should have been no complaints. The twenty-two-year-old center fielder hit twenty-seven home runs—finishing third in the league—and continued to establish himself as one of the league's better hitters with a .300 batting average and 102 runs driven in.

However satisfied they should have been with his batting performance, fans continued to boo Mickey when he did not fulfill their inflated expectations. A particular source of frustration was the growing number of strikeouts that Mantle had during the 1952 season (107). Stengel never tired of using psychological maneuvers to correct Mantle's tendency to reach for bad pitches. (A favorite target of Mantle's frustration with strikeouts continued to be the watercooler in the dugout, and Stengel would repeatedly tell his center fielder, "It ain't the watercooler that's striking you out, son.") But the Yankee manager's observations and advice seemed to have little impact. "Telling Mantle something is like telling him nothing," a frustrated Stengel explained to a reporter.

Still, Stengel had to be pleased with the Oklahoma native's performance in 1955. He had hit thirty-seven home runs by early September—thus generating expectations that he would become the first Yankee to hit forty or more home runs since Joe DiMaggio hit forty-six in 1937. But leg injuries once again foreclosed Mantle from achieving the anticipated home-run milestone. On September 16, he pulled a thigh muscle while trying to drag a bunt down the first-base line, and he never made it past thirty-seven (although he did wind up leading the league in that department, tied teammate Andy Carey for the league lead in triples with eleven, batted .306, and led the league with a .611 slugging percentage). For Stengel, it was a sign of better things to come, and he told sportswriters after the season that Mantle "has not yet reached his peak."

The Yankee manager knew what he was talking about. Mickey opened the 1956 season with two gigantic home runs in the opening game against the Senators in Washington, DC, and by the end of May he had twenty. The last home run of the month was a blast off Senators' pitcher Pedro Ramos that came within eighteen inches of clearing the right-field facade in Yankee Stadium (and would have made Mantle the first player to hit a ball out of the House That Ruth Built). "That hit was unbelievable," said Bob Wolff, who was again providing broadcast commentary for the Senators' game. "The ball was on an acceleration when it hit the facade—it was on the way up. I thought that ball would have gone another hundred feet higher up before it started its descent."

Mantle's performance began to draw national attention—not only because of the magnitude of his blasts but also because he was well ahead of the pace Ruth had set in 1927 when he hit sixty home runs. "Mickey Mantle, the switch-hitter who is electrifying baseball fans everywhere and electrocuting the New York Yankees' opposition," explained veteran sportswriter Tom Meany, "is the most talked-about player in baseball today." And the talk was all in superlatives that had rarely been used. "Baseball has been looking for a long time for the superplayer," said Baltimore Orioles manager Paul Richards. "Now it can stop looking because Mickey Mantle is that player." "For the first time in his career," added *The Sporting News*, "Mantle is the recognized standout player of the majors."

Mantle's accomplishments were all the more remarkable because he continued to bear the burden of his numerous leg injuries—from the osteomyelitis to the twisted knee from the 1951 World Series to the numerous pulled muscles suffered afterward. Never could he play without going through a tedious pregame ritual of wrapping bandages around his right leg from ankle to thigh and then putting a brace around his right knee. "The thing too many people overlook about him," Stengel told Meany at one point, "is that he's been doing all he has been doing this year as a cripple." Early Wynn, one of the stalwarts of the Cleveland Indians' pitching staff, spoke of Mantle's physical handicap after sharing a locker room with him before the 1956 All-Star game. "I watched him bandage that knee—that whole leg," Wynn later said, "and I saw what he had to go through every day to play. And now I'll never be able to praise him enough."

Never, however, would Mantle let his displays of power on the field embarrass the pitcher who had thrown the home-run ball. He would never stand at the plate to watch the ball sail out of the park, point to the sky in celebration, or show any other emotion that might make the pitcher feel uncomfortable. Instead, he would begin his trot around the bases almost immediately after he hit the ball—no matter how far— with his head down and his arms bent at his side. The gesture did not go unnoticed. "I always respected that about him," said Jim Kaat, who pitched in the American League for more than sixteen years.

Mantle's assault on Babe Ruth's home run record dwindled in September, but he ultimately succeeded in winning the triple crown by leading the league in homers with fifty-two, being on top with 130 runs batted in, and, in the last few days of the season, taking the batting crown (with a .353. average) from Boston's Ted Williams (who finished with a .345 average). Williams was gracious in defeat—but he did tell the press, "If I could run like that son of a bitch, I'd hit .400 every year."

By 1956, Mantle had not only matured as an athlete. He had also begun to enjoy the benefits—and suffer the burdens—of fame in New York City.

Mantle had become the object of desire not only for fans but also for young women who would literally throw themselves at him (leading some of his teammates to say toward the end of the 1956 season that "Mickey might be losing ground on Ruth's record on the field but was still well ahead of his home-run pace off the field"). That extracurricular activity was possible because Merlyn, with a dread of flying, had remained home in Oklahoma to take care of the couple's two (soon to be four) sons. Mickey was willing—if not anxious—to exploit that distance from his wife because he was convinced that, like his father and male relatives, he would not make it past his fortieth birthday. "My father died young," he told Hank Bauer at one point. "I'm not going to be cheated."

The attention of fans was another matter. Mantle could never understand why people wanted his autograph—largely because, despite his achievements, he saw himself as just another player. Beyond that, for all his growing sophistication, he had not traveled very far from his roots (and never would he let his fame affect relations with his family—as his brother Ray later told me, Mickey "always remained the same"). "I've always had a private corner," Mickey remarked many years later, "an innate shyness that prevents me from feeling comfortable when talking to strangers." That shyness created considerable discomfort when strangers approached him for autographs and even extended to the young boys who would crowd the door of the players' locker room after a game at Yankee Stadium, trying to secure autographs from the players as they walked to their cars or, in many cases, the nearby Concourse Plaza Hotel. "Of course, the one who was always most aloof when I was a child," remembered Jim Cartelli, who grew up in the shadows of Yankee Stadium (and who befriended Mickey at his baseball fantasy camp decades later), "was Mantle. It was very difficult to get near him."

No one is crowding Mickey Mantle in center field when Jackie Robinson steps into the batter's box to start the fifth inning of the fifth game of the 1956 World Series. After missing the strike zone on the first pitch and then getting Robinson to hit a foul ball that bounces off the railing on the right side of the stands, Larsen throws a slow curve that looks inviting as it approaches the plate, but there is only air when Robinson takes a swing. "A big soft curve sent to Robinson," Bob Neal explains to his radio audience, "and he went fishing for it." Larsen knows, however, that he cannot count on the Dodger third baseman to miss all the pitches, and Robinson's bat squarely meets the ball on the next pitch and sends a high drive to the left side of the stands—but foul—where it hits the top of the facade in the upper deck and then falls back onto the field. "Boy," says Neal, "Jackie really gave that ball a ride." But the threat of a hit ends when Robinson swings at the next pitch and lofts a high fly ball into right field, where Bauer corrals it for the first out of the inning.

Gil Hodges follows Robinson to the plate. The Dodger first baseman is a pull hitter, and Mantle shifts a few feet to his right to account for that tendency. At first, there appears to be little likelihood of a ball reaching the outfield. Larsen fires two fastballs by Hodges which Babe Pinelli calls for strikes. The Yankee hurler thinks he has achieved another strikeout on the next pitch, but the umpire believes otherwise, and the count stands at one ball and two strikes. Larsen misses on the next fastball as well and now, with the count at 2–2, he knows that he has to get the pitch over the plate. But the pitch—a slider—is not nearly as good as Larsen would have liked. "The ball was flat when it drifted into Gil's hitting area," Larsen later recalled. "His brain must have sounded an alarm that this was the pitch that would end up in a home run to tie the score."

His head down, his eyes focused, Hodges swings at the ball with his arms extended and his considerable muscles rippling. There is a loud sound as the bat makes a connection and the ball quickly soars toward left center field. Neal is screaming into the microphone that Hodges "drives one deep into left center field." Sitting in the stands, Joan Hodges, the first baseman's wife, jumps to her feet with thousands of others, believing that the ball is destined to be a home run into the bleachers beyond the 457-foot sign. For his part, Larsen does not think the ball will reach the bleachers, but he does think it will "drop near the base of the fence" for a double or triple or "even an inside-the-park home run."

Mickey Mantle has other thoughts. He gets a good jump on the ball, and Yogi Berra, who is watching from home plate, thinks, "With his speed, Mickey has a chance to catch it." The other person who thinks Mantle can catch up to the ball is Dodger pitcher Clem Labine, who is watching the play from the Dodger bullpen in left center field. "You can tell," Labine later explained, "by where his eyes are—if he was afraid of going into the wall, then you see his eyes off the ball. But when the head is still up and looking for the ball, then you know he's not worried about going into the wall." As the ball dips out of the sky, Mantle, with his head up and his left arm extended, reaches out and snares the ball with his glove at full speed just before it hits the ground. "Sheer robbery," Neal exclaims. "It was," Mickey later said, "the best catch I ever made." And although she is disappointed, Joan Hodges has to agree that it was "a fantastic catch."

Larsen has dodged one bullet. But he is not yet out of the inning. There are only two outs, and Sandy Amoros steps into the batter's box. After taking the first pitch for a ball, Amoros swings hard at the next pitch—another slider—and drives the ball toward the right-field stands. Larsen watches, knowing that the ball has "the legs to get out of the park." But first-base umpire Ed Runge races toward the stands and, as the ball reaches the seats, signals that it is a foul ball. When asked later how close the call was, Runge held up his thumb and index finger— signaling a distance of about four inches. "That shows how valuable it is to have a man down the line in these games," Pinelli says after the game. "If I gotta call that one from the plate, I go the other way."

Larsen has been given another reprieve. After another ball, he throws yet another slider. Amoros swings and sends a routine ground ball to Billy Martin, who pulls it in and makes the throw to first baseman Joe Collins for the out. And so Larsen can now retreat to the security of the Yankee dugout—and as he does so, the fans give him a rousing ovation.

Bottom of the Fifth:
Pee Wee Reese

To the nine-year-old boy, it looked to be like many other trees in the spacious fields of Brandenburg, Kentucky, near the Ohio River. But his father, then a struggling tobacco farmer in the nearby town of Ekron, explained on that long-ago day in the 1920s that this tree—with its strong, low-hanging branches—had a special significance. It was the hanging tree, he said, the one used to lynch blacks who had committed some infraction that the white populace found unacceptable. It was not clear to the young boy whether his father had ever participated in those lynchings. But that was almost secondary. The tree symbolized a violent part of life that contrasted sharply with the boy's otherwise tranquil existence in which blacks lived separate and apart from the white community.

The boy would grow up, move to urban centers where blacks mixed with whites, and learn to respect the contribution of African-Americans to the nation's growth. But he never forgot that tree. "That's something that always haunted my father," the boy's son, Mark, told me decades later. "And I think it's something that dogged my father—to use his expression—his entire life."

As he fields practice ground balls from first baseman Gil Hodges in

Yankee Stadium, Dodger shortstop Pee Wee Reese, now thirty-eight years old, is surely focused on other matters as the Yankees come to bat in the bottom of the fifth inning of the fifth game of the 1956 World Series. There is, of course, tension on the field and in the stands. "Well," says radio announcer Bob Neal, "with such a great thriller, everybody here is going to stay closely glued to their seats." But the pressure of a World Series is nothing new for Reese. Having joined the club in 1940, he has played every inning of every World Series game that pitted the Dodgers against the Yankees. He is now a seasoned professional, and he is not one to be distracted by the huge crowds in the stadium or un-nerved by the importance of the game.

It is a life that Harold Henry Reese could not have imagined when he was growing up on that farm near Ekron, Kentucky. Not that he was there long. It was difficult to eke out a living on a tobacco farm in those Depression days, and by the time his son was seven, Carl Reese gave up the farm and moved his family, which included his wife, Emma, and five children, about fifty miles up the Ohio River to Louisville. There Carl took a job as a detective with the Louisville & Nashville Railroad, but the income was hardly enough to support a family of seven. "We were very poor," Reese later recalled. But it was really of no moment. "Everyone was poor where we lived," he said. Still, all the children worked as soon as they were able and, as Reese remembered, every-body brought in whatever they could earn and "threw it in the pot."

For his part, young Harold would sell box lunches, deliver papers, and take whatever odd jobs he could handle while he went to school. He had an interest in baseball, but, as he remembered years later, "I developed faster at marbles." Before long he was a master at shooting marbles, especially with his smallest marble—the peewee. ("You guys don't stand a chance," he would invariably tell his friends when he ap-proached a game in the neighborhood park. "I've got my favorite pee-wee with me today.") By the time he was eleven, he had won the city championship and his friends were calling him "Pee Wee."

Although it had nothing to do with his physical size, the nickname provided an apt description of young Pee Wee through his high school years. His growth was slow, and even as a seventeen-year-old high school senior he stood only five feet, four inches tall and weighed only

120 pounds. Sometimes he would tag along with his older brother Carl Jr. to neighborhood baseball games, and on occasion the other boys would enlist the younger brother's services if they came up short on players.

Pee Wee enjoyed the game and had a quickness in the field that distinguished him from most of his peers. He soon began playing with an American Legion team and then joined the New Covenant Presbyterian Church team as a shortstop after he graduated from high school. Having grown a few inches and gained some weight, Pee Wee was that much better a player, and he caught the eye of William "Cap" Neal when the church team won an interleague championship in 1937. That was no small matter, because Neal managed the Louisville Colonels, the local minor-league baseball team.

Shortly after the interleague series, Neal asked the young athlete whether he would be interested in joining the Colonels. On the one hand, Pee Wee was excited about the prospect of playing for a professional baseball team. On the other hand, he was concerned that success might lead to his elevation to the Brooklyn Dodgers—with whom the Colonels had a working arrangement at the time. Pee Wee knew all about the Dodgers' history, and, however much he wanted to progress to the big leagues, he did not want to play for that team. The club had not had a winning record in years (which had inspired a sportswriter for a local paper to call them "Bums," a label perpetuated by the paper's cartoonist with an appropriate caricature of a tramp who had an unshaven beard, a dilapidated hat, and a smile that lacked a few teeth). Beyond that, the Brooklyn team seemed to attract eccentric players whose mental lapses were legendary. (There was that memorable game when Dodger outfielder Babe Herman slammed a line drive into right field with the bases loaded. It had all the earmarks of a triple that would drive in all three runners. Instead, only one run scored and the other three Dodgers—including Herman—found themselves at third base, giving the opposing team an easy double play to end the inning. The incident sparked numerous jokes, including one about the ticket agent who leaves Ebbets Field for a cigarette break and, when asked by a cabdriver how the Dodgers are doing, says, "They have three men on base." To which the cabdriver responds, "Which base?")

Still, it was a chance to play professional baseball, and Neal was offering more money than Pee Wee was then making as a cable splicer with the telephone company. Reese's boss did not think that was enough to abandon a job that had considerable security. "Pee Wee," the telephone supervisor said, "I think you're making a mistake by quitting your job and going on to play baseball." Reese did not agree. He had dreams, and they did not include a lifetime job at the telephone company. "I'm young," he responded. "I may as well give it a shot." And so, as he later recalled, "I couldn't get my name on that contract fast enough."

It proved to be a smart decision. In that first year, Reese—now standing five feet, ten inches and weighing about 160 pounds—established himself as one of the best shortstops in the American Association. By the beginning of the 1939 season, the press was reporting that Reese "has fielded and hit sensationally" and that "scouts from everywhere" were "swarming on the youngster's trail."

Cap Neal told anyone who asked that he would demand at least $50,000 for his star shortstop, and many clubs were interested—the Chicago Cubs, the Cincinnati Reds, and the New York Giants. But the acquisition was ultimately made by Larry MacPhail—the Dodgers' volatile, hard-drinking, and often savvy general manager. Reese, MacPhail, told the press, was part of his plan to rebuild the Dodgers into a competitive team, because he was "the most instinctive base runner I've ever seen." Reese did not share MacPhail's excitement. ("Oh, no," he moaned when reporters told him of the trade. "Not Brooklyn.")

His distress did not last long. Indeed, looking back many years later, he acknowledged that the move to Brooklyn "was the best thing that ever happened to me." A key reason was the Dodgers' new manager—Leo Durocher. A fiery player who had started his career with the New York Yankees in the 1920s (with Babe Ruth and Lou Gehrig as teammates), Durocher had a reputation as a slick-fielding shortstop who commanded little respect as a hitter but someone who could inspire a team with his ferocious spirit. It was the same quality that drove teams to hire Billy Martin in later years, and, like those later general managers who pursued Martin, MacPhail decided that Durocher could give the Brooklyn Bums a lift that they sorely needed. And so the thirty-four-year-old Durocher was hired to play shortstop and manage the Brooklyn team for the 1939 season.

Despite the high expectations that surrounded his arrival, Reese was, as he recalled, "scared to death" when he went to spring training in Daytona, Florida, in February 1940. He was, after all, only twenty-one years old and, as one sportswriter explained, with "his pale, thin features and slender build," he looked "more like a choirboy than a professional ballplayer." (When a sportswriter first encountered the smooth-cheeked youth at spring training camp, he asked Reese if he brought a razor with him. "I shave about once a week," Pee Wee explained with a grin.)

That first season was an unimaginable roller-coaster ride. Durocher gave Reese ample opportunity to play at short and made it clear that the rookie was to be the manager's substitute on the field. "I want you to run this team as I would if I were still out there," he told his young protégé. "You're my holler guy." It was enough to give any new player confidence, and Reese appeared to be on his way. Then, at an afternoon game in Chicago's Wrigley Field in the beginning of June, Cubs pitcher Jake Mooty threw a curveball to the right-handed Reese. Reese lost track of the ball against the white shirts of the fans in center field, and it hit him in the head. ("I never saw it," Reese later said.) He slumped to the ground immediately, unconscious and, as the doctors later determined at the hospital, suffering from a concussion. ("They hurt my boy today," Durocher bitterly told his wife afterward.)

After a short stay in the hospital, Reese was sent home to Louisville to recuperate before rejoining the team at the end of June. He brought back with him a determination never to be beaned again—and thus became the first player in the major leagues to wear a batting helmet (which would not be required for all players until the 1950s). Reese also returned with a habit that would later prove to be his undoing: cigarettes. "He started smoking cigarettes," his son, Mark, later recalled, "because he had nothing to do while he was lying in the hospital."

Still, it did not affect his performance when he returned to the Dodgers. Newspapers touted the skills and accomplishments of Reese, calling him the "Boy Wonder" and an "amazing" rookie. For his part, Durocher called Reese "the best leadoff hitter in the National League" and "tops" among shortstops in the last fifteen years. Chicago Cubs manager Gabby Hartnett, a Hall of Fame catcher in his time, agreed, calling Reese "one of the best ballplayers in the major leagues." Pittsburgh Pirates manager Frankie Frisch, who had compiled a sterling record as a National League second baseman, joined the chorus, saying that it was "a delight to watch a kid like that" who was "a great fielder with a great arm" and had "a natural genius for base running."

And then disaster struck again. In a game against the Philadelphia Phillies on August 15, Reese slid hard into second base in order to avoid a force-out on a ground ball. His spikes caught the edge of the canvas base, twisted his leg, and resulted in a fractured heel that prematurely ended his season. Still, in eighty-four games with the Dodgers, he had been able to bat .272, with five home runs and twenty-eight runs batted in—statistics that were all the more impressive in light of his slow start. But more than that, Reese was pleased by his place on the team. "I felt," he said, "that I belonged, that I could play." Which was no small achievement, because the Brooklyn Dodgers of 1940 were a rough-and-tumble group whose players were almost always ready to fight and never willing to give any quarter to opposing teams—or even their own teammates—in the effort to win games. ("We didn't have too many guys who were afraid," Reese later said of his teammates in those early years. "If you were afraid, you didn't stay on the club.")

Reese assumed that his performance would be rewarded by a new contract for the 1941 season with an increase in his salary. But he was only twenty-two years old, had no experience in negotiating contracts, and was "scared to death" of General Manager Larry MacPhail (who was described by one sportswriter as "a part-time drinker and a full-time lunatic"). When he met with MacPhail in the winter at the Dodgers' offices in Brooklyn, Reese decided the best strategy was to be honest. "Mr. MacPhail," he began, "I'd like your advice. How much money do you think I should get?" MacPhail was not interested in giving advice. He slammed his fist on the desk, which only made the young player that much more nervous. "Young man," he scolded Reese, "I've got a job to do and so do you." With that, he handed Reese a contract with the same salary he had made in 1940. "I was so frightened," Reese recalled, "I signed it on the spot."

Pee Wee did not have to endure the same tension on the field when he later reported for spring training. Unlike MacPhail, Leo Durocher was eager to do whatever he could to make his new shortstop feel comfortable. (Durocher reminded Reese early in the season that he was always there to help if needed. "If you have any questions," he said, "don't hesitate. Come up and ask me." A few weeks later, Reese sheepishly approached the manager—an ever-dapper dresser off the field who consorted with gamblers, actresses, and others integral to New York's high life. "What is it, kid?" the manager inquired. "Mr. Durocher," Reese said, "where do you buy your clothes?")

Durocher's interest in Reese's development was matched by his patience. He believed that Reese would only improve with experience, and even as he was singing Reese's praise to reporters in his rookie season, Durocher was also telling them that "Pee Wee will get better."

Reese put Durocher's faith to the test. His play on the field in 1941 lacked some of the finesse that he had shown earlier, and the errors occurred with an uncomfortable frequency. Still, nothing could shake Durocher's confidence in his new shortstop. At one point Reese asked the manager to bench him after he had made some errors in the field. "Pee Wee," Durocher snapped, "if you think I'm going in there to bail you out, you're nuts. You're playing even if you make twelve errors a day." In later recounting the story, Durocher would proudly say, "You know what happened then? Pee Wee didn't just play a good game. He played the game of the century. That's right. The kid played the fucking game of the century."

In time, that kind of superior performance would be Reese's trademark throughout every season. But not in 1941. Reese batted only .229 and led the league's shortstops in errors. ("In spite of me," Reese would later say, "we won the pennant.") Still, he and Pete Reiser, the twenty-two-year-old outfielder who led the National League in batting with a .343 average, were soon being referred to by sportswriters as the "Gold Dust Twins" because of the inspiration they provided to the Brooklyn club.

The World Series against the Yankees was an exciting venture for Reese, and he did have three singles in the first game of that five-game series. But, like the rest of the team, his hopes for victory collapsed when Dodger catcher Mickey Owen failed to hold on to the third strike against Yankee right fielder Tommy Henrich in that critical fourth game. "It looks like we're going to get our ass beat," Reese said to himself as he watched events unfold from the infield. But there was always next year.

Baseball in 1942 was overshadowed by the war that raged in Europe and the Pacific. But not for Pee Wee Reese. He reported to spring training at Daytona in February, but his thoughts were preoccupied by Dorothy Walton, a nineteen-year-old girl with long dark hair, a broad smile, and bright eyes. Pee Wee had met her three years earlier in the backyard of his older sister's home in Louisville. "I saw her on the back porch drying her hair," Reese later explained. "That is the moment I decided: That's the girl for me."

The two began spending time together, and the conversations eventually focused on plans for marriage. It was not something that pleased Dottie's parents. They did not like the idea of their daughter becoming entangled with a baseball player, and they were even more disturbed when their nineteen-year-old daughter decided to visit her boyfriend at the Dodgers' spring training camp in Daytona in March 1942. But Dottie had her own ideas as well as an invitation from the wife of Billy Herman, the Dodgers' second baseman.

The trip took an unexpected twist shortly after Dottie arrived at Daytona. She and Pee Wee went out to dinner one night with outfielder Dixie Walker and his wife, Stelle. The Florida night was warm, the mood was gay, and Stelle did not understand why Pee Wee and Dottie wanted to wait until the fall to get married. "Why don't you two get married now?" she asked. Spontaneity overwhelmed the couple, and they agreed to get married that Sunday, with Dixie Walker as the best man.

The news was not well received in Louisville. "It was not accepted by my mother-in-law," Reese later said with some understatement, "and you could hardly blame her." Not that Pee Wee and Dottie would change anything. The newly married couple found an apartment in the

Bay Ridge section of Brooklyn for the season, and soon enough sportswriters were knocking on the door for an interview with the new Mrs.
Reese. And she was willing to talk about her new life with the Dodgers'
shortstop. Pee Wee, she said, was not one "to talk shop a lot" when he
came home after a game, but he was "a wonderful dancer. Like most
men," she added, "Pee Wee likes to eat at home," and she was only too
happy to oblige, frequently making him steak dinners or Southern-fried
chicken.

Dottie and Pee Wee may have been comfortable with their marriage,
but Larry MacPhail was not. In the general manager's view, marriage
compromised a young man's competitive zeal. "Well," he told Reese,
"there goes the pennant."

MacPhail's prediction proved to be accurate, but no one could blame
it on Pee Wee's marriage. The club won 104 games in 1942—four more
than they had won in 1941 and enough in most years to take the flag—
but the St. Louis Cardinals won 106 games and finished first.

Reese was an integral part of the Dodgers' improved performance.
The twenty-three-year-old shortstop raised his batting average to .255,
reduced his errors in the field, led the league's shortstops in the number
of plays handled, and, perhaps most important, was named to the National League's All-Star team. The statistics, however, failed to capture
the intangible qualities that Reese brought to the game. With his growing self-confidence, his calm demeanor, and his unyielding determination to win, he became the glue that often held the team together.
"Experience and poise, added to his great natural ability," said one
sportswriter during the middle of the season, "make Reese the standout
shortstop in the league." Another sportswriter said later in the season
that "the most valuable Dodger this year is Pee Wee Reese."

In other times and other circumstances, there would be much to
look forward to in the following season. But the nation was at war, and
Reese was called to duty. He joined the navy in January 1943, but, unlike many of his peers, the Louisville native did not have to worry
about armed combat. He was initially stationed at a base in Norfolk,
Virginia, where he supervised intramural athletic events. He was then
shipped to Pearl Harbor, where he played on a baseball team with
other major-league players who toured the Pacific Islands. ("You can

have all the other ballplayers I saw on service teams," said Yankee Hall of Fame catcher Bill Dickey, who managed the team. "I will take Pee Wee Reese.")

Pee Wee was playing cards on a ship coming home from Guam after the war ended when he learned that the Dodgers had signed a contract with Jackie Robinson. "Hey, Pee Wee," yelled a shipmate who had heard the news on a shortwave radio. "Did you hear? The Dodgers signed a nigger." Pee Wee did not give it much thought and continued to play cards. And then the shipmate yelled out, "And he plays short-stop!" To which Reese responded, "Oh, shit."

Pee Wee had never played baseball with a black. In fact, he had never had any real contact with blacks when he was growing up. They lived in separate neighborhoods, went to their own schools, and rode at the back of the bus. He could not even remember ever shaking hands with a black person. Not surprisingly, he would later say that "the first experience I had with Jackie was kind of strange really."

Still, he wanted to be fair. Perhaps it was the lingering memory of that hanging tree. Or perhaps it was just his nature. Whatever. Pee Wee Reese was not going to let the color of a player's skin change his ap-proach. "If he's man enough to take my job," he decided, "I'm not gonna like it, but dammit, black or white, he deserves it."

He did not have to worry about any competition from the new Dodger during the 1946 season. Robinson was dispatched to Montreal to play with the Royals, and Reese resumed his position at shortstop, where he continued his good fielding, improved his batting average to a career high of .284, and was again selected for the National League All-Star team. That performance gave Pee Wee the security he craved. Durocher was not about to replace the Louisville native with Robinson for the 1947 season. Robinson was therefore asked to play first base in that rookie year.

Reese was with the team in Panama when Dixie Walker circulated his petition protesting Robinson's inclusion on the team. Dixie was a close friend, and so Pee Wee was one of the first teammates Walker approached. The Georgia-born Walker no doubt assumed that Reese would be sympathetic. After all, his good friend was from a border state where racial segregation was an integral part of community life.

But Walker probably did not know about that hanging tree. Or perhaps he did not appreciate Pee Wee's fundamental sense of fairness. "Look, man," Reese bluntly told his friend. "I just got out of the service for three years. I don't care whether this man is black, blue, or what the hell color this man is. I have to play baseball." And so Reese told Walker that he would not be signing the petition.

Walker could not have been entirely surprised by Pee Wee's response. The Dodger shortstop was the first one to walk across the field in spring training to shake Robinson's hand. He was also one of the first to play cards with Robinson in the clubhouse before games—something, Reese remembered, that puzzled "some of the Deep South boys" who "wanted to know how in the hell you could do it." For Reese there was no mystery. "After you played with Jackie for a while and realized how sharp he was, what a great competitor he was, what a great athlete he was," he said, "I couldn't just make myself dislike the man."

All of that made it difficult for Reese to stand by idly while his new teammate was subjected to ethnic slurs of the vilest kind from fans and opposing players after the season began. As Durocher had asked in his first days with the club, Reese had taken charge of the team, and he felt obligated to do something when Robinson just stood there silently on the field—turning the other cheek, as Rickey had asked—while the verbal abuse reached a crescendo. Players' memories about when the gestures were made are vague and sometimes inconsistent. Some said it was in Cincinnati. Some said Boston. And yet others said Philadelphia. The location was, however, secondary. Because there is no dispute that Reese would occasionally wander over to Robinson and casually place his hand on his teammate's shoulder or simply stand by his side and stare at the people hurling the abuse. In most cases, that was enough to silence or at least moderate the tension. People now saw that the Dodgers' shortstop—the team leader and, beyond that, someone from Kentucky—was prepared to stand by a black man.

Reese's moral support was critical to Robinson's mental state at the time. "After Pee Wee came over like that," Robinson said many years later, "I never felt alone on a baseball field again." For his part, Reese could never explain why he made the move. He was not one to look for hidden meanings in the hanging tree or some other psychological meandering. "Something in my gut reacted to the moment," he later said. "Something about—what?—the unfairness of it? The injustice of it? I don't know." In time, sportswriters and historians would make much of Reese's support for Robinson. But he never attached much significance to it. "He was embarrassed by the notoriety of that simple gesture," Rachel Robinson told me many years later. "'So what's the big deal?' Pee Wee said. 'He was a teammate.'"

Still, it was the impetus for a close friendship that would endure many trials during their playing years and survive separate paths during their retirement. It was, above all, a friendship that rejected pretense and thrived on candor. At one juncture during the Dodger years—after he had shed his passive response to racial abuse on the field—Robinson complained to Reese that pitchers were throwing at him because he was black. "No," the shortstop replied, "they aren't throwing at you because you're black, Jackie. They're throwing at you because they just don't like you." And later, after they had been teammates for many years, Pee Wee said to him, "You know, I didn't particularly go out of my way just to be nice to you." To which Jackie responded, "Pee Wee, that's what I appreciated most—that you didn't."

It may have seemed spontaneous in retrospect, but dealing with the pressures in Louisville was not so simple. Pee Wee's family did not understand how he could play ball with a black man. "My grandfather would turn over in his grave," he told Rickey at the time, "if he knew I was playing on a team with a colored boy." When Reese went home to Louisville, Pee Wee's older brother Carl Jr. would kid him about the experience, saying, "I bet there will be watermelon seeds around shortstop." Other members of the family made similar remarks, all believing, as Pee Wee's son, Mark, later said, that the integration experiment "was going to blow up in Rickey's face." It may have seemed easy to sidestep those kinds of comments when he was on the field, but Reese could not so casually deflect them at home. "We all know what Jackie had to go through," Mark Reese later explained, "but we don't realize what Pee Wee had to face inside his own head. People have no idea how much my father had to endure."

Despite that inner turmoil, Reese continued to enhance his reputation as the league's best shortstop. In 1947, he duplicated his career-high batting average of .284, slammed a career-high twelve home runs, led the league in walks with 104, and wound up hitting .304 in the seven-game World Series that the Dodgers lost to the Yankees. He had a similar record in 1948 (along with a career-high twenty-five stolen bases), and, more than that, became the recognized leader of the club. Manager Burt Shotton, who wore a shirt and tie in the dugout and was therefore unable to walk out onto the field, had told Reese, "You take charge. You're my man." Branch Rickey gave formal recognition to Reese's leadership role by making him the team captain for the 1949 season.

It was a role that suited Reese well. He would often sit in a captain's chair by his locker in the corner of the clubhouse before and after a game, puffing on a pipe, and reading a newspaper or talking with teammates. "He had a quiet leadership quality about him," Carl Erskine later said. "He didn't say a lot. He didn't yell a lot. He didn't get on guys a lot. But," Erskine continued, "you go in the clubhouse after you had made a mistake, and Pee Wee didn't have to say much. He gave you a look and a couple of words. And you knew what he meant." But there was more to his leadership than constructive criticism. He was there to provide his teammates with encouragement and advice inside the clubhouse (or, as in the case of Duke Snider's earlier comment about Brooklyn fans, try to protect them against their own mistakes). "If anyone had a problem," said pitcher Johnny Podres, "they went to Pee Wee."

His leadership role was evident on the field as well. "Reese was the player I feared most on the Dodgers in those years," said Yankee right fielder Tommy Henrich, who played for the Yankees in the 1941, 1947, and 1949 World Series against the Dodgers. "It was always my feeling that Pee Wee, more than any Dodger, had the ability to make things happen. He was capable of stepping into a pressure situation with the game, the season, or the World Series hanging in the balance and get the key hit, steal the key base, or make the key play in the field that his team needed at that crucial moment."

Pee Wee's willingness to fight for his team was evidenced in other ways as well. If the occasion warranted, he would confront umpires with bad decisions. (There was the time when George Magerkurth, a six-foot-five-inch, 280-pound umpire, called Reese out in a play at second base. The Dodger captain jumped to his feet and started yelling at Magerkurth, telling him how wrong he was. "Get back in the dugout," Magerkurth instructed, "or I'll bite your head off." "If you do," Reese shot back, "you'll have more brains in your stomach than you've got in your head.") And he would be the one to leave his position at shortstop to go to the pitcher's mound if a Dodger hurler appeared to be losing control of the game.

Reese's focus on the pitcher was perhaps epitomized by an occasion in the eighth inning of the second game of the 1949 World Series at Yankee Stadium. The Dodgers were winning, but the score was only 1–0 and two Yankees were on base when Tommy Henrich stepped into the batter's box to face Dodger hurler Preacher Roe. Henrich had hit a home run to win the first series game, and Reese could see the tension in Roe's face. Reese casually walked over to the pitcher's mound. "Let's you and I have a talk," he told Roe. "Sure, Pee Wee," the Dodger pitcher said, obviously welcoming the interruption. "What d'ya wanta talk about?" "Anything at all, Preach," the shortstop replied. "Hunting? Fishing? Anything. Let's just keep Henrich fidgeting up there and wondering what you're going to throw him." The short interlude had its desired effect. After a few minutes, Reese returned to his position and Roe got Henrich to hit a harmless fly ball to the outfield.

The formal elevation to captain in 1949 did not hurt Reese's batting performance. He continued to excel as the team's leadoff hitter, led the league in runs scored (with 132), and managed to hit a career-high sixteen home runs. His record over the next four years reflected the same consistency and contributed to a team record that enabled the Dodgers to come within one game of winning the pennant in two years (1950 and 1951) and then to win the pennant in two other years (1952 and 1953). That high level of consistency was duly noted in the press, and there was little surprise when sportswriters began mentioning Reese as a possible manager after the Dodgers fired Charlie Dressen at the end of the 1953 season. It mattered not to the press that Reese was still an active player. Durocher had been a playing shortstop when he took over the club's managerial reins in 1939, and many other clubs had used player-managers.

Shortly after the 1953 World Series, the *New York Daily News* reported that the Dodgers were moving forward with "the installation of Pee Wee Reese as manager." The report was not mere speculation. General manager Buzzie Bavasi did in fact fly down to Louisville to talk with the team's shortstop about the promotion. Reese was flattered but eventually said no. "Playing is a full-time job," he later explained. "So is managing. You can't do a good job at either if you try to do both." Other factors played a role as well. "He felt he was too close to the players," Bavasi remembered from that long-ago conversation. Trying to discipline players who were his teammates on the field would undoubtedly prove problematic. And then there was the daunting challenge of being a successful manager for the Brooklyn Dodgers. "We just won the pennant two straight years," Reese told Bavasi. "How can you improve on that?"

There was a certain irony in Reese's assessment. The manager's position was eventually given to Walter Alston. He had enjoyed considerable experience as a minor-league manager, but the Dodgers failed to win the pennant in 1954, finishing five games behind the Giants. It was a failure that could not be attributed to Reese's performance. For the first (and only) time in his career, his batting average passed the .300 mark (.309) with a career-high thirty-five doubles. And he continued to play at the same level when the Dodgers took off in the beginning of the 1955 season.

He was, by now, not only the longest-serving Dodger on the team but also the most popular among the fans. Hilda Chester, a boisterous fan who attended virtually every game at Ebbets Field with a cowbell (which she rang regularly), would often call out to the Dodger shortstop, "Pee Wee, have you had your milk today?" When Happy Felton conducted his pregame television show at Ebbets Field (*Happy Felton's Knothole Gang*)—which featured a Dodger player chosen by a Little Leaguer—Reese was the one most often selected. And when his thirty-seventh birthday approached on July 22, the Dodgers decided to give him a special night at Ebbets Field. The decision was made, however, with some trepidation. The Dodgers had tried to have a tribute night many years earlier for Dixie Walker, but the event proved to be a dismal failure. Irving Rudd, the Dodgers' publicity director, promised a better outcome for the Reese event and, as an added inducement, Bavasi told Rudd he would give him a dollar for every fan over the eighteen thousand mark who attended the game.

It was a good incentive for Rudd and a bad bet for Bavasi. By game time, more than thirty-five thousand fans were jammed into Ebbets Field (which officially had a seating capacity closer to thirty-four thousand). The highlight of the evening came in the fifth inning, when a 250-pound cake was rolled out to the infield. The lights were dimmed, and everyone was asked to light a match and sing happy birthday to the Dodger captain. "It was," Carl Erskine remembered, "a tremendous outpouring of affection."

The season had a fitting finale when Reese made the last play in the 1955 World Series for the Dodgers' only championship—a ground ball from Yankee outfielder Elston Howard that Reese fielded and threw to Hodges at first. (In a chance encounter in a bar some years later, Don Hoak, who had played third base for the Dodgers at one point, needled Reese about the play, saying that the ball had bounced in the dirt before Hodges picked it up. It was a point of pride for Reese, who did believe—and wanted to believe—that the throw had been a good one and had not bounced in the dirt. Unable to reach agreement, the two former players picked up the phone at three o'clock in the morning and called Hodges, then in New York as the manager of the Mets. They put the question to Hodges. "It bounced," he said, and hung up.)

The years had begun to catch up with Reese. In an interview with *Parade* magazine during the middle of the 1956 season, he explained the secret to longevity on the baseball field. "The best way to keep your body fit," he said, "is to keep your legs fit. If they're not strong, then you're going to tire more easily." It all sounded so logical, but no amount of exercise could stave off the inevitable. Reese played in 147 games that season—most at shortstop (but a few at third base)—and saw his productivity plummet: a .257 batting average (his lowest since 1942) and only thirty extra-base hits (the lowest number he had ever had in any complete season). After the Dodgers won the 1956 pennant, Reese acknowledged that "[t]his is the toughest one we ever won. We're older."

Pee Wee Reese shows no sign of aging as Enos Slaughter steps into the batter's box to lead off the bottom of the fifth inning of the fifth game of the 1956 World Series. Although Slaughter is a left-handed hitter, Reese knows that the Yankee left fielder can hit to all sides of the field. So there is a chance he could slap a ball to the left side of the infield at Reese. But Slaughter does not hit a ball to any of the Dodger fielders. Instead, he patiently waits out Maglie for the first walk of the game.

Billy Martin steps into the batter's box. Jackie Robinson moves in a little closer to the plate from his position at third base, no doubt thinking that Martin may try a sacrifice bunt to move Slaughter into scoring position at second. Maglie recognizes that possibility as well. He wants to prevent Slaughter from taking a big lead and throws the ball over to Gil Hodges at first base before Martin sees a pitch. Slaughter moves back to the bag safely, and Maglie turns his attention to the Yankee second baseman.

Martin shows no sign of bunting and watches a curveball sail to the outside of the plate for a ball. He then steps out of the batter's box and looks down to third-base coach Frank Crosetti to see if Stengel has given him the sign to bunt. In the meantime, Bob Wolff is reminding his audience that Martin is "always dangerous, particularly, so it appears, when the pressure is really on."

Maglie looks over to Slaughter at first base and then throws a curve which comes in for a called strike. Martin again steps out of the box and looks down to Crosetti in another obvious effort to determine whether the bunt sign is on. Maglie again throws to first base to keep Slaughter close to the bag and then focuses his eyes on the signal from Roy Campanella. The pitch comes in, Martin turns to bunt, and he pushes the ball in front of the plate on the infield grass. Maglie rushes in, fields the ball cleanly, spins around, and throws it to Reese, who is covering second base on the play. But Maglie's throw is high, and for a moment it appears that the ball will sail into center field. But the Dodger shortstop times a leap to catch the ball and force Slaughter out at second. "Pee Wee had to reach high in the air," says Wolff, "and he hauled it in."

Martin is now at first base with one out, and Gil McDougald comes to the plate in the seasonally warm afternoon sun. "Perfect baseball weather," Wolff tells his listening audience. McDougald works the count to two balls and two strikes. Martin is off and running on the next pitch in an attempted steal or hit-and-run play, but McDougald fouls the ball off. Martin retreats to first base, and McDougald waits for the Barber's next pitch.

In a game this close, the Yankee shortstop knows that Maglie will not want to get behind the hitter on the count and risk another walk. So McDougald is ready as Maglie comes in with his pitch. As he no doubt expected, McDougald sees that the ball is in his hitting zone, and he slams a line drive that seems destined to fly over Reese's head at short for another Yankee hit. But Reese again leaps high in the air and grabs the ball with the edge of his glove. As he comes down, the ball pops out of his glove, but, with his quick reflexes, Reese pulls it in and throws to first base to double-up Martin, who was off at the crack of the bat on the understandable assumption that the ball would never be caught. In describing the play for his listeners, Dodger broadcaster Vin Scully says, "It was like Pee Wee Reese was playing catch with himself."

And so Sal Maglie walks off the diamond with the satisfaction that he has given up only one hit in five innings. There is still time to turn the game around.

Top of the Sixth: Yogi Berra

Allie Reynolds went into his stretch on the pitcher's mound at Yankee Stadium, glanced over at Red Sox center fielder Dom DiMaggio at first base (the result of a walk), and then turned his attention to home plate. Reynolds was thirty-six years old, an advanced age for pitchers of his era, and should have been nearing the end of his career. But on this twenty-eighth day of September in 1951, the Oklahoma native was about to become the first American League pitcher to hurl two no-hitters in the same season (Johnny Vander Meer of the National League's Cincinnati Reds having turned the trick in successive starts in 1938). There were two outs in the ninth inning, and only Ted Williams, now poised in the batter's box, stood between the Yankee pitcher and that new record.

In other situations, Reynolds would have given the Boston slugger a pass. ("Usually," Reynolds later told writer Peter Golenbock, "I tried to walk that damn Williams if I could because, I'll tell you, I couldn't pitch to him, and to me it was stupid to let the outstanding hitter get a hit and beat you.") But the Yankees were winning by a score of 8–0, and there seemed little harm in pitching to Williams now. Reynolds threw the Splendid Splinter a fastball. Williams' swing sent the ball into a high pop-up that began to drift into foul territory behind home plate.

Yogi Berra, now twenty-six years old, leaped from his squatting position behind the plate, flipped off his mask, and circled under the ball for what would hopefully be the final out and Reynolds' new American League record. But the ball continued drifting toward the seats, and Reynolds saw that Berra might not make the catch. He rushed in from the pitcher's mound as Berra backpedaled as fast as he could and reached out for the ball with his mitt. But it was too little, too late. The ball glanced off the tip of the mitt and hit the ground, and Berra fell facedown with his arms outstretched. Reynolds, in close pursuit, tried to avoid a collision but inadvertently stepped on his catcher's throwing hand.

Over in a nearby New Jersey hospital, Yogi's wife, Carmen, was getting ready to give birth to their second son. Hearing a scream from Carmen's room, the nurse rushed in, thinking that some medical catastrophe had befallen the pregnant woman. But when she burst through the door, the nurse saw that Mrs. Berra was listening to the radio. The patient looked up at the nurse and exclaimed, "My husband dropped the ball!" The nurse did not understand, but the thousands in attendance at Yankee Stadium certainly did.

With another teammate, Reynolds would have been irate—especially because he now had to throw the dreaded Williams another pitch. But there was no anger or resentment. Only compassion. "The pitcher, who could have been pardoned for slugging Yogi," wrote one sportswriter at the scene, "carefully picked the squat man up, patted him on the fanny, and threw an arm around his shoulders—like a father comforting a small, unhappy boy." "Don't worry about it, Yogi," said Reynolds. "We'll get him again."

The two players walked out to the pitcher's mound, and Berra told Reynolds, "Let's throw him the same pitch." As Yogi resumed his place behind the plate, Ted Williams began to curse him out. "You really put me in a hell of a spot," the Boston outfielder complained. "What am I supposed to do now? I get a base hit and I'm a bad guy." There was nothing for Berra to say or do except wait for the next pitch. Williams swung and again sent a high pop-up into foul territory behind home plate. Berra again jumped to his feet, threw off the mask, and circled under the ball. He was obviously determined to catch this one, and, when he did, he was engulfed by teammates hugging and congratulating him as though he were the one who had pitched the no-hitter. In the clubhouse afterward, Yankee co-owner Del Webb approached Berra. "When I die," said Webb, "I hope I get another chance like you."

As he takes warm-up pitches from Don Larsen in the top of the sixth inning in the fifth game of the 1956 World Series, Yogi Berra knows that there may not be another chance for the Yankees if they lose this game. Still, he has been in seven other World Series and is not overwhelmed by the pressures of the moment. "Except for my first World Series," he later explained, "I had the utmost confidence in myself."

Yogi Berra's faith in himself is hardly surprising. It may have been a product of heredity. Or perhaps the environment in which he grew up. But those who knew Larry Berra from his early days on the Hill—the close-knit Italian neighborhood of small bungalows and family shops in southwestern St. Louis—had a sense that he was someone special. "I think," said his lifelong friend Joe Garagiola, a major-league player who parlayed his wit into a successful broadcasting career, "he could have been a success at anything he put his mind to."

Larry was not the biggest kid in the neighborhood. (Although he would carry about 195 pounds on his frame as a major-league player, Berra never stood taller than five feet, eight inches.) And he certainly was not the best-looking. (In the early days with the Yankees, Berra withstood unmerciful teasing from his teammates and the press about his homely looks. "If I couldn't take anything said about me, cruel or otherwise," he later said, "I figured I wouldn't be in baseball long." And so Berra would brush off repeated comments that he was ugly, saying, "All you've got to do is hit the ball, and I never saw anyone hit one with his face.")

The St. Louis native's perspective did not go unnoticed by his teammates. "Yogi Berra is one of the most secure individuals I have ever known," said Yankee shortstop Phil Rizzuto. Years later, Dave Kaplan, director of the Yogi Berra Museum and Learning Center in Montclair, New Jersey, would pay tribute to that same quality, saying of Yogi, "He is totally comfortable in his own skin."

Whatever one could say about his appearance, there was no dispute that the youngster who roamed the Hill with his friends in those Depression years had a great talent for sports. "I remember him," said Garagiola, "as the best baseball player in the neighborhood, the best football player, the best hockey player—and the best organizer." Organization was critical, because there was no Little League to field teams, provide equipment, and establish schedules. Individual initiative thus became key to the neighborhood kids' enjoyment. During the weekends, the summer, and other times when there was no school, Larry would be up early and go down to a vacant lot or the garbage dump to lay claim to the location for his friends (and, if it were baseball to be played at the dump, Berra remembered, "we used an old car to be the dugout").

However much they wanted to play sports, Larry and his friends could not avoid attendance at St. Ambrose Church on Sunday. Not that Larry was unhappy with that obligation. "When you were at St. Ambrose," he later remembered, "you felt the importance of helping each other, working hard, and doing the right thing. When you were there, you would forget there was a Depression going on." It was a memory not easily forgotten. Throughout his life, attendance at church remained an integral part of Yogi Berra's weekly routine.

But nothing was more important to that young boy on the Hill than his parents. Paulina and Pietro, two immigrants from the small Italian town of Malvaglio near Milan, were devoted to Larry and the rest of their family, which included three older sons and a younger daughter. Pietro had been a tenant farmer in Italy but saw a better life in America for himself and his family (which then included only the two older sons). He ultimately secured a steady job at a factory in St. Louis, and when the factory whistle blew at four thirty in the afternoon to signal the end of the workday, Larry knew that he had to stop whatever he was doing, run to the neighborhood saloon, get his father a tureen of beer, and make sure it was on the kitchen table when his father walked in the door.

Punctuality was equally important if Larry or his siblings wanted to attend a party or other social event in the evenings outside the family's small frame house on Elizabeth Avenue. Before they left, there would always be the question from their father: "What time will you be home?" Never could the children ignore that chosen deadline with impunity. "We didn't have a telephone to call if we were late," Yogi later explained, "so you'd better be home." Excuses were not well received by Pietro. "I didn't make the time," he would tell his children. "You did."

It was a disciplined approach to family life that suited the young athlete and would shape his perspective in later years as well. ("I get pretty ticked if someone doesn't live up to his word," he would say. "You say you're going to be there at five o'clock, you better be there at five o'clock no matter what time it is.") Although he was not always willing to do what his parents asked, Larry's reverence for them never faded. "Wanting to make my folks happy and proud was important to me," he later said, "and it was important until the day they died." He therefore used his first World Series check in 1947 to buy them the car they never had. And when people asked him about his parents—even when he was well into his sixties—Yogi would pull out photographs of each of them that he carried in his wallet.

Despite those strong emotional bonds, Pietro and Paulina never understood their youngest son's obsession with sports. To be sure, it was a way for young children to spend idle time, but it would not, at least so these Italian immigrants thought, lay a foundation for any future as an adult. Seeing little value in sports, they wanted Larry—or "Lawdie," as Paulina called him in her heavy Italian accent—to focus on his education so he could get a job where he could earn enough as an adult to help support their family and ultimately his own family. And so they were disturbed when Larry told them that he wanted to quit school after finishing the eighth grade.

The request could not have been a complete surprise. Larry never had any interest in academics, would often play hooky, and would rarely do well on tests. (A teacher once said to him in exasperation, "Don't you know anything?" To which the young student responded, "I don't even suspect anything.") Never did he try to tell people otherwise. When someone asked him how he liked school, Larry said, "Closed."

Pietro and Paulina had a conference with the principal and the parish priest in an effort to dissuade the young student from quitting, but Larry could not be turned aside. "I was a lousy student and pretty stubborn," he later explained, "and I felt I was wasting my time." And so, at the age of fourteen, Larry Berra joined the employment rolls in St. Louis.

Not that he could hold down a job—employment always took a backseat to baseball. In each case, the job would last until springtime, and then Larry would take off early to play baseball with his friends when they got out of school. His unexcused absences did not sit well with the employers, and in due course Larry would find himself on the street looking for another job.

None of that interfered with his success on the diamond. Ironically, Larry spent very little time as a catcher in the sandlot games and then with the teams organized by the YMCA and, when he turned sixteen, American Legion teams. It was there that he got his nickname. His friend Jack Maguire Jr. noticed that Larry would always sit on the sidelines with his legs crossed and his arms folded, like a Hindu fakir (and yoga disciple) they had seen in the movies. And so the name stuck.

The other quality that people noticed about Yogi Berra was his batting form. It was very unconventional. Like his good friend Joe Garagiola, Yogi hit left-handed even though he threw right-handed (a quirk that neither Garagiola nor Yogi could ever explain). Coaches and managers tried to talk to Yogi about the need to check his swing if the ball was not in the strike zone. But the instruction never had any impact. Yogi would flail away at balls over his head or below his knees and somehow manage to drive the ball into the outfield for a home run or other extra-base hit. (Ted Williams would later say that Yogi "gave hitting a bad name." But Williams would also say that Berra was one of the most dangerous hitters in baseball because "he could move the runner, and move him late in the game, like no one else I ever saw play the game.")

Some critics later said that Yogi was trying to duplicate the batting style of his childhood hero, St. Louis Cardinals outfielder Joe Medwick— a notorious bad ball hitter whose success landed him in the Baseball Hall of Fame and who often bought the local newspaper from Larry on street corners in those early days on the Hill. For his part, Yogi had no complex theories on hitting. When later asked to explain his batting philosophy in a locker room session at one of Mickey Mantle's fantasy camps long after he had retired, Yogi said, "I see the ball, and I hit the ball." And that was it. (There was the time when Dodger pitcher Don Newcombe quickly got two strikes on Yogi during a World Series game at Ebbets Field and then threw a ball low and away that was only a foot off the ground. "A waste pitch to everybody but Yogi," said Garagiola. But Berra—with his unorthodox batting form—reached out for the ball and slammed it over the right-field scoreboard for a home run. As he trotted around the bases, Yogi kept apologizing to an astonished Newcombe, saying, "It wasn't your fault, Newk.")

They may have winced at the batting form, but Berra's coaches and managers could not take issue with the results—which distinguished him from almost all of his peers. "I've got a ballplayer out there," Leo Browne, the manager for Yogi's American Legion team, would say, "I'd like you to see. He swings at everything in sight. His form is all wrong, but he's the best hitter I've ever seen."

With endorsements like that, Yogi thought he had a good chance of securing a professional baseball contract when he and Garagiola went to a tryout for the St. Louis Cardinals at Sportsman's Park in 1942. They caught balls and, as Yogi recalled, "hit the ball pretty good that day." But Branch Rickey—then the Cardinals' general manager—said he was impressed only with Garagiola, giving the seventeen-year-old a promise of a $500 bonus when he graduated from high school. There was no similar offer for Garagiola's good friend. Rickey told Berra that he was "too awkward" and that he "would never become a big league ballplayer." Yogi was "devastated," but, on the other hand, he did not regard Rickey's decision as the last word on his baseball career. "I kept a positive attitude because I thought I was good enough to make it," Berra later explained. "That rejection only made me more determined."

Leo Browne was not prepared to accept Rickey's assessment anymore than Yogi was. So Browne contacted John Schulte, the Yankee bullpen coach who lived in the St. Louis area, and told him about the young prospect on his American Legion team. After consulting Yankee management, Schulte drove down to the Berra home after the 1942

World Series to see if he could strike a deal. "What will it take us to sign you?" Schulte asked the teenager. "$500," said Yogi. "If I don't get it, I don't sign." Schulte yielded to the demand and said the Yankees' offer would include $90 a month to play for the Yankees' Norfolk, Virginia, farm team in the Class B Piedmont League.

Pietro was skeptical about the offer. In his mind, playing games for a living did not seem like a good career path. But Yogi's three older brothers, who had been forced to abandon their own dreams of careers in professional sports, pressed their father to give his youngest son a chance, and Yogi Berra became the property of the New York Yankees. (Years later, Yogi would never tire of saying that his older brothers were better baseball players than he was and that he would periodically tell his father that he could have been a millionaire if he had allowed them to play professional baseball too. To which his father would always say, "Blame your mother.")

Yogi's first professional season was filled with new experiences. To begin with, he was asked to be the team's catcher—even though his primary experience was in the outfield and at third base. (The first game he caught was at night under lights, and a batter hit a high pop-up in foul territory near the third-base line. Berra flipped off his mask, circled under the ball, and kept yelling to the third baseman, who had approached the ball as well, "I got it, I got it." "Okay," said the third baseman. "You got it." And then the ball landed about ten feet from where Berra was standing.) He also learned that there was a condition to the $500 bonus Schulte had promised—the bonus would be paid at the end of the season if, but only if, Berra had not been cut from the team. It was a lesson about contract negotiations never to be forgotten. "When they gave me the business about not getting the money until I stuck with the ball club for a year," Yogi later said, "I made up my mind I was going to see to it I got everything that was coming to me from then on." The Yankees would later learn about that lesson and find that their All-Star catcher was no pushover when it came to the yearly negotiations for the next season's salary.

In the meantime, Berra had to worry about meeting expenses on a monthly salary of $90. He was able to cajole a few dollars a week out of his mother (who extracted a promise from him not to tell his father).

When that proved insufficient, Yogi decided to go on a hunger strike and told his manager one day that he would not play unless he was given some money for food. The manager came through with a few dollars, and in the next two games Yogi had twelve hits (including three home runs) and drove in twenty-three runs. ("When I wasn't hungry," he later explained, "I did good.")

Yogi finished the season with a respectable average and seven home runs (one fewer than the league leader). But he could not look forward to returning the next season. He was drafted into the navy, sent to Bainbridge, Maryland, for basic training, and then to Little Creek, Virginia. One evening after watching a movie, a base commander asked for volunteers to staff a fleet of new thirty-six-foot rocket boats to be used in amphibious landings. Bored with military life, Berra raised his hand, and in due course he was sent to Lido Beach in Long Island and ultimately to England to train for what turned out to be the D-day landing at Omaha Beach on June 6, 1944.

To foot soldiers rushing from amphibious vessels to the shoreline in the early-morning hours of that day, it was a vortex of violence that defied description. But the experience was entirely different to a young seaman on a rocket boat hundreds of yards from shore. As Yogi remembered, the constant barrage of bombs and flares lit up the sky "like fireworks on the Fourth of July." Entranced by the seeming beauty of the display, the St. Louis native sat up in the boat despite the German gunfire that filled the night. His indiscretion did not escape the attention of the commanding officer. "You better get your damn head down if you want to keep it!" he yelled to Berra. Yogi obeyed the instruction and was able to survive the battle with only minor injury.

Yogi returned to the New London, Connecticut, submarine base after the war and was discharged from military service in May 1946—just as he was turning twenty-one. Even before he was discharged, the Yankees had invited Berra to a workout at the stadium during one of his leaves. The first task was to find a Yankee uniform to wear at the workout. Dressed in his shapeless blue navy uniform with the white cap sitting at a tilt on his head, Yogi went to see clubhouse manager Pete Sheehy. When Berra asked for the uniform, Sheehy looked at him in disbelief. "I guess I don't look like a ballplayer," Yogi said with characteristic modesty. "You don't even look like a sailor," Sheehy responded.

Sheehy may have been right, but Berra had the last word. Within days of leaving the navy, he joined the Newark Bears, the Yankees' Triple-A farm team, and, as one sportswriter explained, soon established himself as "one of the league's most dangerous batters." In the remaining seventy-seven games of the season, Yogi batted .314 and hit fifteen home runs. In September, the Yankees called Berra up to the parent club for the final week of the 1946 season. Yogi hit a home run off of the Philadelphia Athletics' Jesse Flores in his first major-league game and then hit another home run in his second game, finishing the week's sojourn in the big leagues with a .364 average. It was only the beginning—and not just for his baseball career.

Yogi was becoming known as much for his personality as for his performance on the field. "Larry was extremely popular with his Newark teammates," said one sportswriter in early 1947, "who took every opportunity to rib him." And how could they not? He had a knack for saying things that caught people off guard and that often made them laugh. (There was the time when Yogi—an avid reader of comic books—was sharing a hotel room with Bear teammate—and future Yankee teammate—Bobby Brown, who was reading a textbook in conjunction with his study to become a medical doctor. Tired from his reading, Brown asked Yogi to turn the lights off. Berra demurred, saying that he had to finish the comic book. When he did, Yogi turned to Brown and said, "This was a good story. How did yours come out?")

Stories of Yogi's comments spread throughout the baseball world, and in time *The Sporting News* would devote a whole column to "Berraisms." "A lot of people thought he wasn't too quick with his brain," Bobby Brown said of his former roommate many years later. "But that's not true. He's got great intelligence. It's just that he didn't have a whole lot of formal education. And if you look at the things that he said, they really mean a lot. It's just that the words are sometimes a little misused."

The Yankees were not concerned about any shortcomings in Berra's verbal skills. Their only interest was to make the most of his considerable talent on the field. Bucky Harris, the Yankees' manager, thought it would be wise to continue Berra's development as a catcher during the 1947 season. But it proved to be more challenging than either Harris or Berra would have liked. "He was in tough shape for two reasons," said Spud Chandler, the first Yankee pitcher to have Berra as a battery mate. "One, he was worried about his catching. And two, he had good reason—he was not a good catcher." Berra agreed with that assessment. "Yeah, I was bad," he would later say of those first two years catching in the big leagues. "I stunk."

Objective evidence supported that assessment. On one occasion he made a wild sidearm throw to second base in an effort to stop a stolen base and beaned the second-base umpire. On another occasion his throw to second was too low and hit the pitcher in the chest. But there were signs of progress—including the time when a St. Louis Browns batter pushed a squeeze bunt toward first base to score the runner on third. Yogi leaped out in front of the plate and completed an unassisted double play by tagging both the batter running to first and the base runner trying to score. (When asked about the play by sportswriters after the game, Berra dismissed the accomplishment, saying, "I just tagged everybody in sight, including the umpire.")

Berra's uneven performance behind the plate sometimes forced Harris to leave the young player on the bench, but he would also play Yogi in right field—because, whatever limitations he had as a catcher, Berra had lost none of his ability to swing a bat. Harris tried without success to correct Berra's habit of reaching for balls out of the strike zone, telling the rookie to think before he swung. It was not useful advice to someone who relied on natural instincts. "How can a guy think and hit at the same time?" Yogi responded. Harris could not quarrel with the rookie's logic. By the time the 1947 season ended, he had hit a respectable .280 in eighty-three games with eleven home runs (and only twelve strikeouts). More than that, he had experienced the elation of a night planned in his honor by family and friends from the Hill. After a night game against the Browns in St. Louis, the young player was feted with a bevy of gifts from local merchants. Yogi had never previously given a speech, and he became so nervous when he got to the microphone that his planned remarks were all but forgotten. As a result, he ended by thanking everyone "for making this night necessary."

Public miscues like that may have enhanced Yogi's reputation for garbled speech, but they had no impact on the camaraderie he enjoyed with the other Yankees. And none of those relationships with team-mates was more important in those early years than the one Berra had with Joe DiMaggio.

Their first memorable encounter was on a station platform in September 1946 as the team was getting ready to board the train to Boston for a series with the Red Sox after Berra had hit his second home run in two days. DiMaggio kept studying the young catcher and then laughed. Berra smiled back, saying, "So what? I can hit homers too." That was the closest Yogi came to a conversation with the Yankee center fielder in those first days. Like Yankee rookies before and after him, Yogi remembered that "you were scared to talk to him." In contrast to Billy Martin's experience a few years later, Yogi explained that "you didn't play jokes" on the great DiMaggio.

Still, the Yankee Clipper was obviously intrigued by this twenty-one-year-old catcher who made funny comments and swung a potent bat. Yogi stayed at the Edison Hotel in Manhattan during his first full season in 1947, and there were many times when DiMaggio would invite him to breakfast, saying that he was making more money than the rookie. And DiMaggio would be there to provide guidance on the proper etiquette for a Yankee player. After he had popped up for an easy out in a game at Yankee Stadium, a frustrated Berra meandered out to right field, where he was playing that day. DiMaggio trotted up beside him. "Always run to your position," he advised the rookie. "It doesn't look good when you walk. The other team may have gotten you down, but don't let them know it." Berra took that and other advice to heart, and, for his part, the Yankee center fielder developed a fondness for this young player that transcended the relationships he had with most of his other teammates. And so, when Tom Horton approached the retired Hall of Fame outfielder in the 1980s about an interview for Berra's autobiography, DiMaggio was happy to cooperate. "If you were doing a book on anybody else in baseball," DiMaggio told Horton, "I would tell you to go to the library. That should tell you how I feel about Yogi."

However much he may have appreciated DiMaggio's support, Berra could not use it to avoid a poor catching performance in the first two games of the 1947 World Series against the Dodgers. Robinson and Reese stole second without much difficulty in the first game, and there were three additional steals in the second game. ("The Dodgers stole everything on me but my chest protector," Yogi later confessed.) Although the Yankees won both games, the reviews on the Yankees' new catcher were not positive. "Worst World Series catching I ever saw," said Connie Mack, a former catcher as well as a veteran of almost fifty baseball seasons as the Philadelphia Athletics' manager.

There was some redemption in the third game. In the seventh inning, Bucky Harris asked Yogi to hit for Sherman Lollar (the Yankees' new catcher), and Berra then became the first player in World Series history to slam a pinch-hit home run. But the guilt returned in the fourth game. Yankee pitcher Bill Bevens was on the verge of the first no-hitter in the World Series when he walked the fleet-footed Al Gionfriddo with two outs in the ninth inning. No doubt aware of the Yankee catcher's shortcomings, Gionfriddo abruptly tried to steal second, and, as he had hoped, Berra's throw to shortstop Phil Rizzuto did not catch him. When Dodger third baseman Cookie Lavagetto later broke up the no-hitter with a double that scored the winning runs, Berra was almost as heartbroken as Bevens. If the Yankee catcher had nailed Gionfriddo at second, Lavagetto never would have had a chance to stand in the batter's box. "He should've made history," Yogi later said of Bevens, "but ended up with a defeat."

Still, Harris was eager to keep Berra's bat in the lineup, and he had the St. Louis native play right field in the remaining series games. But the beleaguered catcher could find no relief there. In the last game of the series, Dodger outfielder Gene Hermanski hit a drive off the low right-field wall in Yankee Stadium that the sometime catcher had difficulty fielding. "Yogi Berra wobbled like a drunk in a hurricane," wrote one sportswriter, "as the ball caromed crazily off the low fence. It went one way and he went the other way, and he fell down. Yogi looked funnier than most of the comic book characters he enjoys."

Despite the comedy of errors, the Yankees won the World Series. And so Yogi was able to take his frustrations and his World Series check back to St. Louis, where he found some solace. Her name was Carmen Short, a confident, brown-eyed, dark blond woman two years younger than the Yankee rookie. He saw her one evening when she was waiting tables at the Club 66, a local restaurant owned by Yogi's friend, Biggie Garagnini. "I was bashful, nervous, and not good-looking," Berra remembered. So he asked Biggie to see if Carmen would go out with him. Biggie did as he was told and, pointing at Yogi across the restaurant, said to the young waitress, "He'd like to meet you and take you out." For reasons that even she did not understand, Carmen thought that the bashful prospect was Terry Moore, the Cardinals' center fielder and, more important, a married man. So Carmen had a quick answer for Biggie. "You go right back and tell him," she said, "I do not go out with married men."

After Biggie assured her that Yogi was indeed single, the two began spending time together, often just sitting at a table in the restaurant talking. Yogi could not have been happier, later saying, "I could hardly believe my luck that Carmen liked me as much as I liked her." An engagement ring was ultimately given (although there were conflicting recollections about how it happened—Carmen telling a reporter in August 1949 that Yogi had given it to her while she was eating a pork chop at the restaurant, and Yogi saying in one of his books many years later that he placed the ring on her plate after she had finished a sumptuous meal at his parents' house). The two were married on January 26, 1949, and for sixty years Carmen has remained Yogi's most trusted confidante. "Carmen is," said Dave Kaplan, "a huge part of who Yogi is."

Yogi certainly needed some moral support when he married Carmen. Despite his hopes to the contrary, he had not eliminated doubts about his catching abilities during the 1948 season. During spring training, Bucky Harris told the press that the St. Louis native would be the Yankees' regular catcher for the entire season. "He knows his failings and is working hard to improve himself," Harris said of Berra. "There will be no more experimenting with Yogi as an outfielder."

It proved to be unfounded optimism. Yogi did improve, but not enough to make Harris feel comfortable. As a result, Berra caught only seventy-one games. He did display considerable success at the plate (with fourteen home runs and a .305 batting average) and an ability to drive in runs (98 in 125 games), but Yogi worried after the season—which saw the Yankees finish third in the standings—when he heard rumors that he might be traded to another team.

Fortunately for Berra, the marriage to Carmen was not the only fundamental change he experienced in 1949. Bucky Harris was fired and Casey Stengel assumed the managerial reins for the Yankees. For reasons never made clear, Casey was prepared to do whatever was necessary to turn Berra into a capable catcher. The first step he took was to hire a new coach to teach the fundamentals of catching to this émigré from the Hill.

Yogi learned of the decision on the first day of spring training when he met Stengel for the first time. "I got Bill Dickey to come in with us, son," said the new Yankee manager. "He's going to help you out." Few men could have been better tutors. A six-foot-two-inch native of Louisiana, Dickey had amassed a sterling record with the Yankees that included a .313 lifetime batting average and an American League season home-run record for catchers (twenty-nine). And more than that, he knew how to catch.

Dickey began by telling Yogi that catching was his ticket to a long career. Good catchers, he explained, were hard to find, and Dickey was going to make Yogi a good catcher. Hour after hour during spring training he showed Berra how to block pitches in the dirt or away from the plate, how to make a clean and accurate throw to each of the bases to pick off runners or to prevent them from stealing, and how to take control of the game by working the pitchers. "He worked my tail off," Berra later remembered. "But I enjoyed doing it." The instruction did not end when the season commenced. "Dickey worked him harder after the game," recalled Yankee outfielder Gene Woodling, "than Yogi had to work during the game." (Years later, Berra would say of Dickey, "Without him, I would have been nothing.")

Berra caught 109 of the Yankees' games during the season and made only seven errors. (Perhaps the best proof of Dickey's tutorial success was the 1949 World Series against the Dodgers. Yogi threw out the first three runners who tried to steal on him, and the only successful attempt during the five-game series was a steal by Pee Wee Reese.) But Berra's growth as a catcher involved more than knowing how to field the position. He also learned how to call the pitches that would enhance a pitcher's chances of success. Part of that effort included a careful study of batters. "I used to watch the hitter," he later explained, "where they'd stand, how they'd stride, and everything." As one example, he was quick to notice that Ted Williams had a batting stance that was slightly different when he played in Yankee Stadium than when he played in Boston's Fenway Park. (And he didn't hide his knowledge from Williams. "Hey," he said as the Boston outfielder settled into the batter's box in a game at the stadium. "What's going on?")

The Yankee pitchers recognized Berra's growing skill as a catcher. "I very seldom shook him off," said Whitey Ford, who began his pitching career with the Yankees in 1950. "I think he knew the batters probably better than I did." Most of the pitchers also appreciated their catcher's ability to ease the pressure in tense situations. The last game of the 1949 season epitomized that ability. The Yankees and the Red Sox had identical records, and the winner of the game would take home the American League pennant. Pitching in relief in the late innings with the score tied, Joe Page had two men on base and Vern Stephens—the hard-hitting Boston shortstop—at the plate. Yogi called time and walked out to the mound. "How long you been married?" the catcher asked a surprised Page. "Eleven years," the pitcher replied in bewilderment. "Any kids?" Berra inquired. When Page said he had no children, Berra added, "You gotta have kids, Joe. Best thing in the world for a family." Page laughed, and Yogi returned to his position behind the plate. And with that, a more relaxed Page proceeded to strike out Stephens. (Not all the Yankee pitchers were receptive to Berra's attempts at psychological counseling. Vic Raschi, one of the Yankees' leading pitchers in the late 1940s and early 1950s, would get angry if he saw Yogi call time and start to come out to the mound. "Gimme the ball, Yogi," he would invariably say, "and get back where you belong." But Berra knew that getting Raschi angry was sometimes the best way to make the Yankee pitcher more focused, and later Yogi would admit that "I never went out to talk to him unless I wanted to fire him up a little.")

Berra's improved performance behind the plate was complemented by consistency in the batter's box. Although he played in only 116 games in 1949 (seven as a pinch hitter), he hit twenty home runs and drove in ninety-one runs—more than any other Yankee. And so he was not pleased when Yankee general manager George Weiss sent him a contract for the 1950 season that included only a $4,000 raise to a salary of $16,000. Yogi sent the contract back with a note saying that he deserved $22,000 (although he told Carmen he would settle for $18,000). Weiss sent his renegade player another contract, which Berra again returned without opening it (assuming, correctly, that it did not include the raise he wanted).

Spring training began with Yogi still in St. Louis. When he saw Berra at a bowling alley one evening, a local sportswriter inquired whether the Yankee catcher was going to join his teammates in Florida. Berra shook his head. "If I go down there," said Yogi, "I'll sign. I know it. So I gotta stay here till I get what I want." Weiss finally called Yogi in St. Louis and, in reassuring tones, urged him to come to Florida for a chat, finally saying that the Yankees would raise his salary to the $18,000 that Yogi wanted.

It was a good investment for the Yankees. Yogi continued to excel in the field and produced a record at the plate that placed him among the league's top hitters—twenty-eight home runs, 124 runs batted in, and a .322 average in 151 games. In other years, it might have been enough to capture the league's MVP award, but Yankee shortstop Phil Rizzuto received the honor because of sterling play in the field and a .324 batting average.

There was a certain irony in the loss of the MVP award to the five-foot-six-inch Rizzuto. The Yankee shortstop was Berra's closest friend on the team. Both of Italian descent, the two players had a natural affinity for each other. They would talk in the clubhouse, socialize after the games, and share rooms on the road. More than that, Rizzuto was able to guide his friend on how to improve his appearance and expand his off-season income. "Phil does everything right," Yogi explained to one sportswriter at the time. "He dresses like I'd like to dress and can't. On him, collars and ties look good. He says the right thing."

Having been with the Yankees since 1941, Rizzuto had come to appreciate the value of being a recognized commodity in the country's largest city. He urged Yogi to move to the New York metropolitan area on a full-time basis so that he could take advantage of business opportunities that would not be available in St. Louis (thus inspiring Yogi and Carmen to purchase a home in the nearby New Jersey suburbs). Phil and Yogi sold clothes in a fashionable men's store in the off-season and made investments in bowling alleys and other businesses that proved profitable over the years. Rizzuto also encouraged his friend to supplement his reading of comic books with newspapers and novels. "Rizzuto made Berra wise in the ways of the world," said one sportswriter in early 1951. "Yogi has learned how to handle himself in hotel dining rooms, how to receive the press, how to maneuver an interview, how to handle the fans. And how to solve certain problems on the field and in the home too."

The new sophistication of the Yankee catcher did not affect his performance on the field. Although he endured a slump in the last two weeks of the 1951 season, he was able to lead the Yankees with twenty-seven home runs and eighty-eight runs batted in—enough to earn him the league's MVP award. Yogi was relaxing at his New Jersey home with a comic book when a horde of reporters converged on his house to advise him of the decision. Like many sportswriters, Yogi had assumed that the award would have gone to Allie Reynolds, who had won seventeen games and pitched five shutouts in addition to the two no-hitters. "It is conceivable," said one sportswriter, "that nobody was more astonished than Mr. Berra himself."

It was the first of three MVP awards that Berra would earn over the course of five seasons between 1951 and 1955. In each year during that period, he would hit at least twenty-two home runs (including thirty in 1952, a new American League season record for catchers that he would duplicate in 1956) and drive in at least ninety-eight runs (with a career high of 125 in 1954, when he won his second MVP award). Not surprisingly, the press began to speculate whether Berra or Roy Campanella was the best catcher in baseball. "Yogi Berra was the greatest catcher in the major leagues in 1954," Dan Daniel wrote in *The Sporting News* on June 15, 1955. "I have seen this Yogi man, year after year, day after day. I have seen the Bombers react to his strong impetus. I have seen them react to his absence, and I know exactly what he can do and what he means to his club and—yes, to the entire American League as well." *The Washington Post*'s Shirley Povich agreed. "There aren't any better catchers than Yogi in the American League now," Povich said. "I think, like Yankee fans," Povich added, "that Campanella could be outhitting Yogi by 40 points and Yogi still would be the more productive hitter. He just seems to get that big one." One record seemed to confirm Povich's judgment: between 1949 and 1955—a seven-year period during which the Yankees won six pennants and five World Series championships—Yogi was the team's leading run producer.

Berra's growing stature in baseball circles did not have any impact on his personality. From his first days with the Yankees, he displayed a humility that spoke volumes about his own self-esteem and his sensitivity to others. (There was the time when Yogi went with a local sportswriter to a father-son dinner sponsored by a church in St. Louis. While he was at the head table signing the bats and balls given to each son, Yogi noticed a corner table that included a group of orphans from a church-supported home. "Ain't they getting anything?" Yogi asked one of the church representatives. Oh, no, said the representative. "We think it's enough of a thrill for them just to be here." Yogi did not agree. "For what he did next," said the sportswriter, "I'll always love him." Berra rose from his seat and went to the orphans' table, where he began talking with the youngsters and signing programs and anything else they handed to him. In due course, one of the church representatives at the head table called out to the Yankee catcher, saying, "We'd like you to come back here and say a few words." Yogi was not interested. "Go on with the program," he snapped. "I'm busy. I'm talking to some friends.")

Compassion was not the only quality that attracted fans to Yogi (who, unlike Mickey Mantle, was never booed as a player). He could still make people laugh. There was the time when the Yankee catcher was invited to appear on a sports radio program to talk about life in the big leagues. "I'm going to throw out a few names," the host explained before the broadcast, "and you just say the first thing that pops into your mind." When the show began, the host explained to the listening audience that he was going to play a "word association" game with the famous Yankee catcher. "All right, then," the host continued with excitement, "here we go." And then the host threw out the first name: "Mickey Mantle." "What about him?" said Yogi.

The characteristics that endeared Berra to the press and the fans were also appreciated by other players. No longer did he have to endure jokes about his homely looks (although he continued to receive friendly barbs about his malapropisms). Instead, he found that teammates and opposing players alike had an affinity for this intense competitor who kept matters in perspective.

Carl Erskine remembered the incident that cemented his view of the Yankee catcher. It was the third game of the 1953 World Series. Dodger manager Charlie Dressen called Erskine over for a conference before the game. "Yogi is digging in," he told his pitcher. "Get a strike on him, and I want him on his back." And so, after getting a strike on Berra during his first at bat, Erskine threw an inside pitch that hit the Yankee catcher in the ribs. When Yogi came to bat again a few innings later, Campanella gave Erskine the knockdown sign. And so there was another inside pitch—this one hitting Berra on the elbow, and Yogi stared at the Dodger pitcher as he trotted down to first base. Erskine was the leadoff hitter in the next inning, and he expected some angry words from the Yankee catcher as he stepped into the batter's box. Instead, Yogi simply looked up at him through the mask and softly asked, "Carl, are you throwin' at me?"

These and other episodes established Berra's reputation as the friendliest of competitors. "Berra," said sportswriter Dan Daniel in 1955, "unquestionably is the most social ballplayer in the business."

Yogi Berra is not concerned with his reputation as Carl Furillo approaches the batter's box as the first hitter in the bottom of the sixth inning of the fifth game of the 1956 World Series. The Yankees are winning, but the margin is slim. The Yankee catcher cannot lose his focus in giving signs to Don Larsen. One mistake and the tables could be turned.

Over in the press box, Bob Wolff tells his listening audience that there have been only eight balls hit to the outfield (including Mantle's home run) and that the crowd "has certainly been treated to a magnificent display this afternoon of pitching and great defensive work." No one has to tell that to the Dodgers. They are talking among themselves in the dugout, and someone says, "You know, we haven't had a base runner yet." Still, the Dodgers are not concerned about Larsen pitching a no-hitter. They have too much experience and too much skill with a bat (and, in fact, have been the victim of only one no-hitter in the post–World War II era—one thrown by Vern Bickford of the Boston Braves in 1950). But they do worry about winning the game—the Yankees have shown an uncanny ability to rise to the occasion when all seems lost in the World Series.

Furillo does not bring hope to his teammates. After fouling off one pitch, he lifts a pop-up to short right field just beyond the infield which Billy Martin corrals for the first out. Roy Campanella steps into the batter's box, and Larsen remembers that Yogi had told him to pitch the Dodger catcher "low and away or in on the hands where he couldn't get much of a swing." For that reason, the Yankee pitcher is not surprised when Berra calls for a curve low and away. Larsen complies, and Campanella lifts a short fly ball just beyond the infield toward center field. Gil McDougald and Martin converge on the ball as it makes its descent, but Martin is the one who makes the catch, and the Yankees have their second out.

The sellout crowd gives Sal Maglie a rousing ovation as he steps into the batter's box, and Wolff reminds his audience that the game represents "one of the greatest pitching duels to this point that has ever been recorded in a World Series game." Ironically, the Dodger pitcher proves to be the most difficult out of the inning. After swinging at—and missing—the first two pitches, Maglie waits out two balls that miss the plate, fouls off two other pitches, and finally goes down swinging on what Larsen remembers as "a good, popping fastball."

Berra takes off the mask and moves toward the Yankee dugout with the satisfaction that Larsen has now retired eighteen Dodgers in a row, but with the knowledge that the Yankees still have only a 1–0 lead.

12

Bottom of the Sixth: Andy Carey

Years later, Andy Carey could remember that moment in the mid-1950s as if it happened yesterday. He was in the batter's box in Boston's Fenway Park in the late innings, with the Yankees losing to the Red Sox and a runner on base. With its short left-field wall (called the "Green Monster" by local fans), Fenway is a park built for right-handed hitters like the Yankee third baseman. Standing almost six feet, one inch tall and weighing about two hundred pounds, the sandy-haired Carey had the tools to take advantage of that short left-field fence. Still, he was surprised when he heard someone yell, "Time-out." He looked to his left to see Billy Martin leaving the on-deck circle on the third-base side of the field and asking him to come over for a conference. Carey stepped out of the batter's box and huddled with the Yankee second baseman. Martin had a message from Casey Stengel. "The old man wants you to hit a home run and win the game," Martin said within earshot of Red Sox catcher Sammy White. "What?" Carey responded in disbelief. "The old man wants you to hit a home run and win the game," Martin repeated. "Get a good pitch and hit a home run."

Carey stepped back into the batter's box and on the next pitch drove a ball into the screen on top of the Green Monster for a home run. As he finished his trot around the bases and stepped on home plate, he saw that White was standing there and laughing. "Well, what are you going to say?" Carey quipped. "The old man says to do it, Sammy!"

The Yankee third baseman does not expect any similar exhortations from his manager as he steps into the batter's box to start the bottom of the sixth inning of the fifth game of the 1956 World Series. With its vast expanse in left center field, hitting home runs in Yankee Stadium is a far greater challenge than blasting one in Fenway. Indeed, despite the earlier experience with Martin in Boston, Carey knows that his desire to hit home runs has proved to be one of the stumbling blocks in maintaining good relations with his manager. Stengel is, at heart, a conservative strategist who believes in getting runs the old-fashioned way—having a man get on first base through a hit or a walk, moving him to second on a sacrifice bunt or hit-and-run play, and then bringing him home with another hit. The Yankee manager had tried to get his third baseman to abandon his desire for the long ball and try instead for singles by spraying the ball to center or right field. But Carey felt more comfortable trying to pull the ball, and the different perspectives had been a constant source of friction. "Ohhh, nice going, Carey," Stengel would invariably sneer when Carey returned to the dugout after hitting a long out to left field. "What happened, Carey?" "They got me." "Well," his manager would reply in a rising voice, "you got to go to all fields!"

It may have been clear in his manager's mind, but that was not the way Andy Carey was brought up in Alameda, California. He was born Andrew Arthur Hexem on October 18, 1931—two days before Mickey Mantle's birth—in nearby Oakland. With its trolley cars, small-town atmosphere, and proximity to San Francisco Bay, Alameda had considerable charm. But in those Depression days, young Andy had other priorities. His family, for one. Relations between his mother and father were not good, and by the time he was five, they were divorced.

His mother worked as a dental nurse in Oakland and never had much money in those early years, but no matter. "I always had a meal there," Carey remembered. And in time, he also had a new stepfather—

Ken Carey, the local attorney who had handled his mother's divorce. It was a good relationship, especially because Ken, like his stepson, was an accomplished athlete. Looking back many years later, Carey would say that "my stepdad was a big influence."

From the beginning, Andy's focus was baseball, and his mother soon realized that her young son had a talent that distinguished him from his peers. "He could throw a ball harder and faster," she remembered, "than any of his playmates." (Years later, when he was playing third base for the Yankees, his teammates would also take notice of Andy's unusually strong arm. "His throws seemed to tear my hands to pieces," said Enos Slaughter, who used to warm up with Carey on the sidelines before games. "In some way, when he threw the ball, it seemed like a large rock hitting your hand." Joe Collins, who caught many of Carey's throws at first base, agreed, saying that Carey's throws would "tear your glove apart.")

With that strong arm, it was only natural that the high school coach would use him as a pitcher. But Andy could also hit with considerable power, and he grew frustrated sitting on the bench in between pitching starts. "Eventually," he later recalled, "I stopped pitching because it didn't give me enough action. I wanted to be in every game, all the way, and I started playing at third all the time." By the time he was a senior, he made the all-county first team as a third baseman, but he had also pitched enough to make the second all-county team as a pitcher— the first time that anyone had made all-county teams in two different positions.

By the time Andy graduated high school in the spring of 1949, several major-league teams had expressed an interest. (One call came to the Carey home from singer Bing Crosby, then a part owner of the Pittsburgh Pirates. Ken Carey was skeptical about the caller's identity and put him to the test. "Sing me a song," the elder Carey demanded. Bing complied, and Ken was satisfied that the caller was indeed the famous crooner.) Despite the interest, Ken Carey was not sure that his stepson should sign a professional contract.

The problem was the major-league bonus rule. If a player received a bonus in excess of $6,000, he could not be placed on a minor-league team but would have to stay with the parent club. Club managers—

eager to provide their new recruits with training in the minor leagues—
were reluctant to offer anything in excess of that amount. Ken Carey
was hopeful that the rule would be changed to allow larger bonuses
and counseled patience. Andy therefore decided to accept a scholarship
offer to play baseball at St. Mary's College in Moraga, California.

Carey played well in his freshman year and expected to spend four
years at St. Mary's. But the school dropped its baseball program, and
the young student's perspective on college suddenly changed. He spent
the summer of 1950 playing with a semipro baseball team in Weiser,
Idaho. Andy hit over .400, and by the end of the summer, as he recalled, "I don't think there was a team that *wasn't* interested in me."

That increased interest coincided with a change in the bonus rule
that eliminated the $6,000 threshold. As Ken had hoped, that proved
beneficial to his stepson, and the offers now being presented to Andy
far exceeded the offers he had received when he had graduated high
school. On the morning of February 5, 1951, Ken and his stepson met
with Joe Devine in a San Francisco hotel to sign a contract to play for
the Yankees' Kansas City farm team with a bonus of $60,000.

After they signed the contract, Devine told his new prospect to
travel to Phoenix, Arizona, where Stengel would convene a special instructional camp. Andy was, of course, anxious to make the trip and,
unlike many players his age, could do so without fear of receiving a
notice to join the military service. The local draft board had decided
that Andy Carey—who now stood at his full height of six feet, weighed
about 180 pounds, and had the skill to play professional baseball—was
unfit for military service.

The problem first surfaced when Andy slid hard into second base
while playing for St. Mary's team. "For whatever reason," Carey later
recalled, "it created this imbalance in my legs. One leg was two inches
shorter than the other one." X-rays showed that cartilage was missing
from his lower spine and that the vertebrae were not properly joined
to the pelvic bone. Some doctors suggested surgery to correct the de-
fect, but Andy and his family were skeptical. They finally accepted the
advice of a physician who proposed using Novocain to relax the muscles and exercise to restore strength to the shorter leg. ("I worked my
ass off," Carey remembered, "trying to get myself in shape again.")

And so, while he would experience back pain from time to time during his baseball career, Carey never needed surgery to correct the ailment. Nor did the back injury handicap the Alameda native at the Yankees' instructional camp in Phoenix. He performed well, and Stengel invited him to join the club in a preseason exhibition tour. ("Imagine how I felt," Carey later said, "appearing before Bay Area fans in the uniform of the world champions.") Still, Stengel decided that Carey needed the benefit of regular play in the minor leagues. When the exhibition tour ended, Andy found himself in Kansas City.

The first half of the season with Kansas City was not what the nineteen-year-old player would have wanted. "My first showing with Kansas City was not good," he later admitted. His batting average was below .250, and, more than that, he failed to display the enthusiasm required for any player to make the grade.

The breaking point came in an away game. Andy dropped a pop fly with the bases loaded, which led to his team's loss. When the club returned to Kansas City, manager George Selkirk called the young third baseman into his office for a chat. "You big, strong son of a bitch," Selkirk began. And for the next hour, as Carey recalled, "he chewed me out unmercifully." Not that Carey could disagree with his manager. "I was getting nonchalant," he remembered. Unaccustomed to a prolonged tongue-lashing for inferior play, Carey began to cry. And then he became angry—with himself. "I left the room with a new slant on baseball," he later told a sportswriter. "I became a hustling, fighting ball player."

The results of Selkirk's lecture were immediate—and dramatic. Andy went on a tear at the plate, getting eighteen hits in his next twenty-two at bats and finishing the season with fourteen home runs (only one of which was hit during the first half of the season). The lesson was not lost on Stengel (who undoubtedly received a report on the bonus player from Selkirk). For the entire time he was with the Yankees, Carey would be the subject of periodic taunts from a manager eager to motivate his third baseman. (Stengel "knew if he made me mad I'd play better," Carey later said. And so, as he recalled, the Yankee manager was "constantly getting me mad.")

Carey failed to appreciate his manager's approach when he came to

the Yankees' spring training camp in 1952. But understanding Casey
Stengel was a challenge to many players and observers, and the prospect from Alameda was no exception. He even had a difficult time in
grasping much of what his manager said. ("Sometimes," said sportswriter Robert Creamer of Stengel, "when he tried to explain something
precisely, his efforts to enhance his listeners' knowledge would get
hopelessly tangled. . . . If you had a general idea of what he was talking
about, it wasn't always that hard to follow him, but at times he could
be very confusing.")

Carey's first clubhouse meetings with the Yankee manager were
nothing short of startling. "I wish I'd have had one of those tiny re-
corders," Carey said with amusement many years later. "He would
rant and rave. A lot of times he'd give some guys names. It took me
about a year to decipher who in the hell he was talking about half the
time." And then there was the time when Stengel walked into the clubhouse bathroom just as Andy was about to take a shave. "Kid," said
the manager, "I want to talk with you." So Carey followed Stengel out
of the bathroom with his face full of shaving lather and sat down to
hear what his manager had to say. "And I'm sitting there and listening," said Carey, "and he goes on and on, and when he went away, I
didn't remember what the hell he said." In the meantime, the lather had
evaporated, and so Carey had to return to the bathroom to start his
shave from the beginning. (In later years, Carey would realize the futility of understanding Stengel's long-winded monologues in clubhouse
meetings and would often start reading a newspaper. This would only
infuriate the Yankee manager, who would eventually yell to his third
baseman, "Pay attention!")

While his remarks may have been incomprehensible on occasion,
Stengel had no trouble in communicating his satisfaction with Carey's
exploits in that 1952 spring training camp. "It is much too early to
make definite statements about new players," Casey told one sportswriter toward the end of March. "But I would be telling you an untruth
if I did not admit that Carey has me ga-ga." Not that anyone should
have been surprised. Carey came to spring training with the confidence
of a seasoned player. "Go ahead, assert yourself," Selkirk had told his
protégé before the camp began. "Let them know who you are." The

twenty-year-old prospect took those words to heart, and, in one of the first camp games, he drew a line in the infield dirt between third base and shortstop. "What are you doing there?" shortstop Phil Rizzuto asked. "I want you to know," said the brash youth, "this is my side here. You stay off my side. This is my territory."

That self-confidence was also evident at the plate. Carey started off the camp by hitting better than any other Yankee player and had a very respectable .324 average by the end of March. That hitting—coupled with fielding described as "brilliant" by one sportswriter—was enough to impress managers of other teams. "I have seen Carey play only one game," said Philadelphia Phillies' manager Eddie Sawyer, "but he does everything right. He has everything to make him a great player." Sportswriters drew similar conclusions. "He has size and strength," *The Sporting News* opined in early April, "can run, is endowed with a strong arm, and he can hit. Andy makes plays which third basemen master only after several years' experience in the majors, and which too many never do achieve." And *The New York Times* labeled Carey as "the No. 1 rookie of the Grapefruit League" who "seems a cinch to open the regular season with the world champions."

Carey's chances of making the club were enhanced by Jerry Coleman's anticipated departure for the military and an injury to Billy Martin that eliminated virtually all competition for the third-base position. ("Carey is confronted," said one sportswriter, "with one of the most remarkable opportunities a kid has faced on the Yankees.") But the opportunity never materialized. Coleman did join the military service, but Martin recovered from his injury and, after sporadic play at the beginning of the season, Stengel decided that the young athlete needed some further experience in the minor leagues. So Andy returned to Kansas City, where he again performed well (hitting .284 with sixteen home runs in only eighty-two games).

Carey had reason to believe that he might be able to stay with the club for the 1953 season. Those hopes should have been buoyed by the Yankees' announcement after the 1952 season that Carey would be groomed to be the club's new shortstop. It was not an idle suggestion. Stengel cherished versatility in his players, and almost all of them could play more than one position. Beyond that, there was the question of

Rizzuto's health. The Yankee shortstop had suffered from a bleeding ulcer at the end of the 1952 season, and sportswriters (as well as Yankee management) began to speculate whether the thirty-five-year-old veteran was nearing the end of his career.

The logic of the proposal may have been compelling in Stengel's mind, but Carey had a different perspective. He wanted to hone his skills at only one position. He did not want the added burden of trying to master two positions. "I'd rather be a good third baseman," he later told Stengel, "than a mediocre shortstop." And so he told his manager to find someone else to replace Rizzuto.

Bold words from a rookie trying to make the club. But Andy had not forgotten Selkirk's admonition to assert himself. Still, it was not a response that would endear Carey to the Yankee manager. Nor was it easily forgotten. Whenever the subject came up in a conversation in the clubhouse or with a sportswriter, Stengel was apt to comment on Carey's stubborn refusal to play more than one position. ("Andy is a one-job man," the manager would tell the press.) Stengel was equally quick to criticize his third baseman if he was not performing well—or sometimes if the team was not performing well. "I was his scapegoat," Carey would later say of his relationship with Stengel. "Whenever he wanted to get on anybody else, he'd always chew me out."

All of which may have explained why Carey found it difficult to break into the lineup in that 1953 season. Martin played almost every game at second base, Rizzuto was well enough to play 133 games at short, and the ever-versatile Gil McDougald started most of the games at third. Andy was forced to spend some time with minor-league teams in Kansas City and Syracuse and saw action in only fifty-one Yankees games (usually for defensive purposes in the late innings). By the end of the year, he had been given only eighty-one at bats (although he did hit .321 and had four home runs in that limited opportunity).

Still, he played enough to be impressed by the camaraderie on the team. "They were always encouraging," he remembered years later. He understood the depth of that team spirit in a game against the Cleveland Indians when he came to bat with a runner on first base and broke his bat hitting a ground ball that resulted in his being thrown out at first but allowing the runner to move to second base. Carey returned to the dugout with disappointment, only to find—much to his surprise—teammates congratulating him for advancing the runner. "Nice going, Carey," they said. "They had their little cliques," Carey observed many years later. "But, to a man, there was nothing like being a Yankee."

Carey's situation changed dramatically in the 1954 season. Martin was in the army, and Stengel now needed another infielder. A torn muscle kept Carey on the bench for the first fifteen games of the season, but he was the regular third baseman when the injury healed, playing 120 games at third and batting .302—the second-highest average on the club. "Andy Carey," said one sportswriter in June, "truly is one of the story book players of the 1954 season."

Carey should have been pleased with his performance, but he had hit only eight home runs, and he could not resist the temptation to hit more. "I should be able to hit more homers and triples," he told Dan Daniel of *The Sporting News* during spring training in 1955. "I have the strength and the weight to put behind a ball to drive those four-baggers into the left-field stand in the Stadium." The reasoning may have been sound, but the reality was far less satisfying. By the middle of May he was hitting .240 with only two home runs, and Stengel urged his third baseman to hit to all fields instead of trying to pull the ball. Carey finally yielded to the pressure. He changed his batting stance and tried to just meet the ball.

The change provided little satisfaction. Carey could not lift his season batting average above .257 (although he did hit eleven triples to tie Mickey Mantle for the league lead). "It was a very hard adjustment for me," he later explained, "but you try to do what they tell you to do." Even more troubling was the inability to regain his earlier—and more satisfying—batting form. "I was screwed up for about two or three years," he said, and had considerable regret that he had succumbed to the pressure. "I look back now," he said many years later, "and I was foolish to have changed. Because if I hit that well being a pull hitter, why change?"

Although his reputation as a pull hitter may have been tarnished,

Carey had no difficulty in retaining his stature as the Yankee player with the biggest appetite. "I've always been a heavy eater," he remarked many years later. "No one ever beat me."

The Yankees learned of Carey's almost insatiable appetite at the 1951 instructional camp in Phoenix. "How much can you eat here?" the nineteen-year-old Californian asked other players when he first arrived. When told that there was no limit, Andy began placing double orders of everything and astounding his teammates with his capacity to eat. ("They never talked about what I did on the baseball field," Carey later remembered of that first spring training experience. "They always talked about my appetite.") Yankee management was not happy to receive restaurant bills for $50 for one player's meal. (Joe Devine, a big cigar in hand, walked over to the youngster at one point and said with some annoyance, "What are you trying to do here?") After one week of receiving bills for Carey's meals, Bill McCorry, the Yankees' traveling secretary, informed the players that they would no longer have an open check but would instead be given only a certain amount of money to cover their meals.

The change in accounting had no impact on Andy's eating habits, and his teammates continued to marvel at Carey's ability to eat large quantities of food without seeming to gain any weight (which he attributed to a schedule of constant workouts). "He could eat," said Hank Bauer, who roomed with Carey and vividly remembered Sunday-night dinners at a New York City restaurant where Carey would consume a five-pound steak with soup, salad, half a dozen eggs, plus dessert. Tony Kubek was equally impressed when he ate with the third baseman. "Carey would order unbelievably," said Kubek. "And I thought to myself: Where's he putting this? Because he wasn't fat."

However much he liked food, Carey was not one to spend long evenings carousing with his teammates. He did not smoke or drink and often went to sleep early. (Years later, when Mickey Mantle, Yogi Berra, and Hank Bauer decided to patronize New York's nightspots to celebrate Billy Martin's twenty-ninth birthday, Carey declined the invitation to join them. "Sure as hell," he said to himself at the time, "something will go wrong and I'll get my name in the newspaper." A prescient thought. Bauer—who was later accused of assaulting a pa-

tron at the Copacabana in the early-morning hours of that evening—
came back to the apartment saying, "Oh, I've got some problems,
roomie.")

There was a certain irony in Carey's distaste for New York's high
life. He was one of the more eligible bachelors on the Yankee club, and
it could not have been entirely surprising when the press began to report in early 1955 that the Yankee third baseman was dating Lucy Ann
McAleer, the twenty-two-year-old budding actress who had appeared
under the name Lucy Marlow in shows and movies (including *A Star
Is Born* with James Mason and Judy Garland).

The relationship evolved from Andy's friendship with heavyweight
boxer Rocky Marciano. During the season, Carey and Bauer would
often travel to the Grossinger's resort in New York's Catskill Mountains after a Sunday-afternoon game and stay there until Monday evening or Tuesday morning. Many times they would encounter the boxer
from Brockton, Massachusetts, who lived nearby and often frequented
Grossinger's facilities. In due course, the famous fighter found himself
playing softball or having dinner with the Yankee players. When Marciano made a trip after the 1954 season to Big Bear, the Southern California ski resort, Carey made arrangements to meet with him. But
there was an unexpected change in plans. Marciano had to return to
the East Coast, and Carey wound up going to a play that featured
Marlow. He was taken with this slim brunette. The evening was followed by letters, telephone calls, and, soon enough, dinners and excursions (including tours of San Francisco Bay on the boat that Carey had
built in the off-season).

The couple was married on October 6, 1955, in Hollywood's First
Methodist Church. The honeymoon was a trip to Hawaii to join the
New York Yankees on an exhibition tour in the Pacific Islands and
Japan. It was an eye-opening experience for the newly married man.
He led the team in home runs with thirteen (hitting three home runs in
a game on three different occasions).

The exhilaration of all those home runs was difficult to suppress.
Andy came into the 1956 season believing that he could duplicate that
performance in Yankee Stadium. But it was not to be. The Japanese
parks were smaller and the American League pitchers much more so-

phisticated. Carey finished the season with a .237 batting average and only seven home runs in 132 games. Stengel was not happy. "I need more punch and more steadiness at third base," he later told one sportswriter. "I wish Carey could go back to his 1955 form."

As he waits for Sal Maglie's pitch to begin the bottom of the sixth inning of the fifth game of the 1956 World Series, Andy Carey is surely eager to vindicate Stengel's decision to keep him in the lineup. The third baseman swings hard at Maglie's first pitch and sends a low line drive over second base into center field for the Yankees' second hit.

Don Larsen lumbers up to the plate and is greeted with cheers and sustained applause from the fans. ("Listen to the crowd," Bob Wolff tells his radio listeners.) The Dodgers assume that Larsen will try to lay down a sacrifice bunt to move Carey into scoring position at second base. Jackie Robinson moves in from third and positions himself at the edge of the infield grass. But Larsen fools his adversaries—he does not square around to bunt but swings hard at Maglie's first pitch and sends a foul ball into the lower box seats just beyond the Dodger dugout on the third-base line. The threat of a bunt remains, however, and Robinson resumes his position on the infield grass as Maglie throws a second pitch. This time Larsen does square around to bunt, but Robinson watches as the ball rolls foul just outside the third-base line.

With two strikes, Robinson assumes that Larsen will abandon any attempt to bunt (because the risk of a foul ball—and a strikeout—are too great). The Dodger third baseman has a brief conference with Maglie on the mound and then takes his position—but this time well behind the third-base bag. As he does so, Larsen steps out of the batter's box for a brief moment to take the sign from third-base coach Frank Crosetti.

Once again the Dodgers have made the wrong guess. As soon as Maglie goes into his motion, Larsen squares around to bunt and now lays down a perfect sacrifice in front of the plate. Campanella pounces on the ball and, having no play at second base to catch Carey, throws the ball to second baseman Jim Gilliam, who is covering first base for Gil Hodges (who has charged the plate in an effort to field Larsen's bunt).

Hank Bauer steps into the batter's box with a chance to increase the Yankees' lead. And he does not let the opportunity pass. After taking a called strike on Maglie's first pitch, the Yankee right fielder drives a ball between Robinson and Pee Wee Reese into left field for the team's third hit. As Carey races around third base for home plate, Sandy Amoros fumbles the ball briefly and then throws it to Reese at second base to make sure that Bauer does not advance. Carey scores easily with the Yankees' second run.

First baseman Joe Collins follows Bauer to the plate, and he keeps the rally alive with a line drive to right center field that Duke Snider cannot catch. Snider grabs the ball on one hop and throws it into second base as Bauer races safely into third. The crowd is alive with anticipation as Mickey Mantle moves toward the batter's box with teammates on each of the corners and only one out. He can put the game on ice with another hit—perhaps another home run that would give the home team a 5–0 lead.

Dodger manager Walter Alston recognizes the risk as well, and he trudges out to the mound for a conference with Maglie. Robinson and Campanella join the huddle and, after a few minutes, Alston starts back to the dugout but then returns to the mound for a few more words. As he does so, Reese comes in from shortstop, and the umpires direct Robinson back to third (because, under World Series rules, only one infielder is allowed to join a conference at the mound). When Alston finally returns to the Dodger dugout, the noise in the stadium escalates, and, as Bob Wolff tells his listening audience, "the crowd certainly is whooping it up."

After taking Maglie's first pitch for a ball, Mantle swings mightily at a curveball just above the knees—and misses. But he catches the next pitch and rips a hard ground ball down the first-base line that pops into Hodges' glove. The Dodger first baseman steps on the bag for the second out and then fires the ball to Campanella to nail Bauer, who is racing for home. Bauer sees immediately that he is a certain out and tries to retreat to third base, but the Dodgers have him cornered. A rundown ensues until Robinson finally tags the Yankee runner out for a double play to end the inning. "How about that one?" Wolff excitedly screams into the microphone.

Top of the Seventh: Jim Gilliam

Jim Gilliam could no doubt remember the moment at will. It was the fifth inning of the seventh game of the 1965 World Series, and he was playing deep behind the third-base bag when Zoilo Versalles, the Minnesota Twins' shortstop, stepped into the batter's box. The Dodgers and the Twins had each won three games. Determined to capture the world championship, Los Angeles manager Walter Alston had turned to southpaw Sandy Koufax to pitch his team to victory in the deciding game.

Koufax had enjoyed another brilliant season—twenty-six victories, a 2.04 earned run average, and a new National League record of 382 strikeouts—and he had already performed well in this series (pitching a complete game shutout and then giving up only one earned run in a losing effort in his second outing). By the fifth inning of the seventh game, the Dodger hurler held a 2–0 lead, but the Twins had runners at first and second bases, and, more critically, Gilliam knew that Koufax didn't have "his good stuff." That increased the pressure for him to protect the third-base line against an extra-base hit—a real possibility if Koufax threw a curve, a pitch that the right-handed Versalles could pull to the left side of the field.

Gilliam could also appreciate the ironies of his situation. He had joined the Brooklyn Dodgers in 1953 as a second baseman. To make room for this new infielder, manager Charlie Dressen moved Jackie Robinson from second to third and benched Billy Cox, who had previously been the Dodgers' regular third baseman. Cox made no secret of his resentment at having been pushed aside for two black players. And yet, twelve years later, here was Gilliam, playing the very position that was at the center of that long-ago controversy.

The further irony was that Gilliam probably would have selected a different position if he had been given a choice. He could play—and did play—every position in the field except pitcher and catcher over the course of thirteen seasons with the Dodgers, and the position he liked the least was third base. "Those balls come at you pretty fast at third," he told a sportswriter at one point, "and it's a case of you do or you don't." (When asked by a sportswriter about the most difficult play to make at third, Gilliam had a quick response: "The tough one is the ball that's hit down the line and over the bag. It has to be back-handed.") But the Dodgers needed him at third, and Gilliam was a team player who would play wherever the manager wanted.

And that was the last irony. Because Jim Gilliam really should not have been playing anywhere. He had retired from active play after the 1964 season and had accepted a contract to be a coach with the Dodgers for the 1965 season. But John Kennedy, the team's third baseman, was placed on the disabled list in May 1965, and Alston had only one infielder left—thus placing the manager in a vulnerable position if he decided to have someone pinch-hit for that last infielder. "So," Alston remembered, "Gilliam kept coming back to my mind more and more." Gilliam was reactivated for the Memorial Day weekend schedule and, without the benefit of any spring training, began to hit the ball at a .400 pace (and eventually finished the season with a .280 average in 111 games).

With the 1965 World Series hanging in the balance, Gilliam watched as Koufax went into his stretch—knowing that he might be the last line of defense in preserving a Dodger victory. With a high kick, the Dodgers' ace fired the ball toward the plate. Versalles' bat met the speeding sphere with a crack and, as one sportswriter later described, sent "a blistering rounder along the third base line." It had all the earmarks of a double that would even the score. But Gilliam fell to his right knee, backhanded the ball with his glove, picked himself up and scampered to third base to beat the runner to the bag. The Twins' threat evaporated, and Koufax proceeded to hold the shutout for a Dodger championship.

In the clubhouse afterward, Alston told the press that Gilliam's grab was "the key play for us," and one sportswriter called it "the fielding gem of the classic." The National Baseball Hall of Fame agreed, and, within twenty-four hours, Gilliam's glove was on display in a glass case in Cooperstown.

Gilliam, wearing number 19 on the back of his uniform, is surely hoping that he can make a different kind of contribution to a Dodger victory as he steps into the batter's box for the start of the seventh inning of the fifth game of the 1956 World Series. His team needs to get someone on base, and Gilliam has proved to be one of the best leadoff hitters in Dodger history. He set a National League record for rookies with a hundred walks in 1953, and over the years he has invariably been one of the Dodgers' leaders in on-base percentage. "He's the best lead-off man I've ever had in Brooklyn," said Charlie Dressen, his first manager. Dressen's successor agreed. "Jim doesn't hit homers and his average isn't high," Alston later told a sportswriter. "But he gets on base and he can put on the hit and run."

It was a role that Jim Gilliam could not have envisioned for himself when he was growing up in Nashville, Tennessee, in the 1930s. His father died when he was two, his mother was a housemaid who struggled to make ends meet, and Jim—the only child in the family—was raised by his grandmother.

School was never a priority, and Jim quit after the tenth grade. While money was always scarce, young Jim did not want to spend his spare time in the workforce. "I had one job," he recalled after joining the Dodgers. "I guess I got $19 or $20 a week as a sort of porter in a five-and-ten-cent store in Nashville." But that job was short-lived. Baseball was Jim Gilliam's principal preoccupation from the time he was a young boy. He grew up only a couple of blocks from Sulphur Dell, the historic Nashville park that was home to the Nashville Elite Giants, the

Nashville Vols, and other teams in the Negro leagues. "I helped around the clubhouse," Gilliam later recalled of those early days in Nashville. "They allowed us kids to play there when the club was on the road."

Jim's first experience in organized baseball was with the Nashville Vols. When he first arrived, Gilliam started as a catcher, but Willie White, the Vols' trainer, thought he was better suited elsewhere. "He was a natural from the very start," White later recalled. "He was fast and could do everything. So I changed him into an infielder quick." (One of those who also took notice of the youngster's skills as an infielder was Roy Campanella, who would often travel to the Nashville park with the Baltimore Elite Giants. "I've been watching you fielding grounders during batting practice," Campanella told his future teammate. "You're gonna be a great ballplayer some day.")

The other change Gilliam encountered in those first days at Sulphur Dell was to his name. He was only sixteen years old when he started playing professional ball, and, as the youngest member of the club, his teammates began to call him "Junior." It was a name that stuck throughout the rest of his career—long after he ceased to be a teenager. After his rookie year with the Dodgers, being called "Junior" infuriated the twenty-five-year-old Gilliam, and he urged sportswriters to abandon the practice. "The name's Jim," he explained, "and Junior is just for kids." Unfortunately, the sportswriters could not be turned aside, and some began referring to him as "Junior ('Call Me Jim') Gilliam." By the time he retired thirteen years later—after publication of hundreds of articles that referred to him as "Junior" Gilliam—the Nashville native said that the reference no longer bothered him.

Whatever name others may have used for him, Gilliam continued to impress people with his talent on the field and at the plate, and by 1946, the seventeen-year-old youth was promoted to the Baltimore Elite Giants. Within two years, Gilliam—now standing almost five feet, eleven inches tall and weighing about 175 pounds—was selected to be on the Negro League East's All-Star team.

Part of that success had to be attributed to George Scales, an Elite coach who persuaded Gilliam—a natural right-handed hitter—to become a switch-hitter. It was not an idle suggestion. "I couldn't hit curves," Gilliam later confessed. And he knew that he would ultimately be able to bat left-handed. "When I was twelve years old," he remembered, "I fell out of a tree and broke my wrist. They put my right arm in a sling. But I didn't want to give up baseball. So I stood out there and swung the bat one-handed with my left hand. After that, I always knew I could do it." He was certainly pleased with the results shortly after he started switch-hitting on the Elites. "I soon discovered," he later explained, "I wasn't missing so many curveballs when I was hitting left-handed against a right-handed pitcher. I could see the ball curving toward me—not away from me. It made them easier to hit."

Not surprisingly, several major-league clubs expressed an interest in Gilliam, and the Chicago Cubs invited him to join their farm club in Springfield, Massachusetts, for the 1950 season. But the Cubs lost interest after two weeks and dropped him from the roster. Gilliam never understood the basis for the decision. "I thought I was playing good ball," he later said. But Jack Sheehan, the manager of the Springfield club, told Baltimore Elite president Richard Powell that "the boy wouldn't be able to hit Triple-A pitching."

There was one dissenting voice: Mickey McConnell, who worked in the Dodger offices with general manager Branch Rickey. McConnell had seen Gilliam play in a Negro National League play-off game in Baltimore and expressed his opinion of the Elite second baseman at a meeting that Rickey had convened with his managers and scouts to review the club's player-development program. In the course of the discussion, Rickey explained that it was important to have a good team in Montreal—where the Royals enjoyed substantial support from the community—but that the team lacked a good second baseman. Rickey asked for suggestions. "When nobody else spoke up," McConnell recalled, "I said Junior Gilliam was a possibility. I explained that he had good running speed, was a switch-hitter who made good contact but didn't hit with power, had good range and good hands and only a fair arm but could get the ball away quickly and throw with accuracy." Rickey liked the suggestion, and the Dodgers ultimately bought the Elite contracts for Gilliam and pitcher Joe Black (both of whom ultimately joined the parent club) as well as an option for pitcher Leroy Farrell (who never made the club). And so Junior Gilliam found himself playing second base for the Montreal Royals in the 1951 season.

His first day with the Brooklyn farm team—at least at the plate—could not have been better. In the opening doubleheader, Gilliam had eight hits—including a grand-slam home run—as well as three walks. His performance in the field was less spectacular. Alston—then managing the Royals—had Gilliam play right field, and he dropped the first ball that was hit to him. Alston cringed as he watched the play. "This kid's gonna have trouble with pressure," he told himself. But Gilliam quickly redeemed himself. "The next ball was hit over his head," said Alston, "and he went back and got it like DiMaggio."

Never again would Alston have to worry about Gilliam's errors in the field. "In the two years I watched him there," said one of Junior's teammates, "I never saw him make a mistake—and I've seen him make some great plays, both at second base and in the outfield." George Shuba, another Royals teammate who would join Gilliam on the Dodgers, agreed that the Nashville native's performance in the outfield was as good as one could expect. "He can run like a streak," Shuba told one sportswriter, "and his arm is very good."

Gilliam's two years with Montreal demonstrated the wisdom of McConnell's recommendation. In 1951, he led the International League in runs with 117 and batted .287, and, in 1952, he batted .301, led the league in runs again with 111, drove in 112 runs, and won the league's Most Valuable Player award. His elevation to the parent club for the 1953 season was all but assured, and Gilliam's play during spring training only confirmed the likelihood of that promotion. "Playing alongside Pee Wee Reese," one sportswriter reported, "Gilliam has looked so smooth, especially feeding double-play balls, that it looked as if the two must have done a lot of rehearsing." Another sportswriter commented that Gilliam "continues to be one of the top sensations of spring training." The former Baltimore Elite's play did not surprise the thirty-four-year-old Jackie Robinson, who knew from the start that Gilliam's addition to the roster might require him to play somewhere else. "I'll have to admit," he told one sportswriter with a grin, "that Junior covers more ground than I could cover."

Sportswriters asked Gilliam after the first regular-season game whether he was nervous about his ability to handle major-league pitching. "No," he replied. "It's still baseball, and I've been playing it for nine years." It was a self-confidence that Gilliam exuded throughout his career. (Years later, teammate Don Drysdale, who used his six-foot-six-inch size and blazing fastball to intimidate batters, remembered that Junior always had the same reaction when told that the opposing team's pitcher had a good fastball. "Sheeet," Gilliam would invariably say. "That guy ain't got sheeet.") With that self-confidence, Gilliam had no difficulty in assuming that he could make a contribution as the new leadoff batter for a team that had won the National League pennant the year before. Indeed, well aware of the power that the Dodger lineup included, Gilliam told his new teammates, "I'm going to have fun leading off for this team because I love to run so much."

And run he did during that rookie season in 1953. He scored 125 runs (fourth in the league), stole twenty-one bases (third in the league), and led the league in triples with seventeen while batting a respectable .278. That productivity continued during the World Series. While the Dodgers lost to the Yankees, Gilliam amassed a .296 average along three doubles and two home runs—which tied the record for the most extra-base hits in a six-game series.

The season's performance distinguished Gilliam from his peers, and he was voted the National League's Rookie of the Year for 1953. For his part, the Nashville native was surprised. "I was figuring Harvey Haddix would get it," he told one sportswriter, with reference to the St. Louis Cardinals' rookie southpaw who won twenty games while losing only nine.

Success did not spoil Gilliam (who was often called "Sweet Lips" by his teammates because of the way he pursed his lips when he swung a bat). He had already learned to take his accomplishments in stride, and that perspective was reinforced by his close relationship with Jackie Robinson. Gilliam roomed with Robinson on the road and made no secret of his admiration for the major league's first black player. But their personalities stood in sharp contrast. Unlike the outspoken third baseman, Gilliam was, as Roger Kahn observed in *The New York Herald Tribune*, "as quiet a rookie as any one could recall." (Kahn recounted that Gilliam would speak to sportswriters in the beginning of the season only after they initiated the conversation but that, by July, "he was saying 'hello' with a sort of reckless abandon.") His teammates had a similar reaction to their new teammate. "He wasn't a holler guy in the clubhouse," Carl Erskine remembered. "He wasn't a holler guy on the bench. Even on the infield, he was a quiet presence who did his job in a workmanlike way."

Still, there was no question that Gilliam treasured his status as a Brooklyn Dodger. "He and Campanella were alike in that way," Erskine said many years later. "They seemed to be saying to themselves, 'There's nothing better than this.' He played like he had a lot of fun."

That sense of fun was also evident when Dodger players gathered around a pool table after a practice session during spring training. Gilliam would walk into the room wearing a large Panama hat tilted to one side, throw a twenty-dollar bill onto the pool table, and say, "Who wants part of the devil's action?" No one could beat the Nashville native other than Alston (reputed to be the best pool player in baseball), and in time his teammates had a new nickname for him: "Devil."

The stability that Gilliam exuded at the pool table and on the field did not extend to his family life. He had met Gloria while she was still attending a Baltimore high school, and by the time he joined the Dodgers in 1953 they had been married for almost five years and had two children. The family initially spent the winters in Puerto Rico so that Gilliam could play baseball there. But Gloria and Jim soon decided that the constant travel was too much for the children and relocated to a home in Rahway, New Jersey. It may have been a wise decision, but the union did not last. In 1957, Gloria sued for (and ultimately received) a divorce, alleging that her husband had confessed to adultery. On April 25, 1959, Jim married Edwina Fields in St. Louis, and in time they had two children as well.

In the meantime, Gilliam was a steady presence in the Dodger lineup, scoring more than or close to a hundred runs in each season, leading the Dodgers in stolen bases, sometimes batting near .300 (with a career-high average of exactly .300 in 1956), and never striking out more than thirty-nine times in a season (despite playing in almost all of the team's games and usually having close to or more than six hundred at bats).

Rarely would he exhibit any anger. ("Jim's calm is his characteristic mark," said one sportswriter during his rookie year, and years later another sportswriter commented that Gilliam's "deportment is exemplary and he's one of the most popular and respected team leaders.") Unlike most of his teammates, he was prone to dismiss verbal assaults and physical challenges with a quip instead of a fist. But there were exceptions—although, even then, Gilliam had learned from Jackie Robinson how to respond to challenges from other players without losing his temper.

There was the time when the Redlegs brought in Raul Sanchez to relieve the starting pitcher in a game at Crosley Field in Cincinnati. In the fifth inning, Gilliam, batting left-handed, dragged a bunt down the first-base line for a hit when he knocked the ball out of the hand of Sanchez, who was trying to make an unassisted out. When Gilliam came up to bat two innings later, Sanchez threw a pitch that was directed at Gilliam's head and required the Dodger second baseman to duck. Junior believed that Sanchez was trying to knock him down in retaliation, and the former Negro league All-Star no doubt remembered Robinson's tactic (used several times with mixed success against Sal Maglie) in responding to pitchers who threw at your head: lay a bunt down the first-base line and, when the pitcher ran to cover first base, barrel into him with enough force to remind the pitcher that there would be a high cost to throwing beanballs.

Gilliam used that tactic to get his revenge on Sanchez's next pitch. As one sportswriter described the scene, "Junior dragged a bunt. It went foul, but Sanchez broke for it anyway, and Gilliam charged down the baseline, bowled the pitcher over, threw a punch at him, wrestled him to the ground, and began pummeling him, bringing both squads to the scene on the run." The melee resulted in fines being imposed on both Sanchez and Gilliam, but the Dodger second baseman had made his point: he would respond in kind if any pitcher intentionally tried to knock him down.

Jim Gilliam is more concerned with getting on base than retaliating against a knockdown pitch as he steps into the batter's box in the top of the seventh inning of the fifth game of the 1956 World Series. But Don Larsen is not making it easy for him. The Dodger second baseman takes a called strike, watches another pitch go by for a ball, and then fouls off a pitch. Now, with the right side of the field encased in shadows created by the towering facade of Yankee Stadium, Larsen throws a slider that tails away from Gilliam just above his knees. Junior knows it is a pitch he can hit. ("I have never been able to hit a bad ball," he once explained to a sportswriter. "And I hit everything I swing at.") He steps into the pitch and lines a low line drive toward the left side of the infield. But the Yankee shortstop is ready. "There's a ball," yells radio announcer Bob Wolff, "which is scooped up by McDougald. A nice play. And a throw to first for the out."

Pee Wee Reese now steps into the batter's box. As the Dodger shortstop later told the press, "When I came up in the seventh, I was looking to punch one into the outfield on the first pitch." Larsen knows nothing of Reese's plan, but it does not matter. Reese swings at the first pitch—a slider—and fouls it off. The Dodger shortstop does not abandon his aggressive strategy, and he swings at the next pitch as well—this one a fastball—and sends a fly into deep center field. Mickey Mantle moves to his right and pulls it in for the second out.

The tension continues to build as Duke Snider comes to the plate. The Yankees respect Snider's power, and Hank Bauer is playing the Dodger center fielder deep in right field. But, after throwing a ball, Larsen sends a fastball to the outside corner of the plate. Snider swings and lofts a fly ball into left field that Enos Slaughter catches with ease.

Bob Wolff watches these events unfold from the press box with growing excitement. He knew from the moment he took over the radio broadcast in the fifth inning that Larsen was pitching a no-hitter. But he resolved that he would never use those words over the air unless and until Larsen actually completed the no-hitter. Part of that perspective was shaped by the mistake made by Dodger broadcaster Red Barber when he was covering Bill Bevens' effort to pitch a no-hitter in the 1947 World Series. Barber kept reminding his listening audience that Bevens was on the verge of a no-hitter, and then—after Cookie Lavagetto crushed those expectations with a game-winning double in the ninth inning—a public outcry had ensued over Barber's commentary.

Wolff is very much aware of Barber's embarrassing experience. And more than that, he does not want to suck the drama out of the game. "If I keep saying it's a no-hitter or it's a perfect game," he later told me, "what do you say at the end? You're giving your punch line away too soon." Wolff explained his perspective to Joe Nixon, the Gillette producer, right before he went on the air. "Joe," Wolff said, "I'm going to let people know there's a no-hitter in progress from this point on, but I'm not going to do it by using those words unless he does it at the end." Nixon agreed. And so, after Slaughter catches Snider's fly ball, Wolff tells his listening audience, "That's twenty-one in a row retired by Don Larsen."

As he walks off the mound, the Yankee pitcher now realizes what Wolff has suspected—that he might throw a no-hitter (although, as he later confessed, he did not know what a perfect game was). After reaching the dugout, Larsen ducks into the tunnel beneath the stands for a cigarette and, as he takes a drag, Mantle walks by. "Well, Mick," the tall right-hander says to his teammate, "do you think I'll make it?" The question violates the superstition among ballplayers that no reference should be made to the possibility of a no-hitter during the game. Mantle stares at Larsen for a moment, says nothing, and then walks away. He, for one, is not going to fool with tradition. Larsen understands, but he is not happy. "It was," he later said, "like a big black shadow surrounded me and kept me apart from everyone else."

14

Bottom of the Seventh:
Enos Slaughter

A haze hung over St. Louis' Sportsman's Park on that October afternoon in 1946. It was the bottom of the eighth inning, and Enos Slaughter stood on first base while more than thirty-six thousand fans watched every move on the field. The tension in the stands and on the diamond was almost palpable—and understandable. The Cardinals and the Red Sox had each won three games in the World Series, and Slaughter represented the winning run of the seventh game—and, ultimately, the world championship.

Slaughter's mere presence on the field was nothing short of extraordinary. In the fifth game at Boston, he had been hit in the right elbow by a fastball. He stayed in the game, but the elbow soon became discolored and swelled considerably. The pain escalated quickly and precluded the thirty-year-old outfielder from getting any sleep on the train back to St. Louis. As soon as the train reached the city, Slaughter went to St. John's Hospital for an X-ray and a conference with Dr. Robert F. Hyland, the team physician. Hyland explained that the pitch had inflicted a deep bone bruise. "I sure hate to tell you this," Hyland told Slaughter, "but you just can't play in the series any more." Hyland added that he even might be forced to amputate the arm if it were re-injured in either of the next two games.

None of that mattered to Enos. The Cardinals had come too far to win the National League pennant by beating the Dodgers in the play-offs after trailing by seven and a half games in July. He could not leave now. The Cardinals were behind, and he had to be there to do whatever he could to change the situation. Somehow, some way, he would get through the sixth game and, if need be, the seventh game as well. ("As long as Enos Slaughter is in a game," one sportswriter later said, "there is a chance that his extra smidgin of hustle will prove the deciding fac-tor.") And so the injured Cardinal rejected any suggestion that he sit on the bench. "I'm playing," he defiantly told Hyland.

And play he did. Slaughter not only fielded balls and swung a bat in that sixth game without incident. He also hit a single to drive in one of the runs in the Cardinals' 4–1 victory over the Red Sox. A seventh game was therefore necessary.

That last game at Sportsman's Park was a seesaw affair. The Cardi-nals pulled ahead 3–1 in the fifth inning, but Red Sox center fielder Dom DiMaggio lined a double to right center field in the top of the eighth to drive in two runs and tie the score at 3–3. The Red Sox were ecstatic, but they paid a high price for that benefit. DiMaggio came up lame at second base with a pulled leg muscle. When Boston took the field in the bottom of the eighth, DiMaggio was replaced in center field by Leon Culberson, a Georgia native who lacked the throwing arm that DiMaggio possessed. It proved to be a critical difference.

The other change for the Red Sox was the pitcher. Bob Klinger strode to the pitching mound, and the first batter he faced was Slaugh-ter. Klinger had pitched for the Pittsburgh Pirates during Slaughter's rookie season in 1938, and that familiarity may have proved helpful to the Cardinal outfielder. He eventually tagged the Red Sox hurler for a sharp single into center field. Still, Klinger seemed to have matters under control. The next two Cardinals were set down without diffi-culty, and with only one out left, Slaughter knew that aggressive action was required.

When Cardinal outfielder Harry Walker stepped into the batter's box, Slaughter resolved to steal second base. And more than that, he committed himself to taking more than one base if the opportunity presented itself. It was not a friviolous decision. To be sure, with a weight of almost 190 pounds on a five-foot-nine-inch frame, Slaughter was not built for speed. But what he lacked in anatomy was balanced by determination. He had hit a triple in the first game of the series and had refrained from trying to score only because third-base coach Mike Gonzalez had held up his hands, signaling for Slaughter to remain at third. In retrospect, it may have made the difference. The Red Sox won the game 3–2 in the tenth inning, and, in the clubhouse afterward, Slaughter registered his complaint with Cardinal manager Eddie Dyer. "Skipper," he said, "I could have scored on that triple if I hadn't been held up." The Cardinal manager understood Slaughter's unflagging drive to win and gave him the freedom to do what he thought best.

The left-handed Walker worked the count to two balls and a strike. As Klinger threw the next pitch, Slaughter was already tearing toward second base with his head down. He heard the crack of Walker's bat and saw a line drive that he knew would land safely for a single in left center field. Under ordinary circumstances, Slaughter could do no better than reach third base. But these were not ordinary circumstances. Culberson—not DiMaggio—would be fielding Walker's hit. "I made up my mind," Enos later said, "that I was going to score the go-ahead run on that play."

Culberson knew nothing of Slaughter's decision as he fielded Walker's hit and casually tossed the ball back to Red Sox shortstop Johnny Pesky, who stood just outside the confines of the infield to take the throw. Pesky's back was to home plate, but no matter. No one scores from first base on a single. "I never expected he'd try to score," Pesky later explained. The other Red Sox infielders could see what was happening but inexplicably did not appear to make any effort to get the shortstop's attention. Any attempt might have been in vain anyway. The noise from the screaming fans, who could see what was unfolding, was deafening.

With the ball in hand, Pesky turned around and began to trot back into the infield when, to his shock, he spotted Slaughter racing for home. But it was too late. By the time Pesky threw the ball to the catcher, Slaughter was sliding across home plate, leaning on his right hand, in a cloud of dust. ("You shudda seen that Slaughter slud home," said former Cardinal pitcher Dizzy Dean.) It was, said *The New York Herald Tribune*, a "mad dash" in "as dramatic a game as the heart can stand." And it made all the difference. The Cardinals won the game 4–3 and became the first team in baseball history to defeat the Red Sox in a World Series.

Slaughter's feat was celebrated around the nation, and forevermore he would be associated with that "mad dash" home. It became a permanent part of baseball folklore that would be referenced in baseball histories, captured in old newsreels at the National Baseball Hall of Fame in Cooperstown, and later memorialized in a bronze statue that sits outside Busch Stadium, the Cardinals' new home. (And when one of Slaughter's daughters took up sailing decades later near their North Carolina home, she named the boat "Mad Dash.")

It was, to be sure, a proud moment in a long career. But Enos Slaughter wanted to make other contributions in other World Series, and ten years later, the forty-year-old veteran—now a member of the American League's pennant-winning team—is delighted when Casey Stengel asks him to play left field in the 1956 World Series. Elston Howard, the Yankees' other candidate for the position, has strep throat, and the former Cardinal wins the assignment through default.

Not that Stengel can be unhappy about the choice. Slaughter hit a three-run home run to win the third game at Ebbets Field, and, by the beginning of the fifth game at Yankee Stadium, he is the leading Yankee hitter in the series with seven hits.

Yogi Berra is the first batter to face Sal Maglie in the bottom of the seventh inning, and he lofts an easy pop fly to the left side of third base which Jackie Robinson catches in foul territory. Slaughter now steps into the batter's box, no doubt believing that he can add to the Yankees' 2–0 lead.

It is a self-confidence born from a childhood in rural North Carolina. Home was a ninety-acre farm in Allensville, a small town just south of the Virginia border. Lonnie Gentry's and Zadok Slaughter's ancestors had been farming the land in North Carolina for generations, and, by the time Enos was born in April 1916, he already had three older brothers (who would soon be joined by a sister and another brother).

Unity was the guiding principle of family life. Each family member had chores to perform—whether milking cows, slaughtering hogs, or planting tobacco, wheat, and corn. It was hard work, but farm life ensured the availability of food on the table and, in the process, taught Enos not to take anything for granted. "When you're a farm boy," he later said, "you learn to appreciate life."

Hunting and fishing were also family affairs, sometimes involving excursions by covered wagon to remote locations. On other occasions, young Enos would travel to nearby woods with his father and brothers to hunt rabbits. "There wasn't enough money to buy me a gun," Enos explained, so he would kill the rabbits by throwing rocks at them. Years later he would say that his throwing arm in baseball was developed by throwing rocks at rabbits.

Although hunting and fishing may have been leisure activities to some, there was nothing casual about the way Enos Slaughter pursued those activities. There was eternal enthusiasm and always boundless energy. And it did not change with age. "He saves a lot of wear and tear on the hound dogs," said Joe Garagiola, who would sometimes hunt with Slaughter when they were teammates in St. Louis. "We let Enos be the retriever. The minute we hit something—bang!—there goes Enos. Through mud and briar bushes and swamp."

It was the kind of attitude young Enos exuded when he participated in sports. That too was a family affair. However much they wanted their children to work the farm, Zadok and Lonnie recognized the need for some respite. During each spring, all work would cease on Saturday at noon, and the family would travel—sometimes by horse and buggy and at other times in the family's 1927 Ford Model T—to a local field where everyone would play baseball.

No one in the family was more excited about those trips than Zadok and Lonnie's fourth child. "I just loved baseball, period," he later said. Although he wrote and did almost everything else right-handed, young Enos found it more comfortable to chop wood left-handed and, not surprisingly, he decided to bat from the left side of the plate. Still, he threw right-handed and was able to become the regular second baseman for Bethel Hill High School in his senior year.

Enos' proficiency at football and baseball was enough to attract a scholarship offer from a local college, but higher education held no allure for the young athlete. "My mind was set," he later said, "on going to work for the mill and continuing to play second base for the company team."

Enos was especially pleased when the sports editor for the *Durham Morning Herald* recommended to Oliver French, the owner of the Cardinals' farm team in nearby Greensboro, that the young player be given a tryout. The eighteen-year-old Enos made the trip in September 1934 with two friends and was elated when Billy Southworth, the Greensboro manager, invited the young player to return for another tryout the following spring—but not as a second baseman. Southworth concluded that the Bethel High School star looked "clumsy" at second base and decided that he had the arm to be an outfielder. With that, Enos Slaughter became—and forever remained—an outfielder.

The Cardinal prospect returned to the family farm and married Hulo Powell, his high school sweetheart. It was not a marriage made in heaven. They were not only young. They also had different visions of their future. "She was in love with Enos Slaughter the farm boy," Enos later said, "not Enos Slaughter the professional baseball player, and the life in that sport would ultimately lead to the end of that marriage." Still, Hulo was with Enos when he traveled to Asheville, North Carolina, the following spring for another tryout with the Cardinal farm team.

It did not start out well. Southworth decided that the young prospect was too slow afoot to become a professional baseball player. But all was not lost. "Did you know," Southworth asked Slaughter one day, "that you've been running flat-footed? Why don't you try running on your toes?" Eager to succeed, Slaughter took the suggestion to heart and spent the next three days trying to change his running style. The results were dramatic. He was now a much faster runner on the base paths—and the recipient of a contract paying him $75 a month to play with the Martinsville Redbirds. ("Those three days," he later said, "saved a long baseball career.")

Hulo returned to the farm in Roxboro, North Carolina, that one of Enos' brothers bought for them, and Slaughter remembered being lonely in that first season of professional baseball. But it did not affect his performance. He made a respectable showing and earned a promotion the following season to the Cardinals' farm team in Columbus, Georgia.

The dream of making the major leagues began to evaporate at the beginning of that second season. Enos was batting a meager .220 and feeling very sorry for himself. During one game, he trotted in from right field after an inning and then slowed down to a walk when he passed first base. Eddie Dyer, the thirty-five-year-old manager, did not hide his disappointment when Enos came into the dugout. "Listen," he said to his twenty-year-old player, "are you too tired to run all the way? If you are," he added with obvious sarcasm, "I'll get some help for you."

The message could not have been more clear. "From then on," Enos remembered, "I kept on running." And not just from the outfield after the end of the inning. He would run to his position in the outfield when the inning began. He would run to first base if he got a walk. And he would expend whatever energy it required to quickly get to wherever else he had to go on the field.

It was a trait that would eventually capture the attention of his teammates, his manager, and even the press. "He is," said one sportswriter after Slaughter had been with the Cardinals for more than seven years, "perpetual motion on the ball field." (Slaughter's hustle also caught the eye of Pete Rose, who later set a major-league record for lifetime hits and became known as "Charlie Hustle" because of his aggressive base running. "I used to watch the Cincinnati Red games on television," Rose told a reporter after his rookie year in 1963. "One day, the Reds were playing the Cardinals. Slaughter drew a walk and ran hard to first base. I decided right then and there," said Rose, "that was what I was going to do as long as I played ball.")

Slaughter's newfound energy in that second season of minor-league ball invigorated his game as well. By the time the 1936 season ended, he had a .325 batting average and the league lead in triples. Although his baseball career appeared to be on track, his marriage was not. Hulo gave birth to a daughter named Rebecca that October, but she died after six days. That misfortune only compounded the problems encountered by the young couple, and by the following summer Hulo was living with her parents in Roxboro while Enos continued his ascent to the big leagues.

The 1937 season brought him closer to his goal. Enos played with the Cardinals' American Association farm team in Columbus, Ohio, and distinguished himself as the league's dominant hitter. He hit twenty-six home runs and led the league in batting average (.382), hits (245), and runs (147). Sportswriters began to refer to him as "slugger extraordinary" and "one of the brightest minor league stars of the year."

Slaughter's exploits on the field made him a fan favorite, and one Columbus sportswriter conducted a contest that asked the reading public for suggestions on a nickname that could be affixed to the town's star player. One of the more popular proposals was "Country," and Slaughter—the sole judge of the contest—agreed that "Country" was indeed the best choice. By the time he reached the major leagues in 1938, teammates and sportswriters alike were referring to the twenty-two-year-old player as Country Slaughter.

The 1938 Cardinals were no longer the hard-charging troupe that had gained fame as the "Gashouse Gang" when they won the 1934 World Series. Manager Frankie Frisch had hoped that constant practice during spring training might enable the team to recapture the glory of that championship team, but it was not to be, and the team finished sixth. ("You can take a doggone mule," outfielder Pepper Martin explained to Frisch, "and work him forty days and forty nights. He ain't going to win the Kentucky Derby.") Still, there was one bright spot amidst the frustration: Enos Slaughter.

Even before spring training had concluded, sportswriters were singing his praises. "Slaughter can throw with about as much force and accuracy," *The Sporting News* reported in March, "as any outfielder the Redbirds have had in years." Enos opened the 1938 season in center field and validated his promotion in the very first game. In the first inning, the New York Giants' batter hit a long drive to center field that seemed destined to be an extra-base hit. "Slaughter was off with the crack of the bat," said one sportswriter. "He turned his back to the grandstand and ran, and when he had gone about as far as he could go without interfering with concrete, he turned, reached out with his glove, and hauled down the drive." Slaughter also made his mark in those first games with a bat by hitting over .300 in the first few weeks of the season (and would finish with a .276 average). By May, the *St. Louis Post-Dispatch* was saying that Slaughter's "potential brilliance may well take some of the sting out of a season already marked by many disappointments for the St. Louis Cardinals."

Slaughter returned to Roxboro after the season ended, pleased with his accomplishments and eager to enjoy life on the farm before he resumed his new life in the major leagues. But unexpected events transformed the homecoming into a tragedy. Shortly before the New Year, he and his father went hunting, caught about twenty-five rabbits, and brought them home to be cleaned for eating. During the process, Zadok cut his finger—in other circumstances, a minor blemish easily disregarded. But, unbeknownst to Zadok and his son, the rabbits were infected with the tularemia bacteria, which produce a condition commonly called "rabbit fever." Zadok contracted the fever, which the local doctors were unable to diagnose. The family took the elder Slaughter to a hospital in Durham, but, as Enos remembered, "his temperature went up to 107 degrees, and when the fever broke, he went with it."

Ironically, Enos himself soon became infected with the disease, suffering from high fever, dizzy spells, and large swellings under his left arm that prevented him from straightening it out. But he would not disclose the ailment to the Cardinals as he prepared to leave for spring training in February. He had secured a new contract for $3,300, and he did not want the team to have any second thoughts about its decision.

Slaughter's silence on his health did not have any adverse impact. He played in 149 games during the 1939 season, batted .320 with 193 hits (fourth in the league), and hit a league-leading fifty-two doubles. That performance helped to lift the Cardinals into a second-place finish and buoyed Enos' spirits. In his first year, he had been intimidated by the atmosphere and almost afraid to converse with the other players. After all, Ducky Medwick, Johnny Mize, and many of the other Cardinals were household names in baseball. "Me being off the farm," Slaughter later said of that first year, "I didn't have too much to say."

But no longer. "I wasn't in awe of the big shots on the club anymore," he remembered. "In fact, the way I was contributing to the success of the ball club, I considered myself to be among them."

There was no change in Slaughter's status as the years progressed. In 1940, he again batted over .300 with thirteen triples and seventeen home runs. By August 1941, he had a .312 batting average, thirteen home runs (the most on the club), and seventy-one runs batted in (second in the league). From all appearances, it would be his best year in the big leagues. But in an afternoon game at Sportsman's Park, a Pirate batter lined a drive into right center field. Slaughter and Cardinal center fielder Terry Moore converged on the ball and, as he realized that Moore was about to make a diving catch, Slaughter tried to jump over his teammate—but landed on his shoulder in the process. Billy Southworth—now the Cardinals' manager—ran out to the field. "Are you okay, Eno?" he asked. Slaughter, ever the stoic, assured his manager that he was fine. But when Southworth asked him to throw a ball, the Cardinal outfielder came up short. And for understandable reasons. An X-ray later showed that Slaughter had broken his collarbone—an injury that sidelined him for the rest of the season and certainly contributed to the Cardinals' inability to overtake the Dodgers for the league lead.

Slaughter and the Cardinals got their revenge in 1942. The Redbirds took the pennant by winning 106 games, and no one was more instrumental in that achievement than the North Carolina native. Slaughter batted .318 (second in the league) with a league-leading 188 hits, a league-leading seventeen triples, and a league-leading 292 total bases.

The Cardinals defeated the Yankees in the five-game World Series, and Slaughter added to his growing reputation with a sterling play in the field. After losing the first game, the Cardinals had rebounded to take a 4–3 lead in the second game at Sportsman's Park. But the Yankees appeared to be on the verge of coming back. Catcher Bill Dickey lined a single to start the top of the ninth inning, and Yankee manager Joe McCarthy sent in Tuck Stainback, his fastest runner, to run for Dickey. Bomber first baseman Buddy Hassett then drove another single into the right-field corner, and Stainback raced past second base with the obvious expectation that reaching third would be easy. But the Cardinal right fielder backhanded the ball quickly, whirled around, and made what one New York sportswriter called "the greatest throw I ever saw." The ball traveled in a perfect arc to Cardinal third baseman Whitey Kurowski, who tagged Stainback out with yards to spare. The Yankee rally died, and the Cardinals won the second game (as well as the next three).

However much he wanted to bask in the glory of that World Series Championship and his burgeoning baseball career, Slaughter knew that a change was required. The nation was at war, and in August 1942 he had enlisted in the Army Air Corps. In January 1943, the twenty-six-year-old outfielder donned a military uniform and abandoned any hope of playing in Sportsman's Park for the foreseeable future. But it was not to be a lonely life. He had met Josephine Begonia, a young woman from Chicago, on a trip to Peoria, Illinois, to make an off-season appearance for the Cardinals after the 1942 season ended. She was playing the piano in the orchestra at the hotel where Enos was staying. The two young people began to talk, a rapport was established, and in March 1943, they were married.

The army assigned Slaughter to be a physical training instructor at what is now the Lackland Air Force Base in San Antonio, Texas. It was a life devoid of combat, and, as victory became imminent in early 1945, he joined a troupe of major-league baseball players in touring the Pacific Islands and entertaining the troops. Even then, however, Enos would not spare any effort to succeed, on one occasion ripping his leg while sliding on a field made of sand and filled with coral. ("These guys are dying for me," he later told a reporter. "The least I can do is give them my best.") He ended his tour on the tiny island of Tinian and was there when—unbeknownst to him—the *Enola Gay* took off one August morning for the flight to Hiroshima.

On February 1, 1946, Slaughter was discharged from military duty and joined the Cardinals for spring training in Florida. But Josephine was no longer with him. The relationship had soured before Enos had been shipped overseas, and, shortly after he arrived at the Cardinals spring training camp in St. Petersburg, he began spending time with Mary Peterson Walker, a widow from Galesburg, Illinois, whose husband had been killed in the war (and who would soon become Enos' third wife and give him a daughter named Patricia).

The changes in his social life may have contributed to Enos' successful transition back to professional baseball. He played that 1946 season without any indication that he had lost any of his skill at the plate or on the field. Chicago Cubs general manager Jim Gallagher grudgingly acknowledged that consistency when he watched Slaughter beat a throw to first base in a game at Wrigley Field. "That big baboon drinks beer, goes away for three years," said Gallagher, "and comes out running faster" (Gallagher not realizing that Slaughter did not drink at the time). Opposing pitchers could have had the same lament. Slaughter batted an even .300 while hitting a career-high eighteen home runs and driving in a league-leading 130 runs. Not surprisingly, those achievements brought him considerable media attention when the 1947 season began. "A throwback to the Gashouse Gang," said one article published in May, "Enos Slaughter is a professional who hustles like a starry-eyed amateur. Ignoring illness and injuries, he plays some of his greatest games when he should be home in bed."

Slaughter's renewed status as a national figure was not the only change in that 1947 season. Jackie Robinson, the Dodgers' new first baseman, had broken the color line. There were, of course, players and managers who objected to racial integration in baseball, and some did what they could to prevent the experiment from succeeding. And so it was easy to accept the credibility of rumors that circulated at the beginning of the season that the St. Louis Cardinals—whose roster included many players from the South—would go on strike when the Dodgers made their first visit to Sportsman's Park in May.

Before that visit, *The New York Herald Tribune* reported that Cardinal owner Sam Breadon had heard about the strike and had traveled to New York City to confer with National League President Ford Frick about possible solutions. Frick, it was said, had responded by sending a telegram to the Cardinal players to warn them about the repercussions if any strike occurred. "If you do this," the telegram reportedly read, "you will be suspended from the league. You will find that friends that you think you have in the press box will not support you, that you will be outcasts. I do not care if half the league strikes. Those who do it will encounter quick retribution."

It was, to be sure, an eloquent endorsement of sound social policy.

Initial reports also indicated that Frick had called several of the Cardinal players, but *The New York Times* soon corrected that impression. "I didn't have to talk to the players myself," Frick reportedly said. "Mr. Breadon did the talking to them. From what Breadon told me afterward, the trouble was smoothed over. I don't know what he said to them, who the ringleader was, or any other details."

There was no work stoppage by the Cardinal players when Robinson made his first appearance at Sportsman's Park. Still, many people in the baseball world assumed that there had in fact been discussions of a strike and that Slaughter and Cardinal center fielder Terry Moore, Slaughter's best friend on the club, were the ones who had tried to organize it. "Tradition had it then, and still has it," said Dodger broadcaster Red Barber in a 1982 book, "that Enos Slaughter led the Cardinals in their threatened revolt against Robinson."

Slaughter dismissed those allegations as "just a lot of baloney." He said he was interested only in playing baseball—not registering social opinions. "I ain't never opened my mouth," he later explained. "It was never brought up in no shape, form or fashion that the Cardinals were going on strike." ("I don't think," said his daughter Gaye many years later, "that my father would have known what a strike was.")

Terry Moore had a similar reaction. In 1994, he retained an attorney when he learned of a book proposing to say that he and Slaughter had "tried to persuade their Cardinal teammates to go on strike in May 1947 to protest Jackie Robinson's admittance to the National League." Moore's attorney advised the publisher that, in his client's view, the allegation was "an out-and-out falsehood."

The recollections of other Cardinal players supported the reactions of Slaughter and Moore. Stan Musial, the team's All-Star first baseman, acknowledged that he heard talk that was "rough and racial" but that the story of the planned strike "was made up." "The facts are," added second baseman Red Schoendienst, "that nothing was said with the Cardinals about going on strike."

Similar sentiments were expressed by Chuck Diering, a rookie outfielder with the team in 1947. "I never heard of anything like that talked among the team members," he told me many years later. Marty Marion, the Cardinal shortstop (and also the National League player representative at the time), agreed, saying that "there was nothing about going on strike." When asked about the possible roles of Slaughter and Moore in the rumored strike, Marion was equally assertive. "That is a mistake," he told me. "I don't care where you got your information from. I was on the team."

In an autobiography published many years later, Ford Frick confirmed that *The New York Herald Tribune*'s story was overblown, that Breadon himself had told Frick that the rumored strike was merely "a tempest in a teapot," and that no telegram had been sent by the commissioner's office to the Cardinal players. Frick quoted Breadon as later acknowledging that "a few of the players were upset and were popping off a bit, but they really didn't mean it. Just letting off a little steam." For his part, Frick said that "the Cardinals were unfortunately marked publicly as the great dissenters when, in reality, their players adjusted more quickly than many of the other players."

There are some who nonetheless maintain that the strike was in fact discussed. Perhaps it was so. But Slaughter was never presented with any information during his lifetime that contradicted his statements concerning a strike to protest Robinson's appearance at Sportsman's Park. Still, rumors of that strike—and Slaughter's alleged leadership role in it—no doubt helped to fuel a furor when Slaughter spiked Robinson in a close game at Brooklyn the following August.

It happened in the eleventh inning with the score tied at 1–1. The Cardinal outfielder was running hard down the first-base line after hitting a ground ball that was fielded by Robinson. Everyone agreed that Slaughter's spikes touched some part of Robinson's right leg when he reached the bag, but there was disagreement about the details. Dodger pitcher Rex Barney, who watched events unfold from the dugout, said that Slaughter "was out by ten feet" but that "he jumped, not on Jackie's foot, but up on the thigh of his leg, and he cut him." Ralph Branca, who was pitching the game, recalled something different, saying that "Enos stepped on his leg just below the calf" but that Robinson was not "cut badly." Robinson himself said that "Slaughter deliberately went for my leg instead of the base and spiked me rather severely." In his *New York Times* story the following day, Roscoe McGowen reported that "Slaughter's foot landed on Robinson's right foot, which was not on the bag but against it. Jackie hopped around a minute or so and Doc Wendler came out, but Robbie stayed in the game, apparently not seriously hurt."

Whatever the details, it was not unreasonable for Robinson and his teammates to assume that Slaughter's action was a manifestation of racism. After all, the Cardinal outfielder was from North Carolina, a state where segregation was still an accepted part of community life and where blacks were commonly referred to as "niggers" (a reference which sometimes sprinkled Slaughter's speech as well). Beyond that, fresh in the team's memory was the vile vituperation that Robinson had encountered—first from his own teammates in spring training and then from almost every team the Dodgers encountered in their drive to win the National League pennant.

Still, some of those who witnessed the incident were unsure of Slaughter's motivation. "My guess," said Red Barber in 1982, "is that if he had been asked if he cut Robinson deliberately, he would have spit tobacco juice and answered two words in that harsh voice of his that rasped and grated, 'Hell, no.'" Barber knew what he was talking about. Five years later, a seventy-one-year-old Enos Slaughter was asked about the incident in an interview for the Hall of Fame. "Whoever said I intentionally stepped on Jackie Robinson," he growled, "I'll look them in the eye and call them a son of a bitch, and I don't give a goddamn. If he wants to fight, I'll knock him on his ass right today."

The denial was rooted in Slaughter's approach to the game. He was a hard-nosed ballplayer who would sacrifice his own welfare for the good of the team—even if it meant spiking an opposing white player (which he had done on many previous occasions). Indeed, a *Saturday Evening Post* article in May 1947—three months before the Robinson incident—highlighted Slaughter's win-at-all-costs approach. "Slaughter, following always his play-to-win code, doesn't spend much time reflecting on ethical values," the article reported. "He is one of the few present-day exponents of that rowdy game which is wistfully recalled by some of the old-timers." Slaughter's base running received particular attention. "Far from the fastest man on the paths," said the article, "he is still the game's most feared base runner."

From Slaughter's perspective, the incident with Robinson was nothing more than a reflection of that competitive zeal. The Cardinal out-fielder claimed that Robinson, a converted shortstop who was still a novice at playing first, had his right foot on the bag (not on the side of the bag) when he took the throw and that Enos had every right to do whatever he could do to break up the play—even if it meant planting his spikes on Robinson's foot. In Slaughter's view, the base paths belonged to the runner, and Robinson had to suffer the consequences if he was even slightly out of position. ("I don't care if my mother had been out there," he later told his daughters. "I would have run *her* over.")

Of course, many eyewitnesses took issue with Slaughter's claim that Robinson was out of position, but there would be other incidents to suggest that the spiking was nothing more than a reflection of Slaughter's excessive zeal. A few years later, he narrowly missed stepping on the foot of Monte Irvin, another black player who was the New York Giants' first baseman, as he was running out a ground ball. "Watch your feet," Slaughter yelled to Irvin. "I'm still catching hell for stepping on Robinson." On another occasion in 1949, the North Carolina native spiked Dodger first baseman Gil Hodges as he ran out a bunt, causing Dodger manager Burt Shotton to say that Slaughter was "a dirty player." And then there was the ground ball that Joe DiMaggio hit in the 1947 World Series. As Roger Kahn reported in one of his baseball books, Robinson was "covering first awkwardly," and the miscue was not overlooked by DiMaggio as he charged down the first-base line. "I could have stepped on his heel," the Yankee center fielder later said. "Play hard. That was my way. But if I did, it could have been a fight and then it would have been the niggers against the dagos, and I didn't want that." It may be that Slaughter, unlike DiMaggio, was more focused on winning the game than worrying about the social consequences of his aggression.

There was, of course, no way to verify Slaughter's actual thoughts as he ran down the first-base line in that 1947 game. Still, many players and writers continued to believe that a man with Slaughter's Southern background had to have been motivated by racially discriminatory motives. Word spread after Slaughter retired that the spiking incident, coupled with his reported involvement in the Cardinal strike, explained his failure to be elected to the Baseball National Hall of Fame despite a statistical record that compared favorably with many other outfielders who had received the honor. And then—after Slaughter was finally elected into the Hall of Fame by the Veterans' Committee—the controversy flared again in 1994 with the broadcast of Ken Burns' celebrated documentary on baseball.

One of the segments focused on the abuse Robinson had endured in his rookie year. According to the documentary, "the most serious incident" occurred in a game against the Cardinals: "Enos 'Country' Slaughter, although out at first by at least ten feet, nonetheless jumped into the air and deliberately laid open Robinson's thigh with his spikes." The dramatic description appeared to mirror Rex Barney's recollection but differed from the observations of other eyewitnesses. But the details were—in one respect—irrelevant. The allegation was racial abuse, and it really mattered not whether Robinson was cut in the thigh, by his heel, or on his foot. Whatever the damage, it was—or so it was said—an intentional infliction of physical harm motivated by racial bias.

Then living in retirement on his farm in Roxboro, the seventy-eight-year-old Slaughter was not pleased when he learned of the statement in the Burns documentary. And he was not one to sit idly by while others accepted as truth something he believed to be inaccurate. As Burns remembered, Slaughter pursued him "relentlessly" in search of a retraction. The former Cardinal was particularly upset because Burns had never contacted him to get his side of the story.

Burns first learned of Slaughter's pursuit at a White House dinner that included many former baseball players. During the dinner, one Hall of Fame veteran warned Burns that Slaughter "was after him." Burns was saddened by the disclosure. From his perspective, there was not much, if anything, he could do. He was a film producer—not an investigative journalist. He did, of course, have a research staff to review books, articles, and other resources. But he did not interview many former baseball players for the documentary. "I wanted writers and historians to provide commentary," he later explained to me. So his failure to contact Slaughter was not an inadvertent omission but a reflection of Burns' artistic approach.

In retrospect, it may not have made a difference. Burns knew, of course, that it was "impossible to know to a certainty" what was in Slaughter's mind at the time of the Robinson incident in 1947. But he rechecked his sources after he first learned of Slaughter's inquiry and found documentation to support the statement in the broadcast. Still, he said that he was prepared to make changes in the documentary if there was proof of error—but Slaughter obviously could not provide any objective proof of his motivations at the time. The statement in the Burns film was not changed and remained a source of frustration to the North Carolina native for the rest of his life.

However much he may have later resented the description in Ken Burns' documentary, the spiking episode did not have any impact on Slaughter's career on the diamond. He remained a stalwart of the Cardinal offense, continued his aggressive ways on the base paths, and played with the same drive that had brought him fame and satisfaction. ("Full of zing as a rookie," said one sportswriter of Enos during spring training in March 1950, "eager for the game to start as though he'd never been in one before.") Slaughter finished the 1947 season with a .294 batting average and thirteen triples, which tied him for second in the league with Stan Musial. He raised his average to .321 in 1948 and to .336 in 1949 (placing him third in the league behind Musial and Robinson, who led the league with a .342 average).

By then he had replaced Terry Moore as the team captain. It was a fitting tribute to Slaughter's achievements on the field and the affection that he felt for the Cardinals. As he told a jammed Sportsman's Park on a night held in his honor in 1948, "I love St. Louis as much as I think St. Louis loves me. Never played for any other team since I came into organized ball, and I hope I never do."

For years afterward, it seemed that Slaughter would get his wish of remaining in St. Louis for his entire career. The Cardinals rewarded his 1949 performance with a $25,000 salary for the 1950 season, and, while his batting average slipped to .290 in that year, he drove in 101 runs—five more than he had in the previous season—and made the National League All-Star team for the seventh consecutive year. Unfortunately, the Cardinal management was not impressed. His 1950 record was not as good as his 1949 record, and so they cut his salary to $20,000.

In retrospect, it may have seemed like the right decision. An assortment of injuries and ailments—the flu, a broken finger, and then a mysterious rash on the lower part of his body that made it "murder to put on the uniform and take it off"—resulted in a 1951 season record that was less than satisfactory: a .281 batting average in 123 games with only four home runs and sixty-four runs batted in. But there was cause for hope. In the last thirty-two games of the season he batted .330 and was credited by manager Marty Marion as one of reasons for the Cardinals' ability to win twenty-three of those games and pull themselves into third place.

Not surprisingly, the thirty-five-year-old Slaughter scoffed at any suggestion that he was nearing the end of his career. "The old kid is far from through," he told one sportswriter shortly after the season ended. "Just wait and see." And see they did. The unyielding drive to succeed paid dividends for the longtime Cardinal in the 1952 season. He raised his batting average to .300 in 140 games, hit twelve triples (second in the league), and drove in 101 runs (fifth in the league). The improved performance did not escape notice in baseball circles, and the Associated Press chose the Cardinal right fielder as "the comeback of the year."

Slaughter's retention of the energy to maintain that high level of play was not a matter of happenstance. It was based on a disciplined lifestyle. His consumption of alcohol was minimal. Although he chewed tobacco, he never smoked cigarettes. He had a daily intake of sunflower seeds and vitamins. He thrived on boiled lean meat, never had anything fried, and rarely ate hamburger meat or pork. He also had a liking for a drink that consisted of skim milk and raw eggs. And—while he had purchased a home in the St. Louis suburb of Belleville, Illinois—he tried to stay in shape during the winters by hunting, fishing, chopping wood, or engaging in some other physical activity. (He did not devote the same attention to his teeth, and many years later—long after he had retired—his daughters would remember with amusement one dinner when he tried to bite into something hard. His false teeth popped out and sailed across the dining room table.)

There was little evidence of Slaughter's age in his performance during the 1953 season. True, he hit only six home runs in 143 games, but he hit thirty-four doubles, drove in eighty-nine runs, and batted a respectable .291. His record and stature also led to his selection for the National All-Star team for the tenth consecutive season (which he more than justified by getting two hits, driving in two runs, stealing a base, and making what one sports historian called "a spectacular diving catch" in the National League's 5–1 triumph over the American League—causing Casey Stengel, who had managed the American League team, to say afterward, "The old feller done us in").

The Cardinals appeared to appreciate Slaughter's dedication and his seemingly ageless talent. The Anheuser-Busch company, makers of Budweiser and other popular beers, had purchased the team shortly before the 1953 season, and Slaughter received special attention when he signed his next season's contract in December. "This is the first Cardinal player contract I've ever handled," President Gussie Busch told a smiling Enos Slaughter at the press conference. "I want you to know that you'll be here as long as I am." Kind thoughts that would not survive spring training.

The North Carolina native was sitting in the dugout in April during the Cardinals' final exhibition game when manager Eddie Stanky approached him. "Slaughter," he said without emotion, "you can go ahead and get dressed. The general manager would like to see you in his office." Slaughter did what he was told and strolled into the office of Cardinal general manager Dick Meyer—"totally unprepared," as he later recalled, "for the news I was about to receive." "Eno," Meyer began, "all good things must come to an end." And then the surprising disclosure: "We've traded you to the New York Yankees."

Slaughter could not believe the words he had heard. He loved the Cardinals. He had been with the organization for his entire career. He had a .305 lifetime batting average in thirteen seasons, and he knew that he was still capable of making a contribution to the team's success. He could not understand why the Cardinals would throw him out.

The answer came in a press conference held later that day. Gussie Busch acknowledged that the club had "just traded one of the greatest baseball players in the history of the St. Louis Cardinals." But the team, he explained, had to look to the future. "We have several very promising outfielders with the Cardinals and in our system," said

Pee Wee Reese batting in his rookie year of 1940. "We didn't have too many guys who were afraid," Reese later said of his Dodger team-mates in those early years. "If you were afraid, you didn't stay on the club."

Enos Slaughter sliding across home plate after the "mad dash" to score the winning run for the St. Louis Cardinals in the seventh game of the 1946 World Series against the Boston Red Sox.

Yankee manager Casey Stengel hugs Billy Martin after the Yankee second baseman hit a single to drive in two runs in the eleventh inning of a game against the Philadelphia Athletics on September 27, 1952, to enable the Yankees to win their fourth straight American League pennant. "That fresh punk," Stengel told reporters when Martin first joined the New York club in 1950, "how I love him."

Corbis

Jackie Robinson and Pee Wee Reese in the locker room on October 1, 1952, after each hit a home run to enable Brooklyn to win the first game of the 1952 World Series against the Yankees. The Kentucky-born Reese made a point of putting his arm around Robinson on the field in a show of friendship when Robinson encountered vile racial epithets during his rookie year in 1947. "After Pee Wee came over like that," Robinson said many years later, "I never felt alone on a baseball field again."

Baseball Hall of Fame

Yogi Berra in the Yankee locker room (with pitcher Bob Turley in the background). "We truly felt like a family, always pulling for each other," Berra later said of his days with the Yankees.

Joe Collins in the locker room on September 8, 1955, after his two home runs accounted for all the Yankee runs in a 5-4 triumph over the Chicago White Sox. "He was a terrific influence inside the clubhouse," Tony Kubek later said of Collins because of his good humor and even disposition.

Jackie Robinson stealing home in the first game of the 1955 World Series with Yogi Berra trying to apply the tag. Whenever he signed the photo in later years, Yogi would invariably add, "He was out!"
GETTY IMAGES

Sandy Amoros catching Yogi Berra's fly ball in the seventh inning of the seventh game of the 1955 World Series at Yankee Stadium. "Lucky, lucky, I'm so lucky," the Cuban-born Amoros later said in his broken English.
BASEBALL HALL OF FAME

Gil McDougald with his unorthodox batting stance. The Yankee management winced when they saw it, but the great Rogers Hornsby, McDougald's minor-league manager, had no qualms. "If you feel comfortable batting the way you do," he told his young protégé, "go ahead."

Mickey Mantle and Hank Bauer hold Bauer's bat before a game on May 10, 1956. Mantle had been using Bauer's bat and already had ten home runs by that point in his march toward the triple crown (with fifty-two home runs).

Mickey Mantle batting right-handed in a game at Yankee Stadium in 1956. Before every game, he had to go through a ritual of wrapping his right leg in tape because of prior injuries. "I watched him bandage that knee—that whole leg," Cleveland pitcher Early Wynn later said when he and Mantle shared a locker room in an All-Star game, "and saw what he had to go through every day to play. And now I'll never be able to praise him enough." CORBIS

Sandy Amoros hoped to enjoy retirement in his native Cuba, but his refusal to accept Fidel Castro's request to manage a local team required him to migrate to the United States, where he lived in virtual poverty.
BASEBALL HALL OF FAME

Andy Carey repeatedly rebuffed the requests of Casey Stengel—who generally wanted his players to be proficient at more than one osition—to play shortstop as well as third base. "I'd rather be a good third baseman," he told the Yankee manager, "than a mediocre shortstop."

BASEBALL HALL OF FAME

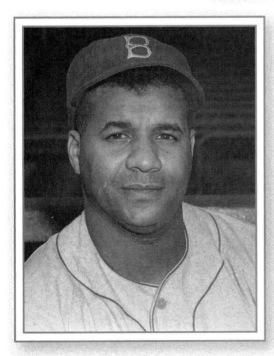

Roy Campanella had a way of relaxing Dodger pitchers with a short conference at the mound—which shortstop Pee Wee Reese invariably attended. "I don't want to miss a word he says," Reese once explained to a sportswriter. "He's funnier than Bob Hope."

BASEBALL HALL OF FAME

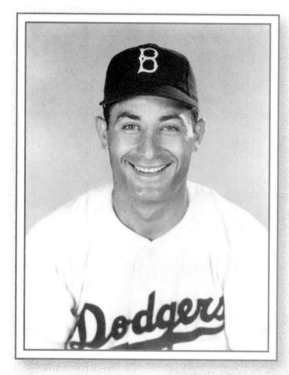

Although respected by his teammates for his talents on the field—especially his rifle arm—Carl Furillo often felt hurt because the other Dodgers did not socialize much with him and his wife, Fern. "We never suspected," said Dodger pitcher Carl Erskine, "that he felt like an outsider."

In addition to his skills on the diamond, Jim Gilliam was reputed to be one of baseball's best pool players and would often throw a twenty-dollar bill on the table and say, "Who wants part of the devil's action?"

Gil Hodges later said that his "biggest baseball thrill" was "the way the Brooklyn fans backed me when I couldn't buy a base hit" during his hitting slump in the springof 1953.

Sal Maglie later complained that Mickey Mantle's home run in the bottom of the fourth inning of the perfect game was "the shortest home run in baseball" and that "in any other field, it would have been an out."

Dale Mitchell loved the camaraderie on the Cleveland Indians but resented the pressure that General Manager Hank Greenberg put on him to hit more home runs.

Home plate umpire Babe Pinelli (who retired after the 1956 World Series) told Duke Snider years after Larsen's perfect game "that he wanted to go out on a no-hitter in a World Series" and that "anything close was a strike."

ogi Berra hitting the 250th home run of his career on July 4, 1957. Ted Williams
would later say that, with his unorthodox batting style, Berra "gave hitting a bad name"
ut added that Yogi was also one of baseball's most dangerous hitters because "he could
ove the runner, and move him late in the game, like no one else I ever saw play the
ame." BASEBALL HALL OF FAME

Enos Slaughter—right
before the start of the
perfect game on October 8,
1956—posing with seven
bats to reflect his seven hits
as the leading Yankee hitter
of the series in the
first four games.
CORBIS

Don Larsen throws the first pitch of the perfect game to Jim Gilliam, with Yogi Berra catching and Babe Pinelli umpiring.

Jackie Robinson's line drive is deflected off Andy Carey's glove to Gil Mc-Dougald, who fires the ball to Joe Collins at first base just in time to beat Robinson to the bag in the top of the second inning of the perfect game.

Billy Martin backpedals to catch Sandy Amoros' pop fly in the top of the second inning as Mickey Mantle and Hank Bauer watch.   BASEBALL HALL OF FAME

Mickey Mantle's catch of Gil Hodges' blast in the top of the fifth inning. Mantle later called it the "greatest" catch in his eighteen-year career.   BASEBALL HALL OF FAME

Don Larsen's no-windup delivery during the perfect game.

The last pitch of the perfect game to Dale Mitchell, with Billy Martin watching from second base.

le Mitchell (*left*) celebrates in the locker room at Fenway Park with pitcher Bob
mon (*center*) and catcher Jim Hegan (*right*) after driving in the winning run in the
th inning to lead the Cleveland Indians to victory over the Boston Red Sox on May 4,
50. Mitchell always maintained that Larsen's last pitch to him in the perfect game
s out of the strike zone—and every Yankee on the field who could see the pitch (other
n Larsen and Berra) agreed. COURTESY OF DALE E. MITCHELL, JR.

Yogi Berra leaps into
Don Larsen's arms
after Dale Mitchell is
called out on strikes.
BASEBALL HALL OF FAME

Don Larsen in the
locker room after the
perfect game.
BASEBALL HALL OF FAME

Busch. "They are knocking at the door of the Cardinals right now and we have to make a place for them."

Busch's explanation was of little solace to Slaughter. Only days shy of his thirty-eighth birthday, the longtime Cardinal right fielder was in tears as he faced the press, repeatedly wiping his eyes with a handkerchief. "This is the biggest shock of my life," Slaughter said. "I've given my life to this organization, and they let you go when they think you're getting old."

The trade was not the only change in Slaughter's life. He had divorced Mary a few years earlier. ("Her parents had come down to our house and started to get into our affairs," Slaughter later explained. "I think that's what broke up our marriage more than anything else.") He subsequently met Ruth Rohleder, a small-time actress who used the name Vickie Van, while he was in Los Angeles on a barnstorming tour after the season had ended. She soon became Enos' fourth wife and traveled with him to New York.

Slaughter was with the Yankees when they opened the 1954 season, and he was eager to show his new team that he was a long way from retirement. "One thing I did when I played ball, regardless of what uniform I wore," Slaughter later told writer Peter Golenbock, "I gave one hundred percent."

Of course, the Yankees were not just any team. They were perennial winners. Still, coming to New York was a mixed blessing. To begin with, Slaughter was not happy with Casey Stengel's platoon system, which often required him to sit out games that included left-handed pitchers and often relegated him to the role of pinch hitter. "My boy," Stengel responded when Slaughter registered his complaint, "you play when I want you to play and you'll be here for a long time." His desire to play was further handicapped by injury—in chasing a long fly ball in Yankee Stadium, he crashed into the scoreboard and broke his arm in three places. The injury required four weeks of recuperation before he could resume play and then additional time for him to regain his batting form. By the time the season ended, he had played in only sixty-nine games and had hit a meager .248 in 125 at bats with only one home run. Not the kind of All-Star season Enos Slaughter had produced year after year when he was with the Cardinals.

Slaughter's adjustment to the Yankees was made that much more difficult by his focus on his statistical record over the course of his long career. He could recite virtually every statistic from his record in both the minor leagues and the National League, and he was not shy about displaying that knowledge. "He always knew his stats," said Hank Bauer, who shared outfield duty with Slaughter. (Bauer, however, agreed that Slaughter "was a great ballplayer," and, when asked at a baseball fantasy camp which ballplayer he would most like to emulate, Bauer pointed to Slaughter.)

Slaughter's record was certainly impressive, but that focus on statistics was not the Yankee way. The Bombers took pride in giving little or no attention to statistics. While Bauer may have been willing to overlook Slaughter's focus on statistics, other Yankees were not. "He talked about himself a little bit," said Bobby Richardson, "where most Yankees didn't do that."

And then there was Slaughter's habit of running everywhere. The Yankees knew, of course, that he had built his reputation on a ceaseless commitment to hustling. But sometimes they could not help but suspect that he used that reputation and his hustle to humiliate them. Gil McDougald remembered the occasion. They were playing in Yankee Stadium, and the Yankee second baseman began his trot toward the dugout on the right side of the field when the inning concluded. Then, seemingly out of nowhere, he felt someone else's spikes on top of his shoe and turned to see Slaughter, who had been playing right field (and presumably would reach the dugout after the second baseman did). McDougald had an explosive temper when wronged, and he did not mince words with his new teammate. "If you ever do that again," he told the former Cardinal, "I'll kill you."

Slaughter understood the resentment that existed among certain Yankees. ("I hustled all the time, ran out every play, ran to and from my position every inning," he later said. "Some players resented that, called me a showboat.") And so he was understandably elated when he learned that the Yankees had traded him to the Kansas City Athletics shortly after the 1955 season began. It was a new club near St. Louis, and, more than that, the Athletics did not have the same abundance of talent as the Yankees. In Kansas City, he hoped, he would have a chance to play more regularly. "The news of the trade really had the adrenaline flowing in me," he told one sportswriter.

He was not disappointed with his second American League club. He batted .322 while playing in 108 games and found himself being appreciated far more than he was in New York. "The people in St. Louis had always been great to me," he later said, "but I never had bigger ovations than those I received in Kansas City's Municipal Stadium." The fans voted the former Cardinal as the team's most popular player and rewarded him with a Chrysler Imperial on the last day of the season.

Enos hoped that he would finish his career playing with the Athletics, and, until August 1956, it appeared that those hopes would be satisfied. Then, as he was getting out of the shower after a game, manager Lou Boudreau asked him to stop by his office after he had dressed. "How would you like to go back to the Yankees?" Boudreau asked when Slaughter came to the office. "I'm satisfied here in Kansas City," he replied. But it was really a rhetorical question. The Yankees, desperate for a left-handed hitting outfielder, had already purchased his contract and released Phil Rizzuto, who could no longer make the long throws from shortstop or get the hits that had made him so valuable earlier in his career.

Slaughter made his first appearance with the 1956 Yankees at a doubleheader with Detroit and quickly vindicated the decision to release Rizzuto. The North Carolina native got five hits, including a home run and a triple, to help his new team win both games. In that final month of September, Slaughter hit close to .300 and finished the season with sportswriters still marveling at his commitment to the game. "Although Enos has not been quite as robust this season as he was last year," said one sportswriter shortly after the trade to the Yankees, "he still was an odds-on favorite who could be counted on to give everything." Slaughter too was pleased with his contribution to the Yankees in that last month of the season. "I really think," he later said, "I helped them win the pennant."

Enos Slaughter is no doubt hoping he can help the Yankees win another game as he waits for Sal Maglie's pitch in the bottom of the seventh inning of the fifth game of the 1956 World Series. After working the count to two balls and a strike, Slaughter swings. "There goes a fly ball," Bob Wolff tells his listening audience with some excitement, "and Amoros is going back for it." There is a pause in the commentary, a signal that the fate of the fly ball is uncertain. But Wolff ends the suspense by saying, "And makes the catch on the cinder path in left field." A few feet more and that fly ball would have been a home run instead of the second out in the inning.

As Slaughter retreats to the Yankee dugout, Billy Martin steps into the batter's box. Martin takes a ball, watches a curveball go by for a strike, and then slams a hard ground ball between Jackie Robinson and Pee Wee Reese that shoots into left field for a single. The Yankees now have their fifth hit, and Gil McDougald comes to the plate. The Yankee shortstop walks on four pitches, and, with runners on first and second bases, the stadium crowd starts to stir. Perhaps this is the beginning of another Yankee rally. But it is not to be. Maglie throws a fastball that forces Andy Carey, the next batter, to jump back from the plate. The Yankee third baseman looks to Babe Pinelli for a ruling that the pitch had hit him, but the home plate umpire shakes his head. Carey steps back into the batter's box and gets ready for the next pitch. Carey swings helplessly at a curveball, fouls off another pitch, and then sends a sharp ground ball to shortstop. Reese fields it cleanly, flips the ball to Junior Gilliam for the force-out of McDougald at second base, and the seventh inning is over.

Top of the Eighth: Gil Hodges

It should have been a happy homecoming. Joan Hodges' husband was coming back from a long trip on the road with the Brooklyn Dodgers. On this last day of August in 1950, they had been married less than two years, and she was still struggling to adjust to the long absences. Still, she had hoped that Gil would remember the gift he had promised—a reward of sorts for her patience. But the twenty-six-year-old Dodger first baseman was no doubt more focused on the fortunes of his club—then vying with the Philadelphia Phillies for the National League pennant—than a shopping trip to find that gift. He came back empty-handed.

The oversight did not sit well with Joan, and she did not hide her disappointment. "It was a pretty one-sided quarrel," she remembered. "I did all the complaining, and Gil remained quiet, keeping everything bottled up inside him." That was, after all, his way. A stoic man not given to outbursts of emotion. But he did give Joan a kiss as he left for the night game at Ebbets Field and said he would look forward to seeing her at the ballpark after the game. But Joan was not yet ready to turn to other matters. "You've been away so long," she replied in a petulant matter that she would later regret, "one more night won't make any difference." And so her husband left the Brooklyn home they shared with her parents without the usual good wishes and walked the few blocks to Ebbets Field in the muggy air.

Gil's mother, still living with his father and older brother in the small town of Petersburg, Indiana, knew nothing of the young couple's squabble when she arrived home that evening. But she did know that the Dodgers were hosting a game against the Boston Braves. It was not something she wanted to miss.

The family did not have a radio to receive a broadcast of a game hundreds of miles away in Brooklyn. Instead, the family had to rely on reports from a local store that had a news ticker. Mrs. Hodges—knowing that her husband was still at work—therefore had only one thought as she walked in the house that August evening. "Call down," she asked her son Bob, "and find out how the game is going." "I was just gonna call you," said the man at the store when he received Bob's call. "He hit one, and Brooklyn's leading 3–1."

Within a short time the man at the store called again. "He hit another one," he told the older brother, "and they're leading 10–1." Bob Hodges did not have to wait long for the next call. The man on the phone was sputtering with excitement. "He's got another," he shouted into the phone, and the Dodgers were winning 14–1. Three home runs in one game. Yankee first baseman Lou Gehrig had hit four home runs in a nine-inning game in 1932, but no one in the National League had ever matched that feat in the twentieth century. But now Gil Hodges had a chance. It was only the sixth inning.

Seated in the box seats with the wives and other family members of the Dodger players, Joan Hodges could hear the "roaring" of thousands of fans when her husband stepped into the batter's box in the seventh inning. They too understood the opportunity that Gil had. But it was not to be—at least not in this at bat. The Dodger first baseman hit a line drive down the third-base line for a hit. In other circumstances, it might have meant something. But not now. Not with history in the making. And so there was disappointment in the stands. "We all thought," said Joan, "it was Gil's last chance."

But the Dodgers could not be restrained. They scored three more runs in the seventh inning, and Hodges came to bat once again in the bottom of the eighth. The crowd was on its feet in anticipation, cheering and stomping. Most of the crowd, that is. Joan was too nervous. So she stayed in her seat, her hands covering her eyes. "I just couldn't look," she remembered. And then she heard the crack of the bat. Almost simultaneous with the familiar sound, Don Newcombe's father, who was standing next to her, began screaming. "Joanie, Joanie," he yelled, "get up and see! It's another one." Indeed it was. The three previous home runs had been hit into the lower left-field stands. This one sailed into the upper deck in left center field—the longest home run of the night.

The game concluded with a lopsided 19–3 Dodger victory, and Hodges was besieged in the clubhouse by the news media, each journalist pushing a microphone in his face or asking questions with a pen and pad at the ready. One television reporter had a personal question. "Did you know you were going to hit those home runs before the game today, Gil?" he asked. "Were you feeling particularly good before game time?" Gil—no doubt remembering the quarrel with his wife only hours earlier—looked over to Joan, who was watching the interview, and the two of them laughed. (In addition to tying a major-league record, the home runs had an unexpected personal benefit for Gil and Joan. *New York Daily News* sportswriter Dick Young asked Joan whether she and Gil, with an infant son and awaiting the birth of another child, had any objection to living with her parents. Joan's wrinkled nose told it all. "There isn't enough room," she told Young. "We've tried everything to get a decent home to rent." Young's headline the next day did not hurt: "Hodges Hits 4 in 1 Tilt. Asks 1 Apartment for 4." As the press later reported, "The Brooklyn ball club's switchboard was swamped, and the office help got writer's cramp signing receipts for telegrams." Within weeks, Gil and Joan had moved their family into a two-story house in Flatbush.)

There are no smiles or laughs as Hodges walks out to the on-deck circle at the start of the eighth inning of the fifth game of the 1956 World Series. Only the growing buzz of the crowd. "There's a hum of expectancy here," Bob Wolff tells his listening audience, "as this eighth inning gets under way as the crowd keeps a careful eye on the playing field and the scoreboard."

Don Larsen is in no rush to proceed as Jackie Robinson moves into the batter's box. The Yankee hurler steps off the mound, takes off his glove, and rubs up the ball. After a few moments, Larsen returns the glove to his left hand, positions himself on the pitching mound rubber, and glares past Robinson for the sign from Berra. After taking a strike and hitting a foul ball to give Larsen a two-strike count, Robinson calls time and walks over to Hodges, who is watching with obvious interest from the on-deck circle. Robinson appears to be rubbing his eye, and then someone from the Dodger dugout throws out a rosin bag (which would probably be the last thing to use if there was indeed a particle in Jackie's eye). The crowd boos, no doubt believing that the ever-competitive Robinson is trying to distract Larsen and avoid another out that will bring the Yankee pitcher that much closer to his ultimate goal. The delay only invigorates Larsen (who later said that the crowd's booing gave him a "comforting feeling" to know that they were on his side). Robinson steps back into the batter's box and taps the next pitch back to Larsen, who makes an easy toss to Joe Collins at first base for the first out of the inning.

Berra has already talked with Larsen about strategy in pitching to Hodges, who is now settled into the batter's box. "Concentrate on throwing good fastballs," Yogi said, "either high or low outside." It was the only way, said the Yankee catcher, to keep Hodges from using his considerable power to pull the ball to the left side of the field.

Larsen understands the merits of his catcher's advice. He had already made the mistake in the fifth inning of letting Hodges pull a long drive to left center field that would have been a hit if someone other than Mickey Mantle had been playing center field. He does not want to give the Dodger first baseman another chance like that.

The first pitch to Hodges is a fastball that catches the outside corner. The crowd roars as home plate umpire Babe Pinelli signals a called strike, and Wolff intones, "The drama rises as this ball game progresses." Another ball, a fruitless swing, and another ball quickly bring the count to two balls and two strikes. And so Gil Hodges, with power enough to drive a ball into the distant outfield seats in Yankee Stadium, concentrates—and no doubt hopes—that he can now do what no other Dodger has done.

It is not an idle hope. His entire baseball career—beginning with those early days in rural Indiana—is a chronicle of exceeding expectations.

Gil's first home was in Princeton, Indiana, located in the southwest corner of the state. Charlie and Irene Hodges were people of modest means when they settled there in the 1920s. Irene would always be there for her family, but Charlie was the one who seemed to have the more dramatic impact on Gil.

The elder Hodges was a man of few words. Rarely was there an overt display of emotion, and, in later years, that would become his second son's trademark as well. Gil was not one, for example, to openly criticize a teammate's play. The message would be conveyed in far subtler ways. "Maybe you realized during a game you made a blunder," said Dodger pitcher Johnny Podres. "You'd look at him and you'd go think about it." And never would Gil tout his success or bemoan his failures. "That's the way Gil is," one of his Brooklyn neighbors told a sportswriter in 1953. "He never shows anything. Let him come home after hitting a couple of home runs or breaking up the ball game, and you'd never be able to tell it from looking at him. He's just a quiet guy who leaves his job behind him at the ball park."

There was the time when Hodges, by now a much-respected member of the Brooklyn Dodgers, had a slump at the end of the 1952 season. Baseball writers had already taken note of Hodges' proclivity to tail off in productivity at the end of the season. ("The big, handsome ex-Hoosier," one sportswriter opined at the beginning of September 1952, "awaits the advent of September with something akin to dread. Not since he took over the first base job in '48 and went on to an All-Star role the following year, has Gil enjoyed a good final 30 days.") But this slump did not end with the beginning of October. It carried over to the 1952 World Series. Twenty-six times Hodges went to the plate in that series, and all he could show for his effort was five walks—and no hits (tying a World Series record for futility). The slump continued into the 1953 season. By the end of May he was hitting a meager .187.

The fans rallied around their slumping star. "It's too warm for a sermon," Father Herbert Redmond told the parishioners at Brooklyn's

St. Francis Xavier church one Sunday morning in May. Redmond did not personally know the Dodger first baseman, but he knew of the widespread frustration in Brooklyn. "Go home," Redmond advised his parishioners, "keep the Commandments—and say a prayer for Gil Hodges."

Those parishioners, as well as other Brooklyn fans, took the advice to heart. The Dodger first baseman not only received hundreds of items from Brooklyn fans during that spring of 1953: letters, telegrams, rabbit feet, rosaries, and other good-luck charms. He also encountered good wishes, sympathy, and even batting tips from fans whenever he went to a restaurant, the store, or anywhere else in the neighborhood. It was an overpowering display of affection that was all the more remarkable because it stood in sharp contrast to the treatment fickle fans would usually give to other local players whose performance did not meet expectations. ("The way the Brooklyn fans backed me when I couldn't buy a base hit," Hodges later said, "is my biggest baseball thrill.")

It was, to be sure, a time of great frustration for the Princeton native. But never once during those many months of anguish did anyone see any evidence of the torment he endured. Unlike Mickey Mantle—who was prone to kick the watercooler, throw his helmet, or toss a bat after one bad plate experience—Hodges' teammates saw the same evenhanded behavior they had witnessed when he was hitting well. "Gil was distraught during his slump," said Carl Erskine, "but he didn't talk about it."

Gil's mood did not change when he went home to Joan. "We didn't talk about it," she later remembered. "We knew it, and it was something he was going through. But not so much that it interfered with our private life." (The slump was finally cured when a movie requested by manager Charlie Dressen showed that Hodges was "stepping in the bucket" when he swung—meaning that he would invariably move his left foot to the left side of the plate instead of stepping toward the ball. Hodges' fortunes improved dramatically when he changed his batting stance, and he finished the 1953 season with thirty-one home runs, 122 runs batted in, and a .302 batting average.)

The quiet manner in which Gil approached life extended to personal conflicts. Like his father, he was slow to anger. ("I never had a fight in my life," he told one sportswriter after he had been with the Dodgers for ten years. "That is," he added with a grin, "since my brother and I used to battle when we were small. I got the worst of that, and maybe that's what cured me.") Still, he was a man of considerable size (six feet, one inch tall and weighing about two hundred pounds), and he was reputed to have the largest hands in baseball—which often inspired sportswriters to engineer photographs with Gil holding boxes or making other demonstrations to show that his hands were much larger than other players. ("I don't know why he ever wears a first baseman's glove," Pee Wee Reese once quipped. "He sure doesn't need one.") With those physical attributes, Gil could command attention if he did get angry. (There was the time when Hodges was clowning around in the clubhouse with Dodger third baseman Don Hoak, who stood six feet tall and weighed 175 pounds. Hoak prided himself on being an accomplished boxer. "Don't fuck with me," he playfully warned his teammate. "These hands are lethal weapons." According to Dodger publicity director Irving Rudd, "Hodges just looked at him, picked him up, and dumped him in a garbage can.")

However infrequent, the anger was invariably aroused by someone else's misconduct. "He was a nice person," Carl Furillo said of Hodges, "but anybody says he never got mad is a lot of baloney. He'd get mad when he would see that somebody was out to harm somebody."

The Dodgers saw evidence of Gil's protective nature during the exhibition tour in the spring of his rookie year. A fight erupted among the players during a game with the club's Fort Worth farm team in Texas. Les Burge, the two-hundred-pound manager of the farm team, made a move toward the much smaller Pee Wee Reese—but he never reached the Dodger shortstop. "I don't know where you're going, Les," Hodges said as he grabbed Burge's shirt and lifted him off the ground, "but it won't be near Pee Wee."

By then, of course, Hodges had left the confines of Indiana and the struggle to escape his father's fate. It was not an easy journey. Charlie Hodges had played baseball in his time, but he did not have the skills to become a professional. So he did what many men in that area did—he worked in the coal mines in nearby Francisco.

It was not a job for the faint of heart. The men would take an elevator hundreds of yards belowground, where they would perform tasks in perilous conditions. Charlie lost an eye in one accident, broke his back in another incident, and then lost four toes in yet another accident. But there was nowhere else to go, especially for a man like Charlie, who wanted to keep food on the table for his growing family—which included two boys and a girl by the time the Depression enveloped the country in 1929. But then disaster struck in 1932. Charlie was changing clothes in the shed around six o'clock one morning to get ready to make his descent into the mines when he heard a loud explosion. "I look out the door," Charlie later said, "and there are flames shooting a hundred feet in the air." Thirty-seven men lost their lives in that explosion, the mine was shut down, and Charlie moved his family—including eight-year-old Gil—to the nearby town of Petersburg to take a job with the Ingle Coal Corporation.

However much he needed that job, Charlie Hodges was determined that his sons would never have to do what he did for a living. When they reached working age and talked about joining him in the mines, Bob and Gil learned that their father had other ideas. "Charlie Hodges' boys," he told them, "will never work in the shafts."

The boys fortunately had other options when high school graduation approached. They each played for the Petersburg High School varsity (Bob as a pitcher and Gil as a shortstop), and, as they got older, Charlie allowed himself to believe that his older son might be able to make it to the big leagues. "Bobby was a good left-handed pitcher," Gil remembered. "He had a live fastball and a good curve. Everybody thought Bobby would be the baseball player in the family." Bob did sign a contract with the Boston Braves to play for one of their minor-league teams, but he did not perform well and left after the first season to enroll in St. Joseph's College in Rensselaerville, Indiana.

Gil, only fourteen months younger than Bobby, joined him in 1941. The two of them starred on the St. Joseph's College varsity team, and Gil's exploits soon caught the attention of Dodger scout Stan Feezle. He approached the young shortstop after one game in the spring of 1943 and asked if he would be interested in attending a Dodger tryout in Olean, New York. Gil came home to Petersburg "breathless," as he recalled. "Dad," he told his father with enthusiasm, "a big-league scout wants me to go east for a tryout."

The nineteen-year-old prospect did not perform well in the field at the tryout. "He ducked away from hot grounders at shortstop," said one sportswriter. "They put him in the outfield, and his wild pegs home, or what was intended for the plate, would have discouraged a lot of people." But not Branch Rickey Jr., the son of the Dodgers' general manager and someone whose views commanded considerable respect in the club's front office. "I went overboard on Hodges," the younger Rickey later recalled, "after I had seen him hit a few a country mile."

The general manager's son took Gil to a hotel in New York City and told him to report to the Dodgers' offices in Brooklyn the next day. It may have seemed like a simple request to Branch Rickey Jr., but this was Gil Hodges' first visit to the Big Apple. "Being a country boy," he later remembered, "I was ashamed to ask for directions, and I got lost. It took me half a day to get to Brooklyn." When he finally arrived, Branch Rickey Jr. offered Gil a contract with a $1,500 bonus—$750 to be paid on signing and the remaining $750 to be paid when he returned from the service (because Hodges was already scheduled to join the marines after the season). After discussing the offer with his father, Gil told Rickey that he would accept the contract, and on September 6, 1943, Gil Hodges became a Brooklyn Dodger.

Gil stayed with the club throughout the month of September, and on the last day of the season, manager Leo Durocher decided to give all the younger players a chance to be in a game. Although Gil had been a shortstop in high school and college, Durocher installed him at third base. The new position did not sit well with Hodges. He made two errors in the field that allowed two runs to score, and those costly miscues were not offset by his batting performance. In his first chance at the plate against Cincinnati Reds pitcher Johnny Vander Meer, Gil looked at a called third strike. He struck out swinging in his next appearance, and in his last effort he was able to draw a walk (and then steal a base).

The young player returned to Petersburg filled with disappointment. In his mind, he had squandered an opportunity to impress Durocher, and he could not help but wonder whether the Dodgers would take him back when he returned from military service. As always, Gil took his concerns to his father, and, as before, Charlie was able to give his son the confidence he needed.

The inspiration was not entirely a matter of logic. Charlie Hodges was a devout Catholic, and, not surprisingly, it was a perspective that stayed with Gil throughout his life. "Yes," Joan Hodges later told me, "he was religious." Years later, long after his father had died, Gil would pay homage to his father's religious teachings. "I prayed the way my father taught us," he explained. "Before each game, I would ask God not to let anyone get hurt and to remember those I love, to give us good health, and forgive us our mistakes." With that perspective, Gil found considerable comfort in his father's simple but definitive response to his second son's misgivings about his future with the Dodgers. "There will," said the senior Hodges, "be more baseball for you."

In the meantime, Gil endured boot camp with the marines in San Diego before being shipped out to Pearl Harbor in 1944 with the 16th Antiaircraft Battalion. From there he was sent to Tinian in the Western Pacific and ultimately to the grueling campaign in Okinawa. When he returned to Petersburg in early 1946, Gil was a sergeant with a bronze star "for heroic or meritorious achievement." Never, however, would he discuss his wartime experiences—not even with Joan. ("Gil just wasn't that way," she later explained.) Joan did not even know about her husband's bronze star until a sportswriter mentioned it to her in conjunction with a story he was preparing three years after she and Gil had been married.

Although he returned from the war unscathed, there was one long-term cost to Hodges' military service: cigarettes. He lit one on his first day home, much to the surprise of his father. "Since when are you smoking?" Charlie asked his son. "Well," came the response, "sitting around in those holes out in Okinawa and those other islands, I had to have something to do." Charlie said nothing, and Gil Hodges continued to indulge a habit of smoking between one and two packs of cigarettes a day.

Gil's prospects for a baseball career did not appear to be bright when he reported for spring training at Sanford, Florida, in 1946. No one was sure what position he should play. "He tried me out every-where," Hodges later said of Branch Rickey's efforts. "He told me he was trying to find a minor league manager who would take me, but he wasn't able to tell 'em what position I could play." Jake Pitler, the man-ager of the Newport News, Virginia, farm team in the Class C Pied-mont League, finally agreed to take the marine veteran and make him the team's catcher. It was a new position for Hodges, and he was not sure that he could succeed as a catcher. His father tried to allay those concerns. "God is giving you the opportunity," Charlie told his son. "Who are you to walk away from it?"

Gil Hodges was not one to disagree with his father, and Charlie no doubt felt a sense of vindication when the 1946 season concluded. His son had learned to handle the new position and, beyond that, con-firmed the belief of Branch Rickey Jr. that the Princeton native could become a professional baseball player. Hodges hit .278 with eight home runs—an impressive accomplishment in light of the dead balls used in the league. With that success, Gil Hodges found himself with an invita-tion to join the Dodgers for spring training in Cuba in 1947.

He did well enough to become the third-string catcher behind Bruce Edwards and Bobby Bragan, but it was not a situation that enabled him to see much play. He caught only twenty-four games in the 1947 season, had only seventy-seven plate appearances, and batted a mea-ger .156 with just one home run.

The situation was vastly different when Hodges joined the team for spring training in the Dominican Republic in 1948. Durocher attrib-uted Hodges' poor performance at the plate in 1947 to an inability to hit curveballs. He therefore had Cookie Lavagetto, one of the team's senior players, give the Indiana native some needed instruction. ("One thing Cookie has taught me," Hodges told a sportswriter during spring training, "is to relax up at the plate.")

The benefits of Lavagetto's instruction were evident in Gil's im-proved performance at the plate. "Hodges is the talk of the Dodgers' camp," one sportswriter observed toward the end of March. "He has been by far the team's best hitter in exhibition games." Durocher was equally impressed. "The boy was weak on curveballs last year," the manager told *The Sporting News*, "but I asked Manager Clay Hopper to instruct his Montreal pitchers to throw Gil plenty of curves, and Hodges has been whacking 'em." There thus seemed little doubt that the Dodgers would keep Hodges on the team—if they could figure out where to play him.

Bragan had been traded away and Edwards had a sore arm—all of which should have provided an opening for the newly minted catcher. But Roy Campanella was now available—until Rickey informed Durocher that the Negro league star would be starting the season with the club's Minneapolis farm team to break the color barrier in the American Association. And so—for the moment at least—Hodges became the team's regular catcher. But he knew all about Campanella's considerable skills, and he did not harbor any hope that he would remain at the position when Campanella made his inevitable return to the parent club. "I was more than a little confused," Hodges later confessed, "about what was going to happen to me."

Fate then intervened. Durocher had initially slated Preston Ward, a twenty-one-year-old rookie from Missouri, to be the team's first baseman. But Ward started to falter at the plate as the season progressed, and Durocher was not happy. In late May, the Dodger manager approached Hodges and, without fanfare or explanation, simply said, "Son, if I were you, I'd buy a first baseman's glove and start working out around there." It was all the advice Gil Hodges needed.

He spent hour after hour doing drills and trying to learn the mechanics of the new position, and that practice soon paid dividends. On June 29, 1948, only days before Campanella made his return to Brooklyn, Hodges started a game at first base. He fared well enough to continue, but the transition was not easy. "I'd never played the position before, or even practiced at it," he told one sportswriter in July, "and I had a time getting my bearings." But he continued to work at it, and within one year he was gaining recognition as an accomplished fielder. "There's little doubt," said one sportswriter in September 1949, "that Gil is the best first baseman in the league." (Hodges did have one glaring weakness—pop flies. For whatever reason, he had difficulty in judging the ball's flight, and he soon entered into an arrangement with Jackie Robinson, who was then covering second base, to pay him five dollars for every pop fly Robinson caught near first base. But then there was the time during the 1952 World Series when Robinson caught a pop fly near Hodges. Buzzie Bavasi, watching events from the stands, noticed that the two players became engaged in a heated argument as they were walking off the field. The Dodger general manager was not happy, and he called the two players into his office before the next day's game. "What's going on?" he bluntly asked. "You embarrassed the club. You embarrassed each other." Hodges then explained that Robinson told him he wanted ten dollars for the catch because it was in a World Series, and Hodges refused, saying that Robinson's demand was unfair. "How did you settle it?" Bavasi asked. "I gave him seven dollars and fifty cents," Hodges replied.)

Some attributed Gil's success at first base to his large hands and his ability to stretch his long body out from the bag to catch throws that might be too short or off the mark. But another factor was Hodges' relationship with the umpires. Never would he argue with the umpire about a bad call in the field or behind the plate. In Gil's mind, it was a matter of respect for authority. "It's the way I've been brought up," he explained. (Years later, when Hodges was playing for the Mets, Rod Kanehl, one of the younger players, referred to his father as "my old man." Gil pulled Kanehl aside and said, "Rod, when you're around me, never refer to your father as your 'old man.' Always refer to him as your father.") It was a perspective foreign to the thinking of most managers, including Charlie Dressen (who assumed Brooklyn's managerial reins in 1951).

A man with an explosive temper, Dressen could not understand why his first baseman would not challenge an umpire's bad decision. The new manager urged, pleaded, and cajoled—all without success in getting Hodges to change his ways. (There was the time when plate umpire Tom Gorman called Hodges out on a third strike with a pitch that appeared to be low. When Gil returned to the dugout, Dressen was on him immediately. "He's taking the bat right out of your hands," said the manager. After an unrelenting torrent of similar exhortations, Hodges finally yielded. "Okay! Okay! Okay!" he told his manager. "The next time I'm up, I won't even ask Tom how his kids and wife are.")

However much it may have frustrated his managers, Hodges' respect for umpires appeared to have incidental benefits. "He was kind of buying into the feeling," said Carl Erskine, "that he was going to get the close ones if he didn't give the umpire a hard time." And there were in fact occasions when Hodges—stretched to the limit in trying to catch a ball thrown by one of the Dodger infielders—would sometimes get the out call from the umpire even though his right foot had been pulled off the bag. (The most notorious incident was the play in the tenth inning of the fifth game of the 1952 World Series. Yankee pinch hitter Johnny Sain hit a slow roller that was fielded by Robinson at second base, but the throw to first was late and short. Although later photographs showed that Sain arrived at the bag before the ball and that Hodges' right foot was off the bag when he made the catch, umpire Art Passarella called Sain out. A Yankee rally was doused before it started, and the Dodgers went on to win the game 6–5 in eleven innings.) The benefits that accrued from Hodges' respect for the umpires did not go unnoticed by the opponents' managers. "That guy steals two outs every game," Phillies manager Mayo Smith complained.

Opposing managers were equally dismayed by Hodges' ability to win games with his bat. His performance in 1948 was not overwhelming—he had eleven home runs and drove in seventy runs but batted only .249. It all changed with the 1949 season—the first of seven consecutive years in which Hodges would be chosen for the National League's All-Star squad. He hit twenty-three home runs (eighth in the league), drove in 115 runs (fourth in the league), and raised his batting average to .285.

Over the next six seasons, he continued to pound the ball with authority, hitting at least twenty-seven home runs each year (with a high of forty-two in 1954 and more than thirty home runs in five of those seasons). The batting barrage during that seven-year stretch included eleven grand-slam home runs—only one short of the National League record of twelve (which Hodges would eclipse before his retirement, leaving the game with fourteen). But home runs were only part of the story. Hodges had an ability to drive in runs that was matched by few other players. For those seven seasons between 1949 and 1955, Gil drove in more than a hundred runs, with a high of 130 in 1954. (Only the New York Giants' Mel Ott, with a string of eight consecutive seasons with more than a hundred runs driven in, could boast a better record in the National League.)

That high level of consistency, coupled with a modest demeanor, made Gil Hodges a perennial favorite among Brooklyn fans—especially because, unlike many other players, he had made Brooklyn his permanent home from the beginning.

The decision to settle in Brooklyn was, in part at least, a reflection of Gil's choice for a wife. He had met Joan Lombardi by accident during the 1948 season. She was working at Macy's at the time, and a fellow employee asked if Joan could come by her house in Brooklyn one afternoon to help make miniature pizzas for her son's birthday party. A native of Brooklyn herself, Joan was happy to oblige, but she had difficulty in hailing a cab to take her back to her parents' home. The inability to find a cab proved to be a stroke of good fortune. Joan's fellow employee had two boarders in her house—Gil Hodges and Eddie Miksis, a utility infielder with the Dodgers. "Gil and Eddie Miksis pulled up in a car," Joan later remembered, "and of course Gil, being the gentleman he was, offered to take me home."

That might have been enough to start a relationship, but there was one complication. Joan was already engaged to someone else. And then another stroke of good fortune (at least for Joan and Gil): a group of friends wanted to see the singer Jane Frohman one evening at a theater in New Jersey. Joan's fiancé was invited, but he was a physician who had an internship at a hospital, and his presence was required in the emergency room that night. So Joan went alone—and spent much of the evening talking with Gil. Telephone calls and other excursions followed, and Joan Lombardi soon had a new fiancé. She and Gil were married on December 26, 1948, and continued to live with Joan's parents in Brooklyn until that summer of 1950.

However much she may have disliked Gil's long absences on road trips, Joan was not unhappy being married to a Brooklyn Dodger. "We were family," she later said of her relationship with the other Dodgers and their wives. That closeness was especially important during those times when the team left town. "When the boys went on the road," Joan remembered, "we'd get together and play bridge or go to the theater or keep in touch with each other. It was absolutely wonderful." And it was never better to be a member of the Dodger family than on October 4, 1955—the day the team won its first World Championship against the Yankees.

There was nothing that Gil and Joan had ever experienced that could compare with the excitement and tumult of Brooklyn when they returned to their home that afternoon from Yankee Stadium, where the seventh game had been played. Joyous fans clogged the streets and wanted nothing more than to touch one of their heroes (Hodges having driven in both runs in the Dodgers' 2–0 victory). "We had to have a police escort," Joan remembered, "and they had to form a human chain for almost two blocks for us to get into our house." They walked in the front door, flush with the exhilaration of the victory and looking forward to the celebration that night at a Brooklyn hotel, only to see their six-year-old son, Gil Jr., sitting in front of the family's black-and-white television set. "Daddy," the young boy exclaimed upon seeing his father, "you're just in time to watch *Ramar of the Jungle.*"

It was a request that Gil Hodges could not refuse. Because, however much he basked in the Dodgers' success and his own accomplishments, it all took a backseat to his family—which ultimately included three daughters in addition to Gil Jr. ("As much as I like my job—and I can't imagine having one that I would like any better," Hodges would say years later when he was manager of the New York Mets, "the job still runs a distant second to my wife and children.") Joan was equally committed to her husband and would devote untold hours after his death in trying to have him inducted into Baseball's Hall of Fame (pointing out to anyone who would listen that her late husband's statistics and accomplishments compared favorably with those of other first basemen who had made the grade).

For a time after that World Series victory in 1955, there was still much in Gil's performance to justify Joan's later crusade on his behalf. Although his batting average dipped to .265 in 1956, Hodges' presence was a major factor in the Dodgers' ability to win the National League pennant—thirty-two home runs and eighty-seven runs batted in. So there was reason to believe that Hodges could help the team duplicate its feat in 1955 of beating the Yankees in the World Series.

Joan Hodges is no doubt anxious as Gil Hodges waits for Don Larsen's next pitch at Yankee Stadium in the eighth inning of the fifth game of the 1956 World Series. With the count at two and two, Larsen knows he has to get the ball over the plate. Berra calls for a fastball, but as soon as it leaves his hand, Larsen is full of fear. "Unlike the previous fastball," he later recalled, "this one was mediocre at best." Then he sees the large shoulders of the Dodger first baseman whip around and hears the "sickening thud" as the bat squarely meets the leather-bound sphere.

The ball zooms off of Hodges' bat in a low line drive toward third base. There is a momentary gasp in the stands as fans sense that Hodges may be the first Dodger to reach base. But Andy Carey is there. He reaches down, his glove just above the infield dirt, and snares the ball. Not sure whether he has trapped the ball or caught it, the Yankee third baseman fires it to Joe Collins at first to remove any doubt—but the third-base umpire has already ruled that Carey caught the ball before it hit the ground. (Carey would later wonder whether he made the right move in throwing to first base—and thus creating doubt in the umpire's mind whether he had in fact trapped the ball instead of catching it. "My God," Carey said to himself, "what if I'd thrown that sucker away!")

Sandy Amoros now steps into the batter's box with two outs. After taking a strike, the Dodger left fielder hits a short fly ball into center field, which Mantle catches with ease. Radio listeners hear the roar of the crowd as Bob Wolff says with obvious excitement, "He's got it."

Larsen walks off the mound toward the dugout, and Vin Scully tells his television audience, "Thus far we've seen the greatest pitching performance I've ever seen. Don Larsen has retired twenty-four consecutive batters."

16

Bottom of the Eighth: Joe Collins

August 2, 1955, was probably the only day in baseball history when a home run saved someone's life. A fan in Asbury Park, New Jersey, sat down in his living room on that day and turned on Channel 11 on his television set to watch the evening game between the New York Yankees and the Cleveland Indians at Yankee Stadium. It was, to be sure, an important game. The Yankees were tied with the Indians for second place in the standings, only one game behind the league-leading Chicago White Sox. Tommy Byrne, the Yankees' colorful thirty-five-year-old southpaw, was slated to face the Indians' Early Wynn, another thirty-five-year-old veteran who, along with teammate Bob Lemon, had led the American League in victories in 1954 with twenty-three, and had already beaten the Yankees three times in the 1955 season.

On the first pitch of the game, Indian outfielder Al Smith slammed a triple and then scored on a sacrifice fly. But the Yankees tied the score in the bottom of the first when Joe Collins, the Yanks' thirty-four-year-old first baseman, drove a ball into the lower right-field stands for a solo home run. And there the score stood for the next nine innings.

Each team had opportunities to break the tie, but neither could bring a runner home.

Yankee second baseman Jerry Coleman started off the bottom of the tenth inning with a fly ball to right field that was caught for the first out. Collins, blue eyed and six feet tall, stepped into the batter's box. He no doubt wanted to duplicate his earlier home run, but success required more than a strong will. Collins understood that. As much as he would have liked to succeed, his performance at the plate in 1955 had been less than spectacular.

He knew the reason. In a game against the White Sox earlier in the season, he had decided to go from first base to third on a single, and, when he saw that the ball might beat him to the bag, he decided to try a headfirst slide. It was not a good decision. "Instead of diving into the bag," Collins later recalled, "I go straight up in the air." The result: he landed hard on his shoulder a few inches from the bag—and was easily thrown out. He could recover from the embarrassment of a bad slide but not from the ensuing pain in his shoulder.

The injury made it difficult for Collins to swing, and, by the time the 1955 season ended, his average had dropped to .234 (from .271 in 1954). Still, he told no one of his injury. "Because," he said simply, "then you don't play." And—more than anything—Joe Collins wanted to play.

Casey Stengel could not be unhappy with that perspective. On that muggy August evening in the House That Ruth Built, Collins' home run was the only reason the Yankees were still in the game. And so Stengel watched as the heavyset Wynn fired a pitch to the Yankee first baseman in the bottom of the eleventh inning, but the ball never reached the catcher's mitt. Collins swung and sent the ball sailing into the right-field stands for another home run—and a Yankee victory.

Satisfied with the outcome, the Asbury Park fan turned off the television set and wandered from his living room into the kitchen for a late-night snack. Minutes later, an out-of-control automobile crashed into the fan's living room at high speed and, as one newspaper later reported, reduced it to "kindling." Everyone agreed—if the fan had still been sitting in that living room and watching the Yankee game, he would have been killed. But Joe Collins spared him from that fate. (And the thankful fan excitedly called the Yankee office the next morning to make sure Collins knew that.)

Collins' role as a savior was nothing new to the Yankees. In ten seasons with the club, he never batted .300, never hit as many as twenty home runs, never drove in a hundred runs, and never led the league in any offensive category. But he was a highly regarded member of a team that won six World Championships and eight pennants in those ten seasons. "The statistics never did quite reflect Collins' contributions to the Stadium tenants," said Arthur Daley in *The New York Times* shortly after Collins retired in 1958. "He spaced his hits judiciously and had the reputation of being formidable in the clutch." Bobby Brown, who played third base for many of Collins' first years with the Yankees, agreed. "He was the kind of guy," said Brown, "who, in big games, could surprise you with a home run or another key hit."

Collins no doubt hopes he can add to that reputation as the Yankees circulate in the dugout in the bottom of the eighth inning of the fifth game of the 1956 World Series. He will be the third batter of the inning, and the Yankee first baseman would surely like to get another hit against Sal Maglie—not only to help the Yankees increase their lead but also to vindicate Stengel's decision to have him play first base instead of Bill Skowron, the club's other first baseman.

True, since Collins was a left-handed hitter, conventional wisdom would dictate that, all things being equal, the Yankee manager should have played him against the right-handed Maglie instead of the right-handed Skowron. But things were not equal. Skowron, known to his teammates as "Moose," had more power at the plate than Collins and was a far more consistent hitter. His record for the 1956 season—twenty-three home runs, ninety runs batted in, and a .308 batting average—far surpassed Collins' performance (a meager .225 batting average with seven home runs). Indeed, in all his years with the Yankees, Collins *never* had a season like Skowron had in 1956.

There was no surprise, then, when Stengel picked Skowron to play the first series game. But the former football player failed to get a hit in four trips to the plate. It may have been just one of those days, but Stengel was not pleased, and Moose found himself sitting on the bench for the second, third, fourth, and fifth games while Collins assumed chores around first base. The change may have made sense to Stengel, but Skowron was mystified. "I was hot," he later confessed.

It was not the first time that Joe Collins found himself on the field while someone else sat in the dugout: he never knew how to stop trying—no matter how impressive the competition.

It all began in the lower-income neighborhoods of Scranton, Pennsylvania, in the 1930s. Joe Kollonige grew up with his brother and sister on the south side of town, which was heavily populated by immigrant families from Poland and Russia. His father, George Kollonige, did what he could to support his wife and children, but it was not easy to make ends meet in the Depression by selling baskets and bags to farmers in the nearby communities. Those early experiences gave Joe an incentive to think about a life that might bring him something more than what his father had.

Baseball was the key. Joe had a talent for the game. But, at five feet, nine inches tall and 135 pounds, he was too small to play for his high school team when he turned fifteen. Mother Nature then intervened. Joe had a growth spurt the next year and soon stood close to six feet (but did not gain much weight). At the age of sixteen, Joe began to play baseball with a semipro team from nearby Minooka. He soon caught the eye of a Cleveland Indians scout and was asked to work out with their local farm team in Wilkes-Barre. But Joe was a Yankee fan at heart and, as luck would have it, his father knew one of the local Yankee scouts. A conversation was held, a decision was made, and, without knowing the details, Joe was invited to practice with the Yankees' Binghamton farm team, which was also training in Wilkes-Barre.

He did well enough in that practice to receive a contract for $75 a month to become a professional baseball player. It was not much money, but Joe was only sixteen and the Depression was in full swing. Hopes for a better future—not to mention jobs—were in scarce supply. So the teenager took a leave from high school to play Class D baseball with the Yankees' Butler farm team in the Penn State League.

Joe was one of the youngest—if not the youngest—player on the team. And he was the smallest player vying for the first baseman's job. "Of course," he later recalled, "me being sixteen years old, about five feet, 10½ inches, 135 pounds, and looking at about six or seven monsters of six foot, three inches, 220 pounds, I say to myself, 'What am I doing here?'—knowing that they're only going to keep one first baseman." But stay he did and, as he remembered with satisfaction, "the other eight were shipped home."

Still, minor-league baseball in western Pennsylvania was a trying experience. The team traveled to each away game by bus, sometimes as much as ninety miles, and then returned home the same night. The money allotted for lunch or dinner was only fifty cents, just enough to buy a hamburger or a hot dog. Playing conditions were less than ideal and helped account for young Joe's first injury—one he never repeated in almost twenty years of professional baseball. "Would you believe," he later said with amusement, "I ran into a light pole?" Unlike major-league parks, the light poles in Butler were located on the field between the stands and the baselines. An opposing batter hit a pop-up in foul territory. Joe wandered over for the play with his eyes focused on the descending ball and never saw the metal structure that suddenly came into his path.

When the season ended, Joe returned to high school, got his degree, and then returned to Butler for the 1940 season and the long but steady climb toward the big leagues. "I played on so many clubs," he said after he joined the Yankees, "that I can't even remember them all." At some point along the way, he also told people that his name was not Joe Kollonige but Joe Collins (and would have his name legally changed in 1954). It was easier to pronounce and perhaps, by eliminating any vestige of foreign extraction, made him feel more comfortable. Whatever the underlying reasons, it was the name by which he was always known in baseball.

The seventeen-year-old prospect hit .320 in that 1940 season and, after another successful year in 1941, was promoted to the Yankees' farm team in Amsterdam, New York, for the 1942 season. It could have been a turning point for the Scranton native. The difference was Shaky Kain, the team's manager. "He was a good manager," said Collins, "but the meanest man I've ever met in my life, barring none." Collins soon learned that his manager had no tolerance for players who failed to be aggressive on the base paths and umpires who made bad calls. "He'd get close to you," Collins remembered, "and just automatically pop you right in the nose. And if the umpire made a bad decision, he'd charge home plate and say, 'Take that mask off.' The umpire would pull that mask off and he'd hit him."

There was one saving grace in Kain's antics: he took an interest in this nineteen-year-old prospect from Scranton, and Collins flourished under the older man's guidance. "He instilled confidence in me," Collins later explained. "I batted .341 that year and might have come up more quickly if it hadn't been for the war." Although he had enlisted many months earlier, Joe did not join the navy until September 1943. Within months he was stationed on an aircraft carrier as a pilot for a fighter plane. Joe was prepared to fight for his country, but the war ended before he could be shipped to the Pacific.

In the meantime, he married Peg Reilley, a vivacious brunette who lived near him in Scranton and became the first—and only—girlfriend Joe Collins ever had. "We were high school sweethearts," Joe later recounted for a sportswriter. "Used to hold hands while sipping sodas at the soda fountain at the drug store." In time, they would have five children over the course of forty-four years of marriage—but those milestones would arrive after Joe made his entry into the big leagues.

The diversion to military service did not help Joe's career. Major-league teams were flooded with returning veterans in 1946, and, however much he may have excelled before joining the navy, Collins was relegated to the Yankees' farm team in Newark. Shortly thereafter he was dispatched to Birmingham when the club decided that Nick Etten, who had been the Yankees' first baseman, needed some minor-league experience in Newark. The change in venue did not hurt Collins. He batted .360 with the Birmingham club (his best mark in the minor leagues) and was selected for the Southern League All-Star team.

It was enough to get him an invitation to spring training with the parent club in St. Petersburg, Florida, in 1948. Unfortunately, it did not start out well. In his very first game in a Yankee uniform, Collins was playing first base in an exhibition game against the St. Louis Cardinals. After the Cardinals got a runner on first base, Yogi Berra flashed a sign to Collins that he was going to throw a ball to him on the next pitch to try to pick off the runner. "I'd say," Collins later recalled, "we had the runner picked off by at least five feet." The umpire did not agree and called the runner safe. Perplexed by the call, Collins approached the umpire for an explanation. "Joe," the umpire said casually, "where's the ball?" Collins looked in his glove and, to his dismay, saw that it was not there. "I turned around," he remembered, "and the runner that I supposedly picked off is holding the ball up in the air."

Although Collins later recalled it as his "most embarrassing" moment in baseball, the incident had no impact on the Yankees' decision to send the Scranton native back to Newark for further seasoning (where he had twenty-three home runs). He did, however, return to the parent club for the last month of the season and made five pinch-hitting appearances. And he received another invitation to the next spring training camp. But when the 1949 exhibition season ended, Collins was sent to the Yankees' Triple-A farm team in Kansas City. He had a good season with the Kansas City club (a .319 batting average with twenty home runs and a league-leading eighteen triples) and was again brought back to the Yankees in September—this time playing a few games in addition to having a few pinch-hitting appearances.

Collins had now seen enough to know that the Yankees were a tightly knit club that approached the game with a detached professionalism. The impression was reinforced in the last two games of the 1949 season. The team was one game behind the Boston Red Sox in the standings and had to play those final two games against the Boston club at Yankee Stadium. Sportswriters and fans speculated on which team would prevail, but not the Yankees. "It may sound a little odd," Collins later recalled, "but everybody had the feeling on the ball club that we had gotten this far and it's only a question of playing two games and winning them." And win them they did.

Having proven himself with the Yankees' top farm teams, Collins earned the right to remain with the parent club for the 1950 season. But he was not the Yankees' only first baseman. Several others were available to fill that role, and Collins found himself sharing first-base duties with Johnny Mize, the former National League All-Star who had led that league in home runs on four separate occasions (with a high mark of fifty-one in 1947).

Although he had already been in professional baseball for almost ten years, Collins was constantly experimenting with his batting stance (and inspired a 1952 article in *Baseball Digest* entitled "Joe Collins and the 97 Stances"). The initial inspiration for the experimentation was frustration. Collins hit only .234 in 1950 (with eight home runs and twenty-eight runs driven in), and the Scranton native no doubt wanted to do better. But no matter how well he did in any particular year, he was always in search of a batting form that would improve his performance. At one point he developed a stance that consisted of a crouch that, in the players' minds, looked like someone sitting on the toilet (thus inspiring his teammates to call it the "shit stance"). "I used to kid Joe about his stances," remembered broadcaster Bob Wolff. "Every year I did my hourly camera interview with Joe, and I said, 'Joe, how about this year?' And he kept saying, 'I'm still looking for that perfect stance.'"

When the Yankees met for spring training in Phoenix in 1951, Stengel was hopeful that the twenty-eight-year-old Collins—using whatever stance he chose—could prove to be the Yankees' regular first baseman. "If I'm going to build up punch around first," the manager told one sportswriter in March, "it may come from Collins. This boy Collins is an improved ball player. This may be his year."

Those words of confidence did not hurt. Collins raised his batting average to .286 in 125 games. Part of that success was an uncanny ability to produce hitting streaks that were critical to the team's success. "When he was hot," said Bobby Brown, "he could carry a team for about ten or twelve days." Still, Collins could never know when Stengel would bench him or play him. (There was the time in 1951 when Collins broke out into a hitting streak during a road trip but, when the team arrived in Detroit for a series against the Tigers, Johnny Mize was playing first instead of him. "Nobody could figure this one out," said Collins. "Nobody." But then Mize proceeded to hit three home runs in the game and missed a fourth by inches, which caused Collins to later say of Stengel, "He was a magician.")

Collins reinforced his value to the team in the 1951 World Series against the Giants, hitting a home run in the second game at Yankee Stadium to lead the Yanks to a 3–1 victory. Still, the Yankees had an abundance of first basemen for the 1952 season (including Mize), and, not surprisingly, rumors swirled during spring training that Collins might be traded to the Philadelphia Athletics. The rumors assumed credibility as the June 15 deadline approached because Collins was batting only .180. But, to his good fortune, Joe then embarked on a hitting streak that included eleven hits (with two home runs) in twenty-two trips to the plate. The streak raised his batting average to .274 and enabled him to evade a trade. "He now may settle down," said Louis Effrat in *The New York Times* on June 16, "and concentrate on playing first base regularly for Casey Stengel."

The release from the trade pressures may have made the difference in Collins' performance. He finished the 1952 season with a .280 batting average in 122 games (along with eighteen home runs—third-highest on the club).

Through it all, Joe preserved his reputation as one of the team's most popular players. Stengel even cited Collins' standing with his teammates as one of the reasons the Scranton native remained with the Yankees. "Collins is popular in the clubhouse," said the Yankee manager. "I don't think that I would have made a good social move if I had traded Joe to Philadelphia."

Much of that popularity was a function of Collins' personality. Sportswriters routinely described him as "one of the most affable members of the Yankees." And for good reason. Nothing seemed to ruffle him. There was always a grin, a quip, or a friendly gesture. (There was the time in early 1955 when rookie Elston Howard hit a game-winning triple in the ninth inning in a game against Detroit. When he returned to the clubhouse, he found a carpet of white towels leading from his locker to the showers—the doings of Collins and Mickey Mantle, who also acted as an "honor guard" for the young player. "When they did that," Howard later recalled, "I figured I was accepted just like everybody else.") "He may never have been a great ballplayer," said one sportswriter of Collins, "but he always was a great guy."

Collins' friendly demeanor proved to be a valuable force in defusing tension among his teammates. "He was a terrific influence inside the clubhouse," said Tony Kubek, who played with Collins in his last few years with the Yankees. All of the Yankees—Collins included—were fierce competitors. But some, like Billy Martin or Gil McDougald, were prone to explode in the face of confrontations with umpires and other players. "Collins was a little laid-back and easygoing," Kubek recalled, "and that tempers some of the atmosphere in the clubhouse."

However soothing his nature on most occasions, Collins could not escape some of the tension in the 1952 World Series against the Dodgers. He played six of the seven series games and failed to get a hit in twelve plate appearances. Those failures at the plate were compounded by his play on the field in the seventh and deciding game. Jackie Robinson hit that high pop-up toward first base in the seventh inning with the bases loaded with Dodgers and two outs. Yogi Berra kept calling for Collins to make the catch while the Dodger runners were circling the bases—and bringing in the winning run—but Collins had lost the ball in the sun. "I was looking for it," he later explained, "but I couldn't find it." Second baseman Billy Martin ultimately saved the day with his shoestring catch, but the experience was not one Collins could easily push aside. "I had nightmares for two or three months," he later said. "I can see that ball dropping and losing the World Series."

The nightmares were gone by the time Collins reported for spring training in 1953. Although Stengel continued to platoon him at first base, Joe performed well when he did play, hitting seventeen home runs (third-best on the club) in only 387 at bats (although his average did slip to .269). He might have played even more games and reached a higher level of performance if injuries had not forced him to spend almost four weeks in the hospital.

The first injury occurred when he bounced a foul ball off his leg. The incident caused phlebitis, and Collins was sent to the Lenox Hill Hospital in New York. After almost two weeks, the doctors advised the Yankee first baseman that he could return home. Joe decided instead to go to Yankee Stadium for the night game against the Red Sox, thinking that he could catch a ride back to Union, New Jersey—where he had purchased a home for his family—with Phil Rizzuto, who lived nearby.

Collins did not expect to play in the game, but Stengel approached him when Boston called in Ellis Kinder to pitch relief. Kinder was one of the American League's best relievers in 1953. But he had one glaring weakness—Joe Collins. "He couldn't get me out no how," Collins later remembered. Joe was sitting on the bench when the Yankee manager approached him midway through the game. "Your buddy's on the mound," said Stengel. "Can you hit?" Collins was not sure. "I'm so weak," he remembered, "I can hardly walk." But he could not turn aside a chance to hit against Kinder. So he took a bat, stepped into the batter's box, and hit the first pitch into the upper deck for a home run. "I was so weak," he recalled, "I could hardly run around the bases." When he returned to the dugout, he slipped and jammed his heel on the dugout steps—an injury that required a return to the hospital for another stretch of almost two weeks.

Collins made another recovery of sorts in the first World Series game against the Dodgers. In a seesaw game played before almost seventy thousand screaming fans at Yankee Stadium on a warm and sunny October afternoon, Collins came to the plate in the seventh inning with the score tied 5–5 and blasted a home run into the right-field seats— thus redeeming his poor performance in the 1952 series. (Ironically, Dodger first baseman Gil Hodges, who also failed to get a hit in that 1952 series, hit a home run in that first series game as well.)

Collins continued to play first base and wield a steady bat in 1954 (twelve home runs and a respectable .271 batting average in 130 games) before succumbing to the injured shoulder in 1955. And he continued to be the subject of trade rumors as the Yankees evaluated numerous candidates for the first-base position. But none of that affected Collins' performance in the first game of the 1955 World Series. His two home runs off Dodger pitcher Don Newcombe made the difference in the Yankees' 6–5 victory.

The press surrounded Collins' locker after that first series game. They not only wanted him to recount the details of his home runs. They also wanted to know if he thought the Yankees, having seen his considerable contribution in the fall classic, should now abandon the never-ending discussions of a possible trade and play him more regularly. "It would be nice," Joe told the sportswriters, "to play every day and not have to walk around feeling a sword was hanging over your head. But we've kept on winning, which counts most. So I have no squawks at all, and, after a long hard fight, I have to join the chorus and say I'm mighty lucky to be a Yankee."

That may have been true in 1955, but Collins' luck was starting to

run out in 1956. His shoulder continued to bother him (so much so that, during the 1955 World Series, he had to pick up his glove hand with his other hand to catch the ball in the field). His batting average continued to fall in 1956, and he knew that the younger Skowron was deserving of more playing time. True, Skowron did not possess the same defensive skills that Collins had in the field. ("I was no gazelle around first base," Moose later acknowledged to me. And so the team sent the former Purdue football player to Arthur Murray Dance Studios during his first spring training in 1954 in the hope that the agility learned on the dance floor could be applied on the baseball field.) But Skowron did wield a more potent bat than Collins. He batted .340 playing part-time in his rookie year of 1954 and .319 playing part-time in 1955. It was inevitable that Stengel would increase the younger player's time in the ensuing years.

Collins did not begrudge the twenty-three-year-old Skowron his due. Quite the contrary. He welcomed him with open arms. "You know, Moose," Collins said one day to Skowron during his first spring training, "you're my competition. But I hope when I play, you'll cheer for me. And when you play, I'll cheer for you." Skowron, accustomed to players who would do anything to squeeze out the competition, was taken aback by Collins' comment. "I never forgot that," he later remarked. And so Skowron would forevermore value the older player's contribution to the club—even when Collins replaced him at first base during the 1956 World Series. "He was a great teammate," Moose later said of Collins.

Unfortunately, that was not enough to guarantee Joe's future with the club. There were moments of glory in 1956, but they were few and far between. One of them included a decision by Stengel to have Collins pinch-hit for Hank Bauer in the third inning of a scoreless game with the Cleveland Indians and with two Yankees on base. Joe responded to the show of confidence with a home run into the Yankee bullpen in right field, leading one sportswriter to say that "never should anyone attempt to outguess Casey Stengel."

No one is second-guessing the Yankee manager as Don Larsen walks to the batter's box in the bottom of the eighth inning of the fifth game of the

1956 World Series. The crowd is standing on its feet and, as Bob Wolff tells his audience, "The applause really rang out to the rafters here."

Larsen's appearance at the plate does not last long. He swings at the first pitch from Sal Maglie without connecting, takes a second strike, and then, after watching a pitch sail outside for a ball, swings wildly at another pitch for the third strike. But none of that matters to the crowd, which again gives him a roar of approval. ("It was," Larsen later said, "the only time in my career when I was applauded by the crowd after I struck out.")

Bauer does not fare any better than the Yankee pitcher. He fouls off one pitch, takes a ball, hits a ball that curves foul into the left-field seats, fouls off another pitch, and then strikes out when Roy Campanella holds on to a foul tip.

Collins goes into a crouch as he steps in the batter's box. He understands the drama that is unfolding and is taking nothing for granted. And he is anything but relaxed. (Collins would later tell one of his sons that the fifth game of the 1956 World Series "was the most intense game he ever played in.")

After taking two balls and then a strike, Collins hits two balls foul toward the Yankee dugout. He then steps out of the batter's box, knocks the dirt off his spikes with his bat, and returns to the batter's box. Maglie takes the sign from Campanella and fires another pitch to the Yankee first baseman. Collins' hopes of adding to the Yankees' lead evaporate as he swings without hitting the ball.

Maglie has struck out the side and, as Wolff intones, is "giving a great pitching demonstration this afternoon." But it pales beside the performance of Larsen, who is sweating profusely in the Yankee dugout. As the Dodgers leave the field, the Yankee hurler picks up his glove and trudges out to the pitching mound—now completely draped in shadows—for the top of the ninth inning. He knows that three outs stand between him and baseball immortality.

Top of the Ninth: Hank Bauer

A s Don Larsen hurls warm-up pitches to Yogi Berra, Joe Collins is throwing the other infielders practice ground balls. The infielders had, as Joe Collins later remembered, "a little huddle" in the dugout before they ran out onto the field. They all understood the significance of the moment. "Nothing gets through," said Billy Martin. If there was a hard-hit ground ball, the infielder would have to block it with his body to preserve the play at first base.

Hank Bauer is in right field, tossing practice fly balls back and forth with Mickey Mantle. An ex-marine, Bauer stands six feet tall and weighs more than 190 pounds. He has the reputation of being a hard-nosed character. (He was, said Mantle, "the toughest and strongest player I ever saw.") More than that, Bauer has the look of a man who can weather any situation. Comedian Jan Murray likened Bauer's face—with its rugged features—to a "clenched fist," and one sportswriter described that face as "a permanent, granite carving of belligerence, aggression and determination."

Maybe so. But in this case, appearances are deceiving. Hank Bauer, one of the Yankees' most fearless competitors, is a victim of the pervasive tension. Like the rest of his teammates, he does not want the ignominy of making a miscue that will ruin Larsen's performance and cost the Yankees the game. That fear engulfs him as Dodger right fielder Carl Furillo makes his way to the batter's box. "Don't hit the ball to me," Bauer says to himself. "Whatever you do, don't hit it to me." Not that Bauer is incapable of playing well under pressure. He has proved that point on more than one occasion, and none are more remarkable than those moments in the sixth game of the 1951 World Series at Yankee Stadium.

The Yankees were leading the New York Giants in games by a 3–2 edge, and the two teams were locked in a 1–1 tie when the twenty-nine-year-old Bauer stepped up to the plate in the bottom of the sixth inning with Yogi Berra, Joe DiMaggio, and Johnny Mize—three future Hall of Fame players—on the bases. Dave Koslo, a left-handed pitcher, was on the mound. Bauer had never faced Koslo before the series, and he did not know that the Giant hurler had a knuckleball in his repertoire. On a count of two balls and two strikes, Koslo threw a knuckleball that fluttered over the middle of the plate while Bauer stood motionless. "I didn't *think* it was a strike," Bauer recalled many years later. "I *know* it was a strike. I'm out—no doubt about it." But the umpire called the pitch a ball. ("Oh, boy," Bauer said to himself. "That's a nice present.") With the count now full, Koslo delivered a fastball and Bauer swung hard. ("I could feel the bat bend a little when I made contact," he remembered.) The ball sailed over the head of Giant left fielder Monte Irvin and hit the 402-foot mark on the left center-field wall for a triple. All three Yankees scored and Bauer's team pulled ahead with a score of 4–1.

The Giants were discouraged but not beaten. They scored two runs in the top of the ninth and had the tying run on second base when Giant manager Leo Durocher called upon twenty-seven-year-old Sal Yvars to pinch-hit for Hank Thompson. Yvars saw little play during the season. But Yankee southpaw Bob Kuzava was on the mound, and Yvars had good success against Kuzava when they played in the minor leagues.

As Yvars had hoped, Kazava came in with a fastball. The Giant catcher was ready. "I hit that son of a bitch solidly," Yvars later recalled, "a line drive over Jerry Coleman's head at second. A base hit for sure." If it proved to be a hit, the runner on second would score the tying run, and the Giants would have the winning run on base.

Bauer watched the ball emerge from the shadows and believed—at first—that he would have no trouble catching it. "But the ball started to fall away from me," he remembered. "And I'm thinking, 'Holy shit. I'm going to have to dive for this.'"

Thus began Bauer's mad scramble to catch up to the ball as it descended. While 61,711 fans watched in almost total silence, Bauer raced to reach the ball before it hit the grass. "Rushing in," said one sportswriter in later describing the scene, "Bauer lunged, stumbled, fell to his knees, slid a good ten feet, and stuck out his glove." It was only a matter of inches. But there the ball was—in his glove. "Then," continued the sportswriter, "like a gladiator displaying the sawed-off head of his enemy, he triumphantly held the glove high in the air to show everyone the ball nestled snugly in the pocket."

The stadium erupted in a deafening roar of applause and cheers as everyone realized that the game—and the series—had concluded with a Yankee victory. "You would have to go back a long way in the history of World Series between the Yankees and the Giants," said one sportswriter the next day, "to find one that, from a dramatic approach, rivaled that which was concluded at the Stadium yesterday." Not surprisingly, Bauer later called the catch his "greatest thrill" in baseball. But it was not his greatest achievement. Not by a long shot. For Hank Bauer, making it out of East St. Louis after the Depression far surpassed the feat of making a shoestring catch during a World Series.

John and Mary Bauer came to the Illinois city from Germany, and they had eight children before Hank arrived in 1922. John had no real skills, and, after suffering an accident with a pickax in the aluminum mill where he worked, had only one leg. The injury forced him to change jobs, and he became a bartender at one of the local saloons. It was not enough to feed a family of eleven. And so, as Hank later remembered, "My oldest sisters used to bring home support."

What the family lacked in money was made up in cohesion. They all looked out for one another—and few family members received as much attention as the youngest child. It was not by happenstance. By junior high school Hank was smoking cigarettes and already displaying the fighting spirit that would become his trademark as a baseball player. "He was a real dead-end kid," said his older brother Joe. "Always going around with a bloody nose." His mother tried to get him to stop smoking by pointing out that he weighed only about a hundred pounds. "That's the reason you're not growing," she would tell her youngest child. But Hank was a teenager and unresponsive to the pleas of a mother who just did not understand. (He did, however, honor his father's command to be home by nine o'clock every evening. "They had a whistle in town that blew at nine o'clock," Hank later recalled. "When that thing started blowing, I started running.")

Hank did, of course, play baseball, but he wasn't very good. He could run, and he could throw a ball with speed and accuracy. ("I learned how to run and throw," he later explained, "throwing rocks.") But the rest was something he had to learn by hard work. "I wasn't blessed with natural ability," he confessed to Peter Golenbock after he had retired. "I had to work like hell." And the effort to preserve his skills never ceased. "Baseball has never been easy for me," Bauer told one sportswriter after he had been playing with the Yankees for almost ten years. "I'm not a natural hitter and have to sweat out every pitch."

Mastering the techniques of hitting and fielding, however, was not enough. Hank knew that success required a commitment that knew no bounds. He had learned that much from the St. Louis Cardinals—his favorite team while growing up. "The only guy I ever saw who hustled more than Bauer," Joe DiMaggio later said of his teammate, "was Enos Slaughter." It was a trait later recognized by opposing players as well. "When Hank came down that base path," said Boston shortstop Johnny Pesky, "the whole earth trembled." Not surprisingly, that competitive spirit endeared Bauer to Casey Stengel, who managed the Yankees during Hank's entire tenure with the team. "He's the hardest-running thirty-six-year-old I've ever seen," Stengel commented during the 1958 season, "and he gives you every ounce of his energy for nine full innings every game."

As a teenager growing up in East St. Louis, Hank used his talent and drive to secure a place on the Central Catholic High School's varsity baseball team and later on the local American Legion team. But no major-league scout was knocking on his door when he graduated from high school in 1940. College was not an option, and his father told him that he should learn a trade. So Hank accepted a job repairing furnaces in a beer-bottling plant. And there he might have stayed if his older brother Herman had not intervened.

Herman (who would later be killed in action during World War II) was a catcher, and he had the natural skills that Hank lacked. (Years later, Bauer would tell Yogi Berra, "You wouldn't have been able to wipe my brother's ass as a catcher.") Herman had won the Most Valuable Player award in 1940 while playing for the Chicago White Sox's minor-league team in Grand Forks, North Dakota. With that stature, the older Bauer was able to engineer a tryout for his youngest brother in the spring of 1941.

Hank's father continued to be perplexed by it all. He did not understand the game of baseball and, more than that, he could not believe that someone would pay his children to play the game. (Years later—after he had joined the New York Yankees—Bauer got his father a box seat ticket near the Yankee dugout when the team came to play the Browns in St. Louis. Hank was proud of his performance that day: a triple and two singles. When he came home that evening, Hank found his father with a beer in hand while sitting in the rocking chair on the front porch. The senior Bauer had a question for his youngest son: "Don't they ever let you walk?")

Hank was delighted to hear about the tryout that Herman had arranged. He traveled to North Dakota and performed well enough to secure a contract playing for the Oshkosh Braves in the Wisconsin State League at a pay of $70 a month. It was not much—Hank would remember eating a lot of "greasy hot dogs and greasy hamburgers" at the Woolworth's five-and-ten-cent store across the street from the stadium—but it was a start.

That first season of professional baseball produced mixed results. "He was a tremendously crude ballplayer," recalled teammate Swede Erikson. Hank batted only .259 and the Braves finished in last place.

("We were just a bunch of kids," Bauer later said, "who had never played professional ball before.") Hank did have one redeeming quality—an ability to hit with power. He hit a team-leading eleven home runs and, as Erikson remembered, "that made him one of the fan favorites." But it was not enough to keep Hank Bauer in professional baseball. When the season ended, the Braves released him.

The uncertainty of Hank's professional baseball career no doubt made the decision on his future that much easier after the Japanese attack on Pearl Harbor on December 7, 1941. Six weeks later, Hank Bauer joined the marines. He knew, of course, that he would soon be drafted in any event. But he also had an interest in shaping his destiny. "I wanted to get in the best outfit," he later said. "And I didn't think the army was the best outfit. I thought the marines were."

Thus began a four-year tenure that would prove to be the most indelible—and rewarding—time of Hank Bauer's life. ("It was a great experience," he later told a sportswriter. "But I don't recommend it if there's a war going on.") He would have many accomplishments and associations of which he could be proud after his military service ended—including almost twelve years with the New York Yankees. But nothing could surpass the satisfaction he drew from those four years with the marines. And so, when the question was posed to him by his children many years later, he would always say that he "was proudest of being a marine."

The marine experience began with boot camp in San Diego and continued with an assignment to the Mare Island Naval Base in Vallejo near San Francisco. Hank had joined the marines to contribute to the war effort, but one of the officers soon learned that the young recruit had played professional baseball. It was not long before he was asked to play for the base team.

Hank was reluctant at first. "I didn't get in here," he said, "to play ball." But pressure was applied, and Bauer soon relented. "What position is open?" he asked. Catcher was the reply. Hank had had only minimal experience as a catcher at Oshkosh, but he was a good marine and immediately agreed to be the team's backstop. (Hank had the same selfless attitude when he played with the Yankees. In fourteen years of major-league baseball, he played only the outfield—except for that one game against the White Sox at Yankee Stadium on September 10, 1955. Yogi Berra was injured and the two backup catchers had been taken out of the lineup for pinch hitters. "Oh, shit," said Stengel to no one in particular in the dugout. "I don't have any more catchers." Although he had not caught a game in more than ten years, Bauer did not hesitate. "Give me the stuff," he told his manager.)

In retrospect, Hank made a good decision to play ball with his fellow marines. The team did well, and the commanding officer was reluctant to allow his star catcher to be shipped overseas. As each combat assignment came across his desk, the officer repeatedly took Hank's name off the list. One of the first assignments would have placed Hank on the USS *Helena*, a light cruiser that sank after being torpedoed in the Battle of Kula Gulf near the Solomon Islands in July 1943. But for his commanding officer's interest in a winning baseball team, Bauer would have been on that ship.

Hank was forever appreciative of that fortuitous postponement of his combat assignment, but he knew it could not continue indefinitely. Beyond that, he was anxious to see action. So he was receptive to the suggestion of Andy Wackenbush, one of his teammates, that they volunteer for a new unit called the Raiders that would play an advance role in anticipated landings on South Pacific islands. Hank went to the first meeting and learned that one of the requirements for joining the unit was an ability to swim. That was a problem. Hank Bauer did not know how to swim. Wackenbush was not pleased when Hank explained the situation. "You gutless son of a bitch," his teammate replied. Hank Bauer was anything but gutless. He returned to the Raiders' commanding officer and said that he could in fact swim. The lie was accepted without question, and the East St. Louis native was made a member of the Raiders' machine-gun platoon.

In time, Bauer would receive stripes as a sergeant and earn the respect of his fellow marines. (Many years after Hank had left the service, Gil McDougald, who roomed with Bauer on Yankee road trips, spoke with some of the men who served with Hank in the Pacific, and the Yankee infielder was understandably curious about his roommate's combat experience. "He was a one-man army," the marine veterans said. "He was a terror.") In the course of almost two years, Hank was involved in four amphibious landings in the South Pacific. The first landing was in New Georgia. That was followed by one in Guam, where he was hit with shrapnel in the back. (All the shrapnel could not be removed, and, as recalled by Tommy Henrich, one of Bauer's teammates when he first joined the Yankees in 1948, "Joe Page used to clown around in our dressing room by picking pieces of shrapnel out of Hank's back.")

The Guam experience was followed by a landing at the island of Emirau off New Guinea and then by a landing on the Japanese island of Okinawa on Easter Sunday in 1945. With more than thirteen hundred Allied ships and more than fifteen hundred Allied planes, that battle represented the largest amphibious assault of the Pacific campaign. Hank was among the marines who landed on the north side of the island, where they were able to secure the local airport with little difficulty. (Hank later recalled that a Japanese pilot landed his fighter plane on the airstrip after it had been overtaken by the Americans. "He never made it out of the cockpit," Bauer remembered.)

As the marines moved south, where the bulk of the population lived, the fighting intensified. Of the sixty-four men in Hank's platoon, only six came back alive. Bauer himself almost became one of those casualties. "I saw this reflection of sunshine on something coming down," he later recalled. "It was an artillery shell, and it hit right behind me." The blast threw him to the ground and a piece of shrapnel cut a jagged hole in his thigh (and could never be entirely removed).

Hank Bauer's fighting days were over. He was sent to Guam for medical treatment, and, after spending two months with the occupational force in Japan, was discharged from the marines on January 19, 1946—exactly four years after he had enlisted—with two Bronze Stars, two Purple Hearts, and eleven campaign ribbons. He also brought back with him a susceptibility to malaria. And, while he could put his marine uniform aside, he could not so easily avoid a recurrence of the dreaded disease (thus requiring him to always maintain access to an adequate supply of quinine water).

Hank returned to East St. Louis and, lacking any prospects in professional baseball, he accepted a job with the ironworkers' union dismantling an old factory. After work he would often stop by the pub where his older brother Joe tended bar. It was there that Danny Menendez, a local Yankee scout, asked Joe about "his little brother." Joe laughed. Hank had put on more than thirty pounds in the marines and had now grown to his full height of six feet. "He's not that little anymore," said Joe. "Stick around."

When Hank arrived, Menendez was impressed by the youngest Bauer's size and made an offer for him to play with the Yankees' farm team in Quincy, Illinois. It would pay $175 a month, with a $200 bonus and another $25 for each month if he made the team. Hank was reluctant at first, saying that he could make as much money with the ironworkers. But Joe—saddened by the loss of his brother Herman, who surely would have continued as a professional baseball player—pushed his younger brother to accept Menendez's offer.

Hank relented and spent the summer of 1946 playing in the outfield for the Quincy team. Hank's batting skills had improved greatly, and he finished the season with twelve home runs, ninety runs batted in, and a very respectable .323 batting average. (There was, however, a moment of panic during a game in July. Hank hit a triple, but by the time he reached third base he was overtaken by the aches and fever that accompany malaria. "You better get me the hell out of here," he told third-base coach Eddie Marleau, who was also managing the team. "I've got malaria." Marleau, who depended on Bauer's presence in the lineup, had no interest in honoring his player's request. The East St. Louis native was too important to the team's success. "Hank," the manager replied, "if I take you out, they'll run me out of town." So Bauer played the remainder of the game under the grip of malaria.)

Bauer's performance at Quincy earned him a promotion to Kansas City for the 1947 season. It was nothing that Hank could not handle. He produced sixteen home runs and a .313 batting average. The next year, his record included twenty-three home runs, a hundred runs batted in, and a .305 batting average. Hank Bauer had demonstrated that he was major-league material.

At the end of the 1948 season, the ex-marine was summoned to the parent club by manager Bucky Harris (inspiring one sportswriter to comment that "Harris has brought up the greatest player in his chain store system"). Hank made his first appearance in a Yankee uniform in the first game of a doubleheader against the Washington Senators on Labor Day. He lined the first pitch to center field for a single to drive in a run. That was followed by two more singles, giving him three hits in his first three plate appearances. "Shit," Hank said to himself. "This is easy."

It proved to be a premature judgment. American League pitchers soon discovered that Bauer had difficulty hitting a curve, and by the time the season ended, Hank had only six more hits and a .180 average. But one of those hits was a home run over the roof of Philadelphia's Shibe Park with Joe DiMaggio and Johnny Mize on base—a display of power that drew uncertain praise from Harris, who was smoking a cigarette when the twenty-seven-year-old rookie returned to the dugout: "It's about time, you son of a bitch."

Hank's late-season stint in New York was not without some emotional strain. He had met Charlene Friede by accident. She was the secretary for Lee MacPhail, the Kansas City Blues' general manager. A petite woman with long dark hair and olive skin, Charlene was sitting at her desk when Hank came into the office. A couple of his marine buddies were in town, and the young player wanted to know if he could get them tickets to a game. The tickets were given, a relationship was ignited, and the wedding ceremony took place on October 22, 1949. But never would Charlene leave her hometown of Kansas City. So she was not there when Hank played for the Yankees in that month of September 1948.

While his batting record for that month was less than spectacular, Bauer remained on the team's roster when the team opened the 1949 season. Casey Stengel had replaced Bucky Harris as the manager, and he could see in spring training that the young man from East St. Louis was big-league material.

His teammates, who had had only limited exposure to Bauer in September 1948, were in no position to disagree. He had a physique that exuded power. ("His strength was the talk of the league," one magazine later reported. "In a playful scuffle one day, he popped a friend on the chest—and sent him to the hospital with a broken rib.") He had a voice that suited his physical attributes. (One sportswriter likened Bauer's voice to "a cement mixer being piped through an echo chamber," and another sportswriter said it "sounds like gravel crunching underfoot.") And when his teammates saw him play, they knew that Hank would do whatever he could to help them win. "When it came to crunching into the stadium wall after a fly ball," said one sportswriter in later recounting Bauer's playing career, "sliding on a raw strawberry to bulldoze a double play, or just plain terrifying the opposition, Bauer was the man."

For all his skill in intimidating the other team, Hank was, at bottom, a gentle soul. "Crusty on the outside," said Andy Carey, who later shared an apartment with Bauer in the Bronx, "but a heart of gold." Gil McDougald, who roomed with Bauer on road trips, agreed, calling him "a supernice guy" who looked out for his teammates.

Elston Howard learned of his teammate's protective spirit shortly after he arrived in 1955 as the team's first black player. Like Jackie Robinson before him, Elston often encountered taunts and other verbal abuse in those first days on the field. "Hank took it personally whenever Elston was heckled," Elston's wife, Arlene, later remembered. "It was not unusual for Hank to come out of the dugout and confront anybody giving Elston a hard time. 'He was my friend,' Bauer would say."

Hank's commitment to his teammates was evident in other ways that were not always apparent to people in the stands. That was particularly true after he had been with the team for a number of years. "As a veteran," said Bobby Richardson, who first came to the Yankees in September 1955 as a twenty-year-old infielder, "he looked out for the younger players. He would not only encourage them but also give them good advice along the way." (There was the time, for example, when Richardson was playing second base and did not get the ball out fast enough to the first baseman in an attempted double play. As the team trotted into the dugout when the inning was over, Bauer caught up to the young player and quietly said, "Throw the ball harder to first base.")

And then there was the money. Being with the Yankees created an expectation that there would almost always be a World Series check. It was not a casual matter for many, if not most, of the players. These were men who had to secure low-skilled jobs in the off-season to make

ends meet. For them, the World Series check was the difference between a comfortable winter and a hard time. Hank, like the other veterans, tried to instill in the rookies the importance of playing the best
they could to win games and keep those series hopes alive. ("Don't
mess with my money," Bauer would invariably instruct the new players.) But Hank was not selfish when the Yankee players gathered in the
clubhouse to allocate the World Series pot and was willing to give a fair
share to rookies and other players who had not been with the club for
the entire season. "When it came World Series time to vote shares,"
Richardson remembered, "he would always encourage his teammates
to be generous with the young players on the team." (Richardson, for
one, was with the club for only two weeks in 1955 and still received a
one-third share. "Hank was behind that," he later told me.)

However much he nurtured relationships with his teammates, Bauer
had one gripe with the Yankees—Stengel's platoon system. In those first
days with the club, the Yankee manager used Bauer interchangeably in
left field with Gene Woodling, who had been named the Minor League
Player of the Year by *The Sporting News* in 1948. Gene was a left-
handed batter, and Stengel was prone to use him against right-handed
pitchers while saving the right-handed Bauer for left-handed pitchers.
That approach reflected conventional wisdom, but there were occasions when the Yankee manager's logic defied scrutiny. (There was the
time in Detroit when Bauer had gone three for three, with two home
runs and a double in a game against the Tigers. With the game tied 5–5
in the eighth inning, Stengel sent Woodling up to pinch-hit for Hank as
he was walking toward the batter's box. "When I saw Woodling come
up," Bauer later said, "I was going to saw his leg off." Instead, he
trudged back to the dugout full of anger and sat down on the bench.
Stengel rambled over to his sulking outfielder and, without fanfare,
said, "I thought you had reached your quota.")

Hank did not hide his distaste for the platoon system, and so, when
later asked what he thought about the Yankee manager in his first days
with the club, Bauer had a quick response: "I didn't care for him." But
there was a method to Stengel's madness. He understood what would
keep his players motivated. "Now you can take that feller over there,"
the manager said to a sportswriter shortly after Bauer had joined the

Yankees. "I got him so mad, sittin' on the bench, that he wanted to hit me with a bat. He wanted to play every day. He wanted to show me. Well, he showed me pretty good."

Bauer eventually understood—and came to appreciate—Stengel's approach. "At the time," he later explained, "I thought he was wrong, and so did Woodling. Stengel used psychology on both of us. He kept us mad. When we did get into a game, we'd bust our asses to stay there." But that was the older, more mature Bauer. In 1949 and the early 1950s, the frustration would often hamper constructive dialogue between manager and player. Especially because Casey was not always good at remembering his players' names.

One incident was particularly telling. "I was on the bench, burnin' up," remembered Bauer, "because Casey insisted on platoonin' me. I'd get so mad at him that I'd go to the far end of the dugout next to the watercooler. I didn't trust myself to sit near him, and I'd stay as far away as possible." But Stengel knew he was there, and late in the game Bauer caught the Yankee manager looking at him. Hank knew the reason. A pinch hitter was needed. Suddenly he heard Stengel's voice. "Woodling," the manager yelled. "Grab a bat." Bauer said nothing and watched as Stengel waddled down the dugout toward the watercooler until he was standing in front of his sometime right fielder. "Woodling, grab a bat," Stengel repeated. Bauer looked up at his manager and said, "I ain't Woodling." To Stengel, that was irrelevant. "Okay, Bauer," Casey responded. "Grab a bat."

For all the platooning, Bauer was still able to play in 103 games in that 1949 season and compile a respectable record with only 301 plate appearances—ten home runs, forty-five runs batted in and a .272 batting average. Hank's record improved dramatically in 1950, when he played in 113 games. He raised his batting average to .320 while hitting thirteen home runs and driving in seventy runs.

Hank could certainly be proud of his performance in 1950. More important, he knew it warranted a substantial increase in his annual salary of $10,000. So he was not happy when general manager George Weiss sent him a contract for the 1951 season with only a $1,500 raise. Hank thought he deserved more.

Charlene typed a letter for Hank stating that the raise was insufficient and that more money would have to be added to the offer. Weiss ignored the letter, plus two others that Bauer sent, and on each occasion returned the contract with the $1,500 raise. After the return of the third letter, Hank received a call at his Kansas City home. It was George Weiss. "How would you like to fly to New York at our expense?" the general manager asked. "I want to talk to you about your contract."

Bauer had never been in Weiss' office at Yankee Stadium, and he was impressed by its size. He also took note of the general manager's refusal to look him in the eye during the discussions. But no matter—the salary was the only issue that counted. Weiss tried to explain why Hank should be satisfied with the proposed salary. To carry his point, Weiss made a comparison to DiMaggio (whose .301 batting average for the 1950 season was actually nineteen points below Bauer's average). "You know the reason we pay DiMaggio $100,000?" Weiss rhetorically asked Bauer. "Because he puts people in the ballpark." The explanation may have been compelling in the general manager's mind, but Hank was not persuaded. "Mr. Weiss," he replied, "Joe DiMaggio is the greatest player I ever saw or hope to play with. But he's not ten times the player I am." Weiss tried to but could not really disagree. Eventually Bauer got a raise of $6,000—a considerable sum for the former pipe fitter.

The salary increase proved to be a good investment for the Yankees. Over the next four years, Bauer never batted below .293, had as many as seventeen home runs but never fewer than ten, and was selected for the American League All-Star team in three of those years (1952, 1953, and 1954). But statistics were only a part of the story. Stengel marveled at Bauer's ability "to do everything right in a tough situation." (There was the game at Yankee Stadium in 1955 when Tiger shortstop Harvey Kuenn slammed a pitch from Bob Turley into right center field toward the scoreboard more than four hundred feet from home plate. "Hank couldn't quite catch up to the ball," Turley remembered. "But somehow, God only knows how, he got close enough to tip it with his bare hand—and flip it right into Mickey Mantle's glove. Hank crashed into the scoreboard, bounced off, and trotted back to right field.") And so, when a sportswriter asked Stengel to identify the three best players he ever managed, the old man rattled off the names of DiMaggio, Berra, and Bauer. Hank was startled when he learned of his manager's response. "Me?" he inquired. "What the hell about Mantle and those guys?" "No," Stengel replied. "You. You gave 110 percent every time you were in the lineup."

Bauer's contribution to the Yankees' success was all the more remarkable because he was usually the team's leadoff batter—a position generally reserved in those days for players with little power and an ability to get on base with singles or walks. Bauer himself was perplexed by his position in the lineup, and one day he posed the question to his manager while the two of them were sitting in the dugout. "First of all," said Stengel, "you can lead the game off with a home run" (and Hank would in fact hit eighteen leadoff home runs in his career). "Second," Stengel continued, "you could lead the game off with a double. Or you could score from first base on an extra-base hit. And you could break up a double play to keep the inning alive. And if you score a run in the first inning, it changes the whole complexion of the game." The explanation was, in effect, a testament to Bauer's drive and versatility.

Hank did not appear to be losing any of those skills as he approached his mid-thirties. His batting average dipped to .278 from .294 in 1955, but he slammed a career-high twenty home runs. In 1956 he hit twenty-six home runs and drove in a career-high eighty-four runs (although his batting average dropped to a career low of .241 in 147 games—the most he had played in any season). And he embarked on a seventeen-game World Series hitting streak in 1956 that would surpass the record of any other player. (Bauer also established a record of sorts of by getting picked off first base twice in the last two games of his streak during the 1958 World Series. "Mr. Bauer has been picked off more often than a tablecloth," said sportswriter John Lardner, "and twice as often as the average toupee." After watching Hank hit a home run that won the seventeenth game, Lardner drew an obvious conclusion: "This goes to show that when Hank runs right around the bases, instead of stopping at first, he can make a lot of trouble.")

Hank Bauer is not thinking about a World Series hitting record as Don Larsen gets ready to pitch in the top of the ninth inning of the fifth game of the 1956 World Series. For his part, Larsen is trying to stay calm, but it is not easy. He walks around the mound and picks up the rosin bag. ("It suddenly felt," Larsen later said, "like it weighed fifty pounds.") He then returns to the pitching rubber, glares down at Yogi Berra's sign, and gets ready to throw the first pitch to Carl Furillo.

The Dodger right fielder fouls off the first two pitches for a two-strike count. Yogi throws a new ball back to Larsen. The Yankee hurler steps off the mound and turns his back to home plate as he rubs the ball. After another quick grab of the rosin bag to keep his right hand dry, Larsen resumes his place on the pitching rubber. After missing the plate for a ball, Larsen throws two more pitches which Furillo fouls off. Furillo steps out of the batter's box momentarily, and, when he returns, Larsen is ready for the next pitch—a slider that the Dodger right fielder swings at and hits. It is a high fly ball that drifts toward the right-field stands. Bauer—only a few feet from the cinder path that circles the perimeter of the stands—keeps his eyes on the ball. There will be no basket catches or other dramatic flourishes from the Yankee right fielder. He holds both hands up and, after what seems like an extraordinarily long time, pulls the ball in for the first out. (Later, Larsen will tell Bauer, "I didn't think that damn thing was ever going to come down.")

Roy Campanella gets comfortable in the batter's box as the crowd roars its approval for the first out. "Our strategy with the great Dodger hitter," Larsen later explained, "was to pitch him inside, even though I had retired Campanella on two outside pitches in both the third and sixth innings." The first pitch conforms to that strategy—a fastball on the inside corner. But Larsen and Berra have to wonder whether they made the right choice. Campanella swings hard and sends a high fly ball that hits the facade at the top of the stadium in foul territory. A slight variation of the pitch or the swing could have made it a home run.

It is a tremendous display of power that Berra takes into account in calling the next pitch. Larsen throws a fastball toward the outside of the plate. The Yankee pitcher anticipates that it will be called a ball, but Campanella swings and sends a harmless ground ball to Billy Martin. The Dodger catcher is thrown out with ease, and there are now two outs. The noise of the crowd reaches a new crescendo as fans realize that Don Larsen is only one out away from doing what no other pitcher in baseball history has ever done.

It is then that Dodger manager Walter Alston turns to Dale Mitchell to pinch-hit for Sal Maglie.

The Last Pitch: Dale Mitchell

With the count of one ball and two strikes, the Dodger pinch hitter has his eyes focused on the ball as it speeds toward the plate.

Dale Mitchell's appearance in Yankee Stadium at that pivotal moment in baseball history represents a true rags-to-riches story. He had grown up poor—"dirt poor," as one of his sons remembered—in Colony, a town in western Oklahoma that the son recalled being little more than "a wide spot in the road." There young Dale shared a small one-room wooden shack with his mother, his sister, and, when he deigned to appear from one of his frequent bouts with the bottle, his father. (Many years later, after he had become an All-Star outfielder in the American League, Mitchell drove his family to the home of his childhood, and, while they all sat in the car and stared at a pile of wood in the otherwise barren field, Mitchell's younger son Bo asked his father what he was looking at. "That was my house right there," Mitchell responded.)

Dale was blessed with superior eye-hand coordination and good physical attributes, eventually carrying almost two hundred pounds on a six-foot-one-inch frame. It was a combination that enabled him to excel at sports, and his considerable athletic skills were evident when he attended high school in nearby Cloud Chief, Oklahoma. He was a forward on the school's varsity basketball team. He ran on the varsity track team and set a record at a state conference by running the hundred-yard dash in 9.8 seconds. And he played the outfield for the school's varsity baseball team. By the time he graduated from high school in 1940, Dale had twelve varsity letters.

The left-handed Mitchell was only a junior in high school when he caught the eye of Cleveland Indians' scout Hugh Alexander. In other circumstances, Alexander would have waited until Dale had graduated before approaching him with an offer. But the boy had unusual talent, and the Indian scout did not want to risk the chance that another team would sign him. A conversation was held, a meeting was arranged with the parents, and a seventeen-year-old Dale Mitchell was signed to a professional baseball contract with the Cleveland Indians in 1939.

Dale was proud of the deal, but he knew he could not disclose its existence to anyone, especially his coaches and friends at Cloud Chief High School. "I had to keep my Cleveland contract a secret," he later remembered, "because it would have made me ineligible for high school or college sports." Dale was willing to take the risk because Alexander had promised the high school student a monthly stipend of $500 until he graduated, and, with his father often unemployed or absent, his family "needed the money badly."

There was, however, one complication. The contract that Dale's parents signed made no mention of the monthly payments that Alexander had promised, and the first month came and went without a check. The ensuing months were no different, and the Mitchells' inquiries about the promised checks went unanswered. When the Cleveland Indians began sending notices for him to report for spring training after high school ended, Dale tore them up as soon as he received them. He believed that a promise was a promise and told Alexander that he would do nothing for the Indians until they made good on the monthly payments. Try as he might, Alexander could not deliver, and Dale accepted a basketball scholarship from the University of Oklahoma instead of the invitation to join the Cleveland Indians.

None of that dampened Dale's interest in baseball. He continued to play in the summer after high school for the semipro baseball team that was sponsored by the Natural Gas Company. It was there that he came under the tutelage of Roy Deal, a former major-league coach and someone who would have a profound impact on Dale's batting style—and his later success in the major leagues. "I had a habit of stepping away from the plate and pulling the bat with my body," Mitchell later told a sportswriter. "Deal taught me how to spread my stance and hit with my wrists. This enabled me to hit outside balls and thus bat better against southpaw pitching."

Deal's instruction was complemented by advice that Dale received when he started playing college baseball in 1941. "My coach at the University of Oklahoma," Dale explained, "was a firm believer in meeting the ball rather than hitting it out of the park." It was a perspective that Dale embraced with enthusiasm, and in later years he would resist pressure from his major-league managers to produce more home runs.

Unfortunately, questions of how to hit a pitched ball were soon eclipsed by other matters. By 1942 the country was at war, Dale had married his high school sweetheart, Margaret Ruth Emerson (much to the dismay of her father, who thought Dale Mitchell was from the wrong side of the tracks and, as one of Dale's sons explained, "was never going to amount to anything"), and then he got drafted into the army. Dale became a quartermaster and spent twenty-six months in England and France. He saw little combat and returned to Oklahoma immediately after being discharged in December 1945.

With military experience now behind him, Dale resumed studies and varsity sports at Oklahoma University in January 1946. As he would later tell his sons, 1946 was his "big year" and one that would forever change the course of his life. He tore up the pitching in the Big Six Conference that spring, batting a phenomenal .507 to establish a new school record. That success was a product of Dale's unusual speed on the base paths and the earlier instruction to focus on getting hits rather than hitting home runs—although there were occasional displays of incredible power. (Arlen Specter, then a student and later the longtime United States senator from Pennsylvania, remembered the time he was walking down Lindsay Street just beyond the right-field fence of the school's stadium when a baseball flew over the fence and hit him in the stomach, knocking him over. He struggled to his feet and called out to the outfielder, "Who hit that damn ball?" "Dale Mitchell," came the response.)

By the end of the season, the Cleveland Indians were knocking on Dale's door again, reminding him of the contract that he had signed many years ago. Dale had not abandoned his dream of becoming a major-league baseball player, but he was still smarting from the Indians' failure to make those monthly payments. It was then that he learned that the Oklahoma City Indians, a minor-league team in the Texas League, had an agreement with the Indians. The proximity of the team to his home was appealing.

Mitchell took his tale of woe to Harold Pope and Jim Humphreys, the Oklahoma City Indians' owners, and they agreed to have the young athlete assigned to their team. There were no regrets there. Dale won the Texas League batting championship with a .337 average.

The Indians called Mitchell up to the parent club in early September. But Pope and Humphreys were not about to leave Mitchell's fate to chance. They knew they had a major-league prospect on their hands. So they personally accompanied the young athlete to Cleveland and told Bill Veeck, the Indians' legendary owner, about the team's failure to make those monthly payments and, more important, the need to give Dale a real chance to play. The plea from Pope and Humphreys could not have hurt. Mitchell later said that Veeck "made amends" for the team's failure to make the monthly payments (Veeck saying that he "couldn't let the world's record for determination go unrewarded"). More than that, the Indians' owner gave Dale that chance to play. Veeck was not disappointed. In eleven games, Mitchell batted .432.

It was enough to make the Indians believe that Mitchell could succeed in the major leagues, and one sportswriter said during spring training in 1947 that Mitchell "is the outstanding candidate for the starting job in center field." But the promise faded quickly after the season began. The Oklahoma native went hitless in the first two games, and manager Lou Boudreau used the inexperienced player only sparingly.

Still, all was not lost. By midseason, Boudreau's choice for left field, Pat Seerey, was not performing well. A replacement was needed, and Dale Mitchell was available. He was inserted in the lineup on July 3.

Dale did not squander the opportunity. ("I'll make good if I have a chance," he had earlier told the *Cleveland Plain Dealer.*) The result: a twenty-two-game hitting streak that represented the longest hitting streak by any American League player in 1947.

By the time the season had ended, Mitchell had mustered a .316 batting average—the highest on the team, the highest among major-league rookies (which included Jackie Robinson), and the sixth-highest in the league. His 156 hits included sixteen doubles and ten triples but only one home run (a prodigious shot that, according to one sportswriter, "astonished" the fans at Cleveland's Municipal Stadium when it hit the facade of the upper deck in the right-field stands).

There was no sophomore jinx for Mitchell. In 1948 he batted .336—third in the league—with 204 hits, only three behind the league leader. Mitchell also had the pleasure that year of playing in what *The New York Times* called "one of the most thrilling pennant races in major league history." The Indians and the Red Sox finished with identical records, forcing a play-off game at Boston's Fenway Park on October 4 to decide the American League pennant winner. Powered by the two home runs and spectacular play by Boudreau, the Indians crushed the Red Sox 8–3, and Mitchell later remembered that game as "the biggest thing I've been involved in." The play-off victory was followed by a World Series triumph over the National League's Boston Braves, and Dale Mitchell had a $7,000 World Series check to go with his $7,000 salary.

Mitchell had reason to be proud of his accomplishments, but he never took his success for granted. "In this game," he once told a reporter, "you never know enough." So he was receptive to Boudreau's proposal that he take some fielding instruction from Tris Speaker, one of the most celebrated players of baseball in the early twentieth century (with a .345 batting average over the course of twenty-two seasons with the Red Sox and the Indians). It was not a casual suggestion. Boudreau was hoping to move the fleet-footed Mitchell to center field, and few players had handled that position as well as Speaker. (Later, a grateful Mitchell would say that "Spoke helped me a lot with my fielding"—although in time Mitchell would be moved back to left field.)

However much he wanted to improve his fielding, Dale was far more interested in hitting (and Speaker himself would say of Mitchell that "the man has one of the best batting eyes in baseball" and that he "may become one of those rare birds—a .400 hitter"). That focus on the science of hitting also helped explain Mitchell's close relationship with Ted Williams—in Mitchell's view, a player with no equal when it came to consistently hitting the ball hard. For his part, Mitchell would study the pitcher's movements, the spin of the ball, and the use of the batter's hands in making contact—all in an effort to sharpen his success at the plate. (After he retired from baseball, Mitchell wanted to impart all he had learned to his young sons, who would later enter professional baseball themselves. At one point Mitchell told Bo that he was going to teach his younger son how to hit the top of the baseball and then the bottom of the baseball—to which Bo replied, "You know, Dad, we're going to have a little trouble with that, because I can barely see the ball.")

There was, however, more to professional baseball for Mitchell than fielding and hitting. The Cleveland Indians encompassed a camaraderie that added an important dimension to the experience. The players would spend time in the clubhouse after the games, smoking cigarettes (or, for Dale, his ever-present black pipe), drinking beer, and recounting the events of the game. If it was a day game, they would often retreat en masse with their families to a restaurant (a local Italian eatery being a favorite). During the summers, the clubhouse would be filled with the players' young sons—although, as Dale Jr. remembered, "When the Yankees came to town there were no kids allowed in the clubhouse. It was a whole different feel. It was serious."

Despite the pleasures and success of being with the Indians, the seeds of discontent were germinating almost as soon as Mitchell arrived in Cleveland. True, he had the best batting average among all Indians as a rookie in 1947, but many people—including Boudreau—complained that too many of Mitchell's hits were soft-liners to left field, a reflection of Mitchell's inclination to slap the ball to the opposite field. A man of Mitchell's size and skill, they said, should have more home runs. And, from watching that one titanic home run in 1947, they knew he could do it—if he tried.

Always eager to please, Mitchell tried to increase his power numbers, telling a reporter at one point during the 1948 season that he had studied the pitchers and now had the confidence to "mash anybody." The statistics seemed to support his confidence—at least to a certain point. He hit four home runs in 1948 along with thirty doubles and eight triples (as well as one of only four home runs that the Indians hit in the 1948 World Series against the Boston Braves), and in 1949 he led the league with twenty-three triples—only three shy of the American League record. In addition to the triples, there was much in Mitchell's performance to satisfy the Indians—a .317 batting average (fourth in the league) with 203 hits (tops in the league). But his home-run production dipped to three in 1949, and the criticism intensified when Hank Greenberg—the power-hitting star of the Detroit Tigers in the 1930s and 1940s—became the Indians' general manager in 1950.

A six-foot-four-inch slugger who had come close to surpassing Babe Ruth's then-record of sixty home runs (with fifty-eight in 1938), Greenberg believed that the Indians needed power to overtake the Yankees in the pennant race. And from Greenberg's perspective, Dale Mitchell should have been doing more to fill the void.

Mitchell's performance in 1950 was certainly respectable—a .308 batting average (marking the fifth consecutive year in which he had batted over .300). But his home-run total was a meager three, and the pressure to hit the long ball intensified when Al Lopez assumed the Indians' managerial reins for the 1951 season. He pushed Mitchell relentlessly to pull the ball to right field instead of slapping at it. ("Swish the bat, Mitch," the manager would repeatedly say when Dale came to the plate. "Use your power.") Mitchell responded by hitting eleven home runs (a respectable level in a season when the league leader hit only thirty-three). But his batting average dropped to .290—an acceptable record for many, but not for the Oklahoma native. Mitchell returned to his earlier batting form in 1952 and was able to raise his batting average to .323, only four points below the league leader. But the home run total dropped to five, and the Indians finished two games behind the Yankees in second place.

Mitchell's higher batting average may have pleased some people, but not Greenberg. He resumed the quest for more home runs, and his displeasure was made known not only to Mitchell but routinely reported in the press. It was not something that endeared Mitchell to the team's general manager. "Greenberg put a lot of pressure on him," one of Mitchell's sons remembered, "and he did not like Greenberg." In the spring of 1953, there was talk about Mitchell quitting after the end of the season, but his performance seemed to make that unnecessary. He hit a career-high thirteen home runs that year while batting an even .300, and before the season was over Mitchell was assuring reporters that he was not about to leave baseball when he was having his best season. "And next year," he promised, "I plan to swing for distance even more."

Sadly, Mitchell never got the opportunity to fulfill that promise. Greenberg remained dissatisfied, and in the beginning of the 1954 season, Mitchell learned that a lifetime batting average of .315 over more than seven full seasons was not enough to keep his position in left field. Instead, the job was given to Al Smith, a younger player who seemed to have the ability to hit more home runs (although that proved to be a false hope, as Smith would hit only eleven home runs in 1954, two fewer than Mitchell had hit the previous season).

In the meantime, Mitchell was relegated almost entirely to pinch-hitting duty, appearing in only fifty-three games and having only sixty at bats with just one home run—ironically, a blast in September that won the pennant-clinching game for the Indians. The next year was no different, with Mitchell appearing in only sixty-one games with just fifty-one at bats, and there was now constant talk about what would happen to one of the Indians' most popular players. "I'm still convinced that I can produce playing regularly," Mitchell told a reporter at spring training in 1956. But he knew that the decision to play him regularly was not his to make and that he could endure only so much frustration. "If I can't get the chance," he added, "I may as well go home and get into a business that will keep me occupied."

Greenberg was not about to give Mitchell that chance to play regularly, and by midsummer Dale had advised the Indians that 1956 would be his last year. Still, he hoped he could finish his career with Cleveland and return to Oklahoma with his pride intact. But it was not to be. Mitchell learned at the end of July that Greenberg had sold the thirty-five-year-old player's contract to the Brooklyn Dodgers for $1,000. Not that Greenberg or anyone else from the Indians' management would tell him. The news came instead from Dodger manager Walter Alston.

He called the Mitchell home in Cleveland and, when Bo answered, Alston identified himself and asked for the young boy's father. Bo, not quite seven, knew enough baseball to know that Walter Alston was the Dodgers' famous manager. He called his father to the phone in the other room and then surreptitiously listened while Alston told Mitchell that he would be moving over to the National League to help the Dodgers, who were then locked in a tight pennant race with the Milwaukee Braves. "Dale," Alston said, "we just purchased your contract, and we need you as soon as you can get here." Mitchell masked his disappointment about leaving Cleveland but felt that some disclosure about his future plans was warranted. "Well," he responded, "I've let it be known that I'll be retiring at the end of this season." Alston was not to be deterred. "I know that," he replied, "but we need you as a left-handed pinch hitter on the team if we're going to win the pennant." "Okay," said Mitchell. "Just so you know that this is my last go-around."

The Cleveland press was not happy. The *Cleveland Plain Dealer* reported on July 30 that the team had sold the contract of "one of the most popular players ever to wear a Cleveland Indian uniform." Mitchell was equally disappointed. He had invested all of his energies and emotions in the Cleveland Indians. He had performed better than most and certainly had reason to feel that he had contributed to the team's success over the last ten years—two American League pennants, one World Championship, and most other years as a contender. Now the Indians had shuffled him off to another team without a word. As Bo Mitchell later recalled, "They certainly cut a piece of his heart out when they mistreated him like that."

But Dale Mitchell was an honorable man. He and Dale Jr., now thirteen years old, drove the next morning from Cleveland to Pittsburgh to join the Brooklyn Dodgers. They reached Forbes Field in the late morning and strode across the empty field to the visitors' dugout, both of them in street clothes and Dale carrying the suitcase with his baseball equipment. They went into the Dodgers' dugout on the third-base side of the field, walked to the back of the clubhouse, and there, with a shaft of summer sunlight coming in from the high windows and illuminating the locker room, they saw Jackie Robinson, Roy Campanella, Carl Furillo, and Pee Wee Reese, each wrapped in a white towel and sitting on a folding chair, playing cards on an overturned crate. It was an informal but striking introduction to the National League.

Brooklyn turned out to be as much as Mitchell could have hoped for in his last "go-around." The Dodgers included many accomplished players who were used to winning and had the talent to keep on winning. Beyond that, they provided some of the camaraderie Mitchell had treasured at Cleveland. "He liked Brooklyn and felt like it was a class organization," one of Mitchell's sons later recalled.

True to his word, Alston began using Mitchell as his left-handed pinch hitter against right-handed pitchers. Mitchell responded to Alston's confidence and performed well, including a hit in his first plate appearance to drive in the winning run in a game against the Braves. He went on to rack up six pinch hits in fourteen at bats in September when the Dodgers came from behind on the last weekend of the season to overtake the Braves. So Mitchell was not surprised that Alston asked him to pinch-hit for Sal Maglie when the Dodgers were down to their last out in the fifth game of the World Series.

Dale Mitchell has no interest in spoiling Larsen's bid for a no-hitter. He and his new teammates are still focused on winning the game. We can beat this guy, they kept telling themselves in the dugout. All we have to do is get someone on base and then we can break this game wide-open. "We were so close," Mitchell later told Peter Golenbock, "that we really felt we were going to win it."

Now, however, the former Cleveland Indian is down to his last strike, and Larsen's pitch is coming toward him. The aging player sees the ball clearly as it approaches, and he begins to lift his right foot slightly in anticipation of taking a swing. But as the ball comes closer

Mitchell sees that it is moving up and away from him—clearly high and outside. He checks his swing and turns back to face Babe Pinelli, assuming that the veteran umpire will confirm Mitchell's almost infallible judgment on the strike zone.

Pinelli hesitates for the slightest second. And then he lifts his right arm and signals a strike. The roar of the crowd explodes as Bob Wolff excitedly yells into the microphone, "Strike three! A no-hitter! A perfect game for Don Larsen!"

As Yogi Berra emerges from his crouch and runs toward Larsen, Mitchell stares at Pinelli, not believing what has just happened. He has been called out on strikes. Realizing the futility of arguing with the umpire, Mitchell slowly walks back to the Dodger dugout. As Berra leaps into Larsen's arms near the pitcher's mound and Yankee players and fans surround the hatless and beaming pitcher, Mitchell shakes his head, complaining to his teammates that he was the victim of a bad call.

Berra, Larsen, and Pinelli, of course, had a different opinion. (Some observers also suggested that Mitchell should have been called out on strikes because his bat crossed the plate when he checked his swing, but Pinelli made no mention of the checked swing after the game, telling reporters only that Larsen's last pitch "was right over the middle" and "an easy call.") But every other Yankee on the field who had a good look at the pitch agreed with Mitchell. "I had a clear view from center field," Mickey Mantle later said, "and, if I was under oath, I'd have to say the pitch looked like it was outside." Andy Carey, who had an even better view from third base (because Mitchell was a left-handed batter), likewise agreed that the "last pitch to Dale Mitchell was high." Gil McDougald, with an equally good perspective from the shortstop position, had the same reaction. "It wasn't even close," said McDougald. "It was high." Even Enos Slaughter, surveying the scene from left field, similarly told a member of the Baseball Hall of Fame staff that the pitch "was high."

No matter. Larsen had made history with a superb and unmatched pitching performance, and there was pandemonium in the clubhouse afterward as dozens of reporters besieged the Yankee players. They of course wanted to know how Larsen felt. ("My legs are still rubbery all over," the Yankee hurler responded, "and I'm so nervous and excited I don't even know what day it is.") The reporters also gathered around Yogi Berra, who took a drag on a cigarette and, with tongue in cheek, said to the reporters assembled around him, "So what's new?" (Berra, however, did not dismiss the significance of the game, and later he would call it one of his "greatest thrills" in baseball.) And, of course, the reporters had questions for manager Casey Stengel as well—some of which bordered on the absurd. ("Is that the best game he ever pitched?" one sportswriter asked the Yankee manager with reference to Larsen.)

Over in the visitors' dugout, the Dodgers likewise felt that the last pitch to Mitchell was a ball. ("High and outside," said Carl Erskine. "No question.") Years later, the Dodgers appeared to get some vindication from the home-plate umpire himself. "Babe Pinelli told me later," said Duke Snider, "that he wanted to go out on a no-hitter in a World Series. That was the last game he was going to umpire. So anything close was a strike."

Whatever their thoughts at the time or later about that last pitch to Dale Mitchell, the Dodgers did not dwell on what might have been. Disagreeing with the plate umpire was nothing new in baseball. They understood that, and they were gracious in defeat. As he sat naked on a stool in the Dodger clubhouse eating a sausage, Maglie was philosophical when asked by a reporter if he was troubled by the no-hitter. "I might have wanted him to get it," the Dodger pitcher responded, "if we hadn't had a chance all the time." But this was, after all, the Yankees. "They are pros," Maglie added. "The way we are. You make one mistake with them and you're in trouble."

The game ended in the afternoon of that fall day in 1956, but it provided a memory that would give Don Larsen untold pleasure for decades, long after he had retired from baseball. He would gladly recount the game and the pressures to untold fans in airports, at memorabilia shows, at Mickey Mantle's fantasy baseball camp in Florida, and wherever else he went. "It makes me happy," he said. "I only wish I had a buck for everyone who tells me they were at the game. If all of those folks were really there, attendance would've been over a million."

The memory of that fifth game of the 1956 World Series did not give the same pleasure to Dale Mitchell. When he reached the dugout steps after the final out, Pee Wee Reese told Dale to let it go. "They're going to be talking about this game for hundreds of years," he said. "You're in the history books." But that was not enough for Mitchell. After an eleven-year career with many accomplishments and numerous accolades (including selection for the 1949 All-Star team), he knew that he would be remembered only for that one at bat in Yankee Stadium.

It was a black mark that forever plagued Dale Mitchell. He would not, really could not, yield in his judgment, always insisting to people who would invariably raise the subject that Larsen's last pitch was high and outside. "He never got over it," his daughter-in-law later recalled. "He was mad about it until the day he died in January 1987." The strikeout was particularly humiliating because Mitchell had so little regard for Larsen as a pitcher. And so the former American League All-Star had a quick response when ABC's *Good Morning America* contacted Mitchell in Tulsa, Oklahoma, in 1986 and invited him to New York to share the spotlight with Larsen and Berra on a segment that would celebrate the thirtieth anniversary of the event: no, thanks. He was not going to travel halfway across the country, he told his family, to talk about striking out.

19

Aftermath

For Don Larsen, the fifth game of the 1956 World Series remained the pinnacle of an otherwise lackluster career. He was able to win nineteen games while losing only ten over the next two seasons for the Yankees, but the mastery he had shown in that World Series contest was gone by 1959, leading Casey Stengel to ask the San Diego native, who hit fourteen home runs in his career as a pitcher, whether he might be interested in switching to the outfield.

The inevitable trade occurred after the 1959 season. Larsen was included in a multiplayer deal with the Kansas City Athletics that brought Roger Maris to the Yankees. Don was neither surprised nor completely unhappy with the trade, in part because he had married Corrine Bruess, a TWA stewardess, who had lived in the Kansas City area.

Over the course of the next six years, Larsen—using his no-windup delivery only sporadically—moved from one team to another in the American League and the National League (but did play a critical role as a relief pitcher when the San Francisco Giants won the pennant in 1962). Unwilling to confront a life without baseball, Larsen continued to play for minor-league teams after the Baltimore Orioles released him in 1966. "I had nothing else to do," he later explained. He eventually found a position as a salesman with the Blake, Moffitt & Towne Paper Company in the San Jose area. He was there for twenty-five years before retiring with Corrine and his son, Scott, to Lake Hayden in northwest Idaho.

In the meantime, the memorabilia craze placed him in great demand at card shows and other events where he would sign baseballs and photos. "It's sometimes fun," he later told me, "but it's hard to sign all that stuff all the time. And my butt gets tired." And then there were the baseball fantasy camps. There too he could sign his name to paraphernalia and reminisce about the glory days with the Yankees (although he did startle the campers on one occasion by saying—in response to a question asking the former Yankees on the dais to identify the greatest player with whom they had played—that it was Willie Mays and not Mickey Mantle).

Sal Maglie never pitched in another World Series. He had a respectable record for the third-place Dodgers in 1957, but the Brooklyn team needed to make room for younger players and sold the forty-year-old's contract to the Yankees on September 1, 1957 (the day after the deadline for World Series eligibility). Sal showed signs of greatness with a shutout of the Cleveland Indians at Yankee Stadium, but Stengel could not fit the former Dodger into the pitching rotation. By 1958 he was wearing a St. Louis Cardinals uniform, but his tenure with the team was brief.

Part of the explanation was Kay. She was diagnosed with cancer and needed a mastectomy. ("Sal," Cardinal manager Fred Hutchinson told his new pitcher, "go home. Your family comes first.") Maglie later took a job with the Boston Red Sox as a pitching coach, but Kay's condition required his full-time attention, and he left the club in 1962 to be with his wife and the two sons they had adopted. He returned to the Red Sox as a coach in 1966 and was with the club when it reached the World Series in 1967. But relations with manager Dick Williams were never good, and Maglie found himself without a job in 1968.

Sal returned to baseball as the pitching coach for the newly franchised Seattle Pilots in 1969. The experiment was not a profitable one for the Pilots or their new pitching coach. The team finished last in the

Western Division and Maglie found himself the subject of biting criticism in *Ball Four*, Jim Bouton's best-selling account of that season. (When his teenage son asked him about the book, the father "gave his typical answer of everyone having their opinion." But to the press, Maglie complained that Bouton "was like a spoiled little brat who always had to have things his own way.")

In the meantime, Kay died in 1967, and Maglie embarked on a new relationship with Doris Ellman, the secretary to the Niagara Falls attorney who handled the closing on the sale of his liquor store. Doris was not a baseball fan and knew nothing of Sal's stature until the time they flew to New York City for a weekend. "There's probably going to be a lot of people stopping to talk to me," he told his future wife. To her surprise, Sal's prediction proved to be accurate. "We couldn't even get down to the corner coming out of the hotel without someone approaching us," she later told me.

Sal remained in Niagara Falls after he and Doris were married, and he tried to spend more time with his two sons, neither of whom showed much interest in baseball. One son eventually pursued a career in the air force, and the other son, Sal Jr., a troubled boy with no direction, met a tragic end by falling to his death from a third-story apartment balcony.

Sal pursued a variety of business ventures in Niagara Falls, including a position as the general manager of a local minor-league baseball team. He also spent a fair amount of time on the golf course, and he came home after one round in 1982 complaining to Doris about "the worst headache I ever had in my life." It proved to be a brain aneurysm that had burst.

Sal did not fully recover from the ensuing surgery, and the situation deteriorated after a stroke in 1985. Routine tasks—even eating—became a challenge. "I would put the plate down in front of him," Doris later explained, "and he would eat all the food on one side and think he was finished. So I would turn the plate around, and he would finish." By 1987, he was in a Niagara Falls nursing home.

News of Sal Maglie's condition was reported in a New York newspaper, which stated—incorrectly—that the former Dodger was in a nursing home in his hometown of Grand Isle (a suburb of Niagara Falls). Doris learned of the mistake when the Grand Isle nursing home called to say that they had some mail for Mr. Maglie. Doris brought home literally hundreds of letters and cards. There was no point in bringing them to Sal because he had already lost most of his cognitive powers. One day Doris began opening up the mail. All were filled with good wishes. And then a five-dollar bill dropped out of one envelope. As she opened the others, more money spilled out—a few dollars here and there—as people offered to do what they could for the pitcher who had given them so much joy in his earlier years.

Sal Maglie finally died in his seventy-fifth year on December 28, 1992.

Jackie Robinson retired after the 1956 season. The Dodgers tried to sell his contract to the Giants, but Jackie had already accepted a position as a vice president with Chock full o'nuts, a coffee shop chain in New York City. An ostensible justification for the retirement was to avoid the constant travel that baseball required and enable him to spend more time with Rachel and his three children. But Jackie was, at heart, a social activist, and there was a steady stream of invitations for him to speak at functions around the country and to work with the NAACP and other public-interest organizations in places far from his home in Stamford, Connecticut.

There was a high personal cost for Jackie's constant travel and the never-ceasing demands of social organizations. Relations with his older son, Jackie Jr., were never good, in part because people were always comparing the son's pedestrian athletic skills to those of his accomplished father. Jackie Jr. joined the army, returned from Vietnam with a demoralizing drug habit, and, just as he was pulling his life together, fell asleep at the wheel one evening in 1971 and died on a New York highway. "Carl," Jackie wistfully told former teammate Carl Erskine at one point, "when I think of the hours I spent with other people's children in a classroom and in youth clinics, I should have been spending more time with my own kids."

Jackie's remorse over his son's death coincided with a deterioration in his health. He had been diagnosed with diabetes shortly after he retired from baseball and was not very diligent in following the doctors' advice for controlling the disease. His weight ballooned and his legs began to throb because of poor blood circulation. In 1968, he had a mild heart attack, and by 1972 the doctors were contemplating the amputation of his legs. But perhaps the most troubling ailment was the growing loss of his eyesight. By 1972, he could barely see.

The end came that October. He and Rachel were watching a football game in their Connecticut home when Jackie detected a flash in his eye—a possible sign that a blood vessel had ruptured. An appointment was made to see a doctor the following morning, and Jackie got up early the next day and began to dress while Rachel cooked breakfast in the kitchen. She heard a noise and looked up to see her husband rushing toward her. Rachel ran to him. He put his arms around her and said, "I love you." And then he dropped to the floor. An ambulance was called, but Jackie Robinson died before he reached the hospital.

Gil McDougald began the 1957 season by hitting line drives to all fields, and by the time the club reached Cleveland on May 7 for a series with the Indians, the Yankee shortstop was batting .368. In his first plate appearance against southpaw Herb Score—the Indians' twenty-three-year-old phenomenon (who had led the American League in strikeouts the previous two years with a fastball that approached one hundred miles an hour)—Gil slammed a line drive that caught Score just below his right eye. "As soon as I hit him," McDougald later said, "I saw blood fly." Score was rushed to a hospital and his eye was saved, but not his career—he would win only seventeen more games over the next five years. Overcome with guilt, McDougald threatened to quit but ultimately knew that he could not because "I had no way of making the bread to support my family."

The experience no doubt helped to give Gil the incentive to pursue the formation of a maintenance company near his New Jersey home that would become a multimillion-dollar venture with twenty-five hundred employees. After the 1959 season, the thirty-one-year-old McDougald informed the Yankees that he would be retiring after the 1960 season. "I woke up one morning," he later said, "and it hit me. What am I trying to prove in this game of baseball?" McDougald became a full-time businessman who devoted his spare time to his family (augmented by the adoption of three children after his four children had grown up) and as coach for Fordham University's baseball team.

The seeds of heartache were immersed in this otherwise fulfilling life: Gil McDougald was losing his hearing. The cause could be traced back to a game at Yankee Stadium on August 2, 1955 (when Joe Collins' home run saved the life of an Asbury Park fan). McDougald had been standing behind Frank Crosetti as he was pitching batting practice. At one point, Gil walked beyond the protective screen to pick up a ball and, as he did so, Bob Cerv—one of the Yankees' more powerful hitters—crushed a Crosetti pitch that hit McDougald in the left ear. Unbeknownst to Gil and the Yankee physician, the blow created holes in the tubes of McDougald's inner ear that eventually stretched to the right ear as well.

By 1985, the hearing loss was complete. Gil did not like his predicament, but he learned to live with it. So he was not receptive to inquiries from Ira Berkow, a *New York Times* reporter, who called some years later to interview him about his physical impairment. Lucille conveyed Gil's decision not to grant the interview request. He can't hear, she explained. No problem, said Berkow. I'll write the questions out. It was a creative proposal but Gil held his ground. But Berkow was a tenacious reporter, and he would not take no for an answer. "Gil," Lucille finally said, "this guy's bugging the life out of me. Would you please sit down with him for twenty minutes and get him off my back?" The article— "McDougald, Once a Quiet Yankee Star, Now Lives in a Quiet World"—appeared in *The New York Times* on July 10, 1994.

The article attracted the attention of a physician at the National Institutes of Health in Bethesda, Maryland, who called to say that the former Yankee might be a candidate for a cochlear implant, a relatively new device that could be surgically implanted in the ear and be used with an external component to enable a person to hear. In due course the evaluation was made and the operation performed in New York City in November 1995. The operation proved successful, and, not surprisingly, there was much excitement when McDougald reached his Spring Lake, New Jersey, home. "Everyone has come to watch Grandpa hear," said Lucille. Gil McDougald now spends his time in retirement with his family, playing golf, and hearing all the sounds that make life complete.

Sandy Amoros never lost his smile but his life took a downward spiral after the 1956 season. He batted .277 with seven home runs as a part-time outfielder in 1957, but he was not part of the Dodgers' plans when they moved to Los Angeles in 1958. Instead, he was sent back to the club's farm team in Montreal. Amoros survived two seasons in Montreal and a few games with the Detroit Tigers in 1960 before returning to Cuba as a celebrity who would attract a trail of young boys wherever he went. There he could enjoy life with his wife, Migdalia, and their daughter, Eloise, on the ranch that Amoros had purchased in Mantanzas. And there too, he hoped, he could continue his baseball career in the Mexican leagues. But Fidel Castro decided otherwise.

The Cuban dictator wanted to form a Cuban baseball league and demanded that Amoros—one of the country's best-known professionals—manage one of the teams. But Amoros rejected the offer. ("I didn't know how to manage," he later explained.) Retribution was quick and costly. No longer was Amoros allowed to travel to Mexico to play baseball. Instead, he was confined to his ranch, a monthly ration of two pounds of meat for his family, and dreams of what might have been.

Sandy eventually secured passage on one of the "Freedom Flights" for his family and arrived in New York City on April 27, 1967. "I no have anything else except my family and my freedom," he told a reporter as he disembarked. "But that is good now." Unfortunately, it was not good enough. Migdalia soon left him and took their daughter to Miami. Left to his own devices, Amoros was forced to subsist in New York City on menial jobs and sometimes on public assistance.

The only bright spot was a decision by the Dodgers to give the thirty-seven-year-old Cuban a monthlong contract for $1,200 so that he could qualify for a pension when he reached the age of fifty. But those future benefits could not change his present life. And so moving to Tampa in 1977 seemed to be a wise move. As Sandy explained, "You don't need so many clothes."

There was no solace for the former Dodger in the Florida sunshine.

He could find only sporadic work and his health deteriorated. Suffering from diabetes, he began to experience poor circulation in his legs that produced excruciating pain. By the time he finally went to Tampa's Memorial Hospital in 1987, the doctors had no choice but to amputate part of his leg because of the onset of gangrene.

Chico Fernandez, one of Sandy's former teammates, brought his plight to the attention of the Baseball Assistance Team, and that charity made arrangements for a prosthetic device as well as a monthly supplement to his baseball pension. And then Brooklyn declared that June 20, 1992, would be Sandy Amoros day in the New York borough. There would be a parade and a ceremony that would culminate in the unveiling of a statue to celebrate Amoros' catch in the 1955 World Series. Amoros was interviewed by a *New York Times* reporter in his daughter's Miami apartment five days before the affair. Sandy still had that same smile, but whatever joy he felt was soon eclipsed by other events. He contracted pneumonia that very day and was rushed to Jackson Memorial Hospital. There he died on June 27, 1992, at the age of sixty-two.

Carl Furillo appeared to have many good years left after the 1956 season. He batted .306 in 1957 (tops on the team) and .290 after the team moved to Los Angeles in 1958. Injuries limited his play in 1959, and in April 1960 he tore a calf muscle as he was running down to first base on a ground ball. He assumed that he would be back in the lineup after the injury healed, but the Dodgers released him.

Furillo exploded when he learned of the Dodgers' decision because he believed it violated his contractual rights. The Dodgers believed otherwise. ("He had his day in the sun," said Bavasi. "It was over.") Carl's teammates counseled conciliation. ("The Dodgers take care of everything," Erskine advised him. "They're not going to let you go hungry.") But Furillo could not abide by the decision. He retained a lawyer and threatened a lawsuit. The ensuing publicity was not favorable to the Dodgers.

The matter was ultimately settled, but the personal cost to the Reading Rifle appeared to be high. Never again would he be able to find a job in professional baseball as a coach or in any other capacity. Bavasi and other major-league officials, of course, denied that Furillo was blacklisted because of his public challenge to the owners' prerogatives. But Furillo believed otherwise.

Carl supported his family with a variety of jobs outside of baseball. (When asked at one point why a man of his stature would work construction, the former Dodger had a quick answer: "I like to eat.") He and his family eventually returned to Stony Creek Mills, and it was there that a physician advised the fifty-four-year-old Furillo in 1976 that the lumps on his neck were a manifestation of leukemia. At Fern's urging, he supplemented the medical treatment with vitamins, and the leukemia was soon in remission. ("I don't know what the hell you're doing," the physician told his patient, "but keep it up.")

Carl felt well enough in 1983 to attend the Dodgers' fantasy camp in Vero Beach, where he quickly became a favorite among the campers (and long after he had made his last appearance in 1987, campers would insist that the Dodgers hang a portrait of Furillo in the locker room). But nothing lasts forever. One morning in January 1989, Fern went downstairs to make breakfast. When Carl did not join her, she trudged up the stairs into their bedroom. "Hey, sleepyhead," she said, "are you going to sleep all day or what?" When her husband did not respond, she leaned over to touch him. His skin was cold, and Fern knew immediately that something was wrong.

The funeral was attended by Koufax, Erskine, and other former teammates. There was, however, no solace for Carl Jr. He had been planning a fishing trip with his father for his sixty-seventh birthday in March, and he could not let go of his father's memory. And then one night he was awakened from a deep sleep, and there, in his bedroom, stood his father, wearing his familiar khaki pants and T-shirt. Carl Jr., now in his thirties, started to cry. "Why are you crying?" his father asked. "Because I miss you so much," the son replied. "Look," said his father. "You've got to stop this. This is not good." And as Carl Jr. tried to reach for his father, the elder Furillo turned him aside. "You can't touch me," he said. "When the time comes, I'll come for you. But you're going to live a long time. So go back to sleep." And with that, Carl Jr. fell into a deep sleep, only to awaken the next morning with a sense of relief that he had not felt since his father had died.

Although the 1957 season was not a productive one for him, Roy Campanella had much to look forward to in Los Angeles before the accident near his Long Island home in January 1958. The left-field foul line was only 250 feet from home plate, and Campanella told one sportswriter before the season began, "I'm looking forward to a real good year."

The automobile accident not only disrupted Campanella's baseball career. It also undermined the prosperous life he had built for himself in New York. He had told his older son that "living well is the best revenge" in combating racism, and he had made considerable strides on that front. He had that large home on Long Island's North Shore (where he catered to his obsession with toy trains and tropical fish), a forty-one-foot powerboat, and a liquor store in Harlem that was a magnet for people who wanted to converse with the famous Dodger. (Roy had entrusted his precocious eight-year-old son with the responsibility for placing wholesale orders, and Roy Jr. later told me that liquor distributors "were shocked" when the young boy handled their calls.)

None of that was the same after the accident. And then he left Ruthe amidst allegations of her adultery and mistreatment of him (which Ruthe attributed to his "suspicious mind"). But he did have a new cause that would remain a focus for the rest of his life: as he explained in the autobiography he dictated after the accident, he had "taken on an even bigger job" than fighting for racial equality— "fighting for the equality, integration, and understanding and acceptance of the severely handicapped."

Events both spontaneous and planned gave Campanella a platform to pursue that new role. One occasion was Roy's visit to Yankee Stadium in October 1958 to cover the World Series for the Hearst newspapers. Arriving after the game had commenced, Campanella's entourage realized that his wheelchair would not fit through the narrow passageway to his box seat. With no other alternative, two large firemen lifted Campanella up and carried him down the aisle while Don Larsen was getting ready to pitch to the batter. At first there was scattered applause and shouts of, "Hi, slugger," and, "Attaboy, Campy," from nearby patrons. But, as the press reported the next day, the display of support for the

former Dodger spread quickly: "Like two mighty waves rolling in opposite directions, the applause and cheers swept down the first-base line
and down the third-base line until they met in the distant bleachers."
Larsen stepped off the mound, the umpire moved back from the plate,
and the game was brought to a halt as the applause and cheering reached
a crescendo that lasted for several minutes.

There was a continuous stream of additional tributes for the stricken
athlete over the next thirty-five years: a ceremony at the Los Angeles
Coliseum in June 1959 attended by more than ninety-three thousand
fans, countless articles, election to the Baseball Hall of Fame, and even
a television movie about his life. Not that Roy was a passive observer
in all this. He had a radio talk show, responsibility as an instructor at
the Dodgers' spring training camps, and, when Tommy Lasorda became the Dodger manager in 1977, a job as a team coach. ("I know you
can't walk," the rookie manager told Campanella, "but there's nothing
wrong with your mind.")

He had a new wife named Roxie who tended to his physical needs,
but her tireless efforts could not eliminate all the problems her husband
encountered. Roy always tried to convey a joyful optimism, but life
was a periodic series of medical traumas that became more frequent as
time progressed. On the last Saturday in June 1993, Roxie called Roy
Jr. and told him that his father, nearing his seventy-second birthday,
had died suddenly of a massive heart attack at his home in Woodland
Hills, California.

Billy Martin knew at the beginning of the 1957 season that his days as
a Yankee were numbered. "One thing goes wrong this year," general
manager George Weiss told him, "you're gone." Ironically, the cause
for Martin's departure was a fight in which he did not participate.
Mantle, Bauer, and other Yankees took their wives out to celebrate
Billy's twenty-ninth birthday in May and found themselves in the Copacabana on New York City's East Side. Verbal confrontations with a
group of bowlers (who were hurling racial epithets at entertainer
Sammy Davis Jr.) led to a challenge for a fight (with those words that
Billy Martin could never resist—"Let's go"). The Copa bouncers decked
one of the bowlers in the men's room before any of the Yankees could

take a swing, but the next day's newspaper headlines enraged Weiss: "Yankees Brawl at the Copa."

Stengel gave Martin news of his trade to the Athletics on June 15 when the team was in Kansas City. Over the next four years, there was no shortage of general managers interested in having the former Yankee on their team—each believing that the fiery second baseman would lead the team to a pennant. ("I never claim a pennant in advance," said Cleveland GM Frank Lane after the Indians acquired Martin in 1959, "but with the acquisition of an experienced second baseman, we are now a sounder club.")

Unfortunately, none of those expectations was fulfilled. Martin could never muster the same drive that he had with the Yankees. "After I was traded," he later confessed, "I wasn't the same player. It felt like my heart was broken."

Martin became a coach for the Minnesota Twins in 1965 and used that opportunity to launch one of the most successful managerial careers in baseball history. The first triumph was in 1969 with the Twins. Billy transformed a mediocre club into an aggressive unit that won the West Division. Despite that achievement, Twins' owner Calvin Griffith fired Martin after the season because of a series of indiscretions (including a well-publicized fight in a bar with Twins pitcher Dave Boswell). Not that Griffith should have been surprised. He told a sportswriter after signing Martin at the beginning of the season that he felt like he was "sitting on a keg of dynamite."

Other owners soon learned to appreciate Martin's talents as well as that volatile personality. He brought the Detroit Tigers winning seasons in the early 1970s but was fired after a series of confrontations with the general manager. That was followed by a miraculous turnaround with the Texas Rangers (who finished second in the division after having lost 105 games in the season before Martin joined the team). Perhaps no incident was more telling of Martin's managerial style than the time when third baseman Toby Harrah was struck on the arm by a pitch and immediately slumped to the ground, writhing in pain. "I'm thinking," Harrah later remembered, "Billy's going to come up and say, 'Hey, Tobe, how ya doin'?" Instead, Martin leaned over Harrah and whispered, "Listen, Toby, when you get on first, I want you to steal second on the first pitch."

The relocation to Texas was as much symbolic as real. "He likened himself to a gunfighter," said his son Billy Martin Jr. And so Martin changed his appearance to match the image—growing a mustache and wearing a cowboy hat, cowboy boots, and other Western garb. It ultimately proved to be too much for the Rangers' management, who could not abide the constant confrontations or Billy's fondness for the bottle. The drinking was especially troublesome. It was a widely known problem that often kept people on edge because they never knew when Martin might explode. "I went out with him a lot," said Tony Kubek, "and you would say, 'Uh-oh. This next drink is going to be the one. And I'm not going to be there when he has that drink.'"

George Steinbrenner surely understood the risks of any association with Billy Martin when he hired him as the Yankees' manager in July 1975. But the Cleveland shipbuilder also had a dream—restoring the now second-rate Yankees to the glory days of their past. And he was sure—like all those previous owners—that Billy had the managerial skills to bring a pennant to Yankee Stadium. Martin did in fact bring the World Series back to New York, but he and Steinbrenner remained locked in a constant state of conflict as each tried to control the team's destiny. And so, over the next fourteen years, he would be fired five times by Steinbrenner, only to be rehired on four separate occasions.

Martin found further success when he assumed the helm of the Oakland Athletics in 1980 after his initial managerial tours with the Yankees. Martin applied the same approach that had worked so well in the past and, as before, the players responded to his incurable optimism. After losing 108 games and finishing last in 1979, the team won eighty-three games, finished second in the division, and drew five hundred thousand more fans to the games—all of which brought Martin recognition as the American League's Manager of the Year. (Billboards in Oakland reflected the city's pride in their new manager: "Nothing but Billyball. Catch it.") And when the team began the 1981 season with a 20–3 record, Billy's face graced the cover of *Time* magazine, which described Martin's transformation of the Athletics as "incredible."

The success was too much for Steinbrenner to ignore, and he lured
Billy back to New York. (Not that Martin played hard to get—when
his son asked the former Yankee why he would want to return to the
tension of a relationship with Steinbrenner, Billy had a quick response:
"I'm not happy anywhere else.") After he was fired by Steinbrenner for
the last time in 1988, the sixty-year-old Martin retreated to the horse
farm he had purchased in upstate New York for his fourth wife. It was
there on Christmas day in 1989 that his pickup truck crashed into a
stone culvert as he was returning from a local bar with Bill Reedy, his
longtime drinking buddy. There remains a question whether Billy or
Reedy was driving. But there is no question that the impact broke Martin's neck and that he died instantly.

Although he hit forty home runs in 1957 (marking the fifth consecutive
year in which he had reached that mark), Duke Snider was not pleased
with the Dodgers' third-place finish. And he was even less pleased by
the Dodgers' move to Los Angeles. He did not relish the thought of
playing in the Los Angeles Coliseum, where the distance down the
right-field foul line was 402 feet.

Still, Snider did well in those first two years in Los Angeles (with
batting averages of .312 and .308), and he hit a home run in the 1959
World Series (thus giving him a National League record of eleven
round-trippers in series play). But his knee continued to restrict his
play, and the Dodgers traded him to the New York Mets in 1963. The
trade reflected more than a change in venue. The Mets were a new
franchise with a propensity to lose and a reputation for comical mis-
haps. "It was," Snider later said, "a miserable experience."

The Mets acceded to Snider's request for a new team, and he
played his last year with the San Francisco Giants in 1964. He had
only 167 at bats and a .210 batting average—the lowest of his career.
And so, when the season ended, Duke packed his bags for the last
time as a player. He had played long enough to have more than two
thousand hits and 407 home runs, but those last few years gave him
little pleasure. "I should have retired," he later told me, "when the
Dodgers sold me to the Mets." But he had four children in school and
needed the money.

Duke's financial concerns were well-founded. An investment in a bowling alley soured. The avocado ranch took too much time for too little profit. And so the only regular income Snider had in those first retirement days was a scouting position with the Dodgers that paid $250 a week. "It made for a lot of sleepless nights staring at the ceiling," he later recalled.

After an unsuccessful tenure as a minor-league coach, Snider found a more suitable role as a broadcaster for the Montreal Expos. A change in job locations was not the only transformation in Snider's life. At Bev's suggestion, he attended a service at the Neighborhood Church near Fallbrook, and, after it was completed, he decided, like his wife, to ask "Christ to come into my life and live in and through me." That decision did not mean that he would become more religious. "Religion," he explained to me, "is different than Christianity. The difference is that it's not what you do. You can't do anything for God. Jesus Christ—you invite him into your heart. He's an in-growing spirit."

The decision to accept Christ coincided with Duke's election to the National Baseball Hall of Fame in 1980. Now content with his place in baseball history, Snider began spending time with his family, attending Dodger fantasy camps in Vero Beach, and, after the memorabilia business exploded in the mid-1980s, attending card shows. The shows generated substantial revenue for the Hall of Fame outfielder, but the Internal Revenue Service later learned that the former Dodger had failed to report $100,000 of income that he had earned from the shows. And so, in July 1995 Duke Snider found himself in a Brooklyn courtroom where he pleaded guilty to a felony for tax fraud. Speaking to a battery of reporters after the arraignment, the sixty-eight-year-old Snider—now heavier than he was in his playing days, with his hair thinning and completely white—confessed that his failing health caused him to make the wrong choice for the benefit of his wife. "One of my concerns," he explained, "was whether she would have enough money."

Although it could not immunize him from a sentence (a fine of $5,000 and two years' probation), the explanation did have a ring of truth to it. Because Duke Snider's health was indeed failing. But he persevered and always tried to be present when the Dodgers held their annual fantasy camps. To ease the pain of traversing the widespread facility at Vero Beach, he used a golf cart to travel from point to point. And so those who came to the camp often saw the Hall of Fame Dodger—the man who had "steel springs in his legs"—whisking up and down the camp's pathways with wisps of his white hair blowing in the breeze.

Mickey Mantle played with the Yankees for twelve more seasons before retiring in March 1969. The statistical record was enough to earn him induction into the Hall of Fame in 1974—his first year of eligibility: 536 home runs (third on the all-time list at the time), 1,509 runs batted in, and a .298 batting average. But much of his allure was what might have been if he had not been plagued by injuries. He played in 150 or more games in only three of those twelve seasons, and often he was still hurting when he did play. "I used to love to run," he told a sportswriter at one point. "Now it hurts to run."

By the time he retired, Mantle was perhaps the most beloved player in baseball. A turning point came in 1961 when he and teammate Roger Maris competed with each other to surpass Babe Ruth's then-magical milestone of sixty home runs in a season. Fans and teammates alike hoped that Mantle would be the one to succeed. And so crowds who had once booed the Yankee center fielder even when he was doing well now cheered his every move—and transferred their jeers to Maris as he came closer to the record. ("Hey," Mantle asked his teammate, "are you trying to steal my fans?")

Mickey remained a fan favorite over the ensuing years even as his performance faltered and he was reduced to almost limping around the bases. "Today," said one sportswriter in 1968, "Mantle is one of the great heroes of America's sports fans wherever he goes. He is cheered louder for hitting homers in batting practice than many players are for hitting them out of the park during the game."

Retirement was not easy at first. A job in an office or any public forum was out of the question. He could not go anywhere without being mobbed by fans. And so he used his fame to make business investments and to garner speaking engagements. ("As he grew older," said Bob Wolff, "this shy guy became one of the premier storytellers.")

The demand for Mickey's signature skyrocketed when the memorabilia craze hit the country in the mid-1980s. Suddenly his autograph on anything—a photo, a baseball, or a bat—would attract hundreds, and sometimes thousands, of dollars. And now more than ever people were eager to be in his presence. (There was time when Bill Liederman—who had opened a restaurant with Mantle in New York City—came to him with a request from a caller who wanted the Yankee outfielder to attend his son's bar mitzvah. "Fuck bar mitzvahs," Mantle responded. "Tell 'em fifty grand"—no doubt thinking that the answer would end the inquiry. But when Liederman passed on the message—without the reference to bar mitzvahs—the caller could not have been more excited. "Deal!" he exclaimed.)

Mantle further exploited the nostalgia obsession with the fantasy camp he and Whitey Ford established in Florida (and which he continued to run after Whitey opened a separate camp). It not only capitalized on his aura but also gave him an opportunity to do something for his former teammates, who could earn needed money as coaches for older Yankee fans who spent thousands of dollars to play baseball for a week with their childhood heroes.

For other people in other circumstances, all of this might have been facile way to make a living. But Mickey Mantle was not one to move easily among strangers. And so liquor became his crutch.

He had, of course, begun his indulgence shortly after he came to the Yankees. The pace of Mantle's drinking accelerated when he left baseball. Everyone wanted to give him a drink. That would have been trouble enough by itself. But Mickey usually had a couple of vodka tonics to calm his nerves before he went to any social event. By nighttime, he was often in oblivion, sometimes impatient and even nasty with strangers, and often forgetful about where he was or what he was supposed to be doing. The low point probably came with a speech in December 1993 when he introduced Reverend Wayne Monroe, who had organized the fund-raising event, by saying, "Here's the fucking preacher."

In the meantime, his marriage with Merlyn disintegrated. ("Mick was one of those men," Merlyn later observed, "who wanted to be married, but only part-time.") His sons were perhaps the real victims in this marital conflict, and Mantle would later bemoan his failure to give them the same attention that Mutt had given him—until they became his drinking partners.

Mantle checked himself into the Betty Ford Center in Rancho Mirage, California, in January 1995. The first task at the clinic was to write a letter to Mutt to explain his situation. "You talk about sad," Mantle later said. "It only took me ten minutes to write the letter and I cried the whole time." But he persevered and returned to Dallas with a new perspective—without alcohol. But it proved to be too little, too late.

On May 28, 1995, Mantle was rushed to the Baylor University Medical Center in Dallas with stomach cramps. The diagnosis: liver cancer. The former Yankee received a liver transplant on June 8, but it did not eliminate the cancer and Mantle was forced to return to the hospital within a couple of weeks to face a disease that could not be controlled. And so the family reached out to the people who meant the most to Mickey Mantle—his former teammates.

One of the first to be called was Bobby Richardson. From all appearances, he and Mantle could not have been more different. But Mickey respected his former teammate's commitment to religion even though Mantle himself had never been one to attend church. The two former players stayed in touch after they had retired, even purchasing a town house together on Grandfather Mountain near Boone, North Carolina.

Richardson received the call in late June 1995 at his South Carolina home. Mickey had returned to the hospital and was asking for him. A few other teammates were there as well. Whitey Ford was particularly taken by the pain Mantle had to endure. There was an intravenous tube that would feed him pain medication, but it would have to be replenished constantly. "You would be talking with him," Ford remembered, "and he would say, looking at the machine, 'How much time do I have left?'" For Ford, it was tough to watch. "As much as I loved him," he later said, "I was glad he finally went."

The passage for the sixty-three-year-old Mantle finally occurred in the early-morning hours of August 13, 1995, with Merlyn and his son David each holding a hand.

Pee Wee Reese played with the Dodgers for two more seasons before retiring. Fortunately, there was an alternative. CBS was televising the Game of the Week and needed someone to join the incomparable Dizzy Dean as a commentator. Dean had been the National League's premier pitcher in the 1930s until Cleveland Indians' outfielder Earl Averill smashed a line drive that hit Dean in the foot in the 1937 All-Star game. And so a promising career was cut short.

Dean was a big man (six feet, two inches and 180 pounds) from rural Arkansas with little education but a gift for gab, and in retirement he became an even bigger man (in excess of three hundred pounds) with a personality that would not quit. It was well suited to television. All he needed in 1959 was a new partner.

Reese seemed to be a perfect fit. He too had a famous name but, more important, he had a sophisticated demeanor that would contrast well with Dean's buffoonery. The two men developed into an engaging team that provided insight and entertainment on the weekly broadcast. ("Podnuh," Dean would often say in his Southern drawl after Reese had finished two innings of on-air commentary, "that wasn't too bad, but I guess I'm going to have to pick things back up.")

For Reese, the experience could not have been better. "He loved working with Dizzy," Mark Reese remembered. And then NBC purchased the Game of the Week in 1966 and replaced Dean with Curt Gowdy, who had been broadcasting the Red Sox games. From Reese's perspective, the arrangement with his new partner seemed to be working well. And then one day in March 1969 he got a telephone call from a reporter after he got off a golf course in Louisville. He had been fired. The former shortstop was incredulous. It was not only the failure to understand the cause of the firing. It was equally difficult for Reese to accept the way in which he was informed—hearing it from a reporter instead of the company. ("Those gutless sons of bitches," Reese complained to intimates. "They didn't have the balls to tell me face-to-face.")

The dismissal did not leave Reese with any financial concerns. He had a variety of business interests in Louisville. He and Dottie also had a lifestyle that left little to be desired. His daughter, Barbara, had grown up and was on her way to giving him grandchildren. His son, Mark, was still in school in Louisville but would soon be playing baseball at the University of Alabama. And then there was golf. Reese was passionate about the game and enjoyed success in being almost a scratch golfer. Still, he wanted some kind of employment, and so, in 1971, he joined the staff of Hillerich & Bradsby, the Louisville company that produced baseball bats (including the celebrated Louisville Slugger).

In all of this serenity, there was only one unsettled issue for Reese: whether he would be inducted into Baseball's Hall of Fame. The first fifteen years of his eligibility passed without an affirmative vote, and in 1983 his name was passed on to the Veterans' Committee. And then, on March 5, 1984, Reese—who was promoting bats at the Boston Red Sox spring training camp in Florida—received a telephone call from a reporter telling him of his election. "You're sure?" Reese replied. "You're not kidding? It's true?" And so, when he gave his speech at the induction ceremony that August, Reese paid tribute to Durocher ("he gave a scared kid from Louisville the opportunity to play") and Dottie ("I wore No. 1 on my back for all those years I played, but she was No. 1 in my heart").

The sixty-six-year-old Reese retired from Hillerich & Bradsby in 1985 and divided his time between homes in Louisville and Florida, playing golf, attending card shows, and making appearances at the Dodger fantasy camps. And then he was diagnosed with prostate cancer. The first doctor told him that it was terminal. But Pee Wee was a fighter. "I just switched doctors," he later told a reporter, "had everything cut out, and now I'm fine." ("Hell," the seventy-five-year-old Reese told his son about the removal of his prostate gland, "I don't need it anyway.")

He resumed life in the belief that he had conquered cancer. But in March 1997 he was diagnosed with lung cancer. By the spring of 1999, the cancer settled in his brain, he became confined to a wheelchair, and, perhaps worst of all, he began to lose his cognitive abilities. "Pee Wee is often delirious, sometimes delusional," Mark Reese wrote to sportswriter Roger Kahn a few months later. "The other day he stared at me with a blank look and said, 'All my life I've pondered sleep.'" The next day—Saturday, August 15, 1999—the eighty-one-year-old Reese slipped away to that permanent sleep.

Yogi Berra remained a stalwart of the Yankee offense for several years after 1956. By 1962, he was playing less and the press was speculating whether he might retire and become a manager. Still, Yogi was caught off guard when Ralph Houk approached him in spring training in 1963 and asked if he would like to manage. "Manage who?" said a surprised Berra. The Yankees, Houk replied. Houk explained that a decision had been made for him to become the team's general manager in 1964, thus creating the vacancy that Berra could fill.

On October 24, 1963, the Yankees announced that the thirty-eight-year-old Berra would retire and become the team's new manager. Yogi left behind a remarkable record of achievement, including 358 home runs (313 as a catcher, a major-league record) and career World Series records for the most hits and doubles. His election to Baseball's National Hall of Fame was never in doubt (and would come in 1972), but there was no similar assurance about his forthcoming performance as manager.

Berra found that managing the Yankees—for all their history and talent—was no guarantee of success. In a roller-coaster season, the Yankees were often chasing the Chicago White Sox for the American League lead. Although there were many factors to explain the club's predicament, much of the blame was placed on the rookie manager. He was, said some, too slow to relieve a starting pitcher who faltered. Others said he made strategic errors in filling gaps created by injured players. And many players found fault because he failed to discipline teammates who were disrespectful. ("A gentle soul," Mantle later said. "He didn't have the heart to bawl out players who deserved it.") By July—with the team struggling to regain first place—Houk decided that Berra would have to be replaced as manager for the 1965 season.

Yogi knew nothing of that decision and continued to push for victories. On the last day of the season, the team won its ninety-ninth game and the American League pennant. The seven-game World Series was lost to the Cardinals, but no one—at least so Berra thought—could complain about that. So he was expecting a new contract, perhaps a raise, and certainly congratulations for a job well-done. Instead, he got fired. ("It was pretty shocking," he later said.) The Yankees offered him a consulting job, but Yogi turned it down and accepted an offer from the New York Mets to join Casey Stengel—that club's first manager—as a coach.

Former Dodger Gil Hodges became the Mets' manager in 1968, and he asked Berra to stay on as a coach. Life took an unexpected turn on April 2, 1972. Hodges died in Florida after an afternoon of golf with three of his coaches. The next day Yogi received a telephone call from Mets owner Don Grant, who offered him a two-year managerial contract. Carmen and Joe Garagiola tried to dissuade Yogi from taking the job. Coaches last forever, they counseled. Managers get fired. None of that mattered to Yogi. "I had a strong desire to take the Mets job," he later said, "and I did."

Berra's first foray as a National League manager was certainly respectable. The Mets battled for first place through much of the season and ultimately finished third. Life spiraled downward in the beginning of 1973 season and by the middle of August, the Mets were in last place. Yogi was not prepared to give up and kept telling his players that "it ain't over till it's over." His optimisim was contagious, and the Mets won twenty-nine of their last forty-three games to finish first in their division. They then defeated the Cincinnati Reds in the play-offs to win the National League pennant.

No one was more proud than Berra. He had taken a team of young and largely inexperienced players to the pinnacle. Still, he knew that much of the team's success was tied to the discipline that had been instilled by Gil Hodges. And so, after the team beat Cincinnati in the fifth game of the play-offs, Yogi went to his office in the clubhouse, closed the door, and called Hodges' widow in Brooklyn. "I did not win this," he said to Joan Hodges in a voice cracking with emotion. "This was your husband's team." It was a gesture she never forgot, and years later Joan Hodges would say of Yogi Berra, "I hope he lives to 150."

Although the Mets lost to the Oakland Athletics in the World Series, Yogi was rewarded with a three-year contract at an annual salary of

$75,000. But the magic was gone. The team finished next-to-last in its division in 1974 and continued to struggle in 1975. Yogi was fired in August after the team lost five games in a row and were all but removed from contention.

Yogi returned to his business interests and his family in Montclair, New Jersey, but not for long. When he learned that he would be the Yankees' manager for the 1976 season, Billy Martin's first call was to ask his former teammate to become a coach. ("Yogi's a rare breed," said the former Yankee second baseman.)

Martin came and went as manager (and came again), but Berra remained a Yankee coach for the next eight seasons, providing some stability to the tumultuous reign of George Steinbrenner. The same attributes that made Yogi a popular player contributed to his high standing as a coach. "I think an hour with him," said Yankee pitcher Catfish Hunter, "can make you feel good all day."

Steinbrenner no doubt appreciated Berra's appeal. And so, when the team faltered under Martin's leadership in 1983, the Yankees' principal owner asked Berra to replace him for the 1984 season. The news was well received in the press, but the results were disappointing. The Yankees finished third, and Steinbrenner was not pleased. Still, the Yankees' principal owner made it clear that there would no change in management for the new season. "Yogi will be the manager this year, period," he told the press in February 1985. "A bad start will not affect Yogi's status either." Reassuring words that were soon forgotten when the Yankees began the season with a record of six wins and ten losses. Yankee general manager Clyde King called Berra after a night game in Chicago to tell him that Billy Martin would be managing the team for its next game in Texas.

To the press, Berra was nonchalant about his firing. "What's the use of getting angry?" he told one sportswriter. But he was bitter about the way he had been fired, saying that Steinbrenner—not some underling—should have been the one to call with the news. And so he vowed never to step foot inside Yankee Stadium again as long as Steinbrenner was the team's owner.

In the meantime, he spent a few years as a coach for the Houston Astros and then had his autobiography published. That was followed by an almost endless stream of best-selling books that capitalized on Yogi's penchant for malapropisms. With the popularity of his books, it was only natural that Aflac—a company that provided insurance for disabled workers—enlist Yogi's services to promote its name in humorous television commercials that featured a talking duck. (In later describing to Bobby Richardson how the commercials were filmed, Yogi took care to explain, "You know, the duck doesn't really talk.")

However much the books and commercials contributed to his fame and income, Yogi took more satisfaction from the museum established in his honor at Montclair State University in New Jersey. The museum not only houses Berra's memorabilia but also provides a learning center for children of all ages. "He is very, very proud of it," said Dave Kaplan, who has been the museum's director since its founding.

Just as the museum was opening its doors in 1998, Yogi received a telephone call from Suzyn Waldman, a Yankee broadcaster, asking whether reconciliation with George Steinbrenner might be possible. "Yogi was a little suspicious at first," said Kaplan. "He thought it was just another scheme to get him to come back to Yankee Stadium." Berra finally consented, and it was agreed that the Yankee owner would meet his former manager at the museum at five p.m. on January 5, 1999. The appointed hour came and went without Steinbrenner's appearance. At five minutes after five o'clock, a very nervous Steinbrenner walked in through the museum's back door accompanied only by his driver. Yogi glanced down at his watch, looked up at Steinbrenner, and said, "You're late." Everyone laughed, and the tension was suddenly lifted.

Yogi, Carmen, and George then retreated to Kaplan's office (later referred to by participants as "Camp David"). "You know, Yogi," Steinbrenner confessed, "what I did fourteen years ago when I fired you and the manner in which I did was probably the worst mistake I ever made in baseball. I hope you will look into your heart and forgive me. We want you back at Yankee Stadium." Yogi had received what he wanted and was gracious in response. "George," he said, "I've made a lot of mistakes too." The two Yankee stalwarts shook hands and hugged.

Thus began a new era in Yogi Berra's life. He became an assistant to the Yankee owner and would make appearances at events, talk with Yankee general manager Brian Cashman about a variety of topics, and provide advice at spring training (during the month of March) and during the season as well. "He is like a clubhouse rat," said Kaplan, who would drive Yogi to the stadium. "He just loves that whole atmosphere and being with the guys."

Health issues began to arise as Yogi aged. His physician diagnosed an arrhythmia shortly before he turned seventy. Although it was not life-threatening, Yogi was sufficiently concerned to change some habits. No longer would he smoke. Drinking was curtailed to a daily glass of vodka. And exercise became a daily ritual.

He continues to attend baseball fantasy camps and spends the month of January playing golf in Palm Springs. And—especially surprising for someone who never made it into high school (let alone out of high school)—he continues to enjoy the status of being one of the country's most quoted individuals.

Andy Carey and Casey Stengel continued to argue about the third baseman's batting style after 1956. "Carey and Casey cannot get together on the batter Andy really is," said one sportswriter in 1957. "Carey thinks he is a power hitter and swings for the circuit. Casey insists that Andy must learn to hit with the pitch."

The Alameda native had some marginal success in 1958 (twelve home runs and a .286 batting average in 102 games), but life took an unexpected turn shortly after the 1959 season began. Andy noticed some spots on his face and suspected measles. "You'll wish it was measles before it's over," said the doctor. The doctor knew what he was talking about. The condition was not measles but mononucleosis, a debilitating illness that stayed with him the remainder of the season and left him unable to play. ("He was weak as a kitten," Gil McDougald remembered.)

Carey geared up for the 1960 season with a daily dose of vitamin B_{12}, but it was too little, too late. The Yankees now had Clete Boyer, a twenty-three-year-old prospect who was a better glove man at third base than Andy. And so Stengel came to him one day toward the end of May and simply said, "Well, Carey, we just traded you to Kansas City."

Carey enjoyed only moderate success with the Athletics but seemed to be doing better with the White Sox in 1961. ("I was hitting the shit out of the ball," he remembered.) And then he sustained a painful injury after sliding into second base in one game. His batting average sank from .340 to .266, and his thoughts drifted to a life outside baseball.

The Philadelphia Phillies sent him a contract for the 1962 season, but the thirty-year-old Carey decided to send it back unsigned. Andy already had many other interests he wanted to pursue, including a position as a stockbroker with a Los Angeles firm. There was the personal side of it too. Lucy had all but abandoned her acting career, and Andy believed that he should also be at their Southern California home with the family (which now included a two-year-old daughter in addition to his five-year-old son). "This kid has definitely decided to give up the game," Phillies manager Gene Mauch told a sportswriter who inquired about Carey's status. "He wants to be home with his wife and family."

There was, however, a qualification to Carey's decision to retire. As he later told *The Sporting News*, "Lucy and I had decided that . . . I would play only with the Dodgers or [the Los Angeles] Angels." And so, as Mauch was telling the press that Carey was hanging up his spikes, the Dodgers were announcing that they had purchased the former Yankee's contract from the White Sox.

Carey saw very little action with the Dodgers. In fact, the season's most memorable moment was a hitless appearance during the team's first game in Philadelphia. Andy Carey was not a well-loved figure in the City of Brotherly Love. He had rejected an opportunity to play for the Phillies with talk about retirement and then signed a contract to play with the Dodgers. Not surprisingly, there were boos and catcalls when he stepped into the batter's box to pinch-hit with the bases loaded. And when he struck out, the fans rose with cheers and applause. "That was," Carey later said with amusement, "the only time I got a standing ovation."

The Dodgers released Carey on October 19, 1962—the day after his thirty-first birthday. Still, there was much satisfaction in his new life. Business flourished, his children got older, and baseball became an almost forgotten part of his past. But the satisfaction was short-lived. By 1974, he and Lucy were divorced, and Andy was on the road to a second marriage with Carolyn Long.

Maintaining good relations with Lucy after the divorce was understandably difficult. The challenge, Andy soon learned, was to retain the love of his two teenage children. They were apparently convinced that their father had made a bad decision for the wrong reason. And so they would have nothing to do with him—a separation that pained their father and caused untold guilt when Jimmy died in tragic circumstances in California in February 1980 at the age of twenty-two. Andy believed that, in some indirect way, he was responsible for his son's death, and never would he discuss the circumstances of the incident with anyone but his closest family members.

In the meantime, his divorce from Lucy coincided with a change in business careers. The securities business was forsaken for a fishing business in the Pacific Islands, and, when that failed, he returned to the United States to pursue a career in insurance, which, like the securities business, required a license. ("I think," said Carey years later, "I've had every license known to man.") That business prospered and, for a time, so did his marriage with Carolyn. But after the arrival of two children, that marriage floundered as well. By the time the millennium had passed, Andy Carey was a single man again.

He had already known Susie Parker as a friend for a couple of years when they began to date. He invited her to a golf tournament in May 2002, and the marriage was held on June 14 of that year.

In the meantime, Carey's business interests were augmented by appearances at card shows because, as Carey had learned almost from the first days of retirement, being a former Bronx Bomber had its benefits. "They always remember you with the Yankees," he later said. And, as the years went by, it became a humbling honor to remember the prominent Yankees who had been his teammates—Joe DiMaggio, Mickey Mantle, Yogi Berra, and Whitey Ford. "Imagine a young kid," he would later say, "and I'm playing on a team with all these Hall of Famers. I look back and think I was the luckiest guy in the world."

Unfortunately, his luck did not hold out. In the spring of 2005, he slipped on the stairs in his Newport Beach villa and fell down. Although seventy-four, Carey had been physically active and should have weathered the incident without serious injury. But the fall precipitated physical repercussions that almost defy explanation. He became paralyzed from the waist down and could not remember anything—even, according to his wife, Susie, the two children by Carolyn Long "that he would live and die for."

The doctors identified the cause as "psychological paralyzation"— Andy's physical response to the guilt he continued to experience over the estrangement from his first two children with Lucy and, more important, the premature death of his son Jimmy.

The road to recovery was a slow and painful one. "He had to learn how to do everything all over again," Susie explained. "How to walk, how to brush his teeth, how to talk." But progress was made, and while he has not regained his prior form, Andy is now able to play golf and talk about those days when he wore Yankee pinstripes.

Jim Gilliam remained an integral part of the Dodger team for many years after 1956. Although he never batted above .282 in any of those years, he continued to command respect for his ability to get on base through walks as well as hits, to steal bases, and to play almost flawlessly in the field. "Gilliam's trouble," said one sportswriter on the eve of the 1959 World Series, "seems to be he's too steady a player. He performs at such a consistently high standard, day in and day out, that he becomes monotonous."

That consistent performance—and Gilliam's willingness to sacrifice his own preferences for the team's good—drew criticism when the Dodgers battled the San Francisco Giants for the pennant in 1962 (ultimately won by the Giants in a three-game play-off series). The criticism arose from Alston's decision to have Gilliam bat second in the lineup behind shortstop Maury Wills, who had an extraordinary ability to steal bases (and would break Ty Cobb's 1915 record of ninety-six steals in a season with 104 in 1962). Gilliam would often take a pitch he would otherwise swing at if he saw that Wills was running toward second for an attempted steal. "Out of the corner of my eye," he later explained, "I might see Maury got a good jump on the pitcher, and I'd let the ball go by." Conversely, if Wills did not get a good jump, he would, as Buzzie Bavasi later explained, "foul the pitch off"—and thus give Wills another chance to make a steal.

Some said that Gilliam's self-sacrifice may have cost the team the pennant. "There must have been twenty times last season," said one umpire in early 1963, "when Wills was on first that I saw Junior Gilliam lay off a pitch. They were pitching outside to Gilliam then, and he can hit an outside pitch as well as any man in baseball—especially with the shortstop covering second, which he always was with Wills."

By 1964, time seemed to be catching up with Gilliam. He struggled at the plate and wound up with a .228 batting average, the lowest of his career. Despite the sagging numbers, the Dodgers valued his knowledge and the quiet manner in which he conveyed advice. The decision to make him a coach for the 1965 season (making him only the third black coach in the major leagues) was announced in September 1964, and Gilliam received well-deserved recognition on the last day of the season with a standing ovation from the fans and his teammates.

Little did they know that Gilliam would be activated early in the 1965 season to help his team win yet another World Championship. The accolades that followed his performance in that World Series did not affect the Dodgers' decision for the 1966 season, and, once again, the Nashville native retired to become a Dodger coach. And once again, Alston changed his mind after the season started and reactivated Gilliam so that there would be someone who could be available in late innings to play third base or pinch-hit.

However understandable Alston's decision may have seemed at the time, Gilliam could not achieve the same glory he had enjoyed in the 1965 season. He saw action in only eighty-eight games and plunged to a career low in batting average (.217). And so, while the Dodgers won the pennant again, Gilliam was disclosing to anyone who would listen that he was *really* going to retire and become a full-time coach in the following season. "I've had it," the thirty-seven-year-old player told one sportswriter. "This time I mean it."

And mean it he did. He became—and remained—the first-base coach for the entire season. And enjoyed it as well. "As a coach," he explained to one sportswriter, "I feel I'm just as much a part of the game as the men on the field. And I get just as much of a kick out of seeing a player I've worked with get a hit or make a tough stop as I would doing it myself."

He also had the time to pursue other interests at spring training or

in Los Angeles' mild climate. "He loved his golf," said former teammate Clem Labine, who frequently played with him. And through it all,
he appeared to be in good physical health. He did not smoke or drink
and kept himself in shape through exercise. But there was one matter
that escaped his disciplined approach to life: high blood pressure.

It was Friday, September 15, 1978. The Dodgers were on the verge
of winning the divisional title that would eventually entitle them to face
the Yankees in the World Series. Gilliam attended a meeting at a down-
town Los Angeles hotel, and, after driving manager Tommy Lasorda to
Dodger Stadium in Chavez Ravine, left to visit a friend before the evening game against the Atlanta Braves. He never made it. He was
stricken by a cerebral hemorrhage and was rushed to Daniel Freeman
Memorial Hospital in nearby Inglewood. He spent seven hours in surgery, but the results were not good. The patient slipped into a coma.
Hours became days, and the hospital reported that it was receiving an
average of a telephone call every minute from people inquiring about
his status.

Jim Gilliam never regained consciousness and died of cardiac arrest
on October 8—only days before his fiftieth birthday.

Enos Slaughter returned to his farm in Roxboro in the fall of 1956 with
a World Series ring—and a new wife. The relationship with Vickie had
soured by early 1955. (A turning point occurred when Enos and Vickie
became embroiled in an argument while driving to spring training and,
as the car flew down the highway at sixty miles an hour, Vickie threw
open the passenger door and spilled out—or, as Enos later said, "jumped"
out). The alternative was Helen Spiker, a TWA stewardess whom Enos
had met in 1955. She became wife number five on December 21, 1955,
and would provide Enos with three daughters in almost twenty-five
years of marriage.

Enos was able to play sporadically for the Yankees for three more
seasons (and bat .304 in 1958 when, at forty-two, he became the oldest
player to be in a World Series). And then, in August 1959, Stengel approached him in the dugout. "We're going to finish third," said the
Yankee manager, "but you might get a chance to play in another World
Series this year." And that was how Slaughter learned that he had been

traded to the Milwaukee Braves, who were locked in a battle with the Dodgers for the National League pennant.

The former Cardinal tried to help his new team, but he was still suffering from a leg injury that hampered his mobility and could not even pinch-hit. And that was the end of Enos Slaughter's career in the major leagues. He would implore major-league owners in later years to give him another chance, but it never came. Retirement might have been bearable if the Cardinals had made good on their earlier promise to give him a job, but the offer never came, and it left the North Carolina native feeling "bitter."

Slaughter managed some minor-league teams and then coached the Duke University baseball team until the school decided not to renew his contract in 1977. And so Enos Slaughter became a full-time farmer in Roxboro. Not that he minded. "I can't go on enough," he said after he reached his seventy-fifth birthday, "about how I enjoy working on the farm." He would get up early in the morning, make coffee and bring a cup to Helen in bed (at least until they divorced in 1980), and start cooking breakfast for everyone. "He went like he was playing the last game of the World Series," said his daughter Gaye.

The only void in those first years of retirement was the question that preoccupied him most—whether he would be inducted into the Hall of Fame. Year after year, it pained him that he could not secure the necessary seventy-five percent of the vote to win election. The favorable decision finally came from the Veterans' Committee in March 1985. "My life is complete now," he told one sportswriter who had called to congratulate him.

Slaughter's election to the Hall of Fame coincided with a change in his schedule. He now found himself inundated with invitations to appear at charity golf tournaments, fantasy baseball camps, card shows, and other events that, as he told one sportswriter in 1992, allowed him "to stay home probably three weekends out of twelve months." The increased travel made it necessary for him to rely on daughters Sharon and Gaye (who lived nearby) to help him with daily chores. And one day in the late 1990s he brought some vegetables from the farm over to Sharon and mentioned that it was time to think about his funeral. "You know," he said, "we ought to go ahead and get a tombstone over at the church because prices keep going up." And so the daughters arranged for the creation of a black granite tombstone that would have the Baseball Hall of Fame emblem, a bat and two cardinals, and an inscription from them: "Take me out to the ball game. We love you, Daddy."

The unwanted event came sooner than any of them would have liked. In June 2002, Enos, now eighty-six, was diagnosed with non-Hodgkin's lymphoma. Recovery would have been difficult enough if cancer had remained the only problem. But the prescribed radiation burned a hole in his stomach, which in turn led to diverticulitis. Surgery at Duke University Hospital corrected the problem with his intestine, but Enos slipped into a coma, needed an artificial respirator to breathe, and required drugs to keep his blood pressure up. The attending physician explained to the four daughters (Patricia, Gaye, Sharon, and Rhonda) that there was no hope for their father to survive without that support system.

Years earlier, Enos had signed a living will that gave his daughters the discretion to withdraw life support if they concluded that the situation no longer warranted artificial assistance. The fateful day arrived on August 11. At midnight, the four daughters—along with Rhonda's husband—joined hands in a circle around the hospital bed while Enos lay there unconscious. "Daddy," Sharon asked her father, "do you want us to sing you a song?" There was, of course, no response. But the five of them—full of sadness and choking back tears—then sang "Take Me Out to the Ball Game." When they had finished, Gaye—the oldest daughter by Helen—placed her hand on her father's head and leaned over him. "Daddy," she said softly, "you can run now. You're going to be safe at home."

The Dodgers may have faltered in 1957, but Gil Hodges did not, lifting his batting average to .299 and finishing with twenty-seven home runs along with ninety-eight runs batted in. And there was reason to believe that Hodges could continue those stellar performances after the team moved to Los Angeles, where the Coliseum's 250-foot foul line in left field seemed ideally suited to a right-handed batter like Hodges. But the Indiana native was now thirty-four, and, while there were moments of glory (including a home run to win the fourth game of the 1959 World Series), his record began to show the signs of age.

Hodges hit his 352nd career home run in 1960—thus establishing a new National League record for right-handed batters—but the Dodgers soon decided that they needed to make room for younger players. And so Hodges was picked up by the New York Mets in October 1961. He struggled with the Mets for two seasons and seemed destined for a forced retirement in May 1963 when he received a call from George Selkirk, general manager for the American League's Washington Senators. The team was foundering in last place, and Selkirk was eager to find a new manager.

The Senators quickly learned that their new manager was a stern disciplinarian (leading first baseman Ken Harrelson to describe Hodges as a "Dr. Jekyll and Mr. Hyde" character who could be "a real gentleman" off the field but who became "a different person" when he put on a baseball uniform). Still, no one could quarrel with the results. After a last-place finish in 1963, the team finished ninth in 1964, eighth in both 1965 and 1966, and in a tie for sixth place in 1967. It was a remarkable accomplishment. So there should not have been any surprise when the Mets pursued Gil Hodges as the manager for their team.

The Mets confronted Hodges with a challenge that surpassed anything he had known with the Senators. Except for a ninth-place finish in 1966, the team had finished last in the standings in every year since its formation in 1961.

It was a situation that demanded change, and Gil was not afraid to experiment. The changes would come in ways large and small. Jackets and ties that had to be worn on the road. Platooning. And a hierarchy that generally required players to communicate with him through his coaches. Not surprisingly, Hodges' managerial style generated different reactions from different players. "He was a big, imposing guy," said outfielder Ron Swoboda, "who scared the shit out of you." In contrast, pitcher Jerry Koosman saw the new Mets manager as "a gentleman's gentleman" who was "happy-go-lucky" and brought "a lot of fun" to the team.

The fruits of the new manager's effort came at a high personal cost. To others, he appeared serene. But he was anything but relaxed during a baseball game. (Duke Snider remembered the time he watched the Dodger first baseman light a cigarette on the bench during a close game at Ebbets Field. "His hands were shaking so much," said Snider, "he could hardly light the cigarette.") Hodges would closely watch events unfold from the dugout, and woe to any player who blocked his vision of what was happening on the field.

The day of reckoning came during a road trip at the end of September. The Mets had arrived in Atlanta to play the Braves. "I had sharp pains in the chest," Hodges recalled, "along with other discomforts that I never experienced before in my life." Before the game was over, he was diagnosed with a heart attack.

Gil was placed in the hospital, and the team finished the season without their manager on the bench. He was in the hospital for three weeks and then took a few weeks of rest in Florida. "I feel great," he told an inquiring sportswriter in November. "I don't feel like I've had a heart attack." Hodges' satisfaction with his physical recovery extended to his hopes for the Mets. When asked for his prediction of team victories in the 1969 season, Hodges said, "A minimum of eighty-five."

The Mets had never won more than seventy-three games in a season, and much of the press was skeptical about that prediction. Hodges nonetheless pushed ahead, and by June sportswriters were beginning to think his prediction might prove to be accurate. Much of the team's success reflected Hodges' continued demand for discipline and commitment. Never would he tolerate a player who made mental mistakes or failed to hustle on every play. The standards were easy to articulate but often difficult to execute, and there were times when he would express his frustrations to Joan when he came home in the evenings. She tried to be philosophical about it. "Gil," she said at one point, "these are grown men. And they each have their own character. They are not your children. You have to understand that." Her husband did not agree. "Well, honey," he replied, "I feel that once they put on that uniform and walk on that field, they represent me. And if they're going to represent me, they are my children."

Cleon Jones—the team's leading hitter with a .340 average—learned about Hodges' perspective in a game against the Houston Astros at Shea Stadium in July. A ball was hit to left field for a double by one of the Astros, and Jones appeared to be very casual in chasing the ball down and then lobbing it back into the infield. Within seconds Hodges, wearing a somber look, emerged from the dugout on the first-base side of the field and began a slow, deliberate walk across the field. The manager passed Nolan Ryan—who was standing on the pitcher's mound and thought Hodges was coming to take him out. And then he passed Bud Harrelson, who was standing in fear at shortstop. ("Oh, my God," he said to himself. "He's coming to get me.") Hodges stopped when he reached Jones in left field and made a simple observation: "I didn't like the way you went after that last ball." He then invited Jones to return to the dugout with him while another Met came out to play left field.

The incident did not hurt the team's performance. They were nine and half games out of first place on August 19. By September 10, the Mets were in first place—to stay. The team finished with a hundred wins (fifteen more than Hodges had predicted), won the divisional series, and then defeated the Baltimore Orioles in the World Series. The achievement of the "Miracle Mets" did not go unnoticed in the press. "In baseball's first 100 years," said one sportswriter, "there was nothing to compare with the spectacular rise of the Mets."

Hodges continued to press for victories in subsequent seasons, but there were no more miracles. The Mets did far better in 1970 and 1971—with identical records of eighty-three wins against seventy-nine losses and a third-place finish—than they had ever done under the team's previous managers. Still, Hodges had hopes that 1972 would be better. But then major-league players threatened to strike and spring training was suspended. Joan returned to Brooklyn to be with her family for Easter Sunday while her husband stayed behind.

Gil was a devoted husband who, as Joan recalled, "sent me flowers for everything and anything." On that Sunday, he ordered flowers for Joan, attended church, and then went to play golf with three of his coaches—Joe Pignatano, Eddie Yost, and Rube Walker—at a course in West Palm Beach.

When they finished, Hodges began to walk to his room at the nearby Ramada Inn. Pignatano turned to Gil and asked, "What time should we meet for dinner?" "Let's say seven thirty," came the response. Those were the last words ever spoken by the Mets manager. He stumbled backward and slumped to the ground. Pignatano and Walker hurried to his side while Yost ran into the hotel to call an ambulance. They rushed him to the nearby hospital, but it was all to no avail. Gil Hodges—just a couple days shy of his forty-eighth birthday—was pronounced dead about forty-five minutes after he had fallen to the ground, the victim of another heart attack.

Back in Brooklyn, Joan was with her family at her mother's house for the Easter festivities and did not see the bulletins being flashed across the nation's television screens. And then, without explanation, she saw Anthony Terranova, Gil's good friend, come into her mother's house. "And I thought," she remembered, "this is very odd. It's Easter Sunday. He should be with his family." But she could see that he had been crying, and she assumed that something had happened to his brother, who, like Gil, had experienced a previous heart attack. "Terry," she implored him, "what's the matter?" He struggled to say something for a few seconds and then blurted out, "It's Gil." "Okay," said Joan, trying to stay calm. "Was he hurt?" Terry could not respond to that simple question. But the answer became clear when tears started to stream down his face. "Is he dead?" Joan asked. "Just nod your head." Terry nodded his head. And, as he did so, her mother's neighbors, having seen the television bulletins or heard the news on the radio, began to stream into the house. Joan stayed there for a long time, but when she finally went home later that evening, she found the flowers that her husband had ordered that morning.

Joe Collins played only sparingly in 1957, and the Yankees announced in March 1958 that they had sold his contract to the Philadelphia Phillies. Within an hour, Collins made his own announcement: he was retiring. "I made up my mind some time ago," he told the press, "that, if I had to leave New York, I would quit." Part of the reason was to stay with his family in Union, New Jersey. The other reason was a shoulder injury. "I couldn't play every day," he later told Peter Golenbock, "which is what I would have to do down there. I would make an ass of myself."

Collins' decision to retire was made that much easier because he already had an alternative to baseball: a job as a public relations executive with People's Express, a Newark trucking company. He had been working with the company in the off-season, and now he would turn the part-time job into a full-time one. The job was tailored to Collins' personality. He was, after all, a gregarious guy with an ever-present smile. Meeting people and getting them to sign contracts could be his forte. And, beyond that, success would involve a lot of time on the golf course—and he loved playing golf. Unfortunately, Joe soon learned that there could be too much of a good thing.

About a year after he retired, the newly minted businessman ran into Gil McDougald, who was still with the Yankees. Collins' former teammate was shocked by what he saw. No longer fit and trim, Collins had gained considerable weight and looked unhealthy (which could not have been helped by Collins' habit of smoking one or two packs of Marlboros every day). The former first baseman told McDougald that he had played 265 rounds of golf over the past year (which included the lunches and dinners and drinks that go with entertaining clients). McDougald subsequently had lunch with Phil Dameo, the People's Express president. "You're killing my buddy," said McDougald. "Get him working in an area where he learns your business." The message apparently had some impact—Collins reduced his time on the golf course and ultimately spent thirty years with People's Express.

In the meantime, Collins continued to enjoy life with Peggy and their five children—which included three boys and two girls. There were dinners, vacations, and, above all, sports and games with the boys, because Joe Collins' departure from the ballfield did not mean an abandonment of his competitive spirit. "He was a ballbuster," remembered Joe Jr., his eldest son. "If you were playing golf with him or anything like that, he didn't want to lose. So if you were getting close to him, he started needling you." (Joe Jr. remembered that his father would not talk with him for two weeks after he beat him in arm wrestling.)

There was no sign of any physical ailment when Joe turned on the television set in his living room and sat down to watch the Yankee game on the evening of August 29, 1989. The team was not faring well and would finish the season in fourth place. Still, they were his team, and he would always be interested in their fate. Joe's younger son Jim came home around ten o'clock, talked with his father briefly, and then went to sleep. Around two o'clock in the morning, Jim awoke and heard the television set. He wandered downstairs and found his sixty-six-year-old father slumped in his chair—the victim of a massive heart attack. (Many of Joe's former teammates would later quip at his funeral that watching the Yankees falter had killed him.)

Hank Bauer's performance continued to slip after 1956, and he was included in the 1959 trade that sent several Yankees to the Kansas City Athletics in exchange for Roger Maris. Hank was not surprised by the trade. "At the age of thirty-seven," he later said, "I was finished." Nor was he unhappy with being in Kansas City. In all those years with the Yankees, Charlene had remained in Kansas City with their children (three boys and a girl) while Hank shared the apartment with Andy Carey in New York. (Still, Hank had managed to make an indelible impression on his children during those years. "He was pretty tough," remembered Hank Jr. "And as the oldest, I got the brunt of his marine-like approach"—which included Bauer's habit of dropping a quarter on his son's bed to see if it would bounce—thus indicating that it was made properly.

Hank played sporadically for the Athletics for the next two seasons and was prepared to retire in 1961 when Athletics' owner Charles O. Finley asked him at the beginning of the season whether he would be interested in continuing to play and simultaneously manage the team. And so, on June 20, Hank Bauer—now sporting a marine crew cut instead of the long dark hair that had been his trademark—became the A's new manager.

The news was well received in the press. ("This is a great break for a great guy," Arthur Daley wrote in *The New York Times*.) For his part, Hank was nervous about being both a player and a manager. And so—after getting a single in a game against the Tigers on July 21— Hank retired as a player to a standing ovation.

The Athletics finished in last place in 1961, but the prospects seemed better in 1962 (and, in fact, the team would finish with seventy-two wins—the second-best performance in the club's history). But Hank had a sense that Finley was making plans to replace him after the 1962 season ended. The Athletics' owner had hired Eddie Lopat to be the pitching coach—a decision usually made by the manager—and Hank could not help but feel that his former Yankee teammate was nothing more than a manager-in-waiting. And so, when Hank saw speculation of the managerial change in the press, he called Finley. "What is it with this article?" he asked. Finley was circumspect, saying only, "I can't answer you at this time."

That was enough of an answer for Bauer. Two days before the season ended, he announced that he was quitting after the 1962 season. "When a man loses his pride," the ex-marine explained, "he loses everything."

Three weeks after leaving the Athletics, Hank's friend Lee MacPhail, now the Baltimore Orioles' GM, made arrangements for him to become an Orioles coach for the 1963 season. And when the season ended with a disappointing fourth-place finish, MacPhail asked Hank to manage the team in 1964. Ironically, one of the new manager's first decisions was to platoon his players. "I hated platooning when I was a ballplayer," he told one sportswriter. "Now that I'm a manager, I know that it's the only way to operate."

It may have made the difference. The Orioles vied for first place throughout the season and finished in third place with ninety-seven wins—but only one game behind the second-place White Sox and two games behind the first-place Yankees. The team may not have won the pennant, but Hank Bauer earned the respect of the players and the press—and was selected by *The Sporting News* as the American League Manager of the Year.

The Orioles finished third again in 1965 with ninety-four wins and then coasted to a first-place finish in 1966. As the season drew to a close, *The New York Times* commented that "Bauer has done a smashing managerial job this year," and *The Sporting News* again selected Hank as the American League's Manager of the Year.

However much he tried, Bauer could not duplicate the success of those first three years in 1967. The team tied for a sixth-place finish, and Hank was left to think about the next season. "I'm gonna be tougher," he told one sportswriter, and, by the middle of July, the club was in second place with a 43–37 record. But the club management was not willing to be patient. And so, during the All-Star break in July,

Hank was in his ranch house in Prairie Village when Orioles general manager Harry Dalton called to say that he was at the Kansas City airport and wanted to come by to talk with the Orioles manager. "I hung up," Bauer later recalled, "and told my wife I was getting fired."

Hank stayed in Prairie Village for the rest of the season, hunting and fishing and waiting for the phone to ring. And ring it did. Charles O. Finley had moved the Athletics to Oakland and was looking for a new manager to breathe fire into his team and bring home a division title. "I'm sticking my neck out," Finley told the press, "and I don't mean to put Hank on the spot, but I'm predicting we'll win our division title next year."

Hank had access to many talented players (including a twenty-three-year-old Reggie Jackson) and was able to develop a winning record after 149 games (with eighty wins and only sixty-nine losses) that surpassed the record mounted by any other Athletics' manager since 1955. But Hank could not produce that division title. And that was the end of Bauer's managerial tenure with the A's.

Hank once again retreated to Prairie Village to wait for the phone to ring. But this time there was no offer from a big-league club. He spent a couple of years managing the Mets' farm team in Tidewater, Virginia (and earning *The Sporting News'* selection as the Minor League Manager of the Year in 1972), before deciding to return to Kansas for good.

The transition to a life without baseball had been made that much easier by Hank's purchase of a liquor store in Prairie Village. ("I made more money in the liquor store," he later explained, "than I ever did in baseball.") And then Mickey Mantle called with an offer for him to be one of the coaches at the fantasy baseball camp that he and Whitey Ford were creating.

When Mantle died in 1995, his sons tried to run the camp, but camp management was not their strong suit. Hank told the Mantle boys that he and Moose Skowron would be happy to take over camp administration (under a new name, "Heroes in Pinstripes"). And so, year after year, Hank would spend countless hours helping plan camp activities.

However much he enjoyed the fantasy camps, they could not insulate him or his family from the problems of advanced age. In 1993, Hank, then seventy-one, was diagnosed with throat cancer. An operation was performed that required the removal of his epiglottis, a small component of the throat that facilitates the swallowing of food, and left Hank with a new voice. ("My biggest recollection of my father," said his daughter Bea, "was his voice," and, remembering that one periodical had compared it to "a rusty wrench," she said the operation made it "rustier.")

Charlene was not as fortunate. She was diagnosed with a brain tumor in 1999 and was gone within a few months.

Hank moved to a ranch condominium in Shawnee Mission near Prairie Village and continued to attend card shows and other events to promote the fantasy camp. One trip took him to Philadelphia in the summer of 2006. He now carried a small bottle of oxygen to assist his breathing, but that proved to be inadequate when he disembarked from the plane. He was placed back on the plane and taken immediately to the hospital when he arrived in Kansas City. The doctors could not determine the cause of Hank's ailment until the following December: advanced lung cancer that would be resistant to chemotherapy, radiation, or any other treatment.

Hank spent most of the next two months in a recliner chair, surrounded by his four children and their families (all of whom lived in the Kansas City area), enjoying sporting events on television and receiving visits from Moose Skowron and other friends. But then the pain increased and breathing became more difficult. On Friday, February 9, 2007, Hank Bauer, five months shy of his eighty-fifth birthday, died at home while surrounded by members of his family.

Dale Mitchell retired after the 1956 season and soon became president of Martin Marietta's lime and cement division in Denver. Even then, however, he could not escape the embarrassment of that strikeout in Don Larsen's game—although he soon realized that, as Pee Wee Reese had predicted, it gave him a place in baseball history that had unanticipated benefits.

The occasion was the construction of a new shopping mall in the Denver area. It was a big project, one that could greatly advance the financial success of Mitchell's company. The problem was the general contractor. He had selected another company to provide the cement and would not give Martin Marietta a chance to submit a bid. To Mitchell, that was unfair. He assumed the fix was in for the other company, but he was not prepared to accept defeat without a fight. Talking to the general contractor in Denver had proved fruitless, so he placed a call to the Las Vegas office of the development company's president—Del Webb, until recently one of two principal owners of the New York Yankees (which had been sold to CBS in 1964).

When the secretary answered the telephone, Mitchell asked for Mr. Webb and was put through immediately. When Webb got on the line, Mitchell began by identifying himself, but Webb cut him off. "I know who you are," he said. Mitchell then explained that the Denver contractor would not provide Martin Marietta with the opportunity to bid. "We're being shut out here," he said. "We can't bid. All we want to do is bid."

Mitchell wanted to believe that Webb would give Martin Marietta that chance to bid. After all, Webb had been a part of the same world of professional sports that had been Mitchell's life for eleven years. He, more than most, surely understood the importance of open competition. But Webb had a different perspective—one that caught Mitchell off guard. "Well, you know," the former Yankee owner responded, "you made me a lot of money with that strikeout." There was a pause and then Webb said, "The job's yours and we're even." So Mitchell had more than an opportunity to bid—he had the contract.

There were other unexpected consequences from Dale's contact with the world of baseball after retirement. There was no better example than the time when the Fellowship of Christian Athletes in Tulsa—where Mitchell had been relocated by Martin Marietta—invited him to moderate a discussion at a luncheon for high school athletes and their fathers. Mitchell immediately invited his friend Allie Reynolds, another Oklahoma native who had achieved fame as a pitcher for the Cleveland Indians and the New York Yankees. Mitchell decided that he would like to invite Ted Williams as well but realized there was one complication—Williams did not like Reynolds, and Mitchell could not help but wonder whether it would be too much risk to put both of them on the same dais.

The family talked about it at great length, and finally Mitchell decided that he should invite the former Boston Red Sox slugger. After all, Ted Williams was one of the greatest hitters in baseball history. It would not be fair to deprive these young boys and their fathers of Williams' presence because he disliked another player. The invitation was duly conveyed, and Williams accepted—perhaps in part because Mitchell did not tell him that Reynolds would also be there.

To minimize the possibility of any conflict, it was arranged that Mitchell would sit immediately to the right of the podium with Reynolds on his right. Williams would be seated on the other side of the podium. It seemed like a reasonable solution to a potential problem, but it failed to account for Williams' keen eye and volatile personality.

The luncheon started off well enough, but Williams was late. He strode in from the back of the gymnasium where the lunch was being held and took his seat on the left side of the podium. As he was eating lunch, Williams caught sight of Reynolds. The reaction was immediate. He leaned over across the back of the podium—not realizing that the microphone was on—and said to Mitchell, "Who invited that cocksucker?" As Williams' question reverberated around the high gymnasium walls, all conversation in the room came to a halt—and the students and their fathers learned something new about life in the major leagues.

Despite the embarrassment of that moment, the interludes with former players were a welcome complement to a life that had most of what Mitchell could have wanted—a good job, a country club membership, and a loving family. But the signs of a dangerous change were evident—especially in retrospect. Mitchell had little exercise except walking on a golf course, and his weight ballooned from the 195 he maintained with the Indians to 220. The lack of exercise was compounded by his continual pipe smoking and by a daily intake of vodka and other alcohol after work, at the club, and with dinner.

The consequences proved to be almost catastrophic. On October 8, 1974—the eighteenth anniversary of his strikeout in Larsen's perfect game—Dale suffered a massive heart attack that required bypass surgery. He was only fifty-three, but the damage to his heart was considerable and impressed on him the need for some changes in his lifestyle. Still, old habits could not be easily changed. He could lose some weight. But he would not abandon his pipe. And he would not, maybe could not, limit his drinking.

Mitchell no doubt wanted the life that he had enjoyed before the heart attack, but it was not to be. Margaret succumbed to cancer in 1976, and that changed almost everything. He was devastated emotionally and was now forced to spend much of his time alone. In search of company—and perhaps the camaraderie he had enjoyed with the Cleveland Indians and the Brooklyn Dodgers—Mitchell would frequently wander by the country club and down three or four drinks in the afternoon before or after golf or while watching card games in the clubhouse. And then the drinking would continue in the evening.

None of that benefited his health, and he had another heart attack in 1980. The heart damage was again considerable, and he was forced to retire from Martin Marietta. That was followed by another episode in 1982, and the doctors were sure that Dale Mitchell did not have long to live. "The doctor called me aside," Dale Jr. remembered, "and said, 'All his arteries are blocked and there's nothing we can do. He could live an hour and a half or he could live ten years.'"

Other people might have made dramatic changes to increase the odds in their favor. But not Dale Mitchell. He continued his pipe smoking, remained committed to his daily drinks, and even took on a new wife named June. His children were now on their own—Dale Jr. as a bank president in Oklahoma City, Bo as director of development for the University of Colorado's Athletic Department, and daughter Lana, his youngest child, as an elementary school teacher in Oklahoma. But he continued to stay in close touch with them and to make the most of whatever time he had left.

January 4, 1987, was a Sunday. The Denver Broncos were in a playoff game that would ultimately lead to the Super Bowl, and Bo had promised his dad that he would call him from home at halftime. But then Bo and his son were given tickets to the game. They made arrangements to travel from Boulder to Denver and then, as they were leaving the house, Bo felt "this supernatural tap on my shoulder" to call his father in Tulsa. Bo knew he would not be able to call him from the stadium, and he wanted to fulfill his promise to make the call. So he returned to the house, called his father, and explained that he was calling early because he and his son were now going to attend the game instead of watching it on television. They talked about the game and, as they closed the conversation, Bo heard himself say, "I love you, Dad." "Well," his father responded, "I love you too." It was the last time that Bo Mitchell ever talked with his father.

The next morning Mitchell awoke, sat up in bed, and asked June to get him a glass of milk. She retreated to the kitchen, but when she came back with the glass of milk, she saw that her husband had fallen back on the pillow, the victim of his last heart attack at the age of sixty-five.

As he was laid to rest in Cloud Chief, the place where it all began, people eulogized Dale Mitchell from many quarters around the country. But as he might have predicted—and often feared—he was remembered most not for his achievements over an eleven-year baseball career but for that one plate appearance on October 8, 1956. As the *Cleveland Plain Dealer* observed, Mitchell had an impressive .312 batting average over those eleven years but was "best known for making the final out in Don Larsen's perfect game in the 1956 World Series."

EPILOGUE

There may, of course, come a time when another pitcher hurls a perfect game in a World Series. Even so, Don Larsen's remarkable accomplishment will remain a unique occurrence in baseball history.

It was, to begin with, a very different time. Baseball was *the* national pastime, the dominant sport of America (even though no major-league teams were located west of Kansas City). Growing up in Livingston, New Jersey, I remember rushing home from school to watch the Yankees on television (because most of the games at that time were played during the day instead of at night), and nothing could compare to the excitement of the World Series. Kids would bring transistor radios to school, and some sympathetic teachers would even bring in a small television set with rabbit ears and a grainy picture so that the class could keep abreast of developments (because, again, all the World Series games were played during the day).

The teams were different as well. The reserve clause gave the owners an unchallenged ability to control the fate of the team's players. And if the player had talent, he was not likely to see a contract with another team for long time—if ever. Of the nineteen men who played in that fifth game of the 1956 World Series, fifteen had never played for any other team. That stability was due in no small part to the considerable skills of those who played in that fifth game. Seven of the nineteen players who were on the field that day were later inducted into the Hall of Fame (and another one—Gil Hodges—probably should have been). And fifteen of those nineteen players had been selected for their league's All-Star team at some point.

The reserve clause may have unfairly limited a player's options to seek better pay with another team, but the clause had the incidental benefit of creating a camaraderie that would be difficult to duplicate in an era of free agency where a player can periodically test the marketplace for his skills. Young men usually came up the ranks through the club's minor-league system and then spent most of their careers with the same teammates. They would not only see each other on the field or in the dugout during games but also spend considerable time with each other traveling by train to the opposing teams' ballparks. There they learned to accept and, for the most part, enjoy each other's company and tolerate each other's idiosyncrasies. "We truly felt like a family, always pulling for each other," Yogi Berra said of his days with the Yankees. Those same sentiments were echoed by Duke Snider in the memoir he later wrote. "Most of all," Duke explained in the introductory chapter, "I want to tell you about our closeness as a *team*, a group of young men mostly in our 20s who were destined to make history, some individually, but all of us as a team whose members genuinely cared for each other."

However much they may have cared for one another, these men were all tough competitors. For most, it was a matter of necessity. Few had a college education, and most had no real prospects for employment that would pay them anything close to what they were making on the baseball diamond. And so success was not merely a matter of winning a game. It was a matter of economic survival.

The unwritten rules of the game reflected that focus. Baseball was not nearly as civilized then as it is today. It was much more a theater for combat than an arena for competition. There is no better illustration than the knockdown pitch. It could be a ball thrown near the batter's head. Or perhaps an inside pitch close to the batter's legs. And on occasion it might even be a pitch that would sail behind the batter's head. Whatever the location, it was a pitch designed to keep the batter off balance. Because a comfortable batter was a batter more likely to get a hit.

Sal Maglie was one of the more notorious—and successful—practitioners, but he was hardly alone. Joe DiMaggio, whose career began in 1936 and ended in 1951, well remembered the pitchers' proclivity to throw knockdown pitches as he watched the Cardinals Mark McGwire chase the single-season home run record in 1998. "Just look at those pitches," the Yankee Clipper complained to confidant Morris Engelberg at one point during that season. "Right down the middle. It's like batting practice. If Bobby Feller were out there, or Allie Reynolds, he wouldn't be smacking those homers. They would dust him off, throw him inside, throw at his head. He wouldn't have been allowed to hit so many homers in my day." But if the pitcher did come in with a knockdown pitch, the batter would often find some way to retaliate. They might (like Carl Furillo did with Maglie) "lose" their grip on the bat and let it sail toward the pitcher's mound. Or they might (like Jackie Robinson did with Maglie) lay down a bunt on the first-base side and then barrel into the pitcher when he tried to field the ball.

Free agency, better training, closer scrutiny by the press, and, most of all, the constant glare of television have transformed baseball in many ways. Players are much more mindful of proper etiquette on the field. But the game still draws millions of fans to ballparks every season and that many more fans to video channels distributed mostly by cable and satellite (with most games now played in evening prime time). It still has its challenges. It can still be imbued with excitement. And I would like to think that recapturing that special moment in the fifth game of the 1956 World Series will not only shed some light on the history of the game and the men who played it but also help explain the allure that the game still holds for millions of fans.

ACKNOWLEDGMENTS

This book has been a wondrous journey. Baseball has always been a passion of mine, surpassed perhaps only by my joy in writing. And so there was much to be said for a project that enabled me to marry those two interests. Over the last six years, I have had the pleasure of being able to delve into memories that remain forever fresh by talking with players who were for so many years merely images on a television screen, reminiscing with family members about other players who are no longer with us, and conversing with others who share a similar interest in the sport.

Like other nonfiction books, this project could not have survived without the generous assistance and support of many other people. First and foremost I have to thank my agent, Jim Donovan. He shared my enthusiasm for the project and maneuvered the shoals of the publishing industry to find the perfect home for it (no pun intended). The team at New American Library has proved to be as good as any author could hope to find. Brent Howard, my editor, was not only adept at proposing changes that made the manuscript more focused but also displayed a keen sense for marketing matters—not to mention an excitement in the project that made the experience that much more enjoyable. Brent was ably assisted by Tiffany Yates, who did a superb job in copyediting, Peter Horan, who handled publicity, and Melanie Koch, who managed subsidiary rights.

Much of the impetus for doing the book evolved from my two sojourns at a baseball fantasy camp in Fort Lauderdale, Florida, that was originally called the Mickey Mantle Memorial Week of Dreams (managed by Mickey Mantle's sons) and then became Heroes in Pinstripes under the watchful eyes (and boundless collegiality) of Hank Bauer and Bill Skowron (affectionately known as Moose), both of whom were perennial coaches at the camp when Mickey was alive. There I was able to meet and have almost daily conversations with several of the players who would figure prominently in the book, including Hank Bauer, Enos Slaughter, and, of course, Don Larsen.

Over the course of time, I was able to talk at length (and often on more than one occasion) with other players as well as family members of those who have passed on and others who had watched the players who would ultimately be profiled in the book. Those interviewed include Marty Appel, Bea Bauer, Hank Bauer, Hank Bauer Jr., Buzzie Bavasi, Dale Berra, Yogi Berra, Bobby Brown, Ken Burns, Roy Campanella Jr., Andy Carey, Susie Carey, Jim Cartelli, Peter Casciato, Joe Collins Jr., Chuck Diering, Carl Erskine, Whitey Ford, Carl Furillo Jr., Fern Furillo, Nancy Gollnick, Joan Hodges, Dave Kaplan, Jerry Koosman, Tony Kubek, Clem Labine, Don Larsen, Ray Mantle, Marty Marion, Doris Maglie, Joe Maglie, Billy Martin Jr., Gil McDougald, Bo Mitchell, Dale Mitchell Jr., Johnny Podres, Mark Reese, Bobby Richardson, Rachel Robinson, Bill Skowron, Gaye Slaughter, Helen Slaughter, Sharon Slaughter, Duke Snider, Bob Turley, and Bob Wolff.

Those interviews were supplemented by tapes provided to me by Peter Golenbock of interviews he had done with many of the profiled players (now deceased) in conjunction with his books on the Yankees and Dodgers. Peter was also prompt in responding to my many questions about some of the comments made by players in those interviews. For all that, I am very grateful. Frances Eddy ably transcribed all the tapes provided by Peter.

Still others were helpful in facilitating many of the interviews—

which was sometimes a challenging experience (because some players were difficult to locate and because, in this Internet age, many former players have been forced to limit their access to the public). Those helpful intermediaries include Buzzie Bavasi, Susie Carey, Dave Kaplan (who oversees the Yogi Berra Museum and Learning Center in Montclair, New Jersey), Mark Langill (the Dodgers' resident historian), Lucille McDougald, Bev Snider, Barbara Tribble (in Rachel Robinson's office), Wanda Greer and Dale Whittenberger (with Heroes in Pinstripes), Rick Wolff, and Jason Zillo (in the Yankees' public relations office).

Words would be inadequate to express my appreciation to the staff at the National Baseball Hall of Fame in Cooperstown, New York, and especially Tim Wiles, the research director there. Tim and his colleagues, including Freddy Borowski and Jeremy Jones, were unfailingly responsive to my many inquiries and eager to assist in ways large and small. Jenny Ambrose, who handles photos in the Hall of Fame's vast collections, was equally prompt in locating photos that could be included in the book.

The personnel at the Montgomery County Public Library in Potomac, Maryland, were similarly responsive to my many requests for books and articles that have long since been placed in archives and other locations that were not easily accessible.

The book also benefited immeasurably from the comments of those who took time from busy schedules to read the manuscript in draft. Those readers include Marty Appel, Peter Casciato, Peter Golenbock, Doug Katz, Dan Okrent, and Charley Phelps. All errors, however, are my responsibility alone.

In all of this, Doug Katz holds a special place. In addition to taking time to review the manuscript, he not only spent untold hours talking with me about every aspect of the project but also provided advice and assistance that, in time, proved to be invaluable.

Marty Appel likewise deserves special recognition. Marty has an encyclopedic memory of players and events that proved immensely useful and, beyond that, expended considerable and much-appreciated effort on the marketing front.

But no one deserves more thanks than my wife, Jan. She shared my interest in the concept for the book from the beginning, read the manuscript in its entirety (and some chapters more than once), and never tired of discussing—and even debating—the many issues that inevitably arise in telling a dramatic story that focuses on the lives of the participants. Whatever success the book has in telling that story of Don Larsen's perfect game—and the players on the field that day—is due in no small part to her involvement.

ENDNOTES

Many of the quotations and stories captured in *Perfect* rely on the memories of players and other observers, which are not always (dare I say it?) perfect. Books, articles, and interviews often include conflicting recollections—sometimes even by the same person. Making choices among those conflicting accounts was not easy, but I have generally tried to select those quotations which are more contemporaneous and, if possible, have the support of another source. One example is Don Larsen's last pitch to Dale Mitchell. Allen Barra's excellent biography of Yogi Berra (*Yogi Berra: Eternal Yankee*) quoted the long-time Yankee catcher from a 2006 event in which he indicated that he called for a fastball even though he thought Larsen's better pitch of the day was his slider. That may be correct, but other sources (including one of Yogi's earlier books and a contemporaneous comment from Larsen) indicated that the fastball was the better pitch, and I have therefore gone with that latter assessment.

Another point concerns articles obtained from the National Baseball Hall of Fame (referred to here as "HOF"). Many of them did not include complete identification. In those situations, I have provided as much detail in the citation as is available in the hope that any interested reader can obtain the article in the appropriate files.

PROLOGUE
The Moment of Truth

2 "Anything can happen"—Interview with Yogi Berra.

2 "I wanted"—Interview with Yogi Berra.

3 "The ball just"—Don Larsen, *The Perfect Yankee*, p. xi.

3 "The guy that kills me"—Interview with Tony Kubek.

3 "The comic book ghoulies"—Don Larsen, *The Perfect Yankee*, p. 98.

3 "excellent stuff"—*Id.*, p. 23.

4 "I don't give a damn"—*Saturday Evening Post*, March 30, 1957.

4 "Casey Stengel always said"—Don Larsen, *The Perfect Yankee*, p. 23.

5 "I'm gonna beat"—*New York Daily Mirror*, October 9, 1956.

5 "Oh, shit"—Interview with Hank Bauer.

5 "flabbergasted"—Interview with Bob Turley.

6 "I knew"—Interview with Yogi Berra.

6 "I had hit off Larsen"—*Sporting News*, October 31, 1981.

6 "Son"—Interview with Bo Mitchell.

7 "We were thinking"—Interview with Andy Carey.

7 "The crowd was"—Mickey Mantle, *My Favorite Summer 1956*, p. 275.

7 "I was so weak"—*New York Post*, June 25, 1976.

8 "most agonizing"—Babe Pinelli, "Kill the Umpire," in Charles Einstein (ed.), *The Second Fireside Book of Baseball*, p. 280.

8 "I'll guarantee"—Tape of radio broadcast.

8 "Roger, what do you"—Interview with Clem Labine.

8 "to distract them"—Interview with Yogi Berra.

8 "I hear"—Yogi Berra, *Yogi: It Ain't Over*, p. 104.

9 "Shut up"—Interview with Yogi Berra.

9 "His sliders were good"—Yogi Berra, *Ten Rings: My Championship Seasons*, p. 151.

9 "Every ball that was hit hard"—Daily News, *Yogi Berra: An American Original*, p. 46.

9 "no man"—Tape of television broadcast.

10 "greatest moment"—*New York Times*, October 19, 2003.

CHAPTER 1
Top of the First: Don Larsen

11 "I make it a rule"—Don Larsen, *The Perfect Yankee*, p. 198.

11 "I didn't pay"—*Saturday Evening Post*, March 30, 1957.

12 "better prospect"—Don Larsen, *The Perfect Yankee*, p. 76.

12 "I was never much"—*Id.*, p. 76.

13 "beating the hell"—Interview with Bob Turley.

13 "I'll never forget"—Don Larsen, *The Perfect Yankee*, p. 83.

13 "You give the best"—Interview with Don Larsen.

13 "Look, Bill"—*Saturday Evening Post*, March 30, 1957.

14 "the only thing"—Peter Golenbock, *Dynasty*, p. 204.

14 "With Turley and"—*New York World Telegram and Sun*, November 18, 1954.

14 "He had probably"—Interview with Gil McDougald.

14 "I'm going to take"—Peter Golenbock, *Dynasty*, p. 216.

15 "Larsen should be"—Interview with Tony Kubek.

15 "I have stretched"—Don Larsen, *The Perfect Yankee*, p. 91.

15 "You want to play"—Peter Golenbock, *Wild, High and Tight*, p. 58.

16 "everybody"—Interview with Bob Turley.

16 "Larsen was easily"—Mickey Mantle, *My Favorite Summer 1956*, p. 219.

16 "He'd never drink"—Peter Golenbock interview with Joe Collins.

16 "Larsen was either"—Don Larsen, *The Perfect Yankee*, pp. 93–94.

17 "I've gotta get home"—*Sporting News*, October 31, 1981.

17 "a devil-may-care"—*New York Daily Mirror*, October 9, 1956.

17 "While this baseball hero"—Roger Kahn, *The Era*, p. 331.

17 "for the sake"—*New York Daily News*, October 9, 1956.

18 "He's very selective"—Don Larsen, *The Perfect Yankee*, p. 37.

18 "sneaky slider"—*Id.*, p. 38.

18 "Larsen will show"—*Id.*

19 "way out"—Tape of radio broadcast.

CHAPTER 2
Bottom of the First: Sal Maglie

20 "the angel"—*Sports Illustrated*, June 6, 1955.

21 "When I'm pitching"—Sal Maglie, BaseballLibrary.com

21 "When I was on"—*Sports Illustrated*, April 15, 1968.

21 "when he pitched"—Interview with Carl Erskine.

21 "When I pitched against"—Jim Bouton, *Ball Four*, p. 30.

21 "I went there once"—*Sports Illustrated*, April 15, 1968.

21 "I've always loved"—*Cavalier*, September 1959.

22 "Kid, are you"—*Sports Illustrated*, April 15, 1968.

22 "Next"—*Bison Tales*, April–May 1993.

23 "That's how little"—*Sports Illustrated*, April 15, 1968.

23 "doing handsprings"—*Bison Tales*, April–May 1993.

23 "In Elmira"—*New York Herald Tribune*, March 28, 1959.

23 "In the dugout"—*Sports Illustrated*, April 15, 1968.

24 "You don't want"—Marshall Smith, "The Meanest Face in the Pennant Race," October 1, 1956 (unidentified HOF article).

24 "hasn't much"—*Bison Tales*, April–May 1993.

24 "a wonderful woman"—*Sports Illustrated*, April 22, 1968; *Saturday Feature Magazine*, July 6, 1957.

25 "For some reason"—*Sports Illustrated*, April 15, 1968.

25 "Luque believed"—*Id.*, April 22, 1968.

26 "We're depending"—*Saturday Evening Post*, May 5, 1951.

26 "And then"—*Sports Illustrated*, April 22, 1968.

27 "deathly quiet"—*Saturday Evening Post*, May 5, 1951.

27 "I was sore"—*Id.*

27 "A train track"—*Sports Illustrated*, April 22, 1968.

28 "You could take"—*Saturday Evening Post*, May 5, 1951.

28 "I was just"—*Id.*

29 "I was in such"—*Id.*

29 "That man"—*New York World Telegram and Sun*, September 22, 1956.

29 "Campanella's"—Carl E. Prince, *Brooklyn's Dodgers*, p. 51.

29 "I didn't dare"—*Cavalier*, September 1959.

29 "the best pitch"—*Id.*

30 "I'm very happy"—*Sports Illustrated*, April 15, 1968.

30 "Where have you"—Russ Hodges and Al Hirshberg, *My Giants*, p. 84

30 "like the barber"—*Sporting News*, September 11, 1957.

30 "shaved the plate"—*Daily Sports News*, December 29, 1992.

31 "Sal, the game's"—*Sports Illustrated*, April 22, 1968.

31 "I picked up"—*Id.*

31 "I was the sort"—*Id.*

31 "plain heavy" and "I believe"—*Id.*

32 "my back feels"—*Niagara Falls Gazette*, January 13, 1953.

32 "Now that dago"—*Fra Noi*, p. 113.

33 "Sal, the time"—*New York World Telegram and Sun*, September 18, 1956.

33 "I'll show"—*Id.*, August 1, 1955.

34 "You've gotta"—Interview with Buzzie Bavasi.

34 "furious"—*Id.*

34 "You dumb"—*Id.*

34 "Carl Furillo"—Peter Golenbock, *Bums*, p. 415.

34 "the strangest"—Interview with Carl Erskine.

35 "I got more"—*Sports Illustrated*, April 22, 1968.

35 "We wouldn't be"—Ronald J. Oakley, *Baseball's Last Golden Age 1946–1960*, p. 240.

35 "Maglie looks"—Tape of radio broadcast.

CHAPTER 3
Top of the Second: Jackie Robinson and Gil McDougald

37 "We can't"—Don Larsen, *The Perfect Yankee*, p. 45.

38 "Looka here"—Roger Kahn, *Boys of Summer*, p. 391.

38 "indoctrinated us"—Jackie Robinson, *I Never Had It Made*, p. 5.

39 "could do things"—Harvey Frommer, *Rickey and Robinson*, p. 21.

39 "Jackie wasn't"—Arnold Rampersad, *Jackie Robinson*, p. 33.

39 "It is doubtful"—*Pasadena Post*, June 16, 1938.

39 "the greatest"—*California Eagle*, October 26, 1939.

39 "looks and"—Jackie Robinson, *I Never Had It Made*, p. 10.

39 "very impressive"—Rachel Robinson, *Jackie Robinson*, p. 22.

40 "He was a big man on campus"—Interview with Rachel Robinson.

41 "There's the nigger"—Jackie Robinson, *I Never Had It Made*, p. 19.

41 "behaving with"—Arnold Rampersad, *Jackie Robinson*, p. 106.

41 "I could see"—*Id.*, p. 94.

42 "a pretty miserable"—Jackie Robinson, *I Never Had It Made*, p. 24.

42 "Damned skin"—Arthur Mann, *The Jackie Robinson Story*, p. 30.

43 "If a black"—Harvey Frommer, *Rickey and Robinson*, p. 104.

43 "Why does"—Peter Golenbock, *Bums*, p. 126.

44 "You got"—*Id.*

44 "by alcoholism"—Roger Kahn, *The Boys of Summer*, p. 98.

44 "I know"—Jackie Robinson, *I Never Had It Made*, pp. 31–33.

44 "thrilled"—*Id.*, p. 31.

45 "Give it all"—*Id.*, p. 44.

45 "I couldn't sleep"—*Id.*, p. 49.

45 "Always"—Peter Golenbock, *Bums*, p. 142.

45 "be a constant"—Rachel Robinson, *Jackie Robinson*, p. 50.

45 "mobbed, trying"—*New York Herald Tribune*, April 19, 1946.

46 "If Jackie Roosevelt Robinson"—Interview with Buzzie Bavasi.

46 "I want you"—Jackie Robinson, *I Never Had It Made*, p. 56.

46 "goddamned fool"—Peter Golenbock, *Bums*, p. 148.

47 "like a fighter"—*Id.*, p. 150.

47 "I don't care"—Roger Kahn, *The Era*, p. 36.

47 "I don't like"—Peter Golenbock, *Bums*, p. 160.

47 "Hey, nigger"—Jackie Robinson, *I Never Had It Made*, p. 58.

48 "You just can't"—Roger Kahn, *The Era*, p. 51.

48 "did more"—Arnold Rampersad, *Jackie Robinson*, p. 173.

48 "You can't"—Carl Erskine, *What I Learned from Jackie Robinson*, p. 80.

49 "Jackie Robinson"—Interview with Bob Wolff.

49 "Robinson was"—Harvey Frommer, *Rickey and Robinson*, p. 163.

49 "As long as"—Peter Golenbock, *Bums*, p. 208.

49 "done more"—*Id.*, p. 165.

49 "His attack"—Roger Kahn, *The Era*, p. 51.

50 "I've got"—Interview with Carl Erskine.

50 "The guy"—*Id.*

50 "From this point"—Peter Golenbock, *Bums*, p. 225.

51 "to give the lie"—Jackie Robinson, *I Never Had It Made*, p. 81.

51 "White people"—Peter Golenbock, *Bums*, p. 228.

51 "very silly"—Jackie Robinson, *I Never Had It Made*, p. 85.

52 "The trouble"—*Id.* p. 96.

52 "have been giving"—Harvey Frommer, *Rickey and Robinson*, p. 181.

52 "The most savagely booed"—Arnold Rampersad, *Jackie Robinson*, p. 269.

53 "one of the greatest"—*Sporting News*, January 2, 1952.

53 "I'm sick"—Carl Erskine, *What I Learned From Jackie Robinson*, p. 96.

53 "That ain't"—Arnold Rampersad, *Jackie Robinson*, p. 256.

54 "How would"—Roger Kahn, *The Boys of Summer*, p. 173.

54 "If that guy"—Jackie Robinson, *I Never Had It Made*, p. 118.

54 "When are"—Peter Golenbock interview with Carl Furillo.

55 "I was getting"—Jackie Robinson, *I Never Had It Made*, p. 118.

55 "to shake things"—*Id.*, p. 120.

55 "breathing life"—*KMOX Sports Digest*, October 2, 1955.

56 "How do you"—Carl Erskine, *What I Learned from Jackie Robinson*, p. 142.

56 "a thinking man's"—Interview with Bob Wolff.

57 "Hey, Indian"—Peter Golenbock, *Dynasty*, p. 89.

57 "could just"—Interview with Tony Kubek.

57 "very, very tough"—Interview with Bobby Brown.

57 "you had everything"—Interview with Gil McDougald.

58 "Pass the ball"—*Id.*

59 "If you feel"—*Sporting News*, May 16, 1951.

59 "Joe"—Interview with Gil McDougald.

59 "Enjoying the bench"—*Id.*

60 "Well, it looks"—*Id.*

60 "What're you doing"—*Id.*

61 "I'm ready"—*Id.*

61 "Don't you have"—*Id.*

61 "Why, Gil McDougald"—*San Francisco Examiner*, May 29, 1958.

61 "Around second base"—*Sporting News*, February 13, 1952.

62 "Right then"—Bob Cooke, "Portrait of a Shortstop" (unidentified HOF article).

62 "spray the ball"—HOF Interview with Gil McDougald.

62 "mad as heck"—*Id.*

63 "You must"—*Id.*

63 "looms as"—*Sporting News*, November 30, 1955.

63 "you're at the center"—HOF Interview with Gil McDougald.

64 "one of the finest"—*Sporting News*, June 13, 1956.

64 "going into the hole"—*USA Today*, April 3, 2006.

64 "His foot"—*New York Times*, December 30, 2001.

64 "I was in"—Interview with Andy Carey.

64 "We would never"—Don Larsen, *The Perfect Yankee*, p. 45.

CHAPTER 4
Bottom of the Second: Sandy Amoros

67 "When he first"—Interview with Johnny Podres.

67 "Little Flying"—*Sporting News*, February 2, 1955.

67 "I run like"—Peter Golenbock, *Bums*, p. 399.

68 "Hold on to"—*New York Daily News*, August 24, 1980.

68 "$100,000 catch"—*Sporting News*, January 4, 1956.

68 "was the biggest"—Pee Wee Reese, "Reese Tells Top Thrill of Series," *NEA Service*, September 28, 1957.

68 "ten greatest"—*New York Times*, October 19, 2003.

68 "Lucky"—*Sporting News*, May 20, 1967.

69 "I saw him"—*Sports Illustrated*, July 10, 1989.

70 "one of the longest"—*Sporting News*, June 25, 1952.

70 "the batter with"—*Id.*, August 27, 1952.

70 "Sandy is always"—*Id.*, May 20, 1953.

70 "He was always"—Interview with Johnny Podres.

70 "He's always"—*Sporting News*, October 10, 1956.

71 "one of the best"—*Id.*, August 27, 1952.

71 "Amoros needed"—*Id.*, April 21, 1954.

71 "He has been"—*New York World Telegram and Sun*, April 8, 1954.

71 "an undercurrent"—L. Moffi and J. Kronstadt, *Crossing the Line*, p. 72.

71 "the Dodgers are reluctant"—*Id.*, March 26, 1954.

72 "the saturation point"—*Sporting News*, April 21, 1954.

72 "For some reason"—*New York World Telegram and Sun*, May 7, 1954.

72 "raced to the"—*Sporting News*, February 2, 1955.

73 "Get him out"—*Pittsburgh Press*, September 30, 1956.

73 "a bad day"—*Sporting News*, October 3, 1956.

73 "He's a streak hitter"—*Id.*, October 10, 1956.

73 "a fine catch"—Tape of radio broadcast.

74 "a real pitchers'"—*Id.*

CHAPTER 5
Top of the Third: Carl Furillo

75 "Rock"—Roscoe McGowen, "Peg O' My Heart—Carl Furillo" (unidentified HOF article)

76 "Who the hell's"—Interview with Carl Furillo Jr.

76 "I would like"—*New York Post*, August 5, 1985.

77 "At that time"—*Boys of Summer* DVD.

77 "state of his health"—Bruce Jacobs, *Baseball Stars of 1950*, p. 68.

77 "He always thought"—Interview with Carl Furillo Jr.

77 "With Pocomoke"—Bruce Jacobs, *Baseball Stars of 1950*, p. 70.

77 "No. It"—Interview with Carl Furillo Jr.

78 "rough grind"—Fred Down, "Furillo's Arm Makes Runners Wary," August 14, 1947 (unidentified HOF article).

78 "thirty uniforms"—Interview with Buzzie Bavasi.

78 "I thought my whole face"—Peter Golenbock interview with Carl Furillo.

78 "the first three waves"—*Id.*

79 "Yes. Very"—Interview with Carl Furillo Jr.

79 "I can't believe"—*Brooklyn Eagle*, April 26, 1946.

79 "I can't even"—Peter Golenbock, *Bums*, p. 96.

79 "I hated"—*Id.*

80 "rifle arm"—*Brooklyn Eagle*, April 26, 1946.

80 "another guy"—Fred Down, "Furillo's Arm Makes Runners Wary," August 14, 1947 (unidentified HOF article).

80 "Reading Rifle"—*Sport Life Album*, January 1951.

80 "the strong Sicilian"—*Daily Sports News*, January 29, 1989.

80 "They were talking"—Peter Golenbock interview with Carl Furillo.

81 "I'd cut"—Peter Golenbock, *Bums*, p. 152.

81 "They pushed"—*Id.*

81 "ringleaders"—Jackie Robinson, *I Never Had It Made*, p. 56.

81 "I can't sign"—Interview with Buzzie Bavasi.

81 "circulated"—Harvey Frommer, *Rickey and Robinson*, p. 126.

81 "backed the revolt"—Arnold Rampersad, *Jackie Robinson*, p. 164.

82 "had players"—Carl E. Prince, *Brooklyn's Dodgers*, p. 65.

82 "I couldn't"—Bruce Jacobs, *Baseball Stars of 1950*, p. 68.

82 "A fly ball"—Peter Golenbock, *Bums*, p. 357.

83 "He was"—Interview with Carl Erskine.

83 "I studied"—Peter Golenbock, *Bums*, p. 357.

83 "I worked"—Roger Kahn, *The Boys of Summer*, p. 339.

83 "I thought you said"—Interview with Buzzie Bavasi.

84 "looked like balloons"—Peter Golenbock interview with Carl Furillo.

84 "Stick it in"—Peter Golenbock, *Bums*, p. 359.

84 "yapping"—*New York Daily News*, February 23, 1975.

84 "I went after"—*Id.*

85 "one guy"—*Boys of Summer* DVD.

85 "I don't ever"—Peter Golenbock interview with Carl Furillo.

85 "I didn't"—Interview with Fern Furillo.

85 "was rough"—Interview with Carl Erskine.

85 "To get"—Interview with Carl Furillo Jr.

85 "I don't want"—Peter Golenbock, *Bums*, p. 152.

85 "We never suspected"—Interview with Carl Erskine.

86 "When he was"—Interview with Carl Furillo Jr.

86 "an entourage"—Interview with Carl Erskine.

86 "Skoonj"—*Daily Sports News*, January 29, 1989.

86 "What's the difference"—*Sporting News*, May 11, 1955.

86 "A thrill"—Peter Golenbock, *Bums*, p. 405.

86 "If the Dodgers"—*Sporting News*, September 26, 1956.

87 "tough out"—Don Larsen, *A Perfect Yankee*, p. 57.

87 "with Mantle's"—Tape of radio broadcast.

CHAPTER 6
Bottom of the Third: Roy Campanella

88 "things went wrong"—*Washington Star*, March 7, 1979.

89 "No one dared"—Carl Erskine, *What I Learned from Jackie Robinson*, p. 52.

89 "Campy is"—Lou Smith, "Sports Sparks," November 25, 1953 (unidentified HOF article).

90 "My dad's work ethic"—Interview with Roy Campanella Jr.

90 "I took"—Roy Campanella, *It's Good to Be Alive*, p. 33.

90 "He was catching"—*Id.*, p. 42.

91 "I didn't know"—HOF Interview with Roy Campanella.

91 "He gives us"—Roy Campanella, *It's Good to Be Alive*, p. 36.

91 "I learned"—*Id.*

91 "You're fourteen"—*Id.*, and HOF interview with Roy Campanella.

92 "I'd sure like"—Roy Campanella, *It's Good to Be Alive*, p. 49.

92 "The Bible"—*American Weekly*, August 3, 1958.

92 "Tom, I need"—Roy Campanella, *It's Good to Be Alive*, p. 58.

93 "But that isn't"—*Id.*, p. 60.

93 "I just couldn't"—*Id.*, p. 70.

93 "What happened"—*Saturday Evening Post*, June 5, 1954.

94 "We just agreed"—Roy Campanella, *It's Good to Be Alive*, p. 81.

94 "I got a family"—*Id.*, p. 88.

94 "You can use"—*Id.*, p. 99.

94 "The social times"—*Saturday Evening Post*, June 5, 1954.

94 "I don't care"—*Time*, August 8, 1955.

94 "Campy is the most"—*Saturday Evening Post*, June 5, 1954.

95 "You know"—*New York Times*, January 29, 1958.

95 "Same team"—Duke Snider, *The Duke of Flatbush*, p. 76.

95 "They were thick"—Roy Campanella, *It's Good to Be Alive*, p. 107.

95 "How much"—*Sporting News*, July 24, 1971.

96 "I've rejected"—Roy Campanella, *It's Good to Be Alive*, p. 109.

96 "Honey"—*Id.*, p. 111.

97 "How did you know"—*Id.*, p. 113.

97 "It's the end"—*Id.*, p. 114.

97 "PLEASE REPORT"—*Id.*, p. 118.

98 "Can they play"—*Sports Illustrated*, September 24, 1990.
98 "Try that again"—*Time*, August 8, 1955.
98 "Good evening"—*Id.*
98 "was perhaps"—Paul Gould, "Negro Catcher a Flock Ace," January 1947 (unidentified HOF article).
98 "He was the best"—*Sports Illustrated*, September 24, 1990.
99 "the outstanding catcher"—*St. Louis Post Dispatch*, June 27, 1949.
99 "the best catcher"—Fred Down, "Campanella to Get Long Test," March 1948 (unidentified HOF article).
99 "it just didn't"—Roy Campanella, *It's Good to Be Alive*, pp. 132–33.
99 "Roy, you're the best"—*Id.*, p. 135.
100 "Mr. Rickey"—*Id.*, p. 136.
100 "Roy Campanella has found"—Tom Briere, "Campanella Blasts Eight Homers in Seven Games," July 1948 (unidentified HOF article).
100 "Ha"—Roy Campanella, *It's Good to Be Alive*, p. 146.
100 "All our pitchers"—*Boys of Summer* DVD.
100 "A catcher must know"—*Saturday Evening Post*, May 26, 1956.
101 "just throw"—Carl Erskine, *Tales from the Dodger Dugout*, p. 208.
101 "I don't want"—*Saturday Evening Post*, June 5, 1954.
101 "I tried"—Roy Campanella, *It's Good to Be Alive*, p. 131.
102 "Campy was"—Interview with Carl Erskine.
102 "Let's have no trouble"—Peter Golenbock, *Bums*, p. 196.
102 "I'm no crusader"—Jackie Robinson, *I Never Had It Made*, p. 96.
102 "nigger"—Roger Kahn, *The Boys of Summer*, p. 365.
102 "always try to get"—HOF Interview with Roy Campanella.
102 "Jackie would get"—ESPN, *The Brooklyn Dodgers* DVD.
102 "often led"—Rachel Robinson, *Jackie Robinson*, p. 86.
103 "Listen"—Interview with Roy Campanella Jr.
103 "if I could let"—*Boys of Summer* DVD.
103 "You don't have to"—*New York Times*, June 28, 1993.
103 "I couldn't swing"—Roy Campanella, *It's Good to Be Alive*, p. 168.
103 "Sink"—*Id.*, p. 171.
104 "Nobody knows"—*Id.*, pp. 176–77.
104 "That's exactly"—*New York Times*, November 26, 1953.
105 "That's fine encouragement"—*Sporting News*, April 14, 1955.
105 "No active player"—*Time*, August 8, 1955.
106 "It meant such pain"—Interview with Roy Campanella Jr.
106 "simply cannot"—*New York World Telegram and Sun*, August 29, 1956.
106 "the Barber"—Tape of radio broadcast.
107 "Larsen is big enough"—*Id.*

CHAPTER 7
Top of the Fourth: Billy Martin

108 "In those days"—Interview with Bob Wolff.
108 "Billy Martin"—*Id.*
109 "I just want"—*Id.*
109 "Pinocchio"—Peter Golenbock, *Wild, High and Tight*, p. 22; *Time,*
    May 11, 1981.
109 "They figured"—*Sporting News*, October 4, 1969.
110 "I have"—David Falkner, *The Last Yankee*, p. 16.
110 "I went"—*Sporting News*, July 5, 1980.
110 "Take shit"—David Falkner, *The Last Yankee*, p. 25.
110 "he was the only one"—*Sporting News*, January 15, 1990.
111 "Because"—Billy Martin, *Number 1*, p. 53.
111 "Because of Jack"—*Id.*, p. 55.
111 "punched him"—*Id.*, p. 60.
111 "the quickest"—David Falkner, *The Last Yankee*, p. 37.
111 "get"—Billy Martin, *Number 1*, pp. 79–80.
112 "Is that the best"—Peter Golenbock, *Wild, High and Tight*, p. 41.
112 "That little"—Billy Martin, *Number 1*, p. 143.
112 "the sensation"—*Sporting News*, June 9, 1948.
112 "That fresh punk"—Peter Golenbock, *Wild, High and Tight*, p. 49.
113 "crossed up"—*Sporting News*, October 4, 1969.
113 "I never saw"—Interview with Tony Kubek.
114 "It wasn't too bad"—Billy Martin, *Number 1*, p. 155.
114 "You big busher"—Tommy Henrich, *Five O'Clock Lightning,*
    p. 272.
114 "No, no"—Mickey Mantle, *The Mick*, pp. 51–52.
114 "was a loner"—Tommy Henrich, *Five O'Clock Lightning*, p. 24.
115 "What about"—Billy Martin, *Number 1*, p. 155.
115 "You'll be back"—*Id.*, p. 141.
116 "You're going"—*Id.*, p. 142.
117 "Hi, pardner"—Bill Liederman and Maury Allen, *Our Mickey*, p. 23.
117 "my best pal"—Mickey Mantle, *The Quality of Courage*, p. 31.
117 "literally tore"—Mickey Mantle, *The Mick*, p. 107.
117 "Only my friendship"—Billy Martin, *Number 1*, p. 176.
118 "If you could drink"—Merlyn Mantle, *A Hero All His Life*, p. 16.
118 "Billy wasn't"—Mickey Mantle, *The Mick*, p. 96.
118 "Hey, Pinocchio"—*Id.*, p. 85.
118 "terrible"—Billy Martin, *Number 1*, p. 172.
118 "It should wake"—Peter Golenbock, *Dynasty*, p. 125.

119 "Enough is enough"—Interview with Moose Skowron.
119 "He was always"—Interview with Andy Carey.
119 "The Yankees"—Daily News, *Yogi Berra*, p. 32.
120 "I know"—*Sporting News*, March 3, 1954.
120 "Martin should"—*Id.*, September 7, 1955.
120 "I don't know"—Billy Martin, *Number 1*, p. 189.
121 "I've written"—Interview with Bobby Richardson.
121 "mediocre" and "a beautiful present"—Don Larsen, *The Perfect Yankee*, p. 63.
121 "deep into"—Tape of radio broadcast.
121 "by six inches"—*New York Times*, July 30, 2002.
121 "I had dodged"—Don Larsen, *The Perfect Yankee*, p. 64.
121 "the first twelve"—Tape of radio broadcast.

CHAPTER 8
Bottom of the Fourth: Duke Snider

122 "felt like rubber"—Duke Snider, *Duke of Flatbush*, p. 86.
123 "I've come"—ESPN *The Brooklyn Dodgers* DVD.
123 "Here comes"—*Id.*
123 "He could swing"—*Id.*
124 "While lots"—*Sporting News*, November 19, 1952.
124 "I never knew"—*Boys of Summer* DVD.
124 "the most amazing"—ESPN *The Brooklyn Dodgers* DVD.
124 "I wasn't excelling"—HOF interview with Duke Snider (2004).
124 "I wasn't so hot"—*Sporting News*, November 19, 1952.
124 "I had been"—*Boys of Summer* DVD.
125 "is definitely"—*Sporting News*, November 19, 1952.
125 "You're going"—Duke Snider, *The Duke of Flatbush*, p. 36.
125 "It didn't"—*Sporting News*, November 19, 1952.
126 "The way"—ESPN *The Brooklyn Dodgers* DVD.
126 "It broke"—HOF interview (2004).
126 "I put"—*Id.*
127 "My number one"—Duke Snider, *The Duke of Flatbush*, p. 46.
127 "Success"—*Id.*, p. 49.
127 "Judas Priest"—*Sporting News*, July 27, 1949.
127 "steel springs"—*Id.*, July 16, 1952; ESPN DVD.
127 "a straightaway"—*Id.*, April 2, 1947.
128 "be the player"—Duke Snider, *The Duke of Flatbush*, p. 18.
128 "I marveled"—HOF interview (2004).

128 "I think"—*Id.*
128 "Don't embarrass"—ESPN The Brooklyn Dodgers DVD.
129 "I was a free swinger"—HOF interview with Duke Snider (2004).
129 "Duke was"—Peter Golenbock, *Bums,* p. 343.
129 "I was always"—Duke Snider, *The Duke of Flatbush,* p. 17.
129 "You two"—HOF interview with Duke Snider (2004); Duke Snider, *The Duke of Flatbush,* pp. 20–21.
130 "a cute"—Duke Snider, *The Duke of Flatbush,* p. 69.
130 "It's a great love"—Interview with Nancy Gollnick.
130 "super wife"—Interview with Duke Snider.
130 "taught me"—Id.
131 "All you need"—*Sporting News,* November 19, 1952.
131 "Make me"—Duke Snider, *The Duke of Flatbush,* p. 79.
131 "Mr. Rickey"—ESPN *The Brooklyn Dodgers* DVD.
131 "Pack your bags"—Peter Golenbock, *Bums,* p. 353.
131 "can run"—*Sporting News,* July 27, 1949.
131 "I was very"—HOF interview with Duke Snider (2004).
132 "I tried to be"—*Id.*
132 "the hardest"—HOF interview with Duke Snider (2005).
133 "Duke Snider"—*New York Times,* June 15, 1998.
133 "When I saw"—ESPN *The Brooklyn Dodgers* DVD.
133 "We plan"—*Sporting News,* October 15, 1952.
133 "What's the matter"—Danny Peary, *Cult Baseball Players,* p. 34.
133 "We never had"—Interview with Duke Snider.
133 "Snider and I"—Peter Golenbock interview with Carl Furillo; Peter Golenbock, *Bums,* p. 349.
134 "was a magnificent"—Peter Golenbock, *Bums,* p. 349.
134 "If he had"—ESPN *The Brooklyn Dodgers* DVD.
134 "My problem"—Peter Golenbock, *Bums,* p. 354.
134 "Duke"—Roger Kahn, *The Era,* p. 25.
135 "Cripes"—Duke Snider, *The Duke of Flatbush,* p. 43.
135 "he certainly"—*Sporting News,* July 16, 1952.
135 "brought a crisis"—*Id.,* November 19, 1952.
135 "grinning"—*Id.*
135 "remember going"—HOF interview with Duke Snider (2004).
136 "a magnificent season"—*Sporting News,* October 7, 1953.
136 "jinx"—Duke Snider, *The Duke of Flatbush,* p. 141.
136 "showmanship"—*Sporting News,* July 7, 1954.
136 "was happy"—HOF interview with Duke Snider (2004) and HOF interview with Duke Snider (2005).
137 "There"—*Sporting News,* May 25, 1955.

137 "the most dangerous"—Duke Snider, *The Duke of Flatbush*, p. 155.

137 "No player"—*Id.*, p. 14.

137 "there's nothing"—HOF interview with Duke Snider (2004).

138 "You guys"—Duke Snider, *The Duke of Flatbush*, p. 158.

138 "No, you're not"—*Id.*

138 "settle down"—*Collier's*, May 25, 1956, and Duke Snider, *The Duke of Flatbush*, p. 217.

139 "until it appeared"—Duke Snider, *The Duke of Flatbush*, p. 172.

139 "I wasn't"—*Sporting News*, May 23, 1956.

139 "Chances are"—*Id.*

140 "Every time"—Ken Burns, *Baseball* video.

140 "It is almost"—Tape of radio broadcast.

140 "There's a drive"—Tape of radio broadcast.

140 "the shortest"—Interview with Joe Maglie.

141 "Snider is digging"—Tape of radio broadcast.

141 "one of the most"—tape of television broadcast.

CHAPTER 9
Top of the Fifth: Mickey Mantle

142 "Hi. This is Mick"—Tony Castro, *Mickey Mantle*, p. 268.

142 "This was"—*New York Times*, August 14, 1995.

143 "lived and died"—HOF Induction Speech, August 12, 1974.

143 "The feeling between"—Merlyn Mantle, *A Hero All His Life*, p. 42.

143 "I just wanted"—David Gallen, *The Baseball Chronicles*, p. 313.

144 "I hope"—Mickey Mantle, HOF induction speech, August 12, 1974.

144 "Don't you ever"—David Gallen, *The Baseball Chronicles*, p. 313.

145 "Look at that guy"—*Sporting News*, January 31, 1951.

146 "The hell"—Mickey Mantle, *The Mick*, p. 18.

146 "I think I've seen"—*Baseball Digest*, June 1962.

146 "How would you like"—Mickey Mantle, *The Mick*, p. 26.

146 "Mick is the kind"—*Sporting News*, January 31, 1951.

146 "Right now"—Mickey Mantle, *The Mick*, p. 27.

147 "He can make"—*Id.*

147 "had to put"—*Id.*, p. 31.

147 "would like"—David Gallen, *The Baseball Chronicles*, p. 314.

147 "They put on"—Whitey Ford, *Slick*, p. 82.

148 "as the No. 1"—*Sporting News*, January 31, 1951.

148 "He was a real"—Interview with Gil McDougald.

148 "I like the idea"—*Sporting News*, March 21, 1951.

148 "I study Joe"—*Id.*, April 25, 1951.

148 "The kid has never"—Merlyn Mantle, *A Hero All His Life*, p. 26.

148 "I hope"—Yogi Berra, *Ten Rings*, p. 87.

148 "I couldn't even"—Mickey Mantle, *The Mick*, p. 44.

149 "Thank God"—Interview with Bob Turley.

150 "He was the perfect"—Interview with Tony Kubek.

150 "was more one"—Yogi Berra, *What Time Is It?*, pp. 19, 59.

150 "I don't know"—Interview with Bobby Brown.

150 "He can't throw"—Mickey's Quotes Web site, p. 2.

150 "Casey kept bragging"—Tony Castro, *Mickey Mantle*, p. 50.

151 "if he wanted"—Yogi Berra, *What Time Is It?*, p. 133.

151 "So Mantle has"—Mickey Mantle, *The Mick*, p. 57.

152 "changed forever"—Merlyn Mantle, *A Hero All His Life*, pp. 37, 89.

152 "I guess"—Mickey Mantle, *The Mick*, p. 71.

152 "This is gonna"—*Id.*, p. 64.

152 "and bawled"—Tony Castro, *Mickey Mantle*, p. 101.

153 "I'm not hitting"—Mickey Mantle, *The Mick*, p. 67.

153 "I don't want"—*Id.*

154 "Mickey, you do"—*Id.*, p. 75.

154 "Take everything"—*Id.*, p. 77.

154 "I got it"and "Don't move"—Mickey Mantle, *All My Octobers*, p. 8.

154 "I wouldn't play"—*Id.*, p. 10.

155 "and let him"—*Id.*, p. 9.

155 "Next to me"—Merlyn Mantle, *A Hero All His Life*, pp. 54–55.

155 "Go chase that"—Peter Golenbock interview with Joe Collins.

156 "a spectacular"—*Sporting News*, October 22, 1952.

156 "You mean"—*Id.*, November 12, 1952.

156 "Yankee candidate"—*Id.*, April 22, 1953.

156 "the saga"—*Id.*, April 29, 1953.

156 "just zoomed"—Interview with Bob Wolff.

157 "Everybody"—Bill Liederman and Maury Allen, *Our Mickey*, p. 117.

157 "565-foot drive"—*Sporting News*, April 29, 1953.

157 "landing with such force"—Roger Kahn, *The Era*, pp. 315–16.

158 "was the longest"—Mickey Mantle, *All My Octobers*, p. 46.

158 "When you're young"—Mickey Mantle, *My Favorite Summer*, p. 9.

158 "capable of taking"—*Sporting News*, April 21, 1954.

158 "It ain't"—Mickey Mantle, *All My Octobers*, p. 42.

158 "Telling Mantle"—David Gallen, *The Baseball Chronicles*, p. 315.

159 "has not yet"—*Sporting News*, September 14, 1955.

159 "That hit"—Interview with Bob Wolff.

159 "Mickey Mantle"—*Collier's*, July 20, 1956.

159 "Baseball has been"—*Sporting News*, August 29, 1956.

159 "For the first time"—*Id.*, May 30, 1956.

160 "The thing too many"—*Collier's*, July 20, 1956.

160 "I watched him"—Mickey Mantle, *All My Octobers*, p. 69.

160 "I always respected"—Bill Liederman and Maury Allen, *Our Mickey*, p. 142.

160 "If I could run"—*Id.*, p. 80.

160 "Mickey might be"—Tony Castro, *Mickey Mantle*, p. 172.

161 "My father died young"—Peter Golenbock, *Dynasty*, p. 271.

161 "always remained"—Interview with Ray Mantle.

161 "I've always had"—Mickey Mantle, *The Mick*, p. 155.

161 "Of course"—Interview with Jim Cartelli.

161 "A big, soft curve"—Tape of radio broadcast.

162 "Boy"—*Id.*

162 "His brain"—Don Larsen, *The Perfect Yankee*, p. 102.

162 "drives one deep"—Tape of radio broadcast.

162 "drop near"—Don Larsen, *The Perfect Yankee*, p. 102.

162 "With his speed"—Interview with Yogi Berra.

162 "You can tell"—Interview with Clem Labine.

163 "Sheer robbery"—Tape of radio broadcast.

163 "It was"—Mickey Mantle, *My Favorite Summer*, p. 269.

163 "a fantastic catch"—Interview with Joan Hodges.

163 "the legs"—Don Larsen, *The Perfect Yankee*, p. 105.

163 "That shows"—*San Francisco Chronicle*, October 9, 1956.

CHAPTER 10
Bottom of the Fifth: Pee Wee Reese

164 "That's something"—Interview with Mark Reese.

165 "Well, with such"—Tape of radio broadcast.

165 "We were very young"—Peter Golenbock interview with Pee Wee Reese.

165 "I developed"—*Look*, March 9, 1954.

165 "I've got"—Unidentified HOF book, p. 20.

167 "Pee Wee, I think"—Peter Golenbock interview with Pee Wee Reese.

167 "I'm young"—Bruce Jacobs, "Captain of the Dodgers," *Sport Life*, 1949.

167 "has fielded"—*Brooklyn Eagle*, May 26, 1938.

167 "the most instinctive"—*Louisville Courier-Journal*, July 27, 1939.

167 "Oh, no"—*Look*, March 9, 1954.

167 "was the best thing"—Peter Golenbock interview with Pee Wee Reese.

168 "scared to death"—*Id.*

168 "his pale, thin"—*Louisville Courier-Journal*, February 22, 1940.

168 "I shave"—*Sporting News*, December 19, 1956.

168 "I want you"—Herb Goren, "Last of the Old Dodgers," unidentified HOF magazine.

168 "I never saw"—Peter Golenbock interview with Pee Wee Reese.

168 "They hurt"—Harold C. Burr, November 1945, unidentified HOF article.

168 "He started"—Interview with Mark Reese.

169 "Boy wonder"—*Brooklyn Eagle*, July 11, 1940, and Hy Turkin, August 29, 1940, unidentified HOF article.

169 "the best"—Edward T. Murphy, August 13, 1940, unidentified HOF article.

169 "one of the best"—*Id.*

169 "a delight"—*Brooklyn Eagle*, July 17, 1940.

169 "I felt"—Peter Golenbock interview with Pee Wee Reese.

169 "We didn't have"—*Id.*

169 "a part-time drinker"—ESPN *The Brooklyn Dodgers* DVD.

169 "Mr. MacPhail"—*New York Daily News*, March 21, 1972.

170 "If you have"—*Look*, March 9, 1954, and *Sporting News*, April 25, 1964.

170 Pee Wee will"—Edward T. Murphy, August 13, 1940, unidentified HOF article.

170 "Pee Wee, if you"—Roger Kahn, *The Boys of Summer*, p. 323.

170 "You know what happened"—*Id.*

170 "In spite"—Peter Golenbock interview with Pee Wee Reese.

171 "It looks like"—*Id.*

171 "I saw her"—*Sporting News*, December 19, 1956.

171 "Why don't"—Peter Golenbock interview with Pee Wee Reese.

171 "It was not"—*Id.*

172 "to talk shop"—Harry Feeney Jr., May 29, 1942, unidentified HOF article.

172 "Well, there goes"—Peter Golenbock interview with Pee Wee Reese.

172 "Experience and poise"—*Brooklyn Eagle*, July 23, 1942.

172 "the most valuable"—*New York Daily News*, August 14, 1942.

172 "You can have"—unidentified HOF article.

173 "Hey, Pee Wee"—*New York Times*, March 31, 1997, and Roger Kahn, *The Boys of Summer*, p. 310.

173 "the first experience"—Peter Golenbock interview with Pee Wee Reese.

173 "If he's man"—*Id.*

174 "Look, man"—*Id.*

174 "some of the Deep South"—*Id.*

174 "After Pee Wee"—Roger Kahn, *The Boys of Summer*, p. 449.

175 "Something in my gut"—*New York Times*, March 31, 1997.

175 "He was embarrassed"—Interview with Rachel Robinson.

175 "No, they aren't"—*New York Times*, March 31, 1997.

175 "You know, I didn't"—*Id.*, July 17, 1977.

175 "My grandfather"—Harvey Frommer, *Rickey and Robinson*, p. 126.

175 "I bet"—Interview with Mark Reese.

175 "was going to"—*Id.*

175 "We all know"—*Id.*

176 "You take charge"—*New York Times*, March 3, 1949.

176 "He had a quiet leadership"—Interview with Carl Erskine.

176 "If anyone"—Interview with Johnny Podres.

176 "Reese was"—Tommy Heinrich, *Five O'Clock Lightning*, p. 180.

177 "Get back"—Buzzie Bavasi, *Off the Record*, p. 73.

177 "Let's you"—*Sporting News*, December 26, 1956.

178 "the installation"—*New York Daily News*, October 16, 1953.

178 "Playing is"—*Look*, March 9, 1954.

178 "He felt"—Interview with Buzzie Bavasi.

178 "We just won"—Buzzie Bavasi, *Off the Record*, p. 53.

179 "It was a tremendous"—Carl Erskine, *Tales from the Dodger Dugout*, p. 124.

179 "It bounced"—*New York Post*, August 10, 1984.

179 "The best way"—*Parade*, August 5, 1956.

180 "[t]his is"—Michael Shapiro, *The Last Season*, p. 293.

180 "always dangerous"—Tape of radio broadcast.

181 "Pee Wee had to reach"—*Id.*

181 "Perfect"—*Id.*

181 "It was like"—Don Larsen, *The Perfect Yankee*, p. 109.

CHAPTER 11
Top of the Sixth: Yogi Berra

182 "Usually"—Peter Golenbock, *Dynasty*, p. 100.

183 "My husband"—Phil Rizzuto, *The October Twelve*, p. 43.

183 "The pitcher"—Daily News, *Yogi Berra*, p. 22.

183 "Don't worry"—Yogi Berra, *Ten Rings*, p. 96.

183 "Let's throw him"—HOF interview with Yogi Berra (2004).

183 "You really"—Yogi Berra, *What Time Is It?*, p. 92.

184 "When I die"—Yogi Berra, *Ten Rings*, p. 97.

184 "Except for"—Yogi Berra, *When You Come to a Fork in the Road*, p. 11.

184 "I think"—*Sporting News*, November 30, 1960.

184 "If I couldn't"—Yogi Berra, *Ten Rings*, p. 16.

184 "All you've got"—*Id.*, p. 26.

184 "Yogi Berra is"—Phil Rizzuto, *The October Twelve*, p. 57.

184 "He is totally"—Interview with Dave Kaplan.

185 "I remember him"—*Sporting News*, November 30, 1960.

185 "we used"—Interview with Yogi Berra.

185 "When you were at"—Yogi Berra, *What Time Is It?*, p. 139.

186 "We didn't have"—HOF interview with Yogi Berra (2004).

186 "I get pretty ticked"—Yogi Berra, *What Time Is It?*, p. 139.

186 "Wanting to make"—Yogi Berra, *Yogi: It Ain't Over*, p. 154.

186 "Don't you know"—Yogi Berra, *When You Come to a Fork in the Road*, p. 3.

186 "Closed"—Yogi Berra, *What Time Is It?*, p. 104.

187 "I was a lousy"—Yogi Berra, *When You Come to a Fork in the Road*, p. 3.

187 "gave hitting"—Yogi Berra, *Yogi: It Ain't Over*, pp. 47, 67.

188 "I see the ball"—Interview with Jim Cartelli.

188 "A waste pitch"—*Sporting News*, November 30, 1960.

188 "I've got"—*Id.*, November 13, 1957.

188 "hit the ball"—Yogi Berra, *Ten Rings*, p. 7.

188 "too awkward"—*Id.*, and HOF interview with Yogi Berra (2004).

188 "I kept"—Yogi Berra, *Ten Rings*, p. 7, and Yogi Berra, *What Time Is It?*, p. 4.

189 "What will it take"—*Sporting News*, November 13, 1957.

189 "Blame"—Yogi Berra, *Yogi: It Ain't Over*, p. 61.

189 "I got it"—HOF interview with Yogi Berra (2004).

189 "When they gave me"—Daily News, *Yogi Berra*, p. 5.

190 "When I wasn't"—Yogi Berra, *Ten Rings*, p. 10.

190 "like fireworks"—Yogi Berra, *When You Come to a Fork in the Road*, p. 67.

190 "I guess"— Mickey Mantle, *All My Octobers*, p. 195.

191 "one of the league's"—Yogi Berra, *Ten Rings*, p. 10.

191 "Larry was"—*Sporting News*, May 25, 1949.

191 "That was"—Interview with Bobby Brown.

191 "Berraisms"—*Id.*, November 6, 1957.

191 "A lot of people"—Interview with Bobby Brown.

192 "He was in tough shape"—Yogi Berra, *Yogi: It Ain't Over*, p. 96.

192 "Yeah, I was bad"—HOF interview with Yogi Berra (2004).

192 "I just tagged"—Tommy Henrich, *Five O'Clock Lightning*, p. 158.

192 "How can"—Yogi Berra, *Ten Rings*, p. 32.

192 "for making"—*Id.*, p. 23.

193 "So what"—*Id.*

193 "you were scared"—HOF interview with Yogi Berra (2004).

193 "you didn't"—*Id.* (1982).

193 "Always run"—Yogi Berra, *Ten Rings*, p. 31.

193 "If you were doing"—Yogi Berra, *Yogi: It Ain't Over*, p. 127.

194 "The Dodgers stole"—Yogi Berra, *Ten Rings*, p. 33.

194 "Worst World Series catching"—*Id.*, p. 34.

194 "He should've made"—*Id.*, p. 35.

194 "Yogi Berra wobbled"—Daily News, *Yogi Berra*, p. 7.

195 "I was bashful"—Yogi Berra, *When You Come to a Fork in the Road*, p. 4.

195 "You go right back"—*Sporting News*, August 24, 1949.

195 "I could hardly believe"—Yogi Berra, *When You Come to a Fork in the Road*, p. 4.

195 "Carmen is"—Interview with Dave Kaplan.

195 "He knows"—*Sporting News*, March 17, 1948.

196 "I got Bill Dickey"—HOF interview with Yogi Berra (2004).

196 "He worked"—*Id.*

196 "Dickey worked him"—Phil Rizzuto, *The October Twelve*, p. 111.

196 "Without him"—Interview with Dave Kaplan.

197 "I used to"—HOF interview with Yogi Berra (2004).

197 "Hey"—*Id.*

197 "I very seldom"—Peter Golenbock, *Dynasty*, p. 163.

197 "How long"—*Sporting News*, August 11, 1954.

197 "Gimme the ball"—*Id.*, November 13, 1957.

197 "I never went"—*Id.*, November 6, 1957.

198 "If I go"—*Id.*

198 "Phil does"—*Id.*, August 10, 1951.

199 "Rizzuto made Berra"—*Id.*, January 10, 1951.

199 "It is conceivable"—*Id.*, November 21, 1951.

199 "Yogi Berra was"—*Id.*, June 15, 1955.

200 "There aren't"—*Id.*, June 29, 1955.

200 "Ain't they"—*Id.*, November 13, 1957.

200 "I'm going to"—Tommy Henrich, *Five O'Clock Lightning*, p. 158.

201 "Yogi is digging in"—Carl Erskine, *Tales from the Dodger Dugout*, p. 95.

201 "Berra unquestionably"—*Sporting News*, June 15, 1955.

201 "has certainly"—Tape of radio broadcast.

202 "You know"—Carl Erskine, *Tales from the Dodger Dugout*, p. 116.
202 "low and away"—Don Larsen, *The Perfect Yankee*, p. 132.
202 "one of the greatest"—Tape of radio broadcast.
202 "a good"—Don Larsen, *The Perfect Yankee*, p. 132.

CHAPTER 12
Bottom of the Sixth: Andy Carey

203 "Time out"—L. Moffi interview with Andy Carey (HOF), and Interview with Andy Carey.
204 "Well, what"—L. Moffi interview with Andy Carey (HOF).
204 "Ohhh"—*Id.*
204 "I always had"—Interview with Andy Carey.
205 "my stepdad"—L. Moffi interview with Andy Carey (HOF).
205 "He could throw"—*Sporting News*, April 9, 1952.
205 "His throws"—Enos Slaughter, *Country Hardball*, p. 158.
205 "tear your glove"—Joe Collins interview with Peter Golenbock.
205 "Eventually"—*Sporting News*, April 9, 1952.
205 "Sing me a song"—*Oakland Tribune*, July 20, 1986.
206 "I don't think"—L. Moffi interview with Andy Carey (HOF).
206 "For whatever reason"—*Id.*
206 "I worked"—Interview with Andy Carey.
207 "Imagine"—*Sporting News*, April 9, 1952.
207 "My first showing"—*Id.*
207 "You big, strong"—L. Moffi interview with Andy Carey (HOF).
207 "I was getting"—*Sporting News*, April 9, 1952.
207 "I left the room"—*Id.*
207 "knew if he"—L. Moffi interview with Andy Carey (HOF).
208 "Sometimes"—Robert W. Creamer, *Stengel*, p. 18.
208 "I wish"—L. Moffi interview with Andy Carey (HOF).
208 "Pay attention"—Interview with Bob Turley.
208 "It is much too early"—*Sporting News*, March 26, 1952.
208 "Go ahead"—L. Moffi interview with Andy Carey (HOF).
209 "brilliant"—*New York Times*, March 26, 1952.
209 "I have seen"—*Sporting News*, April 2, 1952.
209 "He has"—*Id.*, April 2, 1952.
209 "the No. 1"—*New York Times*, March 23, 1952.
209 "Carey is confronted"—*Id.*, March 26, 1952.
210 "I'd rather be"—Interview with Andy Carey.
210 "Andy is"—*Sporting News*, January 18, 1956.

210 "I was"—*Sports Collector's Digest*, May 13, 1994.
210 "They were" and "Nice going"—Interview with Andy Carey.
211 "Andy Carey"—*Sporting News*, June 9, 1954.
211 "I should"—*Id.*, June 15, 1955.
211 "It was a very hard"—L. Moffi interview with Andy Carey (HOF).
212 "I've always been"—*Id.*
212 "How much"—*Id.*
212 "They never"—*Id.*
212 "What are you trying"—Interview with Andy Carey.
212 "He could eat"—Interview with Hank Bauer.
212 "Carey would order"—Interview with Tony Kubek.
212 "Sure as hell"—L. Moffi interview with Andy Carey (HOF).
214 "I need more"—*Sporting News*, February 20, 1957.
214 "Listen to the crowd"—Tape of radio broadcast.
215 "the crowd"—*Id.*
215 "How about"—*Id.*

CHAPTER 13
Top of the Seventh: Jim Gilliam

216 "his good stuff"—*Philadelphia Bulletin*, October 16, 1965.
217 "Those balls"—*Los Angeles Times*, March 5, 1958.
217 "The tough one"—*Baseball Digest*, September 1959.
217 "So Gilliam"—*New York Times*, June 13, 1965.
217 "a blistering rounder"—*Los Angeles Examiner*, April 29, 1966.
218 "the key play"—*Philadelphia Bulletin*, October 16, 1965.
218 "the fielding gem"—*Hartford Times*, October 23, 1965.
218 "He's the best"—*New York Times*, May 24, 1953.
218 "Jim doesn't"—*Sporting News*, October 21, 1978.
218 "I had one job"—*Id.*, April 29, 1953.
219 "I helped"—*Newsday*, September 29, 1965.
219 "He was a natural"—*Sporting News*, April 29, 1953.
219 "I've been watching"—*New York Times*, May 24, 1953.
219 "The name's Jim"—*Sporting News*, January 6, 1954.
219 "Junior ('Call Me Jim')"—*Id.*, January 27, 1954.
219 "I couldn't hit"—*New York Times*, May 24, 1953.
220 "When I was 12"—*Los Angeles Examiner*, June 20, 1959.
220 "I soon"—*Id.*, February 3, 1958.
220 "I thought"—*New York World Telegram and Sun*, March 20, 1958.
220 "the boy"—*Sporting News*, April 8, 1953.

220 "When nobody"—*New York Times*, September 7, 1979.

221 "This kid's"—*Washington Post*, October 12, 1978.

221 "In the two years"—*Sporting News*, March 25, 1953.

221 "He can run"—*New York World Telegram and Sun*, February 24, 1953.

221 "Playing alongside"—*New York World Telegram and Sun*, March 20, 1953.

221 "continues to be"—*Philadelphia Evening Bulletin*, March 20, 1953.

221 "I'll have to"—*New York Times*, May 24, 1953.

221 "No. It's still"—*Sporting News*, April 29, 1953.

222 "Sheeet"—Larry Moffi and Jonathan Kronstadt, *Crossing the Line*, p. 92.

222 "I'm going to have"—Duke Snider, *The Duke of Flatbush*, p. 222.

222 "I was figuring"—*New York Herald Tribune*, December 24, 1953.

222 "Sweet Lips"—Interview with Carl Erskine.

222 "as quiet a rookie"—*New York Herald Tribune*, December 24, 1953.

223 "He wasn't"—Interview with Carl Erskine.

223 "He and Campanella"—*Id.*

223 "Who wants"—*Los Angeles Examiner*, January 9, 1965.

223 "Jim's calm"—*New York Daily Mirror*, May 12, 1953.

224 "deportment is"—*Sporting News*, January 11, 1964.

224 "Junior dragged"—*New York World Telegram and Sun*, July 12, 1957.

225 "I have never"—*Los Angeles Times*, June 18, 1963.

225 "There's a ball"—Tape of radio broadcast.

225 "When I came up"—Don Larsen, *The Perfect Yankee*, p. 151.

225 "If I keep"—Interview with Bob Wolff.

226 "That's twenty-one"—Tape of radio broadcast.

226 "Well, Mick"—Mickey Mantle, *All My Octobers*, p. 75.

226 "It was"—Don Larsen, *The Perfect Yankee*, p. 152.

CHAPTER 14
Bottom of the Seventh: Enos Slaughter

227 "I sure hate"—Enos Slaughter, *Country Hardball*, p. 96.

228 "As long as"—*Sporting News*, October 2, 1957.

228 "I'm playing"—Enos Slaughter, *Country Hardball*, p. 96, and *Saturday Evening Post*, May 17, 1947.

229 "Skipper"—Enos Slaughter, *Country Hardball*, p. 101.

229 "I made up"—*Id.*, p. 101.

229 "I never expected"—*Yankee*, May 9, 1985.

230 "You shudda"—*Los Angeles Times*, August 15, 2002.

230 "mad dash"—*New York Herald Tribune*, October 15, 1946.

231 "When you're a farm boy"—*Sporting News*, July 27, 1976.

231 "There wasn't enough"—Enos Slaughter, *Country Hardball*, p. 7.

231 "He saves"—*Houston Post*, April 8, 1969.

231 "I just loved"—Enos Slaughter, *Country Hardball*, p. 10.

232 "My mind was set"—*Id.*

232 "clumsy"—*Saturday Evening Post*, May 17, 1947.

232 "She was in love"—Enos Slaughter, *Country Hardball*, p. 11.

232 "Did you know"—*Id.*, p. 12.

232 "Those three days"—*Id.*

233 "Listen"—*Saturday Evening Post*, May 17, 1947.

233 "From then on"—*Chicago Tribune*, September 14, 1959.

233 "He is"—*Saturday Evening Post*, May 17, 1947.

233 "I used to watch"—*Sporting News*, December 26, 1963.

234 "slugger extraordinary"—Unidentified HOF article, October 7, 1937.

234 "one of the brightest"—unidentified HOF article.

234 "You can take"—Interview with Enos Slaughter (HOF).

234 "Slaughter can throw"—*Sporting News*, March 17, 1938.

234 "Slaughter was off"—*Id.*, May 19, 1938.

235 "potential brilliance"—*Id.*

235 "his temperature"—Enos Slaughter, *Country Hardball*, p. 34.

235 "Me being"—Interview with Enos Slaughter (HOF).

236 "I wasn't in awe"—Enos Slaughter, *Country Hardball*, p. 47.

236 "Are you okay"—*Id.*, p. 57.

237 "the greatest throw"—*New York Daily Mirror*, December 23, 1942.

237 "These guys"—*St. Louis Post-Dispatch*, August 13, 2002.

238 "That big baboon"—*Id.*

238 "A throwback"—*Saturday Evening Post*, May 17, 1947.

238 "If you do this"—Roger Kahn, *The Era*, p. 59.

239 "I didn't have to"—*New York Times*, May 9, 1947.

239 "Tradition had it"—Red Barber, *1947*, p. 279.

239 "just a lot of baloney"—usatoday.com, August 7, 2002.

239 "I ain't never"—Interview with Enos Slaughter (HOF).

239 "I don't think"—Interview with Gaye Slaughter.

239 "tried to persuade"—Letter from W. Ray Raleigh to William Morrow & Company, June 23, 1994 (HOF).

239 "rough and racial"—Roger Kahn, *The Era*, pp. 56, 341.

239 "The facts are"—Harvey Frommer, *Rickey and Robinson*, p. 138.

239 "I never heard"—Interview with Chuck Diering.

240 "there was nothing"—Interview with Marty Marion.

240 "a tempest"—Ford C. Frick, *Games, Asterisks, and People*, pp. 97–98.

240 "was out by"—Peter Golenbock, *Bums*, p. 163.

240 "Enos stepped"—*Id.*, p. 164.

240 "Slaughter deliberately"—Jackie Robinson, *I Never Had It Made*, p. 67.

240 "Slaughter's foot"—*New York Times*, August 21, 1947.

241 "My guess"—Red Barber, *1947*, p. 279.

241 "Whoever said"—Interview with Enos Slaughter (HOF).

241 "Slaughter, following always"—*Saturday Evening Post*, May 17, 1947.

242 "I don't care"—Interview with Gaye Slaughter.

242 "Watch your feet"—*New York Times*, March 7, 1985.

242 "a dirty player"—*Sporting News*, October 5, 1949.

242 "covering first awkwardly"—Roger Kahn, *October Men*, p. 11.

243 "the most serious"—Ken Burns, *Baseball* video.

243 "relentlessly"—Interview with Ken Burns.

243 "was after him"—*Id.*

243 "I wanted writers"—*Id.*

244 "impossible to know"—*Id.*

244 "Full of zing"—*New York Sun*, March 19, 1950.

244 "I love St. Louis"—Enos Slaughter, *Country Hardball*, p. 117.

245 "murder to put"—*Id.*, p. 138.

245 "The old kid"—*Sporting News*, December 12, 1951.

246 "a spectacular diving"—John Thorn, *Total Baseball*, p. 297.

246 "The old feller"—*St. Louis Post-Dispatch*, January 28, 1979.

246 "This is the first"—*Sporting News*, October 2, 1957.

246 "Eno"—Enos Slaughter, *Country Hardball*, p. 154.

246 "We have several"—unidentified HOF article, April 12, 1954.

247 "This is the biggest"—*Id.*

247 "Her parents"—Enos Slaughter, *Country Hardball*, p. 135.

247 "One thing"—Peter Golenbock interview with Enos Slaughter.

247 "My boy"—Enos Slaughter, *Country Hardball*, p. 157.

248 "He always knew"—Interview with Hank Bauer.

248 "He talked about"—Interview with Bobby Richardson.

248 "If you ever"—Interview with Gil McDougald.

248 "I hustled"—Richard Lally, *Bombers*, p. 104.

249 "The news"—Enos Slaughter, *Country Hardball*, p. 162.

249 "The people"—*Id.*, p. 165.

249 "How would you like"—*Id.*, p. 168.

249 "Although Enos"—*Sporting News*, September 5, 1956.

249 "I really think"—*Yankee*, May 9, 1985.

250 "There goes"—Tape of radio broadcast.

CHAPTER 15
Top of the Eighth: Gil Hodges

251 "It was a pretty one-sided"—*Parade*, August 1, 1954.
252 "Call down"—*Saturday Evening Post*, September 8, 1951.
252 "He hit"—*Id.*
252 "roaring"—*Parade*, August 1, 1954.
252 "We all thought"—*Id.*
253 "I just couldn't look"—Interview with Joan Hodges.
253 "Joanie, Joanie"—*Id.*
253 "Did you know"—*Parade,* August 1, 1954.
253 "There isn't enough"—*New York Daily News*, September 1, 1950.
253 "There's a hum"—Tape of radio broadcast.
254 "comforting feeling"—Don Larsen, *The Perfect Yankee*, p. 161.
254 "Concentrate"—*Id.*, p. 162.
254 "The drama rises"—Tape of radio broadcast.
255 "Maybe you realized"—Interview with Johnny Podres.
255 "That's the way"—*Collier's*, August 21, 1953.
255 "The big, handsome"—*Complete Baseball* (September 1952). (HOF excerpt).
255 "It's too warm"—*Collier's*, August 21, 1953.
256 "The way"—*New York Times*, August 26, 1955.
256 "Gil was"—Peter Golenbock, *Bums*, p. 328.
256 "We didn't talk"—Interview with Joan Hodges.
256 "I never had"—*Sporting News*, March 13, 1957.
257 "I don't know"—*Saturday Evening Post*, September 8, 1951.
257 "Don't fuck"—Peter Golenbock, *Bums*, p. 325.
257 "He was a nice"—*Id.*, p. 283.
257 "I don't know"—*Saturday Evening Post*, September 8, 1951.
258 "I look out"—*Id.*
258 "Charley Hodges' boys"—*Sporting News*, June 15, 1963.
258 "Bobby was"—*Id.*
258 "breathless"—*Guidepost*, September 1960.
259 "He ducked"—*Complete Baseball*, September 1951.
259 "I went overboard"—*Baseball*, January 1950, p. 268.
259 "Being a country boy"—*Guidepost*, September 1960.
260 "Yes, he was"—Interview with Joan Hodges.
260 "I prayed"—*Guidepost*, September 1960.
260 "There will"—*Id.*
260 "Gil just"—Interview with Joan Hodges.
260 "Since when"—*Saturday Evening Post*, September 8, 1951.

260 "He tried me"—*Baseball*, January 1950, p. 268.

261 "God is giving"—*Guidepost*, September 1960.

261 "One thing"—*Brooklyn Eagle*, March 23, 1948.

261 "Hodges is"—Fred Down, March 25, 1948, unidentified HOF article.

261 "The boy was"—*Sporting News*, April 7, 1948.

262 "I was more"—Gil Hodges, *The Game of Baseball*, p. 13.

262 "Son"—*Id.*

262 "I'd never played"—*Sporting News*, July 7, 1948.

262 "There's little doubt"—Gross, "Week-End Personality," unidentified HOF article, September 4, 1949.

263 "What's going on"—Interview with Buzzie Bavasi.

263 "It's the way"—Gil Hodges, *The Game of Baseball*, p. 69.

263 "my old man"—Peter Golenbock, *Amazin'*, p. 131.

263 "He's taking"—Carl Erskine, *Tales from the Dodger Dugout*, p. 126.

263 "He was kind of"—Interview with Carl Erskine.

264 "That guy"—*Id.*

265 "Gil and Eddie"—Interview with Joan Hodges.

265 "When the boys"—*Id.*

266 "We had to have"—*Id.*

266 "As much as"—Gil Hodges, *The Game of Baseball*, p. 105.

267 "Unlike the previous"—Don Larsen, *The Perfect Yankee*, p. 163.

267 "My God"—Larry Moffi interview with Andy Carey (HOF).

267 "He's got it"—Tape of radio broadcast.

267 "Thus far"—Don Larsen, *The Perfect Yankee*, p. 165.

CHAPTER 16
Bottom of the Eighth: Joe Collins

269 "Instead of diving"—Peter Golenbock interview with Joe Collins.

269 "Because"—*Id.*

269 "kindling"—*Sporting News*, March 7, 1956.

270 "The statistics"—*New York Times*, April 28, 1958.

270 "He was the kind"—Interview with Bobby Brown.

271 "I was hot"—Interview with Bill Skowron.

271 "Of course"—Peter Golenbock interview with Joe Collins.

272 "Would you believe"—*Id.*

272 "I played"—*Baseball Digest*, October 1952.

272 "He was a good"—Peter Golenbock interview with Joe Collins.

273 "He instilled"—*Baseball Digest*, October 1952.

273 "We were high school"—*New York Times*, March 27, 1958.

273 "I'd say"—HOF interview with Joe Collins.
274 "It may sound"—Peter Golenbock interview with Joe Collins.
275 "the shit stance"—*Id.*
275 "I used to kid"—Interview with Bob Wolff.
275 "If I'm going"—*New York Times*, March 10, 1951.
275 "When he was hot"—Interview with Bobby Brown.
275 "Nobody"—Peter Golenbock interview with Joe Collins.
276 "He now may settle"—*New York Times*, June 17, 1952.
276 "Collins is popular"—*Id.*, June 25, 1952.
276 "one of the most"—*Id.*, September 29, 1955.
276 "When they did that"—Arlene Howard, *Elston and Me*, p. 40.
276 "He may never"—*New York Times*, April 28, 1958.
276 "He was a terrific"—Interview with Tony Kubek.
277 "I was looking"—Peter Golenbock interview with Joe Collins.
277 "He couldn't get me out"—*Id.*
278 "It would be nice"—*New York Times*, September 29, 1955.
279 "I was no gazelle"—Interview with Bill Skowron.
279 "You know, Moose"—*Id.*
279 "never should"—*New York Times*, June 11, 1956.
280 "The applause"—Tape of radio broadcast.
280 "It was"—Don Larsen, *The Perfect Yankee*, p. 168.
280 "was the most"—Interview with Joe Collins Jr.
280 "giving a great"—Tape of radio broadcast.

CHAPTER 17
Top of the Ninth: Hank Bauer

281 "a little huddle"—Peter Golenbock interview with Joe Collins.
281 "Nothing"—Billy Martin, *Number 1*, p. 197.
281 "the toughest"—Mickey Mantle, *All My Octobers*, p. 57.
281 "a clenched fist"—*Sporting News*, April 13, 1968.
281 "a permanent"—*Los Angeles Times*, September 6, 1964.
282 "Don't hit"—Interview with Hank Bauer Jr.
282 "I didn't *think*"—Richard Lally, *Bombers*, p. 74.
282 "I could feel"—*Id.*
282 "I hit"—*Id.*, p. 73.
283 "But the ball"—*Id.*
283 "Rushing in"—*Time*, September 13, 1964.
283 "You would have to"—*New York World Telegram and Sun*, October 11, 1951.

283 "greatest thrill"—*New York Journal American*, January 3, 1964.

283 "My oldest sisters"—Peter Golenbock, *Dynasty*, p. 150.

284 "He was a real"—*Time*, September 13, 1964.

284 "That's the reason"—*Id.*

284 "They had a whistle"—Peter Golenbock, *Dynasty*, p. 150.

284 "I learned"—*Sports Collectors Digest*, February 14, 1997.

284 "I wasn't blessed"—Peter Golenbock, *Dynasty*, p. 153.

284 "Baseball has never"—*American Weekly*, September 7, 1958.

284 "The only guy"—Tommy Henrich, *Five O'Clock Lightning*, p. 205.

284 "When Hank"—*Time*, September 13, 1964.

284 "He's the hardest-running"—*American Weekly*, September 7, 1958.

285 "You wouldn't have"—Interview with Hank Bauer.

285 "Don't they ever"—*Oshkosh Northwestern*, July 31, 1999.

285 "greasy hot dogs"—*Id.*

285 "He was a tremendously"—*Id.*

286 "We were just"—*Id.*

286 "that made him"—*Id.*

286 "I wanted to get"—Interview with Hank Bauer.

286 "It was a great experience"—*Sports Collectors Digest*, February 14, 1997.

286 "was proudest"—Interview with Bea Bauer.

286 "I didn't get"—Interview with Hank Bauer.

287 "Oh, shit"—*Id.*

287 "You gutless"—*Id.*

287 "He was a one-man"—Interview with Gil McDougald.

288 "Joe Page"—Tommy Henrich, *Five O'Clock Lightning*, p. 205.

288 "He never made it"—Interview with Hank Bauer.

288 "I saw this reflection"—*Time*, September 13, 1964.

289 "his little brother"—Interview with Hank Bauer.

289 "You better"—*Id.*

289 "Harris has brought"—*New York World Telegram*, September 1948.

290 "Shit"—Interview with Hank Bauer.

290 "It's about time"—*Id.*

290 "His strength"—*Time*, September 13, 1964.

290 "a cement mixer"—*New York Times*, October 10, 1966.

291 "sounds like"—*Sporting News*, April 13, 1968.

291 "When it came"—*Time*, September 13, 1964.

291 "Crusty"—Interview with Andy Carey.

291 "a supernice"—Interview with Gil McDougald.

291 "Hank took it"—Arlene Howard, *Elston and Me*, p. 42.

291 "As a veteran"—Interview with Bobby Richardson.

292 "Don't mess"—Yogi Berra, *Ten Rings*, p. 71.

292 "When it came"—Interview with Bobby Richardson.

292 "When I saw"—Interview with Hank Bauer.

292 "I didn't care"—*Id.*

292 "Now you can take"—*New York Times*, June 21, 1961.

293 "At the time"—Yankee, 2000.

293 "I was on the bench"—*New York Times*, March 5, 1968.

294 "How would you like"—Interview with Hank Bauer.

294 "You know the reason"—*Id.*

294 "to do everything"—Peter Golenbock, *Dynasty*, p. 148.

294 "Hank couldn't"—*Time*, September 13, 1964.

295 "Me?"—David Cataneo, *Casey Stengel*, p. 64.

295 "First of all"—Interview with Hank Bauer.

295 "Mr. Bauer"—*Milwaukee Journal*, October 5, 1958.

296 "It suddenly felt"—Don Larsen, *The Perfect Yankee*, p. 171.

296 "I didn't think"—Interview with Hank Bauer.

296 "Our strategy"—Don Larsen, *The Perfect Yankee*, p. 177.

CHAPTER 18
The Last Pitch: Dale Mitchell

298 "a wide spot"—Interview with Dale Mitchell Jr.

298 "That was"—Interview with Bo Mitchell.

299 "I had to keep"—*Cleveland News*, July 11, 1949.

299 "needed"—*Id.*

300 "I had a habit"—*Sporting News*, July 16, 1947.

300 "My coach"—*Id.*, May 10, 1950.

300 "was never"—Interview with Dale Mitchell Jr.

300 "big year"—Interview with Bo Mitchell.

301 "Who hit"—Interview with Dale Mitchell Jr. (based on a conversation with Arlen Specter).

301 "couldn't let"—*Cleveland News*, July 11, 1949.

301 "is the outstanding"—*Sporting News*, March 26, 1947.

302 "I'll make good"—*Cleveland Plain Dealer*, July 20, 1947.

302 "astonished"—*Baseball Digest*, February 1949.

302 "one of the most"—*New York Times*, October 5, 1948.

302 "the biggest"—*Cleveland Plain Dealer*, May 7, 1970.

302 "In this game"—*Cleveland Plain Dealer*, August 20, 1948.

303 "Spoke"—*Id.*

303 "the man has"—*Baseball Digest*, February 1949, and *Sporting News*, November 10, 1948.

303 "You know, Dad"—Interview with Bo Mitchell.

303 "When the Yankees"—Interview with Dale Mitchell Jr.

304 "mash anybody"—*Cleveland Plain Dealer*, July 22, 1948.

304 "Swish"—*Id.*, March 10, 1952.

305 "Greenberg put"—Interview with Dale Mitchell Jr.

305 "And next year"—*Cleveland Plain Dealer*, September 9, 1953.

305 "I'm still convinced"—*Id.*, March 3, 1956.

306 "Dale, we just"—Interview with Bo Mitchell.

306 "one of the most"—*Cleveland Plain Dealer*, July 30, 1956.

306 "They certainly"—Interview with Bo Mitchell.

307 "He liked Brooklyn"—Interview with Dale Mitchell Jr.

307 "We were"—Peter Golenbock, *Bums*, p. 418.

308 "Strike three"—Tape of radio broadcast.

308 "was right over the middle"—*New York Daily Mirror*, October 9, 1956.

308 "I had"—Mickey Mantle, *All My Octobers*, p. 76.

308 "last pitch"—Interview with Andy Carey.

308 "It wasn't"—Interview with Gil McDougald.

308 "was high"—Interview with Tim Wiles, HOF Research Director (who was with Slaughter when he made the comment).

308 "My legs"—Don Larsen, *The Perfect Yankee*, p. 187.

309 "So"—Yogi Berra, *What Time Is It?*, p. 103.

309 "greatest thrills"—*Id.*, p. 99.

309 "Is that"—*Id.*, p. 103.

309 "High and outside"—Interview with Carl Erskine.

309 "Babe Pinelli"—Interview with Duke Snider.

309 "I might have"—*New York Post*, October 9, 1956.

309 "It makes"—*Sporting News*, October 31, 1981.

310 "They're going"—Interview with Bo Mitchell.

310 "He never"—*USA Today*, October 8, 1996.

CHAPTER 19
Aftermath

311 "I had nothing else"—*Sporting News*, October 31, 1981.

312 "It's sometimes"—Interview with Don Larsen.

312 "Sal"—*Sports Illustrated*, April 22, 1968.

313 "gave his typical"—Interview with Joe Maglie.

313 "was like"—*Niagara Gazette*, June 27, 1970.

313 "There's probably"—Interview with Doris Maglie.

313 "the worst headache"—*Id.*

313 "I would put"—*Id.*

314 "Carl"—Carl Erskine, *What I Learned from Jackie Robinson*, p. 127.

315 "I love you"—Rachel Robinson, *Jackie Robinson*, p. 216.

315 "As soon as"—HOF Interview with Gil McDougald.

315 "I woke up"—David Eisenberg, "McDougald a Sharp Businessman," unidentified HOF article, November 7, 1970.

316 "Gil"—Interview with Gil McDougald and Lucille McDougald.

316 "Everyone"—*New York Times*, January 4, 1995.

317 "I didn't know"—*Sports Illustrated*, July 10, 1989.

317 "I no have"—*New York Times*, April 28, 1967.

317 "You don't need"—*Sports Illustrated*, July 10, 1989.

318 "He had his day"—Interview with Buzzie Bavasi.

318 "The Dodgers"—Interview with Carl Erskine.

319 "I like"—*New York Times*, September 1, 1968.

319 "I don't know"—Interview with Carl Furillo Jr.

319 "Hey, sleepyhead"—*Id.*

319 "Why are you"—*Id.*

320 "I'm looking forward"—*Los Angeles Examiner*, January 26, 1958.

320 "were shocked"—Interview with Roy Campanella Jr.

320 "suspicious mind"—*Milwaukee Journal*, August 12, 1960.

320 "taken on"—Roy Campanella, *It's Good to Be Alive*, p. 304.

320 "Hi, slugger"—*New York Daily News*, October 5, 1958.

321 "I know you can't"—*New York Newsday*, June 28, 1993.

321 "One thing"—Billy Martin, *Number 1*, p. 199.

321 "let's go"—Peter Golenbock, *Dynasty*, p. 294.

322 "I never claim"—*Sporting News*, November 28, 1958.

322 "After I was traded"—Billy Martin, *Number 1*, p. 204.

322 "sitting"—Peter Golenbock, *Wild, High and Tight*, p. 167.

322 "I'm thinking"—Michael Demarco, *Dugout Days*, p. 41.

323 "He likened"—Interview with Billy Martin Jr.

323 "I went out"—Interview with Tony Kubek.

323 "Nothing"—Interview with Billy Martin Jr.

323 "incredible"—*Time*, May 11, 1981.

324 "I'm not happy"—Interview with Billy Martin Jr.

324 "It was"—Duke Snider, *The Duke of Flatbush*, p. 256.

324 "I should have"—Interview with Duke Snider.

325 "It made"—Duke Snider, *The Duke of Flatbush*, p. 268.

325 "Christ"—*Id.*, p. 281.

325 "Religion"—Interview with Duke Snider.

325 "One of my concerns"—*New York Times*, July 21, 1995.

326 "I used to"—David Gallen, *The Baseball Chronicles*, p. 309.

326 "Hey"—Bill Liederman and Maury Allen, *Our Mickey*, p. 28.

326 "Today"—*Sporting News*, July 20, 1968.

327 "As he grew"—Interview with Bob Wolff.

327 "Fuck bar mitzvahs"—Bill Liederman and Maury Allen, *Our Mickey*, p. 57.

327 "Here's"—Merlyn Mantle, *A Hero All His Life*, p. 28.

327 "Mick"—*Id.*

328 "You talk"—*Id.*, p. 30.

328 "You would"—Interview with Whitey Ford.

329 "Podnuh"—Vince Staten, *Ol' Diz*, p. 262.

329 "He loved"—Interview with Mark Reese.

329 "Those gutless"—*Id.*

330 "You're sure"—*Sporting News*, March 5, 1984.

330 "he gave"—*Louisville Courier-Journal*, August 13, 1984.

330 "I just"—*Silurian News*, November 1993.

330 "Pee Wee"—Roger Kahn, *The Boys of Summer*, p. 455.

331 "Manage who?"—Yogi Berra, *When You Come to a Fork in the Road*, p. 65.

331 "A gentle soul"—Mickey Mantle, *The Mick*, p. 211.

332 "It was"—Yogi Berra, *When You Come to a Fork in the Road*, p. 47.

332 "I had"—*Id.*, p. 5.

332 "I did not"—Interview with Joan Hodges.

333 "Yogi's"—Billy Martin, *Number 1*, p. 24.

333 "I think"—Yogi Berra, *It Ain't Over Till It's Over*, p. 137.

333 "Yogi will be"—Daily News, *Yogi Berra*, p. 192.

333 "What's the use"—*Id.*, p. 198.

334 "You know"—Interview with Bobby Richardson.

334 "He is very"—Interview with Dave Kaplan.

334 "Yogi was"—*Id.*

334 "You know"—*Id.*

335 "He is"—*Id.*

335 "Carey and Casey"—*Sporting News*, October 9, 1957.

335 "You'll wish"—L. Moffi interview with Andy Carey (HOF).

335 "He was"—Interview with Gil McDougald.

335 "Well, Carey"—L. Moffi interview with Andy Carey (HOF).

335 "I was hitting"—*Id.*

336 "This kid"—*Philadelphia Bulletin*, March 26, 1962.

336 "Lucy"—*Sporting News*, April 4, 1962.

336 "That was"—Interview with Andy Carey.

337 "I think"—*Id.*

337 "They always"—L. Moffi interview with Andy Carey (HOF).

337 "Imagine"—Interview with Andy Carey.

338 "that he would"—Interview with Susie Carey.

338 "He had to"—*Id.*

338 "Gilliam's trouble"—*Newsday*, October 1, 1959.

338 "Out of"—*Los Angeles Times*, June 18, 1963.

338 "foul"—Interview with Buzzie Bavasi.

339 "There must"—*Sporting News*, March 23, 1963.

339 "I've had it"—*New York Times*, October 8, 1966.

339 "As a coach"—*Los Angeles Examiner*, April 26, 1968.

340 "He loved"—Interview with Clem Labine.

340 "jumped"—Enos Slaughter, *Country Hardball*, p. 161.

340 "We're going"—*Id.*, p. 187.

341 "bitter"—Interview with Enos Slaughter (HOF).

341 "I can't"—Enos Slaughter, *Country Hardball*, p. 201.

341 "He went"—Interview with Gaye Slaughter.

341 "My life"—*New York Times*, March 7, 1985.

341 "to stay home"—unidentified HOF *Washington Post* article, 1992.

342 "You know"—Interview with Sharon Slaughter.

342 "Daddy, do you"—*Id.*

342 "Daddy, you can"—Interview with Gaye Slaughter.

343 "Dr. Jekyll"—Unidentified AP article (HOF), February 13, 1969.

343 "He was a big"—Peter Golenbock, *Amazin'*, pp. 194–95.

344 "His hands"—Duke Snider, *The Duke of Flatbush*, p. 59.

344 "I had sharp pains"—Gil Hodges, *The Game of Baseball*, p. 103.

344 "I feel great"—*New York Daily News*, November 22, 1968.

344 "A minimum"—*Id.*, April 5, 1969.

344 "Gil"—Interview with Joan Hodges.

345 "Oh, my God"—YouTube video with Joan Hodges, et al., May 29, 2007.

345 "I didn't like"—*Id.*

345 "In baseball's"—*Sporting News*, November 1, 1969.

345 "sent me flowers"—Interview with Joan Hodges.

345 "What time"—*New York Times*, April 3, 1972.

346 "And I thought"—Interview with Joan Hodges.

346 "I made up"—*New York Times*, March 27, 1958.

346 "I couldn't play"—Peter Golenbock interview with Joe Collins.

347 "You're killing"—Interview with Gil McDougald.

347 "He was a ballbuster"—Interview with Joe Collins Jr.

348 "At the age"—*Sports Collectors Digest*, February 14, 1997.

348 "He was pretty tough"—Interview with Hank Bauer Jr.

348 "This is"—*New York Times*, June 21, 1961.

349 "What is it"—Interview with Hank Bauer.

349 "When a man"—*Time*, September 13, 1964.

349 "I hated"—*New York Times*, September 25, 1966.

349 "Bauer has done"—*New York Times*, September 25, 1966.

349 "I'm gonna"—*Sporting News*, October 21, 1967.

350 "I hung up"—undated *Kansas City Sun* article (HOF).

350 "I'm sticking"—*Sporting News*, November 9, 1968.

350 "I made"—Interview with Hank Bauer.

351 "My biggest"—Interview with Bea Bauer.

352 "I know"—Interview with Dale Mitchell Jr.

353 "Who invited"—*Id.*

354 "The doctor"—*Id.*

355 "This supernatural"—Interview with Bo Mitchell.

355 "best known"—*Cleveland Plain Dealer*, January 6, 1987.

EPILOGUE

358 "We truly felt"—Yogi Berra, *What Time Is It?*, p. 159.

358 "Most of all"—Duke Snider, *The Duke of Flatbush*, p. 20.

359 "Just look"—Morris Engelberg and Marv Schneider, *DiMaggio*, p. 92.

SELECTED BIBLIOGRAPHY

There are a multitude of books about the New York Yankees, the Brooklyn Dodgers, and the players profiled in this book. These are the ones I found most useful, but the list does not in any way purport to be an exhaustive compilation of interesting and informative works on those subjects. I have not included the articles and other sources I used because of the sheer volume, but the endnotes provide some indication of the breadth of the other sources that were reviewed.

Allen, Maury. *Brooklyn Remembered: The 1955 Days of the Dodgers.* Champaign, IL: Sports Publishing, 2005.

Appel, Marty. *Now Pitching for the Yankees: Spinning the News for Mickey, Billy and George.* Kingston, NY: Total Sports Publishing, 2001.

Appel, Marty. *Yesterday's Heroes: Revisiting the Old-Time Baseball Stars.* New York: HarperCollins, 1988.

Barber, Red. *1947: When All Hell Broke Loose in Baseball.* New York: DaCapo Press, 1982.

Barra, Allen. *Yogi Berra: Eternal Yankee,* New York: Norton, 2009.

Bavasi, Buzzie. *Off the Record.* New York: McGraw-Hill, 1987.

Berra, Yogi, with Dave Kaplan. *Ten Rings: My Championship Seasons.* New York: HarperCollins, 2003.

Berra, Yogi, with Dave Kaplan. *What Time Is It? You Mean Now?: Advice for Life from the Zennest Master of Them All.* New York: Simon & Schuster, 2002.

Berra, Yogi, with Dave Kaplan. *When You Come to a Fork in the Road, Take It!: Inspiration and Wisdom from One of Baseball's Greatest Heroes.* New York: Hyperion, 2001.

Berra, Yogi, with Tom Horton. *Yogi: It Ain't Over.* New York: McGraw-Hill, 1989.

Bouton, Jim. *Ball Four.* New York: Dell Publishing, 1970.

Campanella, Roy. *It's Good to Be Alive.* New York: Little, Brown and Co., 1959.

Castro, Tony. *Mickey Mantle: America's Prodigal Son.* Dulles, Virginia: Potomac Books, 2002.

Cataneo, David. *Casey Stengel: Baseball's "Old Professor."* Nashville, Tennessee: Turner Publishing, 2003.

Creamer, Robert W. *Stengel: His Life and Times.* New York: Simon & Schuster, 1984.

Demarco, Michael. *Dugout Days: Untold Tales & Leadership Lessons from the Extraordinary Career of Billy Martin.* New York: AMACOM, 2001.

Durocher, Leo, with Ed Linn. *Nice Guys Finish Last.* New York: Simon & Schuster, 1975.

Eig, Jonathan. *Opening Day: The Story of Jackie Robinson's First Season.* New York: Simon & Schuster, 2007.

Einstein, Charles (ed.). *The Fireside Book of Baseball.* New York: Simon & Schuster, 1956.

Einstein, Charles (ed.). *The Second Fireside Book of Baseball.* New York: Simon & Schuster, 1958.

Engelberg, Morris, and Marv Schneider. *DiMaggio: Setting the Record Straight.* St. Paul, Minnesota: MBI, 2003.

Erskine, Carl. *Tales from the Dodger Dugout.* Champaign, IL: Sports Publishing, 2004.

Erskine, Carl. *What I Learned from Jackie Robinson: A Teammate's Reflections On and Off the Field.* New York: McGraw-Hill, 2005.

Eskenazi, Gerald. *The Lip: A Biography of Leo Durocher.* New York: HarperCollins, 1993.

Falkner, David. *The Last Yankee: The Turbulent Life of Billy Martin.* New York: Simon & Schuster, 1992.

Frommer, Harvey. *Rickey and Robinson.* New York: Macmillan, 1982.

Ford, Whitey, with Phil Pepe. *Slick: My Life In and Around Baseball.* New York: HarperCollins, 1987.

Ford, Whitey, Mickey Mantle, and Joseph Durso. *Whitey and Mickey: A Joint Autobiography of the Yankee Years.* New York: Viking, 1977.

Frick, Ford C. *Games, Asterisks, and People: Memoirs of a Lucky Fan.* New York: Crown, 1973.

Gallen, David (ed.). *The Baseball Chronicles.* New York: Avalon Publishing Group, 1991.

Garagiola, Joe. *Baseball Is a Funny Game.* New York: Lippincott, 1960.

Golenbock, Peter. *Amazin': The Miraculous History of New York's Most Beloved Baseball Team.* New York: St. Martin's Press, 2002.

Golenbock, Peter. *Bums: An Oral History of the Brooklyn Dodgers.* New York: Putnam, 1984.

Golenbock, Peter. *Dynasty: The New York Yankees 1949–64.* New York: Prentice Hall, 1975.

Golenbock, Peter. *George: The Poor Little Rich Boy Who Built the Yankee Empire.* New York: Wiley, 2009.

Golenbock, Peter. *Wild, High and Tight: The Life and Death of Billy Martin.* New York: St. Martin's Press, 1994.

Goodwin, Doris Kearns. *Wait Till Next Year: Summer Afternoons with My Father and Baseball.* New York: Simon & Schuster, 1998.

Henrich, Tommy, with Bill Gilbert. *Five O'Clock Lightning: Ruth, Gehrig, DiMaggio, and the Glory Days of the New York Yankees.* New York: Carol Publishing, 1992.

Hodges, Gil, with Frank Slocum. *The Game of Baseball.* New York: Crown, 1969.

Hodges, Russ, and Al Hirshberg. *My Giants.* New York: Doubleday, 1963.

Howard, Arlene. *Elston and Me: The Story of the First Black Yankee.* Columbia, Missouri: University of Missouri Press, 2001.

Jacobs, Bruce. *Baseball Stars of 1950.* New York: Lion Press, 1950.

Jacobson, Sidney. *Pete Reiser: The Rough-and-Tumble Career of the Perfect Ballplayer.* Charlotte, North Carolina: McFarland and Company, 2004.

Kahn, Roger. *The Boys of Summer.* New York: Harper & Row, 1972.

Kahn, Roger. *The Era 1947–1957: When the Yankees, Giants and Dodgers Ruled the World.* New York: Houghton Mifflin, 1993.

Kahn, Roger. *October Men: Reggie Jackson, George Steinbrenner, Billy Martin and the Yankees' Miraculous Finish in 1978.* New York: Houghton Mifflin, 2005.

Kubek, Tony, and Terry Pluto. *Sixty-One: The Team, the Record, the Men.* New York: Simon & Schuster, 1987.

Lally, Richard. *Bombers: An Oral History of the New York Yankees.* New York: Crown, 2002.

Larsen, Don, with Mark Shaw. *The Perfect Yankee: The Incredible Story of the Greatest Miracle in Baseball History*. Champaign, Illinois: Sagamore Publishing, 1996.

Liederman, Bill, and Maury Allen. *Our Mickey: Cherished Memories of an American Icon*. Chicago, Illinois: Triumph Books, 2004.

Mann, Arthur. *The Jackie Robinson Story*. New York: Grosset & Dunlap, 1950.

Mantle, Merlyn, Mickey E. Mantle, David Mantle, and Dan Mantle, with Mickey Hershowitz. *A Hero All His Life*. New York: HarperCollins, 1996.

Mantle, Mickey. *The Quality of Courage*. New York: Doubleday, 1964.

Mantle, Mickey, with Herb Gluck. *The Mick*. New York: Doubleday, 1985.

Mantle, Mickey, with Mickey Hershowitz. *All My Octobers: My Memories of Twelve World Series When the Yankees Ruled Baseball*. New York: HarperCollins, 1994.

Mantle, Mickey, and Phil Pepe. *My Favorite Summer 1956*. New York: Doubleday, 1991.

Martin, Billy, and Peter Golenbock. *Number 1*. New York: Delacorte Press, 1980.

Moffi, Larry, and Jonathan Kronstadt. *Crossing the Line: Black Major Leaguers 1947–1959*. Charlotte, North Carolina: McFarland & Company, 1994.

The New York Daily News. *Yogi Berra: An American Original*. Champaign, IL: Sports Publishing, 1998.

Ninfo, Bill. *Carl Furillo: The Forgotten Dodger*. Authorhouse, 2002.

Oakley, Ronald J. *Baseball's Last Golden Age, 1946–1960*. Charlotte, North Carolina: McFarland & Company, 1994.

Oliphant, Thomas. *Praying for Gil Hodges: A Memoir of the 1955 World Series*. New York: St. Martin's Press, 2005.

Peary, Danny (ed.). *Cult Baseball Players: The Greats, the Flakes, the Weird and the Wonderful*. New York: Fireside, 1990.

Prager, Joshua. *The Echoing Green: The Untold Story of Bobby Thomson, Ralph Branca and the Shot Heard Round the World*. New York: Pantheon, 2006.

Prince, Carl E. *Brooklyn's Dodgers: The Bums, the Borough, and the Best of Baseball*. New York: Oxford University Press, 1996.

Rampersad, Arnold. *Jackie Robinson: A Biography*. New York: Knopf, 1997.

Rizzuto, Phil, and Tom Horton. *The October Twelve: Five Years of Yankee Glory, 1949–1953*. New York: Forge, 1994.

Robinson, Jackie. *I Never Had It Made: An Autobiography*. New York: Putnam, 1972.

Robinson, Rachel. *Jackie Robinson: An Intimate Portrait*. New York: Abrams, 1996.

Robinson, Sharon. *Stealing Home: An Intimate Family Portrait by the Daughter of Jackie Robinson*. New York: HarperCollins, 1996.

Salant, Nathan. *Superstars, Stars, and Just Plain Heroes*. New York: Stein and Day, 1982.

Shapiro, Michael. *The Last Good Season: Brooklyn, the Dodgers and Their Final Pennant Race Together*. New York: Doubleday, 2003.

Silverman, Jeff (ed.). *The Greatest Baseball Stories Ever Told*. Old Saybrook, Connecticut: Lyons Press, 2001.

Slaughter, Enos, with Kevin Reid. *Country Hardball: The Autobiography of Enos "Country" Slaughter*. Greensboro, North Carolina: Tudor Publishers, 1991.

Snider, Duke, with Bill Gilbert. *The Duke of Flatbush*. New York: Kensington, 1988.

Staten, Vince. *Ol' Diz: A Biography of Dizzy Dean*. New York: HarperCollins, 1992.

Szalontai, James D. *Close Shave: The Life and Times of Baseball's Sal Maglie*. Charlotte, North Carolina: McFarland & Company, 2002.

Testa, Judith. *Sal Maglie: Baseball's Demon Barber*. DeKalb, Illinois: Northern Illinois University Press, 2007.

Thorn, John, Peter Palmer, Michael Gershman, and David Pietrusza. *Total Baseball* (Sixth Edition). New York: Total Sports, 1999.

Tygiel, Jules. *Baseball's Great Experiment: Jackie Robinson and His Legacy*. New York: Oxford University Press, 1997.

INDEX

Aaron, Hank, 86
Abrams, Cal, 132
Adams, Red, 112
Ainsmith, Eddie, 24
Alexander, Hugh, 299
Allen, Mel, 18
Alston, Walter, 34, 67, 178, 216
  Amoros and, 71–73
  bats Campanella eighth in 1955, 86
  bats Furillo eighth in 1954, 86
  in conference with Maglie in sixth inning
    of perfect game, 215
  Gilliam and, 217, 218, 221, 223, 338,
    339
  Mitchell and, 306, 307
  pinch hits Mitchell for Maglie in perfect
    game, 297
  Robinson and, 54–55
  on Snider, 137
Amoros, Eloise, 317
Amoros, Migdalia, 317
Amoros, Sandy, 66–74
  in 1956 regular season, 72–73
  Alston and, 71–73
  batting accomplishments in 1954 season,
    72
  celebrated catch in World Series of 1955,
    67–68

  childhood of, 68–69
  death of, 318
  deteriorating health in later years, 318
  in the field during perfect game, 36, 73,
    74, 215, 250
  first at bat in perfect game, 65
  language barrier and, 70
  Migdalia (wife) and, 317
  as minor leaguer, 69–71
  personality of, 70–71
  post-1956 career of, 317
  power of, 69–70
  second at bat in perfect game, 163
  speculation about Dodger's holding back
    of, 71–72
  speed of, 69, 72
  third at bat in perfect game, 267
Ashburn, Richie, 132
Averill, Earl, 329

Baker, Del, 3
Ball Four (Bouton), 313
Barber, Red, 225, 239, 241
Barnett, Barney, 146
Barney, Rex, 49, 240, 243
Baseball Digest, 275
Bauer, Bea, 351
Bauer, Charlene Friede, 290, 293–94, 348

Bauer, Hank, 281–97
  batting accomplishments of, 293–95
  Berra and, 285
  brought up to Yankees in 1948, 289–90
  cancer of, 351
  Carey and, 212–13, 291
  as catcher in one game for Yankees, 287
  catch in World Series of 1951, 282–83
  Charlene (wife) and, 290, 293–94, 348
  childhood of, 283–85
  commitment to teammates of, 291
  death of, 351
  fantasy baseball camps and, 350–51
  in the field during perfect game, 18, 65, 87, 162, 225, 295
  fighting spirit of, 284
  first at bat in perfect game, 35
  fourth at bat in perfect game, 280
  hustle of, 284, 291
  on Larsen's selection to start perfect game, 5
  as leadoff batter, 295
  malaria and, 288, 289
  as manager, 348–50
  Mantle and, 153
  in the marines, 286–88
  as minor leaguer, 285–86, 289
  negotiates with Weiss, 293–94
  nerves in top of the ninth inning of perfect game, 7, 281–82
  personality of, 291
  physical appearance of, 281
  post-1956 career of, 348–49
  second at bat in perfect game, 139–40
  on Slaughter, 248
  Stengel's platoon system and, 292–93
  strength of, 290
  third at bat in perfect game, 215
  29th birthday celebration for Martin at Copacabana incident, 321–22
  voice of, 290–91, 351
  World Series checks and, 291–92
Bauer, Hank, Jr., 348
Bauer, Herman, 285, 289
Bauer, Joe, 284, 289
Bauer, John, 283, 285
Bauer, Mary, 283
Bavasi, Buzzie, 53, 263, 338
  Campanella and, 95, 97–98, 103
  Furillo and, 78, 81
  Maglie and, 33–34
  Reese and, 178

Robinson and, 46
  on Stark's promotional sign, 83
Berra, Carmen Short, 183, 195, 332, 334
Berra, Paulina, 185–87
Berra, Pietro, 185–87, 189
Berra, Yogi, 60, 182–202, 273
  admired by opposing players, 201
  advises Larsen on Campanella, 202
  advises Larsen on Gilliam, 18
  advises Larsen on Hodges, 254
  advises Larsen on Robinson, 37
  Amoros' catch in World Series of 1955 and, 67
  batting accomplishments of, 198, 199
  batting form of, 187–88
  Bauer and, 285
  as best catcher of his time, 199–200
  Beven's loss of perfect game and, 2
  books written by, 334
  Carmen (wife) and, 183, 195, 332, 334
  as catcher in perfect game, 1–2, 6–10, 65, 184, 201, 202, 254, 267, 296
  catching skills of, 196–97
  childhood of, 185–87
  on closeness of team, 358
  as coach, 331–33
  compassion of, 200
  contract negotiating by, 189, 198
  dialogue with batters of, 8–9
  DiMaggio (Joe) and, 193
  elected to Hall of Fame, 331
  first at bat in perfect game, 66, 73
  Garagiola on, 184, 185, 188
  gets nickname, 187
  on *Good Morning America*, 310
  health of, 335
  on Larsen's no-windup delivery, 3
  leaps into Larsen's arms after perfect game, 308
  as manager, 331–33
  on Mantle's catch in fifth inning of perfect game, 162
  on Mantle vs. DiMaggio as teammate, 150
  Martin and, 113, 333
  as minor leaguer, 188–91
  on Mitchell, 6
  museum established in his honor, 334
  MVP awards of, 199
  in the navy, 190
  on perfect game, 308–9
  personality of, 191, 200
  physical appearance of, 184
  post-1956 career of, 331

receives catching instruction from Dickey, 196
rejected by Rickey in 1942, 188
Rizzuto and, 198–99
second at bat in perfect game, 141
self-esteem of, 184, 200
Steinbrenner and, 333–35
third at bat in perfect game, 230
troubles with catching in first two years, 192
verbal miscues of, 192–93, 200–201, 334
verbal skills of, 191
Williams (Ted) and, 182–84, 187, 197
on winning the game, 2
in World Series of 1947, 194
in World Series of 1949, 196
Bevens, Bill, 2, 194, 225
Bickford, Vern, 202
Bill Taylor's Restaurant, 4
Black, Joe, 220
Black Sox Scandal, 43
Boston Red Sox, 227–30
Boudreau, Lou, 249, 301–3
Bouton, Jim, 21, 313
Boyer, Clete, 335
Boys of Summer, The (Kahn), 138
Bragan, Bobby, 81, 261, 262
Branca, Ralph, 80, 240
Breadon, Sam, 42, 238, 239
Brooke, Holly, 152–54
Brooklyn Brown Dodgers, 43, 44, 95
Brooklyn Dodgers:
  hire Rickey as GM, 42
  lose play-off of 1951, 31, 132–33
  lose World Series of 1941, 125–26, 171
  lose World Series of 1947, 194
  lose World Series of 1952, 119, 135, 156
  lose World Series of 1953, 119–20, 136
  Maglie on, 21, 34
  Maglie traded to, 33–34
  purchase Reading farm team, 78
  Robinson debuts for, 47
  Robinson supported by, 47, 48, 50
  speculation about holding back of Amoros by sportswriters, 71–72
  win pennant in 1955, 55, 105
  win pennant in 1956, 35
  win World Series of 1955, 67–68, 86, 105, 179, 266
Brown, Bobby, 57, 59, 150, 191, 270
Brown, Tommy, 85
Browne, Leo, 188
Bryant, Clay, 69–70

Burdette, Lew, 102
Burge, Les, 257
Burns, Ken, 243–44
Busch, Gussie, 61, 246–47
Byrd, Harry, 113
Byrne, Tommy, 67, 268

Camilli, Dolph, 128
Campanella, Bernice Ray, 93–94
Campanella, Ida Mercer, 89–90, 92
Campanella, John, 89–90
Campanella, Roxie, 321
Campanella, Roy, 56, 88–107, 307
  attitude towards race relations, vs. Robinson's, 101–3
  automobile accident of, 88–89, 320–21
  batting accomplishments of, 104, 105
  on batting eighth in 1955, 105
  beaning of, 103
  Bernice (wife) and, 93–94
  breaks thumb on verge of breaking team's home run record, 103
  breaks up Robinson-Alston confrontation, 54
  brought up to Dodgers as outfielder, 99–100
  as catcher in perfect game, 74, 89, 106–7, 140, 180, 214, 215, 280
  on catching, 100
  catching skills of, 99
  childhood of, 89–93
  coaching offer by O'Malley, 104
  death of, 321
  develops baseball skills as teenager, 91–92
  at Dodgers' spring training camp in 1948, 99
  first at bat in perfect game, 87
  Gilliam and, 219
  as handicapped activist, 320–21
  hand injuries suffered by, 104–6
  handling of pitchers by, 100–1
  Ida (wife) and, 89–90, 92
  joins Bacharach Giants, 92
  as minor leaguer, 97–100
  as National League MVP in 1951, 1953, and 1955, 104, 105
  in Negro National League, 92–94
  personality of, 98, 99
  positive attitude of, 94–95
  racism faced by, 91, 101–3
  Reese on humor of, 101
  Rickey and, 95–100

Campanella, Roy (*cont.*)
  Roxie (wife) and, 321
  Ruthe (wife) and, 92, 96, 100, 320
  second at bat in perfect game, 202
  sent down to integrate American Association league, 100, 262
  as target for Maglie's knockdown pitch, 29
  tension between Robinson and, 102–3
  third at bat in perfect game, 296–97
  told by Robinson about Rickey's plan, 96–97
  tributes to, 320–21
Campanella, Roy, Jr., 100, 320, 321
Campanella, Ruthe, 92, 96, 100, 320
Campanis, Al, 69
Carey, Andy, 159, 203–15
  accepts scholarship at St. Mary's College, 206
  appetite of, 212
  Bauer and, 212–13, 291
  business interests of, 336, 337
  camaraderie on Yankees and, 210–11
  Carolyn (wife) and, 336, 338
  childhood of, 204–5
  father's fake newspaper headline and, 5
  in the field during perfect game, 64, 267, 308
  first at bat in perfect game, 106
  health problems of, 337–38
  leg imbalance of, 206–7
  Lucy (wife) and, 213, 336
  on Martin, 119
  as minor leaguer, 206, 207
  post-1956 career of, 335–36
  press praise in first training camp, 209
  retirement of, 336
  second at bat in perfect game, 204, 214
  self-confidence of, 209
  Stengel and, 203–4, 207–11, 214, 335
  success on Yankees exhibition tour, 213
  Susie (wife) and, 337, 338
  third at bat in perfect game, 250
  on third strike to Mitchell in perfect game, 308
  throwing arm of, 205
  in top of the ninth inning of perfect game, 7
  troubles with batting stance of, 211
Carey, Carolyn Long, 336, 338
Carey, Jimmy, 337
Carey, Ken, 205, 206
Carey, Lucy Ann McAleer, 213, 336, 337

Carey, Susie Parker, 337, 338
Cartelli, Jim, 161
Cashman, Brian, 334
Cerv, Bob, 316
Chandler, Albert B. "Happy," 27–29, 43
Chandler, Spud, 192
Chapman, Ben, 47–48
Chester, Hilda, 178
Chicago Tribune, 156
Cleveland Indians, 32–34
Cleveland Plain Dealer, 302, 306, 355
Cobb, Ty, 338
Cochrane, Mickey, 144
Coleman, Jerry, 15, 59, 61, 115, 116, 118, 209, 269
Coleman, Rip, 4
Collier's, 138
Collins, Jim, 347–48
Collins, Joe, 268–80
  batting accomplishments of, 275–78
  batting stances of, 275
  on Carey's throwing arm, 205
  childhood of, 271
  clutch hitting of, 270
  death of, 347–48
  embarrassing pickoff incident in first spring training, 273–74
  fan saved by home run of, 268–70
  in the field during perfect game, 18, 64, 163, 254
  first at bat in perfect game, 35
  fourth at bat in perfect game, 280
  friendly demeanor of, 276–77
  hits home run injured, 277–78
  in huddle before taking field in ninth inning of perfect game, 281
  injured in headfirst slide in 1955, 269
  on Larsen's drinking, 16
  and Mantle act as Howard's "honor guard," 276
  Mantle and, 155
  as minor leaguer, 271–74
  in the navy, 273
  Peg (wife) and, 273, 347
  with People's Express, 347
  popularity among teammates of, 276
  retirement of, 346–47
  second at bat in perfect game, 140
  Skowron and, 270–71, 279
  Stengel and, 270–71, 275–79
  third at bat in perfect game, 215, 270
  trade pressures on, 276
  in World Series of 1951, 275

in World Series of 1952, 277
in World Series of 1953, 278
in World Series of 1955, 278, 279
Collins, Joe, Jr., 347
Collins, Peg Riley, 273, 347
Connors, Chuck, 82
Corbitt, Claude, 98
Costas, Bob, 143
Cox, Billy, 53–54, 217
Craft, Harry, 147
Craig, Roger, 8
Creamer, Robert, 20, 208
Crosby, Bing, 205
Crosetti, Frank, 5, 106, 114, 180, 214, 316
Culberson, Leon, 228

Daley, Arthur, 104, 270, 348
Dalton, Harry, 350
Dameo, Phil, 347
Daniel, Dan, 199, 201, 211
Davis, Sammie, Jr., 321
Deal, Roy, 300
Dean, Dizzy, 230, 329
Devine, Joe, 58, 206, 212
Dickey, Bill, 173, 196, 236
Diering, Chuck, 239
DiMaggio, Dom, 182, 228
DiMaggio, Joe, 32, 58, 60, 158, 242
   Bauer and, 284
   Berra and, 150, 193
   on knockdown pitches, 359
   Mantle and, 148–49, 154
   Martin and, 114–15
   Slaughter and, 284
   Snider and, 122
   Weiss on salary of, 294
Dixon, Tom, 92
Doby, Larry, 156
Downey, Jack, 111
Downey, Tom, 125
Dressen, Charlie, 53–54, 95, 103, 134–35, 177, 201, 217, 256
   Hodges and, 263
Drysdale, Don, 222
Durham Morning Herald, 232
Durocher, Leo, 60, 82, 167–70, 178
   Campanella and, 99–101
   Furillo and, 79, 84
   Hodges and, 259, 261–62
   Maglie and, 29–33
   Reese and, 168–70, 330
   Robinson and, 46–47, 50

Dyer, Eddie, 229, 233
Dykes, Jimmy, 14

Ebbets Field, right-field wall of, 82–83
Edwards, Bruce, 49, 99, 261, 262
Effrat, Louis, 276
Engelberg, Morris, 359
Erikson, Swede, 285, 286
Erskine, Carl, 21, 56, 314
   Berra and, 201
   Campanella and, 89, 101, 102
   Furillo and, 83, 85, 86, 318, 319
   Gilliam and, 223
   Hodges and, 256, 264
   Maglie and, 21, 34
   Reese and, 176, 179
   Robinson and, 102
   Snider and, 137
   on third strike to Mitchell, 309
Etten, Nick, 273

Farrell, Leroy, 220
Feezle, Stan, 258
Feller, Bob, 33, 359
Felton, Happy, 178
Fernandez, Chico, 318
Finch, Bob, 97–98
Finley, Charles O., 348–50
Flores, Jesse, 191
Ford, Whitey, 2, 55, 149, 197, 327, 328, 350
Free agency, 358, 359
French, Oliver, 232
Frick, Ford, 238–40
Frisch, Frankie, 169
Furillo, Carl, 67, 75–87, 307
   batting accomplishments of, 83, 86
   on being brought up to Dodgers, 79
   Campanella explains Negro League teams to, 93
   childhood of, 76–77
   death of, 319
   on Durocher, 79
   in early years with Dodgers, 79–83
   eye operation of, 83–84
   Fern (wife) and, 75–76, 79, 319
   in the field during perfect game, 74
   fight with Durocher, 84
   first at bat in perfect game, 75, 87
   on Hodges, 257
   leukemia of, 319
   on Maglie, 34
   negotiates with Rickey, 82

Furillo, Carl (*cont.*)
   as neighborhood celebrity, 86
   petition to bar Robinson and, 81
   plays in minor leagues, 77–78
   post-1956 career of, 318
   retaliation against Maglie by, 359
   right-field wall at Ebbets Field and, 82–83
   Robinson and, 80–81
   second at bat in perfect game, 201, 202
   sensitivity of, 85
   "Skoonj" nickname of, 86
   Snider and, 85, 133–34
   social isolation from other Dodgers, 85
   sues Dodgers on release, 318–19
   third at bat in perfect game, 296
   throwing arm of, 77, 80, 82
   wins batting championship in 1953, 84
   on World Series win in 1955, 86
   in World War II, 78–79
Furillo, Carl, Jr., 77, 79, 86, 319
Furillo, Fern Reichart, 75–76, 79, 85, 319
Furillo, Jon, 77, 79

Gallagher, Jim, 238
Garagiola, Joe, 184, 185, 188, 332
Garagnini, Biggie, 195
Garcia, Mike, 33
Gehrig, Lou, 64, 117, 122, 128, 132, 135,
   150, 167, 252
Gilliam, Edwina Fields, 223
Gilliam, Gloria, 223
Gilliam, Jim ("Junior"), 67, 216–26
   Alston and, 217, 218, 221, 223, 338,
      339
   batting accomplishments of, 223
   childhood of, 218–19
   as coach, 339
   death of, 340
   dislike for playing third base, 217
   divorced from Gloria, 223
   Edwina (wife) and, 223
   in the field during perfect game, 36, 214,
      250
   first at bat in perfect game, 17–18
   as minor leaguer, 220–21
   nickname of, 219
   personality of, 222–24
   plays in Negro league, 219–20
   post-1956 career of, 338
   retaliates against Sanchez, 224
   retirement of, 339
   Robinson and, 221, 222, 224
   rookie season of, 221–22

   second at bat in perfect game, 121
   self-confidence of, 221–22
   sense of fun of, 223
   as switch hitter, 219–20
   temperament of, 223–24
   third at bat in perfect game, 218, 224–25
   wins Rookie of the Year in 1953, 222
   in World Series of 1965, 216–18
Gionfriddo, Al, 194
Golenbock, Peter, 182, 247, 284, 346
Gollnick, Nancy, 130
Gomez, Ruben, 84
Gonzalez, Mike, 229
Good Morning America, 310
Gowdy, Curt, 329
Grant, Don, 332
Greenberg, Hank, 33–34, 304–6
Greenwade, Tom, 146
Griffin, John, 128
Griffith, Calvin, 322
Grim, Bob, 67

Haddix, Harvey, 222
Happy Felton's Knothole Gang, 178
Haring, Josh, 77
Harrah, Toby, 322–23
Harrelson, Bud, 345
Harrelson, Ken, 343
Harris, Bucky, 191–92, 194–96, 289, 290
Hartnett, Gabby, 169
Hassert, Buddy, 236
Hausmann, George, 26
Hearn, Jim, 133
Heffner, Don, 12
Henrich, Tommy, 114, 126, 148, 171, 176,
   288
Herman, Babe, 103, 166
Herman, Billy, 171
Hermanski, Gene, 50, 194
Hoak, Don, 179
Hodges, Bob, 252, 258
Hodges, Charlie, 255, 257–61
Hodges, Gil, 68, 99, 164, 179, 242, 251–67
   batting accomplishments of, 264–65
   childhood of, 255, 258
   death of, 332, 345–46
   disappoints in first season, 259
   in the field during perfect game, 36, 214,
      215
   first at bat in perfect game, 64–65
   heart attacks of, 344–46
   hits four home runs in game, 252–53
   importance of family to, 266

Joan (wife) and, 251–53, 256, 260,
  265–67, 345, 346
large hands of, 257, 263
learns to play first base, 262
as manager, 332, 343–45
military service of, 260
as minor leaguer, 261
pays Robinson to catch pop flies, 262–63
post-1956 career of, 342–43
protective nature of, 257
receives hitting instruction from Lavagetto, 261
relationship with umpires of, 263–64
religiousness of, 260
Rickey and, 129
second at bat in perfect game, 162–63
supported by fans during slump, 255–56
temperament of, 256–57
third at bat in perfect game, 254, 267
tries out for Dodgers, 258–59
in World Series of 1953, 278
Hodges, Gil, Jr., 266
Hodges, Irene, 255
Hodges, Joan Lombardi, 162, 163, 251–53,
  256, 260, 265–67, 332, 345, 346
Hodges, Russ, 30
Hopp, Johnny, 153
Hopper, Clay, 261–62
Hornsby, Rogers, 58–59, 131
Horton, Tom, 193
Houk, Ralph, 14, 331
House Un-American Activities Committee,
  51
Howard, Elston, 149–50, 179, 230, 276,
  291
Hubbell, Carl, 30
Humphreys, Jim, 301
Hunter, Catfish, 333
Hutchinson, Fred, 312
Hyland, Robert F., 227–28

"I Play Baseball for Money—Not Fun"
  (Snider), 138, 139
Irvin, Monte, 242, 282

Jackson, Reggie, 350
Johnson, Billy, 59
Jones, Cleon, 344–45
Jorgensen, Spider, 129

Kaat, Jim, 160
Kahn, Roger, 54, 138, 157–58, 222, 242,
  331

Kain, Shaky, 272–73
Kaline, Al, 8
Kanehl, Rod, 263
Kaplan, Dave, 184, 195, 335
Kennedy, John, 217
Kinder, Ellis, 277–78
Kiner, Ralph, 49
Klinger, Bob, 228, 229
Knockdown pitches, 29, 358–59
Kollonige, George, 271
Koosman, Jerry, 343
Koslo, Dave, 282
Koufax, Sandy, 216, 217, 319
Kubek, Tony, 57, 113, 149, 150, 212, 276,
  277, 323
Kuenn, Harvey, 294
Kurowski, Whitey, 237
Kuzava, Bob, 119, 282–83

Labine, Clem, 8, 162–63, 340
Landis, Kenesaw Mountain, 43
Lardner, John, 295
Larsen, Charlotte, 11
Larsen, Corrine, 312
Larsen, Don, 1–19
  baseball ambitions as child, 12
  baseball fantasy camps and, 312
  on demotion from Yankees, 14
  drafted during Korean war, 13
  drinking of, 16
  in eighth inning of perfect game, 253–54,
    267
  fails to make support payments, 17
  in fifth inning of perfect game, 143,
    161–63
  finds out he's starting game, 6
  first at bat in perfect game, 106–7
  in first inning of perfect game, 17–19
  in fourth inning of perfect game, 121
  on Good Morning America, 310
  as high school athlete, 12
  on his slider during perfect game, 9
  hitting ability of, 13–15
  on Hodges' fly ball in fifth inning of per-
    fect game, 162
  makes predictions the night before perfect
    game, 5
  memorabilia shows and, 312
  as minor leaguer, 12–13
  in ninth inning of perfect game, 1–2, 6–10,
    282, 295–98, 307–10
  no-windup delivery of, 3
  personality of, 13, 14, 16

Larsen, Don (*cont.*)
  physical appearance of, 1
  on pitching perfect game, 308–9
  plays for Baltimore Orioles, 14, 17
  plays for St. Louis Browns, 13–14
  post-1956 career of, 311
  second at bat in perfect game, 214
  in second game of World Series of 1956,
    3–4
  in second inning of perfect game, 37, 56,
    64–65
  selected to start game, 4, 5
  in seventh inning of perfect game, 224–26
  in sixth inning of perfect game, 184,
    201–2
  on Snider's near home run in fourth inning
    of perfect game, 121
  social habits of, 13, 14, 16
  socializes the night before perfect game,
    4–5
  statistics in 1956 regular season, 16
  on superstition regarding no-hitters during
    games, 226
  third at bat in perfect game, 279–80
  in third inning of perfect game, 75, 87
  traded to Kansas City Athletics, 311
  traded to Yankees, 14
  during Yankee's 1955 season, 14–15
Larsen, James, 11, 12
Larsen, Scott, 312
Larsen, Vivian, 17
Lasorda, Tommy, 340
Lavagetto, Cookie, 2, 194, 225, 261
Lemon, Bob, 33, 268
Liddle, Don, 33
Liderman, Bill, 327
Lobert, Hans, 94
Loes, Billy, 68
Look, 52
Lopat, Eddie, 15–16, 348–49
Lopata, Stan, 132
Lopez, Al, 304
Lown, Turk, 103
Luque, Dolf, 25, 27

McCarthy, Joe, 236
McConnell, Mickey, 220, 221
McCorry, Bill, 17, 212
McCulley, Jim, 30
McDougald, Gil, 56–64, 67, 68, 117, 118,
    210
  approach to playing the infield, 56–57
  batting stance of, 58–59, 62
  Bauer and, 287, 297
  childhood of, 57–58
  Collins and, 347
  competitiveness of, 57
  expresses desire to play second base,
    61–62
  in the field during perfect game, 18, 56,
    64, 202, 225, 308
  first at bat in perfect game, 106
  hearing loss of, 316–17
  hits Herb Score with line drive, 315
  Lucille (wife) and, 58, 60
  as minor leaguer, 58–59
  plays basketball in college, 58
  plays in semipro league, 58
  retirement of, 315–16
  rookie season of, 59–61
  second at bat in perfect game, 181
  spiked by Slaughter, 248
  Stengel and, 59–63
  takes over at shortstop, 63–64
  temperament of, 276–77
  third at bat in perfect game, 250
  on third strike to Mitchell, 308
  wins Rookie of the Year in 1951, 61
  in World Series of 1951, 60–61
McDougald, Lucille Tochilin, 58, 60
McGowan, Jack, 92
McGowan, Roscoe, 240–41
McGraw, John, 113, 144
McGwire, Mark, 359
Mack, Connie, 61, 194
Mackey, Biz, 92–93
MacPhail, Larry, 167, 169–70, 172
MacPhail, Lee, 147–48, 349
Magerkurth, George, 177
Maglie, Doris Ellman, 313, 314
Maglie, Kay Pileggi, 24, 27, 312, 313
Maglie, Sal, 6, 20–36, 73
  as basketball player in youth, 21–22
  brain aneurysm and stroke of, 313–14
  business ventures of, 313
  celebrates winning the pennant in 1951, 31
  confidence in Campanella of, 89
  curveball of, 28–30
  death of, 314
  Doris (wife) and, 313, 314
  in eighth inning of perfect game, 270, 280
  on feelings toward Dodgers, 21, 34
  in fifth inning of perfect game, 165,
    180–81
  first at bat in perfect game, 87
  in first inning of perfect game, 1–2, 35–36

in fourth inning of perfect game, 139–41
on Furillo, 34
Kay (wife) and, 24, 27, 312
knockdown pitch of, 29, 359
on Larsen's perfect game, 309
on Mantle's home run in fourth inning of
    perfect game, 140
in Mexican League, 26–28
as minor leaguer, 22–24, 28
on New York Giants team, 24–26, 29–33
personality of, 20–21
as pitching coach, 312–13
plays for Dodgers in 1956 regular season,
    34–35
post-1956 career of, 312
Robinson's retaliation tactic and, 224
second at bat in perfect game, 202
in second inning of perfect game, 66,
    73–74
in semipro leagues, 22
in seventh inning of perfect game, 230,
    249–50
in sixth inning of perfect game, 214–15
"The Barber" nickname of, 30–31
in third inning of perfect game, 89,
    106–7
traded to Brooklyn Dodgers, 33–34
traded to Cleveland Indians, 33
in World Series of 1951, 31–32
in World Series of 1954, 32–33
Maglie, Sal, Jr., 313
Maguire, Jack, Jr., 187
Malamud, Bernard, 52
Mantle, David, 145, 329
Mantle, Lovell, 144–46
Mantle, Merlyn (Johnson), 118, 143, 151,
    153, 160–61, 327–29
Mantle, Mickey, 60, 142–63
  on always trying for home runs, 140
  on attention of fans, 161
  batting accomplishments of, 156–60
  on Berra, 331
  Brooke Holly and, 152–54
  brought up to Yankees in September 1950,
    147
  cancer of, 142–43, 328
  on catch in fifth inning of perfect game,
    163
  childhood of, 143–46
  and Collins act as Howard's "honor
    guard," 276
  comparison with Snider and Mays,
    136–37

  death of, 328–29, 350
  DiMaggio (Joe) and, 148–49, 154
  draft status of, 151
  drinking of, 117–18, 327, 328
  elected to Hall of Fame, 326
  as fan favorite, 326
  fantasy baseball camp of, 327, 350
  in the field during perfect game, 87, 143,
    161–63, 225, 267, 308
  in first at bat of perfect game, 36
  friendship with Martin, 116–18
  frustration with strikeouts, 151, 158
  Greenwade on, 146
  home-run trot of, 160
  joins Yankees' instructional camp in 1951,
    148
  on Larsen's drinking, 16
  with Larsen the night before the game, 4
  leg injuries of, 154, 157–60
  long-distance home runs of, 150,
    155–59
  Lopat confronts, 15–16
  Lovell (mother) and, 144–46
  on Martin, 110
  memorabilia shows and, 327
  Merlyn (wife) and, 151–52, 155, 160–61,
    327–29
  as minor leaguer, 146–47
  Mutt (father) and, 143–47, 153–55
  named after Mickey Cochrane, 144
  nervousness in top of the ninth inning of
    perfect game, 7, 9
  osteomyelitis of, 145–46, 151
  plays in Ban Johnson League, 146
  post-1956 career of, 326
  power of, 145, 146, 155–57
  pressure from publicity on, 150–51
  refuses to talk to Larsen during seventh in-
    ning of perfect game, 226
  relationship with teammates, 149–50
  retirement of, 326–27
  second at bat in perfect game (home run),
    140–41
  sent down to minors, 152–53
  shifted to the outfield, 148
  shy personality of, 148–49, 161
  speed of, 145
  Stengel and, 148, 150–52, 154, 155,
    158–60
  switch-hitting of, 144
  third at bat in perfect game, 215
  on third strike to Mitchell in perfect game,
    308

Mantle, Mickey (*cont.*)
  29th birthday celebration for Martin at
    Copacabana incident, 321–22
Mantle, Mutt, 143–47, 153–55, 328
Mantle, Ray, 161
Marion, Marty, 13, 150, 239–40, 245
Maris, Roger, 326
Marleau, Eddie, 289
Martin, Alfred Manuel, 110
Martin, Billy, 15, 62, 67, 108–21, 149, 167,
  210, 211
  aggressiveness of, 118–19
  batting accomplishments in World Series
    of 1952 and 1953, 119–20, 277
  Berra and, 113, 333
  brought up to the Yankees in 1950, 114
  childhood of, 109–12
  competitiveness of, 118
  confidence in locker room of, 114–15
  confusion about name of, 110–11
  death of, 324
  DiMaggio (Joe) and, 114–15
  drinking of, 117–18, 323
  emulation of Stengel's managerial style by,
    113
  exuberance of, 114–15
  faces uncertain future on the Yankees in
    1956 season, 120–21
  in the field during perfect game, 18, 65,
    121, 163, 202, 296–97
  fighting ability of, 109–11, 118
  first at bat in perfect game, 74
  friendship with Mantle, 116–18
  in huddle before taking field in ninth in-
    ning of perfect game, 281
  intensity of, 108–9, 276–77
  Jenny (mother) and, 110, 111
  Lois (wife) and, 116
  as manager, 322–24, 333
  as minor leaguer, 112
  reaction to divorce, 117
  recalled to active service, 120
  relays Stengel's home run request to Carey,
    203
  released from army on hardship grounds,
    116
  second at bat in perfect game, 180–81
  sent down to Kansas City, 115–16
  small size of, in childhood, 109
  Stengel and, 112–14, 118–20, 322
  thanks Wolff for advice, 109
  third at bat in perfect game, 250
  traded to Kansas City Athletics, 322
  29th birthday celebration at Copacabana
    incident, 321–22
Martin, Billy, Jr., 323
Martin, Jackie, 111
Martin, Kelly, 117
Martin, Lois Berndt, 116
Mathews, Eddie, 86
Mauch, Gene, 123, 336
Mays, Willie, 33, 89, 136, 154
Medwick, Joe (Ducky), 187, 235
Menendez, Danny, 289
Mexican League, 26–28
Meyer, Dick, 246
Meyer, Russ, 157–58
Miksis, Eddie, 265
Minoso, Minnie, 69
Mitchell, Bo, 6–7, 298, 306, 354–55
Mitchell, Dale, 298–310
  anger about strikeout in perfect game,
    309–10
  in the army, 300
  athletic abilities of, 298–99
  batting accomplishments of, 302–5
  brought up to Cleveland Indians in 1947,
    301–2
  childhood of, 298
  as college baseball player, 300–301
  criticized for not using power, 303–4
  death of, 355
  drinking of, 353, 354
  embarrassing comment by Williams (Ted)
    at Fellowship of Christian Athletes func-
    tion and, 352–53
  focus on science of hitting by, 303
  Greenberg and, 304–6
  heart attacks of, 354
  June (wife) and, 354, 355
  on Maglie, 24
  Margaret Ruth (wife) and, 300, 354
  with Martin Marietta division, 351–52
  as minor leaguer, 301
  pinch hits in ninth inning of perfect game,
    6–10, 298, 307–10
  receives fielding instruction from Speaker,
    302–3
  retirement of, 351
  signs deal with Cleveland Indians who
    withhold payments, 299
  sold to Dodgers in 1956, 306–7
  on third strike in perfect game, 308–10
Mitchell, Dale, Jr., 303, 306–7, 354
Mitchell, June, 354, 355
Mitchell, Lana, 354

Mitchell, Margaret Ruth Emerson, 6–7, 300, 354

Mize, Johnny, 60–62, 235, 274, 275

Monroe, Wayne, 327

Moore, Terry, 195, 236, 239, 244

Mooty, Jake, 168

Mueller, Don, 136

Murray, Jan, 281

Musial, Stan, 30, 239, 244

Natural, The (Malamud), 52

Neal, Bob:
  on Larsen-Maglie battle, 74, 106
  on Larsen's batting prowess, 107
  on Larsen's change of pace pitch to Snider in first inning, 19
  on Maglie's pitching in fourth inning, 140
  on Maglie's pitch to Bauer in first inning, 35
  on Mantle's catch in fifth inning, 163
  on Mantle's catch in third inning, 87
  on Mantle's home run in fourth inning, 140
  on Reese's catch in second inning, 73
  on retiring of first twelve Dodger batters, 121
  on Robinson at bat in fifth inning, 161, 162
  on Snider's catch in fourth inning, 141
  on tension in the fifth inning, 165

Neal, William "Cap," 166, 167

Newcombe, Don, 73, 98, 188, 278

New York Daily News, 30, 52, 80, 86, 178, 253

New York Giants:
  lose World Series of 1951, 31–32
  Maglie plays for, 24–26, 29–33
  win play-off series of 1951, 31, 132–33
  win World Series of 1954, 32–33

New York Herald Tribune, 138, 139, 222, 230, 238, 240

New York Times, The, 10, 53, 68, 104, 209, 239, 270, 276, 302, 318, 348

New York Yankees:
  Berra as manager of, 331, 333
  competitiveness of, 15–16
  Larsen traded to, 14
  lose World Series of 1955, 67–68
  Martin as manager of, 323, 331
  Robinson on, 52
  win World Series of 1941, 125–26, 171
  win World Series of 1947, 194, 236–37
  win World Series of 1951, 31–32, 283

win World Series of 1952, 119, 135, 156

win World Series of 1953, 119–20, 136

"Now I Know Why They Boo Me" (Robinson), 52

Oakland Athletics, 323

O'Malley, Walter, 53, 69, 104, 133, 135

O'Neill, Steve, 22, 29

Ott, Mel, 24, 26, 27, 29, 264

Owen, Mickey, 126, 171

Pafko, Andy, 133

Page, Joe, 197, 288

Parade, 179

Parrott, Harold, 85, 102

Pasadena Post, 39

Pasquel, Bernardo, 26–28

Pasquel, Jorge, 26, 28, 93

Passarella, Art, 264

Patchell, George, 91

Patterson, Red, 157

Pennock, Herb, 48

Perfect game:
  first inning (Dodgers at bat), 17–19
  first inning (Yankees at bat), 1–2, 35–36
  second inning (Dodgers at bat), 37, 56, 64–65
  second inning (Yankees at bat), 66, 73–74
  third inning (Dodgers at bat), 75, 87
  third inning (Yankees at bat), 89, 106–7
  fourth inning (Dodgers at bat), 121
  fourth inning (Yankees at bat), 139–41
  fifth inning (Dodgers at bat), 143, 161–63
  fifth inning (Yankees at bat), 165, 180–81
  sixth inning (Dodgers at bat), 184, 201–2
  sixth inning (Yankee at bat), 204, 214–15
  seventh inning (Dodgers at bat), 224–26
  seventh inning (Yankees at bat), 230, 249–50
  eighth inning (Dodgers at bat), 253–54, 267
  eighth inning (Yankees at bat), 270, 279–80
  ninth inning (Dodgers at bat), 1–2, 6–10, 282, 295–98, 307–8

Pesky, Johnny, 229–30, 284

Philadelphia Phillies, 47–48

Piersall, Jimmy, 118

Pignatano, Joe, 345, 346

Pinelli, Babe, 7–8, 18, 65, 87, 140, 163, 250, 254, 308, 309

Pitler, Jake, 261

Podres, Johnny, 67, 68, 70, 176

Pope, Harold, 301
Povich, Shirley, 200
Powell, Richard, 220

Queen, Mel, 80

Racial integration of baseball, 43–48
  strike rumors, 238–40
  Walker's petition and, 46–47, 81, 128
Ramos, Pedro, 159
Raschi, Vic, 197
Redmond, Herbert, 255–56
Reedy, Bill, 324
Reese, Carl, 165
Reese, Carl, Jr., 166, 175
Reese, Dorothy Walton, 171–72, 330
Reese, Emma, 165
Reese, Mark, 164, 168, 175, 329–31
Reese, Pee Wee, 34, 50, 85, 124, 164–81, 307
  Amoros' catch in World Series of 1955
    and, 68
  batting consistency of, 177
  brought up to Dodgers, 167
  on Campanella's humor, 101
  cancer of, 330–31
  childhood of, 164–66
  as commentator, 329
  death of, 331
  decline in 1956 season, 179–80
  Dorothy (wife) and, 171–72, 330
  Durocher and, 168–70, 330
  elected to Hall of Fame, 330
  in the field during perfect game, 35, 36,
    73, 165, 180–81, 215, 250
  first at bat in perfect game, 18
  as first player to wear batting helmet, 168
  hanging tree memory and, 164, 173, 174
  Hodges and, 257
  intangible qualities brought to the game
    by, 172
  leadership ability of, 176–77
  on longevity in baseball, 179
  marble shooting and nickname of, 165
  mentioned as possible manager of Dodg-
    ers, 177–78
  as minor leaguer, 166–67
  Mitchell and, 309
  in the navy, 172–73
  negotiates with MacPhail, 169–70
  as one of the "Gold Dust Twins," 170
  popularity of, 178–79
  reputation as league's best shortstop, 172,
    175–76

  retirement of, 329
  Robinson and, 173–75
  second at bat in perfect game, 121
  Snider and, 124–26, 137, 138
  third at bat in perfect game, 225
  in World Series of 1941, 171
  in World Series of 1955, 179
Reichart, Charlie, 76
Reiser, Pete, 46, 81, 125, 127, 131, 170
Reserve clause, 357–58
Reynolds, Allie, 21, 57, 135, 182, 352–53,
  359
Richards, Paul, 99, 159
Richardson, Bobby, 120–21, 143, 291, 292,
  328, 334
Richman, Arthur, 4, 5
Rickey, Branch, 53
  Berra and, 188
  Campanella and, 95–100
  Gilliam and, 220
  Hodges and, 129, 261
  lectures on "Dodger way," 128
  negotiates with Furillo, 82
  Reese and, 176
  Robinson and, 42–46, 50
  Snider and, 125–27, 130, 131
Rickey, Branch, Jr., 127, 259, 261
Rizzuto, Phil, 59, 63, 184, 194, 198–99,
  209, 210, 249, 277
Roberts, Robin, 132
Robertson, Charlie, 2
Robeson, Paul, 51
Robinson, Jackie, 37–56, 302, 307
  Alston and, 54–55
  appears before House Un-American Activ-
    ities Committee, 51
  in the Army, 40–41
  athletic abilities of, 39
  attitude towards race relations, vs. Cam-
    panella's, 101–3
  batting accomplishments of, 51–53
  becomes outspoken on racial issues, 50–53
  childhood of, 38–39
  death of, 315
  debuts for Dodgers at Ebbets Field, 47
  deterioration of health in later years, 314–
    415
  Dressen and, 53–54
  Durocher and, 46–47, 50
  fading abilities in 1955-1956, 55–56
  in the field during perfect game, 35, 36,
    106, 214, 215, 230, 250
  first at bat in perfect game, 37, 56, 64

Gilliam and, 221, 222, 224
Jackie Jr. and, 314
moves to third base, 53–54, 217
movie of life of, 81
paid by Hodges to catch pop flies,
    262–63
personality of, 39
petition incident and, 46–47, 81, 128
playing style of, 48–49, 55
plays for Kansas City Monarchs, 41–42
plays in minor leagues, 44–46
pressure endured by, 45
Rachel (wife) and, 39–41, 44–45, 315
racism faced by, 38, 40–41, 44–50,
    174
Reese and, 173–75
religiousness of, 38
retaliation tactic of, 224, 359
retirement of, 314
Rickey and, 42–46, 50
screamed at by Martin, 114
second at bat in perfect game, 161–62
on Snider not running out groundballs,
    134
Snider on, 128
as social activist, 314
spiked by Slaughter, 240–44
strike rumor incident and, 238–40
tells Campanella about Rickey's plan,
    96–97
tension between Campanella and,
    102–3
third at bat in perfect game, 253–54
at UCLA, 39
weight problems of, 49, 55
wins Rookie of the Year in 1941, 49
Robinson, Jackie, Jr., 314
Robinson, Jerry, 38
Robinson, Mallie, 38
Robinson, Rachel Isum, 39–41, 44–46, 102,
    175, 315
Roe, Preacher, 177
Rose, Pete, 233
Rosen, Al, 158
Rozelle, Pete, 124
Rudd, Irving, 179, 257
Runge, Ed, 163
Ruth, Babe, 47, 117, 122, 135, 137, 150,
    156, 167, 304
Ryan, Nolan, 345

Sain, Johnny, 264
St. Louis Dispatch, 235

Salvini, Jenny, 110, 111
Sanchez, Raul, 224
Savitt, Alan, 152
Scales, George, 219
Schoendienst, Red, 145, 239
Schulte, John, 188–89
Schwartz, Art, 12
Score, Herb, 33
Scully, Vin, 9–10, 181, 267
Selkirk, George, 207, 343
Shaughnessy, Frank, 99
Sheehan, Jack, 220
Sheehan, Tom, 56
Sheehy, Pete, 60, 117, 190–91
Shotton, Burt, 47, 50, 53, 82, 176, 242
Shuba, George, 67, 221
Silvera, Charlie, 6
Sisler, George, 51
Skowron, Moose, 5, 119, 147, 270–71, 279,
    350, 351
Slaughter, Enos, 227–50
in the army, 237
base running of, 241, 242
batting accomplishments of, 233–36, 238,
    244–47, 249
becomes outfielder, 232
on Carey's throwing arm, 205
childhood of, 230–32
"country" nickname of, 234
death of, 342
disciplined lifestyle of, 245
elected to Hall of Fame, 341
in the field during perfect game, 18, 225,
    226, 308
first at bat in perfect game, 18
focus on statistics of, 248
as hard-nosed player, 241
Helen (wife) and, 340, 341
Hulo (wife) and, 232–34
hustle of, 233, 238, 248
infected with tularemia bacteria, 235
Josephine (wife) and, 237
"mad dash" home in World Series of
    1946, 229–30
Mary (wife) and, 237, 247
as minor leaguer, 232–34
post-1956 career of, 340–41
resented by Yankees, 248
retirement of, 341
Ruth (wife) and, 247
as St. Louis Cardinal, 234–46
second at bat in perfect game, 180
self-confidence of, 230

Slaughter, Enos (*cont.*)
  spiking controversy with Robinson and,
    240–44
  Stengel and, 230, 246, 247, 340
  strike rumors concerning Robinson and,
    238–40
  third at bat in perfect game, 230, 249–50
  on third strike to Mitchell in perfect game,
    308
  throwing arm of, 231
  traded to Kansas City, 248–49
  traded to Yankees, 246–47, 249
  Vickie (wife) and, 340
  in World Series of 1946, 227–30
Slaughter, Gaye, 239, 341, 342
Slaughter, Helen Spiker, 340, 341
Slaughter, Hulo Powell, 232–34
Slaughter, Josephine Begonia, 237
Slaughter, Lonnie Gentry, 230–31
Slaughter, Mary Peterson Walker, 237
Slaughter, Patricia, 237
Slaughter, Rebecca, 233–34
Slaughter, Rhonda, 342
Slaughter, Ruth Rohleder, 247
Slaughter, Sharon, 341–42
Slaughter, Vickie, 340
Slaughter, Zadok, 230–31, 235
Smith, Al, 268, 305
Smith, Mayo, 137, 264
Smith, Red, 139
Snider, Beverly Null, 129–30, 133, 135, 325
Snider, Duke, 54, 67, 122–39
  on Amoros, 70
  athletic ability in high school, 124
  attitude of, 134–35
  batting accomplishments of, 131, 132,
    136
  Beverly (wife) and, 129–30, 133, 135, 325
  as broadcaster, 325
  camaraderie with teammates, 133
  childhood of, 123–24
  on closeness of team, 358
  compared with Mantle and Mays, 136–37
  disappointment in performance during
    World Series of 1949, 131–32
  as Dodger fan in teen years, 125–26
  Dressen and, 134–35
  elected to Baseball Hall of Fame, 325
  failing health in later years, 325–26
  in the field during perfect game, 74, 122,
    139, 141, 215
  first at bat in perfect game, 18–19
  first visit to Yankee Stadium, 122–23

Furillo and, 85, 133–34
  on ground balls, 124
  on Hodges, 344
  lack of success in first days on the Dodg-
    ers, 128–29
  lashes out at Dodger fans, 138, 139
  as Major League Player of the Year in
    1955, 137
  memorabilia shows and, 325
  as minor leaguer, 126, 127, 129
  moodiness of, 129
  in the navy, 126–27
  on Pinelli's comment about third strike to
    Mitchell in perfect game, 309
  post-1956 career of, 324
  propensity to feel sorry for himself, 134
  reaction to sportswriters' criticisms,
    137–39
  receives nickname from father, 12
  refuses to sign Walker's petition against
    Robinson, 128
  requests number 4, 128
  Rickey and, 125–27, 130, 131
  on Robinson, 128
  second at bat in perfect game, 121
  sent down to minors, 129–31
  signs with the Dodgers, 125
  taught baseball fundamentals by father,
    123
  tax fraud and, 325
  third at bat in perfect game, 225, 226
  Thomson's pennant winning home run
    and, 132–33
  traded to New York Mets in 1963, 324
  traded to San Francisco Giants in 1964,
    324
  on wearing Dodger uniform, 128
  in World Series of 1952, 135
Snider, Florence, 125
Snider, Kevin, 133
Snider, Ward, 123, 125
Soar, Hank, 64
Southworth, Billy, 232
Speaker, Tris, 302–3
Specter, Arlen, 300–301
Sport, 52
Sporting News, The, 49, 67, 68, 72, 120,
    136, 137, 139, 156, 159, 191, 199, 209,
    211, 234, 261, 336, 349, 350
Sports Illustrated, 20, 137
Stainback, Tuck, 236–37
Stanky, Eddie, 47, 246
Stark, Abe, 83

Steinbrenner, George, 323, 324, 333–35
Stengel, Casey, 14, 57, 312
  bats Larsen seventh during 1956 season, 15
  Bauer and, 284, 290, 292–95
  Berra and, 196, 294, 295, 332
  Carey and, 203–4, 207–11, 214, 335
  Collins and, 270–71, 275–79
  on Cox, 53
  on DiMaggio (Joe), 294
  incomprehensible remarks of, 208
  on Larsen's car accident, 16
  McDougald and, 59–63
  managerial style of, 113
  Mantle and, 148, 150–52, 154, 155, 158–60
  Martin and, 112–14, 118–20, 322
  replaces Larsen in second game of Series, 4
  selects Larsen to start game, 4, 5
  Slaughter and, 230, 246, 247, 340
  use of Larsen during 1956 regular season, 16
  warms up Ford in the ninth inning of perfect game, 2
Stephens, Vern, 197
Stirnweiss, Snuffy, 115, 116
Stobbs, Chuck, 156
Stoneham, Horace, 31
Sukeforth, Clyde, 43
Swoboda, Ron, 343

Terranova, Anthony, 346
Thompson, Fresco, 94–95
Thomson, Bobby, 31, 103, 132–33
Time, 105, 323
Toot Shor's, 34
Truman, Harry S, 78–79
Turley, Bob, 3, 5, 13, 14, 16, 60, 149, 294
Turner, Jim, 3

Vander Meer, Johnny, 182
Veeck, Bill, 13, 301
Vernon, Mickey, 158
Versalles, Zoilo, 216–18

Wackenbush, Andy, 287
Waitkus, Eddie, 52–53
Waldman, Suzyn, 334
Walker, Dixie, 25, 46, 49, 81, 128, 171, 173–74, 179
Walker, Harry, 228, 229
Walker, Rube, 103, 345, 346
Walker, Stelle, 171

Ward, Preston, 262
Washington Post, The, 200
Webb, Del, 184, 352
Weiss, George, 14, 115–16, 120, 198, 293, 321
Wendler, Doc, 241
Wertz, Vic, 33
White, Sammy, 203, 204
Williams, Dick, 312
Williams, Ted, 3, 8–9, 94, 160, 182–84, 187, 197, 303, 352–53
Wills, Maury, 338
Wolff, Bob:
  on Collins' batting stances, 275
  on crowd cheering in sixth inning, 214, 215
  on the crowd in the ninth inning of perfect game, 8
  on crowd noise in eighth inning, 253, 280
  on drama in eighth inning, 254
  hired by Gillette to broadcast World Series, 108
  on Maglie's pitching, 280
  on Mantle's catch in the eighth inning, 267
  on Mantle's long-distance home runs, 156–57, 159
  on Mantle's storytelling ability, 327
  on Martin in fifth inning, 180
  on Martin's intensity, 108–9
  on McDougald as "thinking man's" player, 56
  on McDougald's fielding play in seventh inning, 225
  on Mitchell striking out, 308
  on not mentioning the words "no hitter" in seventh inning, 225–26
  on Reese in the fifth inning, 181
  on Robinson being most exciting player, 49
  on Slaughter's fly ball in seventh inning, 250
  top of the sixth inning comments by, 201–2
Woodling, Gene, 196, 292, 293
Wynn, Early, 33, 160, 268, 269

Yost, Eddie, 345, 346
Young, Dick, 52, 80, 86, 253
Yvars, Sal, 98, 282–83

Zimmer, Don, 29, 67
Zimmerman, Roy, 26

Lew Paper is a graduate of the University of Michigan and Harvard Law School and holds a master's degree in law from Georgetown University Law School. He has held a variety of positions in the public and private sectors, including a fellowship with Georgetown University Law School's Institute of Public Interest Representation, Legislative Counsel to Senator Gaylord Nelson in the United States Senate, and Associate General Counsel at the Federal Communications Commission. He is the author of *John F. Kennedy: The Promise and the Performance*; *Brandeis: An Intimate Biography*; *Empire: William S. Paley and the Making of CBS*; and *Deadly Risks* (a novel). His articles and book reviews have appeared in numerous publications, including *The New York Times*, *The Washington Post*, *The New Republic*, and *The American Scholar*. He currently practices law in Washington, D.C.